THE HIDDEN PLACES OF THE

PEAK DISTRICT AND DERBYSHIRE

By Samantha Russell

Regional Hidden Places

Cornwall
Devon
Dorset, Hants & Isle of Wight
East Anglia
Lake District & Cumbria
Northumberland & Durham
Peak District and Derbyshire
Yorkshire

National Hidden Places

England
Ireland
Scotland
Wales

Country Living Rural Guides

East Anglia
Heart of England
Ireland
North East of England
North West of England
Scotland
South
South East
Wales
West Country

Other Guides

Off the Motorway
Garden Centres and Nurseries
    of Britain

Published by: Travel Publishing Ltd, Airport Business Centre,
10 Thornbury Road, Estover, Plymouth, Devon PL6 7PP

ISBN13   9781904434795

© Travel Publishing Ltd

First published 1991, second edition 1994,
third edition 1997, fourth edition 1999,
fifth edition 2002, sixth edition 2005,
seventh edition 2007, eighth edition 2009

Printing by: Latimer Trend, Plymouth

Maps by: ©MAPS IN MINUTES/Collins Bartholomew (2009)

Foreword

This is the 8th edition of the *Hidden Places of the Peak District and Derbyshire*. The guide has been been fully updated and in this respect we would like to thank the Tourist Information Centres in Derbyshire for helping us update the editorial content. The guide is packed with information on the many interesting places to visit in the area. In addition, you will find details of places of interest and advertisers of places to stay, eat and drink included under each village, town or city, which are cross referenced to more detailed information contained in a separate, easy-to-use section to the rear of the book. This section is also available as a free supplement from the local Tourist Information Offices.

The *Peak District National Park* was the very first of Britain's National Parks covering an area of 540 square miles. The *Dark Peak* covering north Derbyshire and small parts of Cheshire and South Yorkshire is an area of windswept moorland, steep river valleys and impressive crags. Futher south is the *White Peak* a limestone-based undulating green landscape criss-crossed by miles of dry stone walls and gently flowing rivers whilst to the west can be found the beautiful valleys and rivers of the *Dales* as well as the *Staffordshire Moorlands*. In contrast the rest of Derbyshire offers the visitor an intriguing mix of villages and towns packed with cultural and industrial heritage and should certainly not be missed.

The *Hidden Places of the Peak District and Derbyshire* contains a wealth of interesting information on the history, the countryside, the towns and villages and the more established places of interest. But it also promotes the more secluded and little known visitor attractions and places to stay, eat and drink many of which are easy to miss unless you know exactly where you are going.

We include hotels, bed & breakfasts, restaurants, pubs, bars, teashops and cafes as well as historic houses, museums, gardens and many other attractions throughout the area, all of which are comprehensively indexed. Many places are accompanied by an attractive photograph and are easily located by using the map at the beginning of each chapter. We do not award merit marks or rankings but concentrate on describing the more interesting, unusual or unique features of each place with the aim of making the reader's stay in the local area an enjoyable and stimulating experience.

Whether you are travelling around the area on business or for pleasure we do hope that you enjoy reading and using this book. We are always interested in what readers think of places covered (or not covered) in our guides so please do not hesitate to use the reader reaction form provided to give us your considered comments. We also welcome any general comments which will help us improve the guides themselves. Finally if you are planning to visit any other corner of the British Isles we would like to refer you to the list of other *Hidden Places* titles to be found to the rear of the book and to the Travel Publishing website.

Travel Publishing

Did you know that you can also search our website for details of thousands of places to see, stay, eat or drink throughout Britain and Ireland? Our site has become increasingly popular and now receives over **500,000** visits annually. Try it!

website: www.travelpublishing.co.uk

Location Map

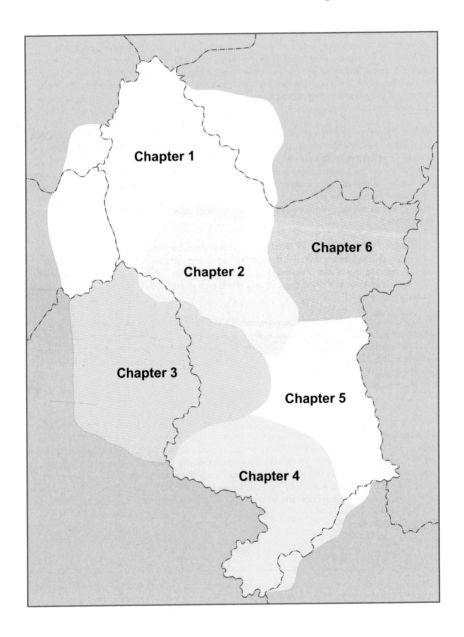

Chapter 1

Chapter 6

Chapter 2

Chapter 3

Chapter 5

Chapter 4

Contents

iii   Foreword

iv   Regional Map

I   Contents

GEOGRAPHICAL AREAS:

3   Chapter I: Buxton and the Dark Peak

37   Chapter 2: Bakewell, Matlock and the White Peak

77   Chapter 3: Dovedale and the Staffordshire Moorlands

105   Chapter 4: The Trent Valley

127   Chapter 5: The Amber Valley and Erewash

155   Chapter 6: Derbyshire Coal Mines

ADVERTISEMENTS:

172   Peak District and Derbyshire Advertisements

INDEXES AND LISTS:

283   List of Tourist Information Centres

284   Index of Towns, Villages and Places of Interest

ADDITIONAL INFORMATION:

290   Order Forms

291   Reader Comment Forms

297   List of Advertisers

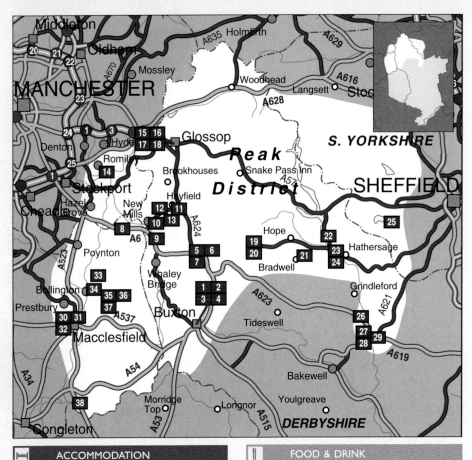

🛏 ACCOMMODATION

6	The Roebuck Inn, Chapel-en-le-Frith	p 10, 178
10	The Torrs, New Mills	p 14, 181
11	The Royal Hotel, Hayfield, High Peak	p 14, 182
12	The Printers Arms, Thornsett, High Peak	p 15, 183
13	Sycamore Inn, Birch Vale, High Peak	p 15, 184
17	The Star Inn, Glossop	p 17, 186
19	Causeway House, Castleton, Hope Valley	p 20, 187
21	Bowling Green Inn, Bradwell, Hope Valley	p 24, 188
22	Ladybower Inn, Bamford, Hope Valley	p 24, 189
24	The Little John Inn, Hathersage, Hope Valley	p 26, 190
28	Rutland Arms, Baslow	p 29, 194
29	Devonshire Arms Hotel, Nether End, nr Baslow	p 29, 195
35	The Robin Hood, Rainow, nr Macclesfield	p 34, 200
37	Common Barn Farm, Rainow, nr Macclesfield	p 34, 200

🍴 FOOD & DRINK

1	Eagle Public House & Restaurant, Buxton	p 5, 176
2	Cafe @ The Green Pavilion, Buxton	p 5, 177
3	The Old Sun Inn, Buxton	p 6, 177
5	In a Pickle, Chapel-en-le-Frith	p 10, 178
6	The Roebuck Inn, Chapel-en-le-Frith	p 10, 178
8	Dandy Cock Inn, Disley, nr Stockport	p 13, 179
9	The Crossings, Furness Vale, High Peak	p 13, 180
10	The Torrs, New Mills	p 14, 181
11	The Royal Hotel, Hayfield, High Peak	p 14, 182
12	The Printers Arms, Thornsett, High Peak	p 15, 183
13	Sycamore Inn, Birch Vale, High Peak	p 15, 184
14	Duke of York, Romiley, nr Stockport	p 16, 185
16	The Hare & Hounds, Simmondley Village, nr Glossop	p 17, 185
17	The Star Inn, Glossop	p 17, 186
18	The Beehive & Hague Bistro, Glossop	p 17, 186

Buxton and the Dark Peak

The Peak District is a truly topographically diverse tract of land in the Southern Apennine Range, also known as the 'Backbone of England'. It divides the rugged north from the softer pastoral countryside of the south and lies mostly in the county of Derbyshire but extends its reaches into the neighbouring counties of Staffordshire, Cheshire, South Yorkshire, and as far north as West Yorkshire and Greater Manchester.

At its hub is the Peak District National Park – the first in Britain covers an area of 555 square miles (1,438-km). The land itself is divided into two distinct regions that take their names from the underlying rocks: the Dark Peak and the White Peak. The contrast could not be more marked, and it gives the Peak District a unique, dual personality which is constantly changing, yet as comfortably enduring as the rocks themselves.

The northern area of the Peak District National Park, known as the Dark Peak or High Peak, is a landscape of moorland and deep valleys edged with escarpments of dark sandstone and shale. The rugged millstone grit moorland and crags enclose the softer limestone plateau of the White Peak like a horseshoe. The ancient, originally pagan custom of well-dressing and the mysterious Castleton Garlanding Ceremony are found mainly in these limestone areas of Derbyshire, where the streams frequently disappear through the porous rock.

There are spectacular rock formations, picturesque villages and historic churches and castles. The Romans left their roads and the remains of their forts and baths, there are Saxon and Norman churches, and the Civil War raged through the area leaving a trail of destruction. The National Park is scattered with the remains of ancient settlements. Mainly agricultural for hundreds of years, with some coal mining and ironworks, the industrial revolution transformed the place as mills, mines and works sprang up everywhere. As the population of the towns grew, the factory and mine owners built houses for the workforce, churches and grand civic buildings, and left a rich legacy of Victorian architecture.

FOOD & DRINK

21	Bowling Green Inn, Bradwell, Hope Valley	p 24, 188
22	Ladybower Inn, Bamford, Hope Valley	p 24, 189
23	Pool Cafe, Hathersage, Hope Valley	p 26, 189
24	The Little John Inn, Hathersage, Hope Valley	p 26, 190
25	The Three Merry Lads, Lodge Moor, nr Sheffield	p 26, 191
26	The Eating House, Calver Bridge, Hope Valley	p 28, 192
28	Rutland Arms, Baslow	p 29, 194
29	Devonshire Arms Hotel, Nether End, nr Baslow	p 29, 195
30	The Jolly Sailor, Macclesfield	p 31, 196
31	Dolphin Inn, Macclesfield	p 31, 197
32	Puss in Boots, Macclesfield	p 31, 197

FOOD & DRINK

33	Coffee Tavern, Pott Shrigley	p 33, 198
34	The Holly Bush, Bollington	p 34, 198
35	The Robin Hood, Rainow, nr Macclesfield	p 34, 200
36	Rising Sun Inn, Rainow, nr Macclesfield	p 34, 199
38	Boars Leigh Restaurant, Bosley, nr Macclesfield	p 35, 200

PLACES OF INTEREST

4	Buxton Museum and Art Gallery, Buxton	p 8, 178
7	The Chestnut Centre, Chapel-en-le-Frith	p 11, 179
15	Glossop Heritage Centre, Glossop	p 16, 182
20	Treak Cliff Cavern, Castleton, Hope Valley	p 22, 187
27	Avant Garde of Baslow, Baslow	p 29, 193

3

The Amber Valley, the Erewash and the Trent Valley, to the east and south of Derbyshire, although not part of the National Park, have many pleasant walks and magnificent stately homes for visitors to enjoy. Derbyshire was at the forefront of the Industrial Revolution, and its history is recorded in the Industrial Museum at Derby. It is reflected, too, in many of the villages with their rows of 18th and 19th century workers' cottages. To the northeast of Derbyshire is the heart of the coal-mining area, which prospered during the 19th and early 20th centuries. Sometimes overlooked, this part of Derbyshire is well worth exploring for its industrial architecture alone.

On the southern edge of the Peak District, the undulating pastures and crags of the Staffordshire Moorland are ideal places to walk, cycle or trek. It is a mixture of charming villages, historic market towns, ancient farms and relics of the Industrial Revolution, including the reservoirs of Rudyard and Tittesworth. They were originally the water supply for the Midlands, but are now peaceful havens for wildlife and leisure.

The Dark Peak, or High Peak, is not as forbidding as its name might suggest. These high moors are ripe for exploring on foot, and a walk from the Kinder Reservoir will lead to the western edge of Kinder Scout. This whole area is really a series of plateaux, rather than mountains and valleys, with the highest point on Kinder Scout being some 2,088 feet above sea level. In this remote and wild area the walker can feel a real sense of freedom - however, it is worth remembering that the moors, with their treacherous peat bogs and unpredictable mists, which can rise quickly even in summer, should not be dismissed as places for a casual ramble.

It was at Kinder Scout, in April 1932, that the single most important action in securing access rights for ordinary people to the English countryside took place. Seventy or so years ago, the unique sense of freedom offered by the beckoning Dark Peak moors was available only to a privileged few, for most of the moorland was the strictly-private game reserve of a handful of wealthy owners. 'Trespassers will be Prosecuted' and 'Keep Out' signs were abound, but these didn't ward off over 400 walkers who took part in what became known as the "Mass Trespass", by walking over the land. Five of the leaders received prison sentences ranging from two and six months, they immediately became martyrs to the cause of free access, and their actions led to legislation which opened up England's countryside to walkers. The Peak District National Park was also formed as a direct result of the trespass, and nowadays the Pennine Way passes directly over Kinder Scout.

To the eastern side of this region are the three reservoirs created by flooding of the upper valley of the River Derwent. Howden, Derwent and Ladybower provide water for the East Midlands but their remote location, along with the many recreational activities found there, make them popular places to visit. The Derwent dam is particularly famous as the site of practice exercises for the Dambusters of the Second World War. Even those who have not visited the area before will be familiar with some of the place names, as they feature heavily in winter weather reports. Snake Pass (the A57), one of the few roads that run through this northern section of the National Park, is often closed during the winter; even in spring, conditions can deteriorate quickly to make driving hazardous.

The Peak District National Park is now one of the most visited areas in the world. There are up to 30 million visits each year - only Mount Fuji National Park in Japan has more visits!

BUXTON

Although not actually situated within the National Park itself, the elegant Georgian town of Buxton is the largest habitation that lies within what is widely know as, "The Peak District", where it is possibly one of the best centres to base a short, or even long term stay within the area. Referred to as the heart of the Peak District, Buxton, like Bakewell, is right on the divide between the Dark Peak and White Peak areas of the National Park. A large part of the White Peak lies between the two towns. The reason why Buxton was excluded from the National Park becomes obvious as you approach it from the south on the A6. As you drop off the limestone plateau, enormous quarry faces open up on your right at Tunstead. Buxton in fact is almost ringed by gigantic quarries, so the Park boundary was drawn neatly around it. At 1,000 feet above sea level, Buxton is also England's second-highest market town (only Alston in Cumbria is higher), and provides a wealth of things to do.

Both the Peak District and the Peak District National Park are filled with much of historical interest, some of which dates back several thousand years. For its gracious architecture, the town of Buxton wears the crown, and can be attributed mainly to the 5th Duke of Devonshire, who hoped to establish a northern spa town that would rival, and possibly surpass, the attractions of Bath. In both locations it was the Romans who first exploited the healing waters of apparently inexhaustible hot springs as a commercial enterprise. They arrived in AD70, and called the place *Aquae Arnemetiae* that translates as "The Spa of the Goddess of the Grove". It is one of only two places in Britain which had the Roman prefix aquae (meaning "waters") - the other being *Aquae Sulis*, or Bath. The waters still bubble up at Buxton, always maintaining a constant temperature of 82°F (28°C). Buxton water is reputed to be particularly pure and especially effective at relieving the symptoms of rheumatism. Countless rheumatism sufferers are on record attesting that Buxton water has helped to soothe their symptoms but it wasn't until the Tudor period that the reputation of the spa waters was enhanced when Mary, Queen of Scotland, under the custodianship of the 6th Earl of Shrewsbury, was given leave to take the waters for her numerous ailments. The Hall, now the Old Hall Hotel was specially built to house her visits between 1573 and 1584. The people of Buxton also say that it makes the best cup of tea possible, and collect bottles of it to take home. Experts have calculated that the water that bubbles up nowadays fell as rainfall over 5,000 years ago.

In the 18th century, the 5th Duke of Devonshire was inspired to build **The Crescent** and **Great Stables** to ensure that visitors would flock here. Between 1780

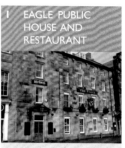

1 EAGLE PUBLIC HOUSE AND RESTAURANT

Buxton

Great beer in great surroundings and the central venue for live music.

see page 176

2 CAFÉ @ THE GREEN PAVILION

Buxton

Opposite The Crescent in the town centre this tiny modern café, with outside seating, offers bistro-style food prepared from locally sourced ingredients.

see page 177

Among the other notable architectural features of the town are The Colonnade and the Devonshire Royal Hospital. They were originally built as stables for hotel patrons of The Crescent and, after their conversion by the 6th Duke in 1858, the largest unsupported dome in the world was built to enclose the courtyard in 1880.

3   THE OLD SUN INN

Buxton

Traditional English pub some 400 years old serving great value food and up to 6 real ales.

see page 177

and 1811 he was also responsible for the development of the Square, Hall Bank and St John's Church. Built to the designs of John Carr of York, **The Crescent** was the first 'resort' hotel in Britain and was at the heart of Buxton's aspirations to become a fashionable spa town. The building is similar to the architecture found in Bath and, after suffering from neglect, underwent a huge restoration programme. Next to The Crescent, the Thermal Baths are now the Cavendish Shopping Centre, and the former town house of Bess of Hardwick and her husband the Earl of Shrewsbury, The Hall, is now the Old Hall Hotel. **Turner's**

Memorial stands opposite, and commemorates Samuel Turner, treasurer to the Devonshire Hospital. It was built by Robert Rippon Duke in 1879, a very good friend of Turner. During 1959, a local motorist crashed into the memorial, the choice was made to demolish it at the time. When the area received its pedestrian modernization some years later however, it was repaired and reinstated to its former glory, being part of Buxton's important heritage.

The Railway arrives - Georgian Buxton enjoyed only modest success but after 1850 visitors started to arrive in substantial

The Pavilion Gardens, Buxton

numbers to holiday and take the waters. New baths, a Pump Room, churches and hotels were built to accommodate them. The Great Stables were converted into the Royal Devonshire Hospital and had its magnificent slate roof added in 1881. The Pavilion and Gardens were laid out and in 1903 the **Opera House** was opened to much acclaim.

The attractive **Buxton Opera House** was designed by the renowned theatre architect, Frank Matcham. Gertrude Lawrence, Gracie Fields and Hermione Gingold all played here and on one memorable occasion, the famous Hollywood screen stars Douglas Fairbanks and Mary Pickford were in the audience to watch the Russian ballerina, Anna Pavlova. However, in 1932 it became a cinema and, apart from an annual pantomime and a handful of amateur performances, showed films only. In the late 1970s it was restored to its former Edwardian grandeur and was officially opened by Princess Alice in 1979. Today it is one of Britain's leading provincial theatres, practically bursting at the seams with around 450 performances each year including dance, comedy, children's shows, drama, music, pantomime, opera and even shows on ice!

St John the Baptist Church was built in Greek style, with pediment, in 1811 by Sir Jeffrey Wyatville. That same year Wyatville laid out The Slopes, the area below the Market Place in Upper Buxton. The grand Town Hall was built between 1887 and 1889 and dominates the Market Place. Further down Terrace Road is the **Buxton Museum**, which reveals the long and varied history of the town and its surrounding area. As well as housing an important local archaeology collection, the museum also has a fine collection of Ashford Marble, Blue John ornaments, paintings, prints, pottery and glassware.

It is not known for certain whether well dressing took place in Buxton before 1840. There are stories that Henry VIII put a stop to the practice, but it has certainly been a part of Buxton's cultural calendar since the Duke of Devonshire provided the townsfolk with their first public water supply at **Market Place Fountain**. From then on, High Buxton Well (as the fountain came to be called) and St Anne's Well were decorated sporadically. In 1923 the Town Council set about organising a well-dressing festival and carnival that continues to this day. Every year on the second Wednesday in July, this delightful tradition is enacted.

St Anne's Church, built in 1625, reflects the building work here before Buxton's 18th century heyday when limestone was the most common construction material, rather than the mellow sandstone that dominates today.

Buxton is surrounded by some of the most glorious of the Peak District countryside. These moorlands also provide one of the town's specialties - heather honey. Several varieties of heather grow

The attractive Buxton Pavilion Gardens have a conservatory (built in 1871) and octagon within the grounds. Antique markets, brass band concerts and arts shows are often held here, and it is a very pleasant place to walk at any time of year. Laid out in 1871 by Edward Milner, with money donated by the Dukes of Devonshire, it includes formal gardens, serpentine walks and decorative iron bridges across the River Wye. The conservatory was reopened in 1982 following extensive renovation; there is also a swimming pool filled with warm spa water.

4 BUXTON MUSEUM AND ART GALLERY

Buxton

Explore the history of the area from pre-history to the Victorian era and enjoy displays of art works.

 see page 178

on the moors: there is ling, or common heather which turns the land purple in late summer; there is bell-heather which grows on dry rocky slopes; and there is cross-leaved heather which can be found on wet, boggy ground.

The town is also the starting point for both the Brindley Trail and the Monsal Trail. Covering some 61 miles, the Brindley Trail, which takes its name from the famous canal engineer, leads southwest to Stoke-on-Trent, while the Monsal Trail, beginning just outside Buxton at Blackwell Mill Junction, finishes at Coombs Viaduct near Bakewell, some 8 miles away.

AROUND BUXTON

Less than one mile to the west of the town, on Green Lane, is Poole's Cavern. Since the 16th century, the cavern has been known as "the first wonder of the Peak". It is a natural limestone cave, said to be over 2 million years old, which was used by tribes from the Neolithic period onwards. Archaeological digs have discovered Stone Age, Bronze Age and Roman artefacts near the cave entrance. Art Hacker's "Buxton Thro' Other Glasses" (turn of the century) says …

"A kind of abandon-hope-all-ye-who-enter-here sort of feeling assails you as you pass beneath the low arch of rock."

The spectacular natural formations in the cavern include a large stalactite called the 'Flitch of Bacon' and the 'Poached Egg Chamber', with blue grey and orange formations, coloured by manganese and iron soaking down from the lime-tips above.

Axe Edge Moor, which receives an average annual rainfall of over four feet, is strictly for hardened walkers. It should come as no surprise that this moor is the source of several rivers which play important roles in the life of the Peak District including the River Dove, River Manifold, River Dane, River Wye and River Goyt. The moor actually spreads over three counties, and at Three Shire's Head, to the south east, the counties of Derbyshire, Staffordshire and Cheshire meet.

The entire length of the River Goyt can be walked, from its source to its confluence with the River Etherow to the north and just outside the boundaries of the National Park. Once marking the boundary between Derbyshire and Cheshire (which now lies just to the west), a walk along the Goyt takes in sections of the riverbank as well as the Errwood and Fernilee reservoirs before leaving Derbyshire just north of New Mills. Although the two reservoirs look well established and very much part of the landscape, they are relatively recent additions: the Fernilee was opened in 1938 while the Errwood was flooded in 1967.

The highest point in this area is **Shining Tor**, overlooking Errwood Reservoir and standing some 1,834 feet above sea level. To the north is **Pym Chair**, the point at which an old packhorse road running east to west crosses this gritstone ridge. An old salters' route, it was used for transporting salt from the Cheshire plains across the Peak District moorlands to the industrial and well-populated areas of south and west Yorkshire. Pym's chair is said to be named after a highwayman called Pym, who used to sit here awaiting travellers whom he could rob. During the 19th century, the Goyt valley with its natural resources of both coal and water, developed rapidly into one of the nation's major textile production centres. In order to service this growth, the valley also developed an intense system of transport, including canals and railways. The rugged terrain that had to be negotiated has made for some spectacular solutions to major engineering difficulties.

NORTH OF BUXTON

TAXAL

5 miles NW of Buxton off the A5004

Overlooking the Goyt Valley, Taxal is home to the church of **St James**, the tower of which dates from the 12th century. Inside are a series of fascinating memorials - the earliest to William Jaudrell, who died in 1375, and Roger Jaudrell, a soldier killed at Agincourt in 1415. This is the same family that gave its name to Joddrell Bank, where the radio telescope can be found. An unusual memorial is one dated 1768 to the "Yeoman of the King's Mouth" or "food taster" to George II. West of Taxal are **Windgather Rocks**, a

gritstone outcrop popular with trainee rock-climbers. East of the village is the elegant and gracious **Shallcross Hall**, dating back to the 18th century and at one time home of the Shawcross family.

COMBS

3 miles N of Buxton off the A6

Combs Reservoir is situated near to the village, just outside Chapel-en-le-Frith and is crossed at one end by Dickie's Bridge. 'Dickie' is said to have resided at a farm in Tunstead where he was known as Ned Dixon. Apparently murdered by his cousin, he nevertheless continued his 'working life' as a sort of guard-skull, alerting the household with a series of knockings on the walls whenever strangers drew near. Of course, Dickie's little 'security' alarm was a problem at times, for instance, labourers had to be recruited for harvest time but were unable to sleep with the noises they heard. They left very quickly. Strange occurrences are said to have ensued when attempts were made to move the skull.

CHAPEL-EN-LE-FRITH

5 miles N of Buxton off the A6

This charming town stands on a high hill, near the High Peak, adjacent to the Buxton and Whaley-Bridge railway. It sprang from an ancient chapel within the Peak 'frith' or forest when in 1225 the guardians of the High Peak's Royal Forest purchased land from the Crown and built a chapel here, dedicating it to St Thomas à Becket

•

To the west of Buxton lies Axe Edge, the highest point of which rises to 1,807 feet above sea level. From this spot on a clear day the panoramic views of Derbyshire are overwhelming. Just beyond, at 1,690 feet above sea level, the Cat and Fiddle Inn is the second highest pub in England.

•

9

5 IN A PICKLE

Chapel-en-le-Frith

Are you 'in a pickle' over your lunch routine? Sick of the same old offerings? Then pay a visit to this new coffee shop and deli and you won't be disappointed.

🍴 see page 178

6 THE ROEBUCK INN

Chapel-en-le-Frith

A 17th century coaching inn, we offer a selection of fine cask ales, traditional home cooked foods and contemporary B&B accommodation.

🍴 ⋈ see page 178

of Canterbury. A century later the chapel was replaced with a more substantial building; further modernisation took place in the early 1700s. The building of the original chapel led to the foundation of the town and also its name, which is Norman French for 'chapel in the forest'. Although the term 'forest' suggests a wooded area, the 'frith' or forest never really existed, but referred to the Royal Forest of the Peak, hunting grounds that extended over much of north Derbyshire during the Middle Ages.

One piece of its heritage is the Peak Forest Tramway. This connected the limestone quarries around Dove Holes, with the canal basin at Buxworth, and provided a further means to getting the stone to market where it was needed.

A great scandal occurred here, in 1648, when Cromwell's men used the church as a gaol for 1,500 prisoners of the Scottish Army who had fought at the Battle of Ribbleton Moor. The conditions were appalling, few could even lie down because of the overcrowding and they were left there for 16 days before being released. No fewer than 44 died during this period and another 10 were too weak to survive the forced march back to Scotland. The dead were buried in the churchyard and after that the church became known as 'Derbyshire's Black Hole'.

Chapel Brow is a steep and cobbled street lined with picturesque little cottages leading down from the church onto Market Street and the modern section of the town, this is the true centre of Chapel. Visitors to this part of the town will notice several curious relics from a bygone era, notably the old stocks on the market place, put there by the town elders to meet out justice to wrong doers, and the old market cross. A more recent curio can be seen over the doorway of a premises on the Market Place. A Bull's head stares out over the street, and is all that remains of the inn that once stood here in pre war years.

Looming over the town is the prominent **Eccles Pike** (1,250 feet high) which, every year in August, is the site of the Eccles Pike Fell Race, one of the oldest fell races in the country – renowned for being tough and demanding. The road up to the Eccles Pike from Chapel-en-le-Frith has stunning views of the surrounding valleys and hills. From the top, and from Castle Naze, you can see as far as Manchester 20 miles to the northwest.

On the Castleton Road just a few miles northeast of the village lies the **Chestnut Centre**, a

Stocks, Chapel-en-le-Frith

fascinating wildlife conservation centre. Set in 50 acres of landscaped grounds and home, not only to a unique collection of birds and animals, but to many wild birds and mammals.

CHINLEY

6 miles N of Buxton off the B6062

Chinley is beautifully situated with plenty of walking close at hand, and a walk up **Chinley Churn** or **Cracken Edge** gives an excellent view across the area. This small north Derbyshire village lays claim to the superb **Chinley Viaducts**, a masterpiece of Victorian engineering. Chinley Station was once an important railway junction; from here you would have been able to catch a train to Sheffield, Manchester, Derby or even London. However, the railway is now a shadow of its former self, with the line to London closed since 1968 and the Manchester - Sheffield service much reduced from its heyday. Nonetheless, a legacy of fine railway bridges and viaducts can be seen around Chinley, and it must have been an amazing sight in the era of the steam engine.

The most important building around Chinley is probably the Elizabethan Hall at nearby Whithough which was built by the Kyrke family in the 16th century but is now the Old Hall Inn.

Another notable residence in the area is **Ford Hall** which was home to Reverend William Bagshawe (known as the "Apostle of the Peak"). He served as vicar

The Chestnut Centre, Chapel-en-le-Frith

of Glossop from 1652 until his ejection in 1662 under the Act of Uniformity. Bagshawe's successor as Nonconformist minister at Chinley, Dr James Clegg, built **Chinley Chapel** in 1711. Chinley Chapel, a simple Georgian building, looks deceptively like an ordinary house from the outside.

BUXWORTH

6 miles N of Buxton off the B6062

The village name has had a chequered history, starting off as Buggesworth in 1222, then to Bugsworth in 1625, but it was in the summer of 1929 when the villagers had a choice of 'Bugsworth' or 'Buxworth', according to the original petition document, which was rescued from a refuse bin in the late 1980's, there were 365 signatures for 'Buxworth' and only 3 against.

During 1999, there was an attempt to put the 'bug' back in Buxworth in order to commemorate the Millennium, but villagers voted the idea down, so it

7 THE CHESTNUT CENTRE

Chapel-en-le-Frith

Set in 50 acres of stunning, unspoilt conservation parkland, The Chestnut Centre houses Europe's largest collection of otters and owls

🏛 see page 179

Above Roosdyche, to the east of Whaley Bridge, is Bing Wood, a charming name until the true meaning of "bing" is revealed - it means 'slag heap' - a name that harkens back to the prominence of the coal industry during the 19th century.

remains 'Buxworth' to some and 'Buggy' to others.

Buxworth is the site of the terminal basin for the Peak Forest Canal (see Whaley Bridge), finished in 1800. It became one of the largest ports on the English narrow canal network during the 19th century, and remains unique as the only complete example of a canal and tramway terminus in Britain. 'Bugsworth Basin' was granted the status of a Scheduled Ancient Monument in 1977.

Buxworth used to have several public houses. Nowadays there is one inn, the Navigation, and a war memorial club known as 'Buggy Club'.

WHALEY BRIDGE

7 miles N of Buxton off the A5004

Known locally as the *'Gateway to the Goyt Valley'*, this Area of Outstanding Natural Beauty is a magnet for walkers, tourists and those seeking adventure. The village grew up around the coal-mining and textile industries. Both have now gone, but many feel the real glory of Whaley Bridge is the **Peak Forest Canal,** flowing through the town. Many visitors come by water, and there is a thriving barge-restaurant base at the canal head; boats can also be hired to those who want to explore the delights of the waterways in the area.

The **Toddbrook Reservoir,** often seen in summer with small yachts, is in an exceptionally beautiful setting. It was built in 1831 to be a feeder for the Peak Forest Canal, and is situated to the west of the town. The wharf here is dotted with picturesque narrowboats.

The whole area round the canal basin is very historic, with a large conservation area. Every year, usually in June, the basin provides the setting for one of the biggest local events, the **Whaley Water Weekend**. It is their starting point for the annual **Rose Queen Carnival**, which usually follows a week later.

To the east of the town lies a weird natural feature on the hillside, the curiously named **Roosdyche** is a strange flat-bottomed valley, 3/4 mile long, 40 yards wide and with sides sloping up to 30 feet high. Local legend decrees that The Roosdyche was a Roman racecourse as nobody could explain its creation but it is now believed the great scoop taken out of the hillside was the result of glacier erosion dating from the last ice age.

A map detailing many of the walks in and around Whaley Bridge

Peak Forest Canal, Whaley Bridge

is available from many outlets in the town.

LYME PARK

8 miles NW of Buxton off the A6

Lyme Park is an estate and park in the county of Cheshire, although the estate lies wholly within the Peak District National Park. It is an ancient estate that was given to Sir Thomas Danyers in 1346 by a grateful King Edward III after a battle at Caen. Danyers then passed the estate to his son-in-law, Sir Piers Legh, in 1388. It remained in the family until 1946, when it was given to the National Trust. The principal feature of the park is **Lyme Hall**, it offers a memorable glimpse of a genteel and extravagant age and has now become even better known since its use as the location for "Pemberley", the home of Mr. Darcy, in 1995 the BBC production of Jane Austen's novel *Pride and Prejudice*. The grounds now form a country park owned and managed by the National Trust and supported by Stockport Metropolitan Borough Council. A leaflet has been produced to help you get the best out of the grounds and gardens.

Not much remains of the original Elizabethan manor house; in the 18th century the house was redesigned to resemble an Italian palazzo, the work of Venetian architect Giacomo Leoni. Not daunted by the bleak landscape and climate of the surrounding Peak District, Leoni built a corner of Italy here in this much harsher countryside. Inside the mansion there is a mixture of styles: the elegant Leoni-designed rooms with rich rococo ceilings, the panelled Tudor drawing room, and two surviving Elizabethan rooms. Much of the three-dimensional internal carving is attributed to Grinling Gibbons, though a lot of the work was also undertaken by local craftsmen. Another glory of the house is the collection of early 17th century Mortlake tapestries, produced in what was then the village of Mortlake outside London.

As well as the fantastic splendour of the manor house, the estate includes a 17-acre Victorian garden, laid out with impressive bedding schemes, a sunken parterre, an Edwardian rose garden, Jekyll-style herbaceous borders, a reflection lake, a ravine garden and Wyatt conservatory. The garden is surrounded by 1,400 acres of medieval moorland, woodland and parkland, and is home for many Red Deer and Fallow Deer. Also within the garden is an unusual landmark, **The Cage**: built as a hunting lodge, it served as a watchtower from which to follow the stag hunts but was later used as a lockup for poachers. After years of disuse it has been recently restored.

NEW MILLS

9 miles N of Buxton off the A6015

Situated by the River Sett, New Mills takes its name from Tudor corn mills that once stood on the riverbanks, though an earlier mill,

8 DANDY COCK INN

Disley

The Dandy Cock Inn is a very traditional English Pub with good wholesome food and regular entertainment for all to enjoy.

see page 179

9 THE CROSSINGS

Furness Vale

As the website states, "The Crossings - a great little village pub" - and one can't argue with that!

see page 180

10 THE TORRS

New Mills

A friendly inn, offering comfy beds, real ales and fine food.

‖ ⊨ *see page 181*

11 THE ROYAL HOTEL

Hayfield

Where modern hospitality and traditional values; Good food and Fine wine; Comfort and Luxury, all come together.

⊨ ‖ *see page 182*

known as the "Berde Mill", built in 1391, gave it the name New Mill before that. Later, in the 18th and 19th centuries, water power was used to drive several cotton-spinning mills in the town and, as New Mills grew, the textile industry was joined by engineering industries and the confectionery trade. There is still a rich legacy of this industrial heritage to be found in the town. The Torr Mill is featured on the millennium series of postage stamps issued by the Post Office. The elevated **New Mills Millennium Walkway**, built on stilts rising from the River Goyt, sits directly opposite the Torrs Mill. The walkway answered public demand for a route through the impassable gritstone **Torrs Gorge**, reached by the **Torrs Riverside Park**. The gorge is an area of exceptional natural beauty and unique industrial archaeological heritage. The 175-yard-long steel walkway is fixed to the rock face and adjoining railway retaining wall at a height of about 20 feet from the base of the 100-feet deep gorge. The **New Mills Heritage Centre**, near the walkway, contains a fine model of how the town looked in the 1840s.

The **Little Mill** at Rowarth still retains a working water wheel, although the mill building is now a well-known public house. Opposite the library is the Police Station, where the ringleaders of the 'Kinder Trespassers' were kept in the cells, following their arrest in 1932, after the mass public trespass on Kinder Scout. Although it is

now a private house, the site is identified by a plaque on the wall. The trespass was a significant factor in the creation of National Parks, to allow public access to the countryside (see also the introduction to this book).

The serious walker or stroller can use New Mills as a starting point for various way-marked walks. **The Goyt Valley Way** leads south to Buxton via Whaley Bridge and the Goyt Valley north to Marple. There are local signposted walks below the Heritage Centre and the **Sett Valley Trail** follows the line of the old branch railway to Hayfield and then on to Kinder Scout. Opened in 1868, the single track line carried passengers and freight for over 100 years. However, by the late 1960s much of the trade had ceased and the line closed soon afterwards. In 1973, the line was reopened as a trail and is still used by walkers, cyclists and horse riders and it takes in the remains of buildings that were once part of the prosperous textile industry.

HAYFIELD

9 miles N of Buxton off the A624

Beneath the western slopes of **Kinder Scout**, Hayfield sits peacefully in the narrow valley of the River Sett surrounded by some of the wildest hills in the Dark Peak. The first written record of the place is to be found in the *Domesday Book* when it was called 'Hedfeld' and was a natural clearing in the vast forest that once covered the whole of North Derbyshire. It was once a staging post on the packhorse route across the Pennines. The old packhorse route went up the Sett valley and by Edale Cross, where the remains of an old cross can still be seen, down to Edale by Jacob's Ladder. Some ancient cottages still survive around the centre of the old village, and some local farmhouses date from the 17th century.

Things were much different in its industrial past, when cotton and paper mills, calico printing and a dye works made it a busy and anything but a peaceful place. As the 1700s progressed Hayfield began to share in the great expansion of textiles, which was taking place in its neighbour town, New Mills. Three-storey weavers' houses replaced many of the thatched cottages; three woollen mills were built by the river and later in 1810, a dye works. However, the prosperity did not last and handloom weaving began to decline, although Hayfield still had woollen mills until the mid 1800s.

A curious building can be found in Market Street, on the left of a small square known as **Dungeon Brow**. Built in 1799 this was the town's lock-up and was referred to as the new prison. However, the stocks in front of the building appear to be somewhat newer than the prison itself.

The elegant parish **Church of St Matthew** was completed in 1818, and is a reminder of this Pennine town's former prosperity. It stands on the site of a medieval church built in 1386 at the command of Richard II. The freemen of the parish had the right to appoint their own vicar, recommending him to the local bishop. This right was given to the freeholders when the church was built.

Tourists now come to walk on Kinder Scout, which at 2,088 feet is the highest point in the Peak District National Park, or to explore the much gentler valley of the River Sett. Hayfield is a popular centre for exploring the area and offers many amenities for hill walkers. The old station site has been turned into a picnic area and information centre. For many years Kinder Scout was barred to walkers, being preserved as a grouse moor. Until the peace was interrupted on 24th April 1932 by the famous 'Mass Trespass', when four hundred ramblers set off walking across the moors. Five ramblers were later arrested and imprisoned for their part in the demonstration. But it was not made in vain: as a result of the trespass access restrictions were gradually reduced. The walk started from **Bowden Bridge Quarry**, just to the west of the village centre and is now a car park with public toilets and a Peak Park campsite opposite.

Three miles northeast of the town is **Kinder Downfall**, a spectacular waterfall and at over 90 feet is the highest waterfall in the county. It lies on the River Kinder, where it flows over the edge of **Kinder Scout**. The waterfall was

12 THE PRINTERS ARMS

Thornsett
Conveniently situated mid way along the Sett Valley Trail, the Printers Arms is the perfect place to stop and recharge the batteries.

🍴 🛏 see page 183

13 SYCAMORE INN

Birch Vale
Bringing city style and luxury to the English countryside, The Sycamore Inn fuses warm, traditional hospitality with fine dining and contemporary elegance.

🍴 🛏 see page 184

Kinder Scout

14 DUKE OF YORK

Romiley

The Duke of York and Mediterranean Restaurant is conveniently located ½ mile from junction 27 on the M60 motorway.

see page 185

15 GLOSSOP HERITAGE CENTRE

Glossop

The Heritage Centre, in the town's central square, houses a permanent exhibition illustrating the rich history of Glossop

see page 182

formerly known as *'Kinder Scut'*, and it is from this that the plateau derives its name. In winter when the fall freezes solid it forms an imposing and fascinating sight – one not to be missed! In such conditions, climbers use it for ice-climbing training. It is also renowned for its blow-back effect, hence the phrase 'Kinder blow-back': where the prevailing wind forces the fall's water back against the rock so the water appears to run uphill! Not far from the bottom of the fall is a small lake known as **Mermaid's Pool**. Legend has it that those who go to the pool at midnight on the night before Easter Sunday will see a mermaid, or water sprite, swimming in the dark waters. The legend is said to date back to the times when pools and lakes were places of worship.

CHARLESWORTH

12 miles N of Buxton on the A626

Located on the western edge of the Pennines, Charlesworth has many old and typically Pennine cottages. The cotton mills established in the 19th century have long since ceased to operate but the village has two rows of small cottages where the occupants used to weave cotton.

As well as the neat mock-Gothic **St John the Baptist Parish Church** (1849), there is also a Catholic church (1985), which was built primarily for the many Irish immigrants who came over to this country after the potato famine to work in the nearby mills.

The site of a Roman fort, **Melandra Castle** is situated nearby and can be reached by a path from the Glossop to Stalybridge road.

GLOSSOP

13 miles N of Buxton off the A624

Glossop stands at the foot of an exhilarating stretch of road with hairpin bends, known as the **Snake Pass** and is an interesting mix of styles: the industrial town of the 19th century with its towering Victorian mills and the 17th century village with its charming old cottages and cobble streets. The name Glossop is thought to be of Saxon origin, derived from "Glott's Hop" - where 'hop' is a small valley and 'Glott' was probably a chieftains name.

Further back in time, when the Romans arrived here the area was under the control of the Brigantes, who were in the midst of a civil war, which lead to Roman intervention and the establishment of a fort, now known as Melandra Castle, but it is thought that the Roman name for the fort was

'Ardotalia'. The early, wooden fort probably dates from the seventies of the first century AD in the course of the 'pacification' of Brigantia. The timber fort has disappeared completely under the present stone fort and very little survives today but the stone foundations. The settlement developed further as part of the monastic estates of Basingwerk Abbey in north Wales and the village received its market charter in 1290. Subsequently there was a decline in its importance, and little now remains of Old Glossop except the medieval parish **Church of All Saints**.

Planned as a new town in the 19th century by the Duke of Norfolk, the original village stood on the banks of the Glossop Brook at the crossing point of three turnpike roads. The brook had already been harnessed to provide power for the cotton mills, as this was one of the most easterly towns of the booming Lancashire cotton industry. Many still refer to the older Glossop as Old Glossop and the Victorian settlement as Howard Town, named after the Duke, Bernard Edward Howard.

Latest news suggests that Glossop is set to become one of the country's most attractive areas for birdlife with the creation of a huge nature reserve bordering the National Park. The Royal Society for the Protection of Birds (RSPB) is believed to be in the final stages of negotiations and it hopes to turn a huge swathe of land into a conservation area where normal activities such as farming can continue but always with the birdlife in mind. The proposed site will stretch from Saddleworth in the north to Glossop in the south, taking in the Arnfield and Dovestones reservoirs and the Chew Valley. These areas are rich in wildlife, especially moorland birds such as the curlew, ring ouzel and the golden plover. There are also peregrine falcons, short-eared owls and many wetland birds. And in addition to the many species of birds there is also an abundance of roe deer, which were first spotted in the area by locals twenty years ago.

The **Glossop Heritage Centre** in Henry Street highlights the way the town has developed over the years. There are resources for family history research, an art gallery and café. You can read all the latest news from the centre on the website at www.glossopheritage.co.uk, or keep yourself up-to-date with daily news worthy stories about what's going in the area at, www.glossopadvertiser.co.uk.

DINTING

13 miles N of Buxton off the A624

The village is well served by the Dinting Railway Station, which is notable for the impressive **Dinting Arches**: a 120 feet viaduct built to carry the main Sheffield to Manchester railway line, which crosses the narrowest point of the valley, to the west of Glossop. It's graceful yet sturdy and even structure lends its name to a pale

16 THE HARE & HOUNDS

Glossop

One of the finest pubs in North Derbyshire offering great food, a selection of real ales and a traditional welcome.

🍴 *see page 185*

17 THE STAR INN

Glossop

Traditional street-corner inn close to town centre – offering 5 real ales it's a place able to quench any thirst!

🍴 🛏 *see page 186*

18 THE BEEHIVE AND HAGUE BISTRO

Glossop

Glossop's best kept secret, fine dining in a traditional pub atmosphere.

🍴 *see page 186*

The one main street in Hadfield looks unchanged since the 1950s but all was to change when a roving BBC location researcher wandered into town. Hadfield became the home of the cult TV series **The League of Gentlemen,** *a quirky comedy in which visitors were frowned upon and murky secrets dwelt behind every door. In the series, the town was known as Royston Vasey, and some of the local shops have maps showing the locations of many of the scenes, as well as souvenirs of the programme. Fame has now fleeted from the town since the shows popularity peaked in 2000, but many residents still remember and tell lengthy stories about what happened when Hadfield was also known as Royston Vasey.*

medium strength beer that is hugely popular in the county. The village church of the **Holy Trinity** was built in 1875 in Victorian gothic style and has a tall and elegant spire.

HADFIELD

14 miles N of Buxton off the A624

Once upon a time this was a small, inconspicuous town at the dead end of a branch railway line.

The main attraction of Hadfield is that it marks the start of the **Longdendale Trail**, which follows the line of the former Manchester to Sheffield railway line and forms part of the longer Trans-Pennine Trail that runs from coast to coast (Liverpool to Hull). It is now a safe, traffic-free trail for biking and walking. Its level sandy surface makes it suitable for wheelchair users and less agile people, as well as for families with small children and pushchairs. You can get onto the Longdendale Trail at Platt Street, Hadfield.

Longdendale itself is the valley of the River Etherow, and is a favourite place for day-trippers. Along the footpath through this wild and desolate valley there are many reminders of the past, including **Woodhead Chapel**, the graveyard of which has numerous memorials to the navvies, and their families, who died in an outbreak of cholera in 1849 while working on the two tunnels on the Sheffield to Manchester railway line. The chapel was originally built in 1487, though it has been rebuilt several times since.

NORTH EAST OF BUXTON

From Glossop, the A57 east is known as Snake Pass, and is an exhilarating stretch of road, with hair-pin bends. The road is frequently made impassable by landslides, heavy mist and massive snowfalls in winter but weather permitting, it is an experience not to be missed. For much of the length of the turnpike road that Thomas Telford built across Snake Pass in 1821, the route follows the line of an ancient Roman road, known as Doctor's Gate, which ran between Glossop and a fort at Brough. The route was so named after it was rediscovered, in the 16th century, by Dr Talbot, a vicar from Glossop. The illegitimate son of the Earl of Shrewsbury, Talbot used the road with great frequency as he travelled from Glossop to his father's castle at Sheffield.

EDALE

8 miles NE of Buxton off the A625

Edale is a justly popular destination for people who want to walk, climb, mountain bike, hang-glide or just sit and admire the magnificent scenery. Though the valley has changed over the centuries, it remains unspoilt, and there are many places where even in the bustle of today it is possible to escape from the crowds. Many travellers have spoken of Derbyshire as a county of contrasts, and nowhere is this more apparent than at Edale. Not only

Grindsbrook Booth Packhorse Bridge, Edale

does the landscape change dramatically within a short distance from the heart of the village, but the weather - as all serious walkers will know - can alter from brilliant sunshine to snowstorms in the space of a couple of hours.

Edale is famous for being the start of the **Pennine Way National Trust Trail**. Opened in 1965, this long-distance footpath winds up the watershed of England to Kirk Yetholm, across the Scottish border. The 300-year-old Nag's Head Inn is the traditional start of the 270-mile (435-km) Pennine Way. Though the footpath begins in the lush meadows of this secluded valley, it is not long before walkers find themselves crossing the wild and bleak moorland of featherbed Moss before heading further north to Bleaklow.

The village, nestling at the foot of Kinder Scout, is in the heart of dairy-farming and stock-rearing country, began as a series of scattered settlements. The five hamlets, which punctuate its length, are all called 'booths', an old word meaning a temporary shelter for herdsmen. The true name of the village is actually Grindsbrook Booth, but it is commonly known by the name of the valley. Tourism first came to Edale with the completion of the Manchester to Sheffield railway in 1894, though at that time there was little in the way of facilities for visitors. Today there

Southern End of Pennine Way, Edale

19

19 CAUSEWAY HOUSE

Castleton

A warm welcome awaits you at this traditional, family-run B&B. It retains a real flavour of days gone by and a relaxed and friendly atmosphere.

see page 187

are several hotels, camping sites, a large youth hostel and adventure and walking centres. **The Moorland Centre** is a new visitor and learning centre at Fieldhead, replacing the former National Park Information Centre. The Duke of Devonshire, speaking at the opening ceremony in September 2006, said: "In order to love these uplands properly we need to learn about them and educational facilities and functions are high on the list of priorities here and rightly so".

Not far from the village is the famous **Jacob's Ladder**. Nearby is the tumbledown remains of a hill farmers' cottage; this was the home of Jacob Marshall, who some 200 years ago cut the steps into the hillside leading up to **Edale Cross**, an ancient boundary marker erected by the monks of Holywell abbey, Flintshire, who owned lands here in medieval times.

CASTLETON

8 miles NE of Buxton off the A62

Situated at the head of the lovely Vale of Hope, Castleton is sheltered by the Norman ruin of **Peveril Castle** (English Heritage). The castle, originally called *'Castle of the Peak'* was built as a wooden stockade in 1080 by William Peveril (illegitimate son of William the Conqueror). In 1155 Henry II, thinking that the Peverils had become too powerful, seized the castle and its lands. Later rebuilt in stone, the keep was added by Henry in 1176. It was originally about 60 feet high and faced with

gritstone blocks, which still remain on the east and south sides and still dominates the view across Castleton. In Tudor times the building fell into disrepair, and the keep was used as a courthouse. Soon after, the castle was abandoned completely, with the stone being used for building cottages. In 1832 Sir Walter Scott published *Peveril of the Peak*, set in and around the castle. The foundations of the Great Hall and kitchens can be seen inside the courtyard. It remains the only surviving example of a Norman castle in Derbyshire, and is among the best preserved and most complete ruins in Britain.

Approaching Castleton from the west along the A625, the road runs through the **Winnats Pass**, a narrow limestone gorge hemmed in on both sides by steep limestone hills. It is thought to have been created when huge caverns, carved out by swift flowing underground rivers, collapsed. The gorge, over a mile in length, has been used as a road for centuries and is still the only direct route to the village from the west.

Aside from the castle, some of the older buildings in the village are the Castle Hotel, one of 6 pubs, dating back to the 17th century and Castleton Hall, a fine 13th century house, now a YHA Youth Hostel. Two and a half miles west of the village at Rushup Edge, is **Lord's Seat,** a Bronze Age burial mound. **St Edmund Parish Church** was heavily restored in 1837, but retains its box pews and a fine Norman arch, as well as a Breeches Bible.

Castleton has a lot to offer visitors in terms of interest and history. **Castleton Visitor Centre** is situated at the very heart of the village. The centre houses a fascinating museum as well as a full range of tourist information services including accommodation bookings, local theatre bookings, brochures, up to date information on events, attractions and the Peak District National Park. To cap it all, there are constant changing displays in the exhibition room, which shows off the talents of local artists, photographers and crafts people.

If you visit Castleton you can learn about the numerous traditions, customs and annual events for which Castleton has become famed. Where else will you find a Garland Ceremony held on **Oak Apple Day** or the ancient practice of ringing a curfew bell?

On Oak Apple Day, 29th May, the ancient ceremony of garlanding takes place in the village, and after the three feet high Garland has been paraded though the streets, it is hoisted to the top of Saint Edmund's Church tower. The ceremony celebrates the ending of winter, and the restoration of Charles II to the throne in 1660 after the rule by the parliamentarians.

The Garland is a wooden frame, with bunches of wild flowers attached and a small wreath of garden flowers on top called the "Queen". The 'King', dressed in Stuart costume, with the garland on his shoulders, tours the village on horseback followed by a procession and a band. At the end of the ceremony the garland is left on the top of the tower of St Edmunds Church to wither and the Queen's wreath is placed on the war memorial.

The hills to the west of Castleton are famous for their caves, which have been in the hands of the Ollerenshaw family for many years, and are probably one of Derbyshire's most popular attractions. Amazing trips down into the caves themselves can be made. During these trips, as well as seeing the incredible natural beauty of the caverns and the unique rock formations, there are collections of original 19th century mining tools. Above ground, in the gift shops, various items can be bought made with the distinctive "Blue John" fluorspar with its attractive purplish veining, which is only found in the Castleton area.

The **Blue John Mine** is a natural cavern system with some old workings. The name "Blue John" was given to the fluorspar in the 18th century by two miners, John Kirk and Joseph Hall. The best caverns within the system are the Crystallised Cavern and the Variegated Cavern.

At the bottom of Winnats Pass, only 1,000 metres (0.6 miles) from the centre of the village, lies **Speedwell Cavern.** It is a very gentle walk along the road to this former lead mine, which used boats on an underground canal to ferry the miners and lead ore to and

The village of Castleton is overlooked by the mighty bulk of Mam Tor, from which there are tremendous views. Known as the "shivering mountain", it rises to a height of 1,691 feet, and has the remains of an Iron Age fort at the top.

The Ollerenshaw Collection in Castleton is a collection of huge vases and urns made with the Blue John stone. Once prized by the Romans, it is said that Petronius paid the equivalent of around £40,000 for a wonderfully ornate vase carved from the stone. It is said that in a fit of petty-mindedness, he preferred to smash the vase rather than relinquish it to the Emperor Nero.

20 TREAK CLIFF CAVERN

Castleton

This spectacular underground cavern contains a wealth of rock formations, minerals and fossils. A fascinating day out for all the family.

 see page 187

•

Peak Cavern was used by the BBC, who filmed an episode of The Chronicles of Narnia *series there. Over the years successive Kings and Queens would entertain deep within the belly of the cave, which would be festooned with candles and other open flames - visitors can see the ledge on which the Royal musicians would perch.*

•

---

from the rock face. Half way along is a small chamber known as Halfway House, which allows boats to pass as they go in and out. The mine had a short life: it started up in 1771 and, following an investment of £14,000, closed in 1790 after only £3,000 worth of iron ore had been extracted. This underground canal is about 800 metres long, finally reaching a glorious cavern with a huge subterranean lake known as the Bottomless Pit.

Treak Cliff Cavern is on the Mam Tor Road, and contains superb stalagmites and stalactites. The cavern is not a natural formation, as it was dug by miners for the Blue John fluorspar. However, while digging in 1926, the miners broke through into some natural caverns, which have some features now known as the Frozen Waterfall and Aladdin's Cave.

Only **Peak Cavern** is a true cave. Directly beneath the castle, it has an awe-inspiring entrance and is said to have the widest opening of any cave in the British Isles. More recently the cave has been promoted using its older, more vulgar name the "Devil's Arse" (called so because of the flatulent-sounding noises from inside the cave). Up until the 17th century, little cottages used to stand within the entrance. The ropemakers who lived in these tiny dwellings used the cave entrance for making rope, the damp atmosphere being a favourable environment for rope making. Bert Marrison, the last rope maker in Castleton, worked

here and his ashes, along with some of his tools, are buried here. The ropewalk, which dates back some 400 years, can still be seen and guides re-enact the process of making rope. One ropemaker's cottage still exists.

HOPE

9 miles NE of Buxton off the A625

Tradition says that a great battle took place here in the 7th century between the troops of Mercia, under King Penda, and Northumbrian troops under King Edwin. The tradition further states that two hills to the north of the village, **Win Hill** and **Lose Hill,** were so named because of the battle. However, the village gets its first recorded mention in a charter dated AD 926, where it mentions a great battle won by King Athelstan. By the time of the *Domesday Book* of 1086, the parish of Hope had extended to embrace much of the High Peak area and included places such as Buxton, Chapel-en-le-Frith and Tideswell, and was one of the largest parishes in England. It remained so until the 19th century, though a market charter was not granted it until 1715.

The parish **Church of St Peter** was built at the beginning of the 13th century. The only part remaining from that original church is the Norman font. Its tower is 14th century with a squat spire on top and, though the chancel was rebuilt in 1881, 14th century piscina and sedilia are incorporated into the walls. The Latin inscription on a chair in the north aisle reads (in translation), 'You cannot make a scholar out of a block of wood', and is said to have been carved for Thomas Bocking, the vicar and schoolmaster here during the 17th century. His name also appears on the fine pulpit, and his Breeches Bible is displayed nearby. From the outside, the squat 14th century spire gives the church a rather curious shape. In the churchyard can be found the shaft of a Saxon cross.

The **Hope Agricultural Show** is held every year on August Bank Holiday Monday, and offers something for all the family.

BROUGH

9 miles NE of Buxton off the A6187

Brough is the site of the Roman fort of **Navio**, meaning 'place by the river'. Excavations of the site in the early 20th century revealed an enclosure with walls six feet thick, though little can be seen today. This rectangular fort was built in AD 158 to control the Romans' lead mining interests in the area. You can visit the riverside fort and wonder what the garrison thought of the surrounding hills as they kept lookout.

BRADWELL

9 miles NE of Buxton off the B6049

'Bradder' as this Hope Valley village is known locally, has a long and chequered history. People have taken baths in Bradwell ever since the Romans built the fort of *Narvio* at nearby Brough (also see Brough). Near the New Bath

Saxon and Steeple Cross, Hope

Hotel, where there is a thermal spring, the remains of a Roman Bath were found. Legend has it that Bradwell was also once a Roman slave camp, with the slaves working in the lead mines.

Later, when the Roman Empire fell, just after AD400, Bradwell became a tribal border and the mysterious earthwork known as the **Grey Ditch** was constructed north of the village. The boundary is a massive embankment that runs from Bradwell Edge to Mick Low to protect the limestone plateau from the north. We still don't know who built it or when.

21 BOWLING GREEN INN

Bradwell

Traditional country pub located in the Peak District National Park, popular with visitors and locals alike. Accommodation available. Food is locally sourced. Children's menu also available.

 see page 188

22 LADYBOWER INN

Bamford

The Ladybower Inn feels a world away from the city but it's an easily achievable destination for some fresh air and a change of pace and to tuck into the sort of food you'd have at home if you had the time.

 see page 189

During the Middle Ages and later, Bradwell was an important centre for lead mining, is famous as the place where miners' hardhats - hard, black, brimmed hats in which candles were stuck to light the way underground - were made; thus these hardhats came to be known as 'Bradder Beavers'.

The centre of the village is a maze of narrow lanes with tiny cottages. A narrow street called Smalldale follows the line of the Roman road between Brough and Buxton.

Most buildings in Bradwell date from the 1800s. Built in 1549, Hazelbadge Hall is one of the oldest houses in the area. Bradwell is also the birthplace of Samuel Fox, the 19th century inventor of the modern umbrella. His house is marked with a plaque and lies just off the main street.

A key attraction here is the massive **Bagshawe Cavern**, a cave reached by descending a flight of 98 steps through an old lead mine. It was named after Sir William Bagshawe, who owned the land when it was discovered in 1806 by lead miners. For the more adventurous, caving trips are available.

On the Saturday before the first Monday in August, four wells are dressed in the village. Although wells were dressed even at the turn of the 20th century, the present custom dates back only to 1949, when the Bowling Green Well was dressed during Small Dale Wakes. The village has its own particular method for making the colourful

screens, section by section, so that the clay does not dry out.

BAMFORD

11 miles NE of Buxton off the A6187

Bamford is a hillside village beneath the **Bamford Edge** and on the road to the **Ladybower** and **Upper Derwent** dam. When the Derwent and Howden dams were built in the early years of the 20th century, the valley of the Upper Derwent was flooded, submerging many farms under the rising waters. The 1,000 or so navvies and their families were housed at Birchinlee, a temporary village which came to be known locally as 'Tin Town', for its plethora of corrugated iron shacks. During the Second World War the third and largest reservoir, the **Ladybower**, was built. This involved the inundating of two villages — Derwent and Ashopton. Many buildings were lost including ancient farms and Derwent Hall, dating from 1672 and made into a youth hostel in 1931. The spire of the parish church was visible at first, but was demolished in 1947.

St John the Baptist Parish Church in Bamford was built between 1856 and 1860, and is unlike any other in Derbyshire. It was designed by the famous church architect William Butterfield, with a slender tower and an extra-sharp spire. It was here, within the churchyard, that the dead from Derwent's church were re-interred. The survivors were re-housed in Yorkshire Bridge, a purpose-built hamlet located below the embankment of the Ladybower Dam. The **Visitor Centre at Fairholmes** (in the Upper Derwent Valley) tells the story of these 'drowned villages'. Here you can also learn all about **The Derwent Dam**, built in 1935 and was the practice site for the Dambusters, who tested their bouncing bombs here.

Also worthy of note, particularly to lovers of industrial architecture, is **Bamford Mill**, just across the road by the river. This cotton mill, built in 1780 and rebuilt in 1791-1792 after a fire, retains its huge waterwheel and also has a 1907 tandem-compound steam engine. It ceased to operate as a cotton mill in 1965 and was used by an electric furnace manufacturer until a few years ago. It has now been converted for luxury housing.

Along the A57 towards Sheffield, the road dips and crosses the gory-sounding **Cutthroat Bridge**. The present bridge dates back to 1830, but takes its gruesome name from a 400-year-old murder (16th century), when the body of a man with his throat cut was discovered under the then bridge.

Bamford Sheepdog Trials, held on Spring Bank Holiday Monday, are among the best-attended and most famous in the Peak.

HATHERSAGE

12 miles NE of Buxton off the A625

The fictional home of **Little John**, loyal friend of Robin Hood. According to legend Little John,

after he had buried his comrade Robin Hood at Kirklees Priory, made his way sadly back to Hathersage where he spent his last remaining days. Whether or not the legend is to be believed, it is worth mentioning that when the grave in the churchyard was opened in the 1780s, a 32-inch thighbone was discovered. This would certainly indicate that the owner was well over seven feet tall. The whole area surrounding Hathersage has features with such names as Robin Hood's Cave, Hood Valley, Hood Brook and Robin Hood's Moss.

As well as its historical association to Robin Hood it also

Little Johns Grave, Hathersage

25

23 POOL CAFÉ

Hathersage

A child-friendly café that sells teas and coffees, light snacks and lunches, and possibly the finest fish and chips in the area!

see page 189

24 THE LITTLE JOHN INN

Hathersage

Whether you're after a quiet drink with friends, a romantic dinner or a place to stay in the heart of the beautiful Peak District, they can cater to your every need.

see page 190

25 THE THREE MERRY LADS

Lodge Moor

Truly a hidden gem, set amongst beautiful countryside, the Three Merry Lads offers a good pint, excellent food and magnificent service.

see page 191

has interesting literary connections. **Charlotte Brontë** stayed at Hathersage vicarage in 1845, and the village itself appears as 'Norton' in her novel *Jane Eyre*. The name Eyre was probably gleaned from the monuments to the prominent local landowners with this surname, which can be seen in the village churchyard.

The Eyre family has been associated with this area for over 800 years. Legend has it that the family was given their name by William the Conqueror. During the Battle of Hastings, so it is said, William was knocked from his horse and, wearing his now battered helmet, found it difficult to breathe. A Norman, Truelove, saw the King's distress and helped him take the helmet off and get back on his horse. In gratitude the King said that from thenceforth Truelove would be known as 'Air' for helping the King to breathe.

Later the King learned that Air had lost most of a leg in the battle, and made arrangements for Air and his family to be cared for and granted land in this part of Derbyshire. The name became corrupted to Eyre over the years, and the family's coat of arms shows a shield on top of which is a single armoured leg. The 15th century head of the family, Robert Eyre, lived at Highlow Hall. Within sight of this Hall he built seven houses, one for each of his seven sons. **North Lees** was one, which Charlotte Brontë took as a model for Rochester's house, Thornfield Hall. It is one of the finest

Elizabethan buildings in the region - a tall square tower with a long wing adjoining and the grounds are open to the public. Another was **Moorseats**, where Charlotte Brontë stayed on holiday and used as the inspiration for Moor House in *Jane Eyre*.

St Michael's Parish Church is said to date from 1381, though it has been much altered and extended over the years. There are brasses of the Eyre family, and an Eyre family chapel once stood on the north side of the chancel, on the other side of the tomb to Robert Eyre, dating from 1459.

Highlow Hall is a fine, battlemented manor built in the 1500s by the Eyre family. It is said to be haunted by a ghost known as The White Lady, thought to be the older sister of the wife of Nicholas Eyre, founder of the Eyre family. Nicholas had promised to marry her, but instead jilted her in favour of her younger sister. She was so humiliated she killed herself.

Until the late 18th century Hathersage was a small agricultural village with cottage industries making brass buttons and wire, until in 1750 a Henry Cocker started the **Atlas Works**, a mill for making wire. By the early 19th century it had become a centre for the manufacture of needles and pins. Though water power was used initially for the mills, by the mid-19th century smoke from the industrial steam engines enveloped the village. The fragments of dust and steel dispersed in the process of sharpening the needles destroyed the lungs of the workers, reducing their life expectancy to 30 years. There was also a paper mill, with the paper being used to wrap the needles and pins. The last mill here closed in 1902, as needle making moved to Sheffield, but several of the mills still stand, including the Atlas Works.

EAST EDGES OF THE DARK PEAK

FROGGATT

5 miles N of Bakewell off the B6054

Froggatt Village Hidden by Winter Mist

This neat village sits below the gritstone escarpment known as **Froggatt Edge** - a favourite place for climbers. The village's position has lead to its name - there are 17 fresh water springs in the village of which three can still be seen. The river Derwent is close by together with its attractive 17th century bridge, which is rather unusual in that it has two different shaped and sized arches.

The Froggatt show is held on August Bank Holiday and is an offshoot of the former village 'cow club'. There are very few pubs or shops but the quaintness still attracts many tourists on hot summer weekends.

Nearby **Stoke Hall**, situated high above the Derwent Valley, was built in 1757 for Reverend John Simpson. The Hall is now a hotel and restaurant, but remains home to a ghost, said to have been haunting the building for well over 100 years. The ghost is claimed to be that of a maid at the Hall who, while pining for a soldier fighting overseas, was brutally murdered. Her employers at the Hall were so shocked by this that they built a memorial to her in the front garden. However, the memorial was seen to move not long after it had been erected, and so it was rebuilt in a quiet corner of the estate, where it remains undisturbed.

CURBAR

5 miles NE of Bakewell off the A623

Although it is Eyam that is famous as the 'Plague Village', Curbar suffered much the same way, though about 30 years earlier. During the height of the infection bodies were taken away from the centre of the village, and usually as quickly as possible, to prevent the spread of the disease. Many of the graves were left unmarked, but at Curbar the **Cundy Graves** (dating from 1632) can be seen on the moors above the village. They are named after the Cundy family, who

27

Walkers atop Curbar Edge, Curbar

26 THE EATING HOUSE

Calver Bridge

The Eating House at the Derbyshire Craft Centre has a tiled floor, exposed stonework, smart wooden benches and newspapers to read while you relax.

❙❙ see page 192

farmed nearby. Below the Wesleyan Reform Church there are other graves.

Missionaries have trained at **Cliffe College,** since 1883. It is now a theological college and conference centre sponsored by the Methodist Church. Interesting older features of the village include a circular pinfold or stock compound on top of Pinfold Hill, where stray animals were kept until claimed by their owners. There is also a covered well and circular trough, and an unusual village lock-up with a conical roof.

The coarse gritstone ridge of **Curbar Edge,** which shelters the village, is popular with rock climbers and walkers alike.

CALVER

4 miles NE of Bakewell off the A623

In 1870 James Croston, in his book *'On Foot Through The Peak'* noted that the air at Calver was 'full of pale blue smoke that wreathed itself into a variety of fantastic looking clouds' - a reference to the lime-burning and lead-smelting which still took place in late Victorian times. Sixty years later just before the Second World War, travel writer Thomas Tudor remarked, "Calver is not pretty for it has mills and lime works and ugly houses, and gives little suggestion of the rural charm which agriculture and its attendant interests can throw over these Derbyshire dales".

These days the polluting smoke of industry is consigned to Calver's past and despite heavy traffic over the **Calver Bridge,** built in 1974, the village still wears a cloak interwoven with threads of rural charm.

Calver is also home to one of the most sinister buildings known to television viewers with long memories. The handsome, though austere, **Georgian Cotton Mill,** which is now converted into luxury flats, was the infamous Colditz Castle of the television series of that name. It was built between 1803 and 1804 by Arkwright to replace a mill built in the 1780s.

BASLOW

4 miles NE of Bakewell off the A619

Standing at the northern gates to Chatsworth, Baslow is inextricably linked with the fortunes of the Cavendish family. The village has three distinct parts – Bridge End, the oldest part around the church,

27 AVANT GARDE OF BASLOW

Baslow
A wonderful shop full of your entire gift and home needs. Every turn of the head leads to another surprise.

🏛 see page 193

Rhododendrons, Calver

28 RUTLAND ARMS

Baslow
A glorious country pub, with one of the best riverside beer gardens you will ever see.

🍴 🛏 see page 194

29 DEVONSHIRE ARMS HOTELS

Nether End, nr Baslow
A superb hotel with twelve beautiful en-suite rooms, fine dining and a great range of real ales for you to enjoy.

🍴 🛏 see page 195

Over End, a residential area to the north of the village and Nether End, next to the Chatsworth Estate. At Nether End, near one of Baslow's two fine bridges over the Derwent River, you can see one of the few remaining thatched cottages in the National Park.

The **Old Bridge** was built in 1603. It is the only bridge across the Derwent that has never been destroyed by floods. It replaced a wooden bridge, and one of the tasks of able-bodied men in the village at one time was to guard this bridge to ensure its weight limit was not exceeded. The watch house still exists, and it has an entrance that is only three-and-a-half feet high. The **Devonshire Bridge** was built just after the First World War, and carries most of the traffic across the river nowadays.

The parish church of **St Anne's** dates partly from the 15th century, and has an unusual clockface decorated with the legend 'Victoria' and '1897' in place of numerals - the idea of a local man, Lieutenant-Colonel E. M. Wrench. These were added to commemorate Queen Victoria's Diamond Jubilee. It is beautifully situated by the River Derwent, and has a squat broach spire that dominates the village. The fragment of an ancient Saxon cross shaft can also be found in the porch. Inside the church another unusual feature is preserved: a whip that was used to drive stray dogs out of the church during services in the 17th and 18th centuries. Some people claim it was also used to waken people who fell asleep during a service and snored.

Baslow sits beneath its own Peakland 'edge', which provides fine views across the Derwent Valley towards Chatsworth House. From the **Eagle Stone,** a 6 metre high block of gritstone on Baslow Edge, to the north of the village, there are wonderful views.

29

In pre-Saxon times, Macclesfield was known as "Hameston" – the homestead on the rock, and on that rock is set the church founded by King Edward I and Queen Eleanor - the Parish Church of St Michael and All Angels. From the modern town, a walk to the church involves climbing a gruelling flight of 108 steps. The core of the church is 14th century, but it was extended in the 1890s. The Legh Chapel within it dates from 1442, when Pierz Legh, who fought at Agincourt and was killed at the Siege of Meaux, was interred within it. Another chapel contains the famous Legh Pardon brass, which recalls the medieval practice of selling pardons for past sins, and even for those not yet committed. The inscription on the brass records that, in return for saying five Paternosters and five Aves, the Legh family received a pardon for 26,000 years and 26 days.

Climbing to the top of this isolated rock was a test for every young Baslow man before he married. It is here that the same Lieutenant-Colonel Wrench who had the unusual clock face installed, erected the **Wellington Monument** in 1866 to celebrate the Duke's victory at Waterloo and to counterbalance the monument to Nelson on Birchen Edge not far away. It is in the form of a ten-feet-high cross.

THE CHESHIRE PEAK DISTRICT

MACCLESFIELD

The earliest written reference to Macclesfield is found in the *Domesday Book* of 1086. Macclesfield is a medieval town, as evidenced by its street patterns and their names. Look to the end of Macclesfield's historic streets and you'll see the dramatic Peak District hills. Macclesfield is the major market town for East Cheshire and was once an important silk manufacturing town.

Charles Roe built the first silk mill here, beside the River Bollin, in 1743 and for more than a century-and-a-half, Macclesfield was known as *the* silk town, renowned for the skill of its designers and for its richly patterned woven fabrics. Whilst Macclesfield established its reputation many years ago as the greatest silk weaving centre in England, this industry has now declined in international attention.

Some of the early mill buildings survive and a number of them are of great architectural interest. It's appropriate then, that Macclesfield can boast the country's only **Silk Museum** where visitors are given a lively introduction to all aspects of the silk industry, from cocoon to catwalk! Originally the Macclesfield School of Art, built in 1877 to train designers for the silk industry, the museum has an award-winning audio-visual presentation, fascinating exhibitions on the Silk Road across Asia, silk cultivation, fashion and other uses of silk. A shop dedicated to silk offers a range of attractive and unusual gifts – scarves, ties, silk cards and woven pictures along with inexpensive gifts for children.

The silk theme continues at nearby **Paradise Mill**. Built in the 1820s, it is now a working museum demonstrating silk weaving on 26 restored jacquard hand looms. Exhibitions and restored workshops and living rooms capture the working conditions and lives of mill workers in the 1930s. It is also possible to buy locally-made silk products here. Within the town's **Heritage Centre** is another silk museum, which has some interesting displays on Macclesfield's rich and exciting past, (the town was occupied for five days by Scottish troops during the Jacobite Rebellion of 1745, for example). The Heritage Centre is housed within a former Sunday School which was built in 1813 and finally closed in 1970.

The Heritage Centre is situated

in the centre of Macclesfield. The Silk Museum, Paradise Mill and West Park Museum are situated within easy walking distance of the Heritage Centre.

One of the Macclesfield area's most famous sons is **Charles Frederick Tunnicliffe**, the celebrated bird and wildlife artist, who was born at the nearby village of Langley in 1901. He studied at the Macclesfield School of Art and first came to public attention with his illustrations for Henry Williamson's *Tarka the Otter* in 1927. A collection of Tunnicliffe's striking paintings can be seen at the **West Park Museum** on the northwest edge of the town. This purpose-built museum, founded in 1898 by the Brocklehurst family, also includes exhibits of ancient Egyptian artefacts, as well as fine and decorative arts.

Much less well-known is **William Buckley,** (the 'Wild White Man') who was born in Macclesfield around 1780. As a young man he joined the army and became a respected soldier. However, his military career came to an abrupt end in 1802, when he took part in a mutiny at Gibraltar against the Rock's commanding officer, the Duke of York, father-to-be of Queen Victoria. The mutiny failed and Buckley was transported to the convict colony of Australia. There he escaped into the outback and became the leader of an aboriginal tribe (the Wathaurung people) who took this giant of a man, some 6 feet 6 inches tall, as the reincarnation of a dead chief. For 32 years Buckley never saw a white man or heard a word of English. When the explorer John Bateman, on his way to found what is now Melbourne, discovered him, Buckley had virtually forgotten his mother tongue. He was pardoned, given a pension and was killed in an accident at Hobart at the age of 76. His survival against the odds, his determination to be free, and his life with the Wathaurong make his story remarkable.

AROUND MACCLESFIELD

PRESTBURY

3 miles N of Macclesfield off the A538

Prestbury, several times voted one of Cheshire's best-kept villages, has riverside walks along the Bollin Valley towards Wilmslow and includes a great deal of dairy-farming country. Widely known as one of the most attractive villages in the northwest, with its atmospheric and historic landscape, 13th century church and ancient buildings including the timber-framed **Priest's House**.

Dominating the centre, however, is the **Parish Church of St Peter**, a building largely of the 13th century but restored in 1879 by Sir George Gilbert Scott. In the churchyard is the church's Norman predecessor, a chapel largely rebuilt in 1747. Even today, it still maintains a tradition that began in 1577, every autumn and winter evening at 8pm a curfew bell is rung, with the number of

30 THE JOLLY SAILOR

Macclesfield

The regulars are the salt of the earth at the Jolly Sailor. It's a traditional Macclesfield pub that has lost none of its character and warmth while at the same time offering quality service and real value for money.

see page 196

31 DOLPHIN INN

Macclesfield

One of the best little pubs is the Dolphin Inn in Macclesfield: Robinsons beers feature here - including the mind blowing Old Tom at 8.5% in winter, which is dispensed by gravity.

see page 197

32 PUSS IN BOOTS

Macclesfield

A cosy yet spacious pub near the centre of Macclesfield with a canal-side beer garden, serving wholesome food and real ales.

see page 197

Norman Church, Prestbury

is the **Reading Room**, a building erected in 1720, which is now housing a branch library, a bank, an estate agent's and the Parish Council Chamber.

Prestbury Hall is in a commanding position facing down the village street. Ford House is at the other end of the street, near Prestbury Bridge, which crosses the River Bollin. And although not a listed building, it has a pleasing appearance and is an important component of the Conservation Area.

Charles Edward Stuart's Jacobite army passed through the village in late November 1745 on its way south to London. Four or five regiments marched through, followed by the prince and his bodyguard. An eyewitness described him as being a 'very handsome person of a man', in Highland dress, with a blue waistcoat trimmed in silver and wearing a blue Highland bonnet.

chimes corresponding to the date of the month. Close by is a building known as the **Norman Chapel** with a striking frontage carved with the characteristic Norman zigzags and beaked heads. Even older are the carved fragments of an 8th century Saxon cross, preserved under glass in the graveyard.

Opposite the church is the Priest's House, a remarkable building dating back to about 1448 and is now a bank. Also of interest

Saxon Cross, Prestbury

The village has several excellent restaurants and is a favourite destination for sightseers.

ADLINGTON

4 miles N of Macclesfield off the A523

Adlington Hall is one of the country's most popular attractions, with a history that can be traced back to 1040 when the Legh family of Adlington chose the site for a hunting lodge in the Forest of Macclesfield. The present structure, (quadrangular in shape) dates back to 1315, and incorporates both Medieval and Tudor architecture, further wings and rooms having been added down the centuries. There is much to see as you tour the hall, with beautifully polished wooden floors and lovely antique furnishings, enhancing the air of elegance and grandeur. The Great Hall is a breathtaking sight, a vast room of lofty proportions that sets off perfectly the exquisitely painted walls. One of Adlington Hall's most interesting and historic possessions is the organ in the Great Hall, standing in the balcony supported at each end by the two original oak trees, their roots still in the ground. It is one of the finest examples of a large 17th century organ in Britain as well as being one of the oldest. Being virtually unaltered since it was built, it now re-creates the authentic sounds of its day and has responded to the touch of many maestros, none more famous than George Frederick Handel who visited the hall in the 1740s.

Equally impressive are the Hall's gardens. Landscaped in the style of 'Capability Brown' in the 18th century, these are truly a delight to behold, with a Lime Avenue planted in 1688, and the splendid folly 'Temple to Diana' with its painted ceiling. More recent additions to the gardens include a maze, rose garden and the beautiful Father Tiber Water Garden.

It wasn't long after Handel's visit to Cheshire that the county was gripped by a mania for building canals, a passion that has left Cheshire with a uniquely complex network of these environmentally friendly waterways.

BOLLINGTON

4 miles NE of Macclesfield on the B5091

Known to its residents as the Happy Valley, this town as the name suggests, lies on the River Bollin, which flows from here down across the Cheshire plain. It's difficult to determine if this is a town or a village, because its 7,300

33 COFFEE TAVERN

Pott Shrigley
The Coffee Tavern, a curious structure - perhaps a former non-conformist chapel? - Now housing a tearoom and craft shop. This quaint building is like taking a step back in time! And is a haven for walkers and cyclists due its rural location.

¶ *see page 198*

Adlington Hall, Adlington

34 THE HOLLY BUSH

Bollington

Traditional village hostelry noted for its excellent food and real ales.

see page 198

35 THE ROBIN HOOD

Rainow

A great place for pub goers and walkers alike to sample fine food and drink.

see page 200

36 RISING SUN INN

Rainow

Predominantly a food house but has a good regulars base of clientele who come to enjoy a drink at the bar. Three real ales available. Parties and walking groups very welcome.

see page 199

37 COMMON BARN FARM

Rainow

For an unforgettable break in the Cheshire Peak District, visit Common Barn Farm, beautiful self-catering cottages and Bed & Breakfast rooms, situated on a traditional working sheep farm.

see page 200

population is strung out over a distance of about two miles, giving the feeling of one long village. Present day Bollington is really based around three villages that became merged together – Bollington, West Bollington and Bollington Cross.

Like Macclesfield, in its 19th century heyday, there were 13 cotton mills working away at Bollington but producing cotton rather than silk. Two of the largest mills, the Clarence and the Adelphi, still stand, although now adapted to other purposes. The Victorian shops and cottages around Water Street and the High Street recall those busy days.

A striking feature of the town is the splendid 20-arched viaduct which once carried the railway over the River Dean. It is now part of the **Middlewood Way,** a ten-mile, traffic-free country trail that follows a scenic route from Macclesfield to Marple. The Way is open to walkers, cyclists and horse riders and during the season cycles are available for hire, complete with child seats if required.

Just as remarkable as the viaduct, although in a different way, is **White Nancy.** This curious dome-shaped, whitewashed monument stands on Kerridge Hill, more than 900 feet above sea level. It was erected in 1817 and has been the subject of considerable discussion though it is generally believed to have been built to commemorate the Battle of

Waterloo, and was named Nancy after a member of the Gaskell Family.

Today, Bollington enjoys a strong sense of community spirit and this is no more apparent that at the **Discovery Centre** in Clarence Mill. It was opened by cousins John & Terry Waite, in 2005 and provides an insight into Bollington's heritage.

Visit the "Happy Valley" site (www.happy-valley.org.uk) for maps, pubs and restaurants, local history, organisations, businesses and artisans, and to learn about a local heritage initiative.

SUTTON

2 miles S of Macclesfield off the A523

Sutton Hall is honoured by scholars as the birthplace of **Raphael Holinshed**, whose famous *Chronicles of England, Scotland & Ireland* (1577) provided the source material for no fewer than 14 of Shakespeare's plays including the plot of *Macbeth*, and for portions of *King Lear* and *Cymbeline*. As well as drawing heavily on the facts in the Chronicles, the playwright wasn't above plagiarising some of Holinshed's happier turns of phrase.

This semi-rural village includes the hamlets of Gurnett and Jarman and it was in Gurnett that the notable engineer James Brindley did his apprenticeship in about 1733. A plaque commemorating this fact can still be seen on Plough Cottage.

BOSLEY

6 miles S of Macclesfield on the A523

Bosley takes its name from the wild boar that used to be prevalent in the area; in the *Domesday Book* of 1085 it was described as 'Boslegh'. Whilst Bosley is technically part of Macclesfield, it is on the Leek Road, and is a stones-throw from Congleton via the Bosley Crossroads.

To the east of Bosley town centre is the **Macclesfield Canal,** one of the highest waterways in England, running for much of its length at more than 500 feet above sea level. It was one of the last canals to be built and was designed by Thomas Telford. Between Macclesfield and Congleton, the canal descends over 100 feet in a spectacular series of 12 locks at Bosley, before crossing the River Dane via Telford's handsome iron viaduct. Also to the east of the village is the reservoir created to feed the canal. It is used by anglers and is visited by ornithologists.

Other unusual features of this superbly engineered canal are the two "roving bridges" south of Congleton. These swing from one bank to the other where the towpath changes sides and so enabled horses to cross over without having to unhitch the tow-rope.

38 BOARS LEIGH RESTAURANT

Bosley

The Boars Leigh Restaurant is in a beautiful country position, a friendly restaurant serving Continental cuisine.

see page 200

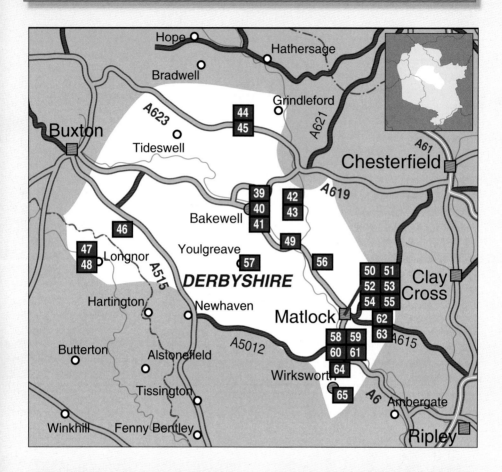

🛏 ACCOMMODATION

40	The Manners Hotel, Bakewell	p 38, 200
43	Ball Cross Farm Cottages, Chatsworth Estate, nr Bakewell	p 41, 202
44	The Miners Arms, Eyam, Hope Valley	p 43, 203
46	Bull I' th' Thorn, Hurdlow, nr Buxton	p 53, 204
47	The Black Grouse, Longnor, nr Buxton	p 54, 205
48	Ye Olde Cheshire Inn, Longnor, nr Buxton	p 54, 206
51	Glendon Guest House, Matlock	p 57, 208
54	The Duke of Wellington Residential Country Inn, Matlock	p 58, 210
57	The Bulls Head, Youlgreave, nr Bakewell	p 62, 211

🍴 FOOD & DRINK

39	The Bean & Bag, Bakewell	p 38, 201
40	The Manners Hotel, Bakewell	p 38, 200
44	The Miners Arms, Eyam, Hope Valley	p 43, 203
46	Bull I' th' Thorn, Hurdlow, nr Buxton	p 53, 204
47	The Black Grouse, Longnor, nr Buxton	p 54, 205
48	Ye Olde Cheshire Inn, Longnor, nr Buxton	p 54, 206
50	Stones Restaurant, Matlock	p 57, 207
52	The Horseshoe, Matlock	p 57, 208
53	The Sycamore Inn, Matlock	p 58, 209
54	The Duke of Wellington Residential Country Inn, Matlock	p 58, 210
55	Tawney's Coffee Shop, Matlock	p 58, 209
56	Tall Trees Coffee Shop & Restaurant, Two Dales, nr Matlock	p 59, 211
57	The Bulls Head, Youlgreave, nr Bakewell	p 62, 211

Bakewell, Matlock and The White Peak

These regions of the Derbyshire Dales occupy the central area of the Peak District National Park between the two major towns of Ashbourne and Buxton. It is altogether a more gentle, feminine kind of landscape than the Dark Peak. Its rich lands are more intensely farmed, and sheep and cattle dot the fields, which are separated by dry-stone walls. The estimated 26,000 miles of dry-stone walls in the White Peak are believed to make the most lasting impression on first-time visitors to the Peak District.

Considered to be part of the White Peak, Bakewell and Matlock are built on sedimentary rock deposited 350 million years ago, when the land lay under a warm tropical sea. Today Bakewell is nearly 400 feet above sea level, but it is by no means among the highest in the Peak District – parts of which rise to over 2,000 feet. The landscape is a geologist's dream, displaying the effects of millions of years of change.

The two main rivers, the Wye and the Derwent, which both have their source farther north, are, in this region, at a more gentle stage of their course. Over the centuries, the fast-flowing waters were harnessed to provide power

Peak District National Park, Youlgreave

to drive the mills situated on the riverbanks; any walk taken along these riverbanks will not only give the opportunity to discover a wide range of plant and animal life, but also provide the opportunity to see the remains of buildings that once played an important part in the economy of north Derbyshire.

Most of the White Peak is now used for dairy farming (for which calcium soil is essential). In the past it supported a number of creameries and the famous Hartington cheese factory survives today (see also Chapter 3, Hartington).

🍴	FOOD & DRINK	
58	The Princess Victoria, Matlock Bath	p 67, 212
59	Riverside Tea Rooms & Old Bank Cafe Bar, Matlock Bath	p 68, 213
60	Heights of Abraham, Matlock Bath	p 68, 212
61	The Peak District Mining Museum, Matlock Bath	p 69, 214
62	Scotland Nurseries Garden Centre,Restaurant & Chocolate Shop, Tansley, nr Matlock	p 70, 215
63	The Gate, Tansley, nr Matlock	p 70, 214
64	The Old Bakery Coffee Shop and Restaurant, Cromford	p 71, 216

🏛	PLACES OF INTEREST	
41	Haddon Hall, Bakewell	p 40, 201
42	Chatsworth House, Edensor	p 41, 202
45	Eyam Museum, Eyam, Hope Valley	p 43, 204
49	The Wind in the Willows Attraction, Rowsley	p 56, 207
62	Scotland Nurseries Garden Centre,Restaurant & Chocolate Shop, Tansley, nr Matlock	p 70, 215
65	The National Stone Centre, Wirksworth	p 73, 216

39 THE BEAN & BAG

Bakewell

Home of the famous
Bakewell pudding! Indulge in
a lovely fresh coffee,
homemade snacks or light
bites.

🍴 see page 201

40 THE MANNERS HOTEL

Bakewell

A lovely little pub offering,
good food, a full selection
of drinks, letting rooms and
holiday accommodation.

🍴 🛏 see page 200

BAKEWELL

World famous puddings, annual shows, steeped in history and packed with attractions - Bakewell is a 'must see' town at the geographical (and spiritual) heart of the Peak District National Park. The Park Authority has its headquarters here at **Aldern House** on Baslow Road, but these modern planners are following in the footsteps of an administrative history that goes back to Saxon times.

During Saxon times, Bakewell was in the Anglican kingdom of Mercia, and by Norman times had gained a great level of importance, with the town itself, and its church, being mentioned in the *Domesday Book*. An entry refers to the town as 'Badequella', meaning 'Bathwell', which is said to derive from a cluster of thermal springs in the area.

The **All Saints Parish Church** dates from the 10th century (although most of the building is medieval, it was restored in 1841).

The site, on which the church stands contains the largest and most varied group of medieval monuments in Britain. Inside the church, there are many references to the 'Manners' and 'Vernon' families, the story of the elopement of John Manners and Dorothy Vernon being one of the Peak District's most romantic tales.

The Romans had a station here and the town became established as a meeting and crossing point on the River Wye. The three original fords were eventually superseded by bridges and two of these remain: the distinctive **Five-Arched Bridge**, at around 800 years old is one of the oldest in the country, and the **Old Packhorse Bridge** further upstream.

There has been a market in Bakewell since 'time immemorial', but King Edward III granted its market charter in 1330. Held every Monday, the farming community flocks from miles around for the weekly sale of livestock, domestic goods and provisions. In 1826 the market was moved to a site in

Medieval Wye Bridge, Bakewell

Granby Road to clear the streets and relieve congestion. In recent years the livestock market has moved across the river to the new award-winning **Agricultural Business Centre**, and is currently enjoying something of a resurgence with the recent revival of monthly farmers' markets.

Today, Bakewell attracts a multitude of visitors and tourists, and has gained fame as being the unofficial 'Capital of the Peak'. It contains many interesting historic buildings and monuments. A couple of miles east of Bakewell is one of Britain's most celebrated and best loved historic houses and estates, **Chatsworth**. Offering something for everyone to enjoy from world famous works of art and spectacular fountains to miles of free walks.

The Rutland Arms was built in 1804. It is claimed that Jane Austen stayed there in 1811 and she based *Lambton* in *Pride and Prejudice* on the town. However the Rutland Arms' (known then as the White Horse Inn) chief claim to fame is as the place where the **Bakewell Pudding** was stumbled upon. Legend has it that the dish was an accidental invention during the 1860s. The story goes that a nobleman visited the Inn and ordered a strawberry tart. The cook, instead of stirring the egg mixture into the cake as would normally happen, spread it over the jam, and the Bakewell Pudding was born. However similar puddings were made in the area as early as the 16th century and this 'accident' story is now seen as doubtful.

This popular dessert is traditionally served with hot custard, but smaller versions (usually known as Bakewell tarts or Bakewell slices) can be bought in bakeries and supermarkets throughout the country. Two shops within the town each claim to have the oldest recipe: **The Old Original Bakewell Pudding Shop** on Bridge Street, and **Bloomers Original Bakewell Pudding Shop** on Water Street.

Those who enjoy old buildings should take time to look at the

Saxon Cross in Churchyard, Bakewell

39

In the churchyard of St Peter's Church in Edensor is buried the late President John F. Kennedy's sister Kathleen (known as "Kick"), who had married the Marquis of Hartington, heir to the 10th Duke of Devonshire, in 1944. Kathleen's mother, Rose Kennedy, objected to the marriage because the Marquis was a Protestant. When the marquis was killed by a German sniper four months later, Rose saw it as divine retribution. She later became engaged to the 8th Earl Fitzwilliam, and both of them were killed in 1948 in an airplane crash in France.

41 HADDON HALL

nr Bakewell

Haddon Hall is thought by many to have been the first fortified house in the country, although the turrets and battlements were actually put on purely for show.

 see page 201

town's historic **Alm Houses** (King Street) – a classic sandstone terrace built by charity 300 years ago to give shelter to destitute townsfolk.

Other places of historical interest include **Bagshawe Hall**, a fine 17th century house built by a rich lawyer, and the **Old House** in Cunningham Place, behind the parish church. The latter building is one of the few genuinely medieval buildings of the area and serves as the local history museum and is in the care of the Bakewell Historical Society. **Old House Museum** (as its known today) houses a fascinating collection of rural bygones.

Also worth a visit is the **Market Hall,** which adjoins the Market Square, originally built as an open sided market hall. Since those early days, it has been used as a washhouse, dance hall and library before taking on its latest lease of life as the **Bakewell Information Centre**.

Not all of Bakewell's attractions are immediately obvious. Take the 'pink building', tucked away behind the walls of a picturesque medieval courtyard. With its lopsided walls and latticed windows, the house (now a florist's shop) has all the charm of a gingerbread cottage – and Kings Court is just one of many secluded squares to be discovered in the higgledy-piggledy backstreets of Bakewell.

There is little evidence of industry in the town, which is not very surprising considering Bakewell is surrounded by farming

country, but the remnants of **Lumford Mill** can still be seen. Originally built in 1778 by Sir Richard Arkwright as a cotton spinning mill, over 300 hands, mainly women and children, were employed here. Badly damaged by fire in 1868, the Mill has been rebuilt and it is used as offices today. Here can also be found a very fine example of a low-parapeted packhorse bridge across the Wye, dating from 1664. **Holme Hall** to the north of town dates from 1626. This Jacobean hall faces the water meadows of the Wye.

Just down the A6 toward Matlock is the romantic pile of medieval **Haddon Hall**, home of the Duke of Rutland. Haddon Hall is the star of many films. *Jane Eyre, Elizabeth* and *Pride and Prejudice* have all recently been shot in the lavish surrounds.

Bakewell has an annual well dressing and carnival, held in late June.

NORTH OF BAKEWELL

EDENSOR

2 miles E of Bakewell off the B6012

Pronounced 'Ensor', this pretty village was demolished then re-built in a different location by the 6th Duke of Devonshire between 1838 and 1842, after he deemed the original village was too close to **Chatsworth House** and spoiled the view. Only Park Cottage remains in its original location.

Unable to decide on a specific design for the buildings, an eccentric, though somehow pleasing, mixture of architectural styles characterises the village, with the graceful spire of Sir George Gilbert Scott's **St Peter's Church** dominating the scene.

PILSLEY

2 miles NE of Bakewell off the A619

There are two Pilsleys in Derbyshire, one being in northeast Derbyshire near Chesterfield and the Chatsworth Estate Village which this description covers. Pilsley is a pretty, unspoilt village with magnificent views over the Derwent Valley. It lies about one mile east of Chatsworth House, and along with Edensor and Beeley makes up the three Chatsworth Estate villages. The village is in a sheltered position and the limestone cottages are enriched by gardens full of colour. The Shire Horse Stud Farm, built by the 9th Duke of Devonshire in 1910, has been converted into a variety of craft workshops and the Chatsworth Estate Farm Shop.

HASSOP

3 miles N of Bakewell off the B6001

This little village is dominated by its fine Roman Catholic **Church of All Saints** (1818) and **Hassop Hall,** which is now a luxurious country house hotel. The church was built by the Eyre family who, as well as being devout Catholics, also owned some 20 manors in the area. Dating from the 17th century, Hassop Hall was garrisoned for the King by Thomas Eyre during the

View from Chatsworth Park, Edensor

Civil War and it remained in the family until the mid-19th century when there were a series of contested wills.

GREAT LONGSTONE

3 miles NW of Bakewell off the B6465

This one-street village has attractive 18th and 19th century houses, notably **Longstone Hall** built in 1747 of red brick and was the home of the Wright family. Nearby, Longstone Edge is being quarried for fluorspar, the mineral lead miners threw away as waste, but the National Park Authority wants to stop damage being caused here. On 28 July 2008, the Authority was granted leave to appeal against an earlier High Court decision that permitted quarrying. Although a date has not yet been set, it's likely that the appeal will be heard before the end of the year – watch this space!

---

42 CHATSWORTH HOUSE

nr Edensor

Magnificent stately home containing a wealth of art treasures including furniture and porcelain.

🏛 see page 202

---

43 BALL CROSS FARM COTTAGES

Chatsworth Estate, nr Bakewell

Superbly restored cottages enjoying breathtaking views of Chatsworth Park.

🛏 see page 202

Village Cross, Great Longstone

STONEY MIDDLETON

4 miles N of Bakewell off the A623

This village, known simply as "Stoney" locally, is certainly well named as, particularly in this part of **Middleton Dale**, great walls of limestone rise up from the valley floor. Further up the Dale there are also many disused limestone quarries as well as the remains of some lead mines. Not all industry has vanished from the area, as this is the home of nearly three-quarters of the country's fluorspar industry. Another relic from the past also survives - a shoe and boot-making company operates from the village and is housed in a former corn mill.

An ancient village, the Romans built a bath here, and it is mentioned in the *Domesday Book* as Midletune. It is thought that the place originated when a motte and bailey castle was built on **Castle Hill**, but was abandoned in the 14th century due to the Black Death. Nearby is the odd octagonally-shaped **St Martin's Parish Church**. Joan Eyre built it in thanksgiving for the safe return of her husband from the field of the Battle of Agincourt in the 15th century. It is said that she actually built the church at a place where she and her husband-to-be met and courted in secret, as her family did not approve of him.

Middleton Hall dates originally from about 1600, but was much altered by the Denman family in the 19th century. The most famous Denman was a lawyer who became Lord Chief Justice of England in 1832.

During the Great Plague of 1665-1666, the 17th century villagers of Stoney Middleton left food and clothing out for those quarantined in nearby Eyam.

In January 2007 some of the houses in the village were ruined when a wall of mud pounded the village after a dam near the top of the dale burst following heavy rainfall. Despite this, Stoney Middleton has preserved its village identity and character and also partakes in the custom of well-dressing, when two wells around

The Nook are dressed in late July/ early August.

EYAM

5 miles N of Bakewell off the B6521

Eyam, pronounced 'Eem', cannot escape its infamous label as 'the **Plague Village**'. In 1665, a local tailor, George Vicars, received a bundle of plague-infected clothing from London. Within a short time the infection had spread and the terrified inhabitants prepared to flee the village. However, the local rector, William Mompesson, and his predecessor Thomas Stanley persuaded the villagers to stay put and, thanks to his intervention, most neighbouring villages escaped the disease. Eyam was quarantined for over a year, relying on outside help for supplies of food which were left on the village boundary (see Stoney Middleton).

Out of a total of 350 inhabitants, only 83 survived. Whole families were wiped out, and there were no formal funerals. People were buried close to where they died without ceremony. At Riley Farm, the farmer's wife buried her husband and six children within eight days. The **Riley Graves**, as they are called nowadays, are still there.

An open-air service is held each August at Cucklet Delf to commemorate the villagers' brave self-sacrifice, and the well-dressings are also a thanksgiving for the pureness of the water. Taking place on the last Sunday in August, known as Plague Sunday, this also commemorates the climax of the plague and the death of the rector's wife, Catherine Mompesson.

The village itself is quite large and self-contained, and typical of a mining and quarrying settlement. For all its plague associations, it is said that it was the first village in England to have a public water system. In the 16th century a series of troughs were placed

•

The nursery rhyme 'Ring a' ring a' roses' describes the symptoms of plague. One sign of the infection was a dark red rash like a 'ring of roses'. A 'pocketful of posies' was a bunch of herbs people carried to ward off the disease. 'Atishoo, atishoo' was the sound of sneezing as the plague took hold. Finally came death – 'we all fall down'.

•

44 THE MINERS ARMS

Eyam

A 17th century inn & restaurant, steeped in history with many tales to tell! As well as fine accommodation and great food.

🍴 🛏 see page 203

45 EYAM MUSEUM

Eyam

Learn the full story behind this village, once devasted by plague.

🏛 see page 204

Mompessons Well, Eyam

Padley Chapel, Grindleford

•

Padley Chapel in Grindleford is all that remains of the manor house of Padley Hall, from where two priests, Robert Ludlam and Nicholas Garlick, were taken to be hung, drawn and quartered in 1588 at the height of the Reformation. There is a pilgrimage each year in July to Padley Chapel to commemorate two of the Catholic martyrs.

•

throughout the village, with water being brought to them by pipes. An interesting place to stroll around, there are many information plaques documenting events where they took place. **Eyam Museum** tells the story of the heroic sacrifice and the **Parish Church of St Lawrence** dates partly from the 12th century and restored in the 19th century, houses an excellent exhibition of Eyam's history, including Mompesson's own chair and the plague register. Also inside the Church are two ancient coffin lids;

the top of one of the lids is known as St Helen's Cross. Born in what is now Turkey, she is said to have found a fragment of the cross on which Jesus was crucified. In the churchyard is the best-preserved Saxon cross to be found in the Peak District, along with an unusual sundial which dates from 1775. There is also a memorial to Catherine Mompesson and Thomas Stanley.

The home of the Wright family for over 300 years, **Eyam Hall** is a wonderful, unspoilt 17th century manor house that is now open to the public. As well as touring the house and seeing the impressive stone-flagged hall, tapestry room and the magnificent tester bed, there is also a café and gift shop. The Eyam Hall Crafts Centre, housed in the farm building, contains several individual units which specialise in a variety of unusual and skilfully-fashioned crafts.

A mile or two north of the village is **Eyam Moor**, where there are cairns and stone circles.

GRINDLEFORD

6 miles N of Bakewell off the A625

Strung out for 2 miles along the River Derwent, Grindleford gets its name from the grindstones that were quarried from nearby Froggatt and Curbar Edges for many years.

Across from Padley Chapel is **Brunt's Barn**, a conservation centre founded in 1981 in memory of Harry Brunt, a local man who helped found the Peak District National Park.

ASHFORD IN THE WATER

1 mile NW of Bakewell off the A6

Not exactly in the water, but certainly on the River Wye, Ashford is another candidate for Derbyshire's prettiest village. It developed around a ford that spanned the river and was once an important crossing place on the ancient Portway. Originally a medieval packhorse bridge, **Sheep Wash Bridge** crosses the Wye, with overhanging willows framing its low arches. It is one of three bridges in the village, and a favourite with artists. There is a small enclosure to one side that provides a clue to its name, as this is still occasionally used for its original purpose - crowds gather to witness sheep being washed in the river to clean their fleece before they are shorn. The lambs would be penned within the enclosure and the ewes would be thrown in the water at the other side. Seeing their offspring, they would swim across, their wool getting a good wash as they went.

So-called Black Marble, or Ashford Marble, actually a highly polished grey limestone from quarries near the village, was quarried nearby for some considerable time, and particularly during the Victorian era when it was fashionable to have decorative items and fire surrounds made from the stone. It was also exported all over the world. Within the village there was once a thriving cottage industry inlaying Black Marble with coloured marbles, shells and glass. Another industry

Padley Gorge, Grindleford

was candle making, and the house that now stands on the site of the factory is called The Candle House. It stands in Greaves Lane, "greaves" being the unusable dregs of melted tallow.

The great limestone **Parish Church of the Holy Trinity** was largely rebuilt in 1871 but retained the base of a 13th century tower and a 14th century north arcade. A fine Ashford Marble table is on show as well as a tablet to the memory of Henry Watson, the founder of the marble works who was also an authority on the geology of the area. Several of the pillars within the church are made of the rare Duke's Red marble, which is only found in the mine at Lathkill Dale owned by the Duke of Devonshire. The church also boasts a Norman tympanum, complete with Tree of Life, lion and hog, over the south door. Hanging from the roof of Ashford's church are the remains of four 'virgin's crantses' - paper garlands carried at the funerals of

Sheepwash Bridge over River Wye, Ashford in the Water

early 1950s. It now belongs to the Olivier family. **Thornbridge Hall** dates from 1781, but was extensively refurbished in Victorian times. It has been a teacher training college and a conference centre but is now a private residence once more.

The village also has a pleasant range of mainly 18th century cottages, and a former tithe barn.

MONSAL HEAD
3 miles NW of Bakewell off the B6465

Monsal Head, standing high above the dale, affords the best viewpoint for admiring **Monsal Dale**, through which the River Wye flows. The view is spectacular, with the river far below, winding through a steep-sided valley with many rocky outcrops. It forms part of the **Monsal Trail**, a popular route with walkers at weekends. The viaduct here is now an accepted feature of the landscape, but when the railway was built in the 1870s, John Ruskin campaigned against the damage done to this unique environment, simply "so that any fool from Bakewell can be in Buxton by lunchtime".

WARDLOW
6 miles NW of Bakewell off the B6465

At a crossroads near Wardlow, the body of Anthony Lingard (who had earlier been hanged at Derby) was publicly gibbeted in 1815 for the murder of a local widow. The body was placed in a cage and hung from the gibbet, a sight that drew an enormous crowd - so large that the

unmarried village girls. One of them dates from 1747.

Near the village is **Churchdale Hall**, which dates from the 18th century and was once part of the vast Chatsworth estate. It was also the home, until his death in 1950, of the 10th Duke of Devonshire who never resided at Chatsworth. Churchdale Farm is now a working sheep farm tucked down a private drive and is a haven of rural peace. The Monsal Trail is at the end of the drive and it offers gentle walks to Monsal Head and Bakewell, wild flowers in profusion and safe cycle riding for the children. To the south of Ashford is another manor House, **Ashford Hall** overlooking a picturesque lake formed by the River Wye. Built by the Dukes of Devonshire in 1785 to a design by Joseph Pickford of Derby, it was occupied by them for a time, but then sold in the

local lay-preacher at Tideswell found himself preaching to virtually empty pews. Determined not to waste this opportunity to speak to so large a congregation, he made his way to the gibbet and gave his sermon there.

A wonderful track leads from Wardlow to the edge of Cressbrook Dale, known as **The Pingle**. In spring the sides of this wonderful dale are covered with orchids and cowslips.

LITTON

6 miles NW of Bakewell off the A623

Although this is only a small village there is a real sense of spaciousness about Litton; a wide grass verge runs down the side of the street of this attractive village, situated almost 1,000 feet above sea level. An old world village pub, The Red Lion, and attractive triangular green complete with its ancient

cross and village stocks make up Litton's idyllic picture.

Equally attractive are the stone built cottages, though the oldest house dates from 1639 - many of the buildings have date stones - most date from the mid-18th century, a time of prosperity for the area when the local lead mining industry was booming.

A macabre historical reference is that of **Litton Mill**. The mill still stands beside the Wye Mill stream about 2 miles from Litton village (also see Millers Dale).

Litton was the also birthplace, in 1628, of **William Bagshawe**, who earned the title the "Apostle of the Peak" (see also Chapel-en-le-Frith).

CRESSBROOK

5 miles NW of Bakewell off the B6465

Clinging to the slopes of the Wye Valley, the village cottages of

Cressbrook Dale is renowned for its wonderful wild flowers, and is one of Derbyshire's finest dales for botanical interest. Some of the flowers are exceptionally rare including Bird's Foot Sedge (Carex ornithopoda). However, in spring the sides of the dale are literally covered with spotted orchids and cowslips. Cressbrook's well-dressing takes place during the first week in June.

Litton Village, Litton

Cressbrook are found in terraces amongst the ash woodland. The handsome **Cressbrook Mill**, built in 1815, was closed down in 1965, and has now been converted into flats. The apprentice house, used to house the pauper children from London and elsewhere who worked long hours in the mill, also exists. The owner of the Mill, William Newton, known as the "Minstrel of the Peak" because he wrote poetry, saw that the apprentices were treated well (see also Tideswell), unlike those at the nearby Litton Mill. The stretch of the River Wye between Cressbrook and Litton mills is known as Water-Cum-Jolly Dale.

TIDESWELL

8 miles NW of Bakewell off the B6049

Dubbed 'the Cathedral of the Peak', the magnificent 14th century **Parish Church of St John the Baptist** has a wealth of splendid features, and is one of the grandest parish churches in Derbyshire. The tower is impressive, the windows are beautiful and there is a fine collection of brasses inside. The 'Minstrel of the Peak', William Newton, is buried in the churchyard (see also Cressbrook).

In other parts of Derbyshire, natives of Tideswell are said to come from 'Tidsa', which takes its name from a Saxon chieftain called Tidi. Over 900 feet above sea level, the surrounding countryside offers many opportunities to wander, stroll, or take a leisurely (or energetic) hike through some varied and impressive scenery.

The village is one of the most ancient in the Peak District, and was granted its market charter in 1251. This was where the Great Courts of the Royal Forest of Peak met during the reign of Edward I, and some of buildings in the village may have foundations going back to that time.

Eccles Hall, overlooking the Market Place, was built in 1724 and became the home of the headmaster of the Grammar School in 1878.

By the 14th century the village was a flourishing centre for the local wool trade. Today it is home

Tideswell Church, Tideswell

to a number of craftspeople working in buildings converted from other uses. The excellence of their work is apparent, not only in the items they make, but also in the splendid well-dressing they help to arrange annually on the Saturday nearest St John the Baptist's Day, 24th June.

PEAK FOREST

11 miles NW of Bakewell off the A623

Despite its name, Peak Forest doesn't boast any trees. Instead, it takes its name from the medieval Royal Forest of the Peak, which was an open area used as a Royal hunting park rather than a forested area. At Chamber Farm, rebuilt in the 18th century, the Forest courts were held, attended by some 20 foresters whose job it was to maintain the special laws of the area.

The village grew from an earlier settlement called Dam, a hamlet that still exists. The **Parish Church of King Charles the Martyr** speaks of the fierce independence of the village inhabitants, and is one of the few in England dedicated to someone who was never a saint, but who was, nevertheless, revered by many. It was built in 1657 by the wife of the 2nd Earl of Devonshire, during a time when there was a ban on building churches. It became known as the 'the Gretna Green of the Peak', because of a quirk of ecclesiastical law - it was not subject to the laws regarding posting the banns before marriage. The church that stands today was built in 1878 on the site of the former chapel.

Within walking distance of Peak Forest is one of the original 'Seven Wonders of the Peak' as described by the poet Charles Cotton in 1682. **Eldon Hole** is the largest open pothole in Derbyshire, it was once thought to be bottomless and home to evil spirits. In the 1500s the Earl of Leicester had a man lowered on a rope to find the true depth. He went crazy and died speechless shortly afterwards. A traveller was fatally thrown in here after being robbed by two villains in the 1700s. Local legend also tells how a goose was thrown down Eldon Hole and reappeared inside Peak Cavern (also called the Devil's Arse) 2 miles (3 km) away. It had been singed down to its pimples by some infernal flames. Potholers, who view the hole as no more than a practice run, maintain that it is, in fact, 'only' 245 feet deep (75 metres).

TADDINGTON

5 miles E of Buxton off the A6

Now lying just off the main Bakewell to Buxton road, Taddington was one of the first places to be bypassed, and it has made a great improvement to village life. An ancient village and one of the highest in England at 1,100 feet, the cottages here are simple but the **Parish Church of St Michael and All Angels** is well worth looking at. Like many in the Peak District, it was rebuilt in the 14th century with money gained from the then-booming woollen

• *About 2 km west of the village of Taddington, on the escarpment lies Five Wells chambered cairn. Reputed to be the highest megalithic tomb in England, it is now a shadow of its former self after the mound was robbed for stone around 200 years ago. Only one of the chambers is still fully standing. Twelve burials were found in the tomb when it was excavated.* •

Church and Carved Pillar, Taddington

a hessian factory from the Hall and one day they quarrelled. The next day one of the brothers, named Isaac, was found dead in the cellar. The other brother was found guilty of the act. It is said that Isaac has been heard wandering around the passages of the Hall from time to time. The other ghost is of a drunken farmer who fell from his horse on his way home from Bakewell Market. Intriguingly, it was the farmer's ghost that revealed to his wife that he was dead before she knew about it.

MILLERS DALE

7 miles NE of Buxton off the B6049

Millers Dale is very near to the infamous **Litton Mill**. The original 19th century mill became notorious during the Industrial Revolution for its unsavoury employment practices. It was at Litton Mill where Robert Blincoe arrived as a child from a London poorhouse. He later wrote a harrowing tale of the cruelty and inhumane treatment meted out to the mill workers, many of the children died as a result of the harsh treatment they received at the hands of Ellis Needham and his sons. They were buried away from the mill to try and hide the truth about what went on, though in reality in those days, few people cared as long as these children were not a burden on local parishes. The mill, now luxury apartments, is said to be haunted by the ghosts of the orphans who were exploited as cheap labour.

The hamlet takes its name

and lead industries in the area. In 1891 it was considerably restored. The churchyard entrance is through a magnificent lych-gate, a gift to the church from Samuel Bramwell in 1910, and the churchyard is one of the best kept in the county.

Taddington Hall, one of the smaller of the Peak District manor houses, dates back to the 16th century though much of the building seen today was constructed in the 18th century. As with all good halls, Taddington has its share of ghost stories. One in particular concerns two brothers. The pair ran

from one of several charming and compact dales that lie along the River Wye and provide excellent walking. The nearby nature reserve occupies land that was originally a limestone quarry, which was last used in 1971. This tiny settlement, situated in the narrow valley of the River Wye, began life as late as the 1860s when it was built to provide housing for the workers building the London to Manchester railway. All this has now gone but the dramatic **Monsal Dale Viaduct** (built in the 1860s to carry the railway line) remains and is now used by walkers taking the Monsal Trail. It has stone piers and a wrought iron superstructure. There is another viaduct to the north, built in 1905, to cope with increased traffic on the line.

The disused railway has been converted to a track for walkers, cyclists, horse riders and less active people, including wheelchair users. Between Blackwell and Monsal Head the trail follows the deep limestone valley of the River Wye for eight-and-a-half miles. It is unsuitable for cycling and wheelchairs at its western half, with rocky diversions around tunnels. Level access is available from Miller's Dale Station, for half-a-mile west or two miles east.

The **Parish Church of St Anne's** is on a hillside, and is modern, dating from 1879.

WORMHILL

4 miles E of Buxton off the A6

Wormhill, originally named 'Wolfhill', is a sleepy village with an attractive village green, old Church and majestic Hall. Its original name is thought to have been taken from the numerous wolves which roamed the nearby woods – rest assured there are no wolves here today!

The village is surrounded by varied scenery of rocks known as **Chee Tor** and the beautiful dale through which runs the River Wye. The Bagshawes have been chief land owners in this village for several generations, they built **Wormhill Hall** in 1679, a stone mansion (privately owned) that can be seen on the approach to the village.

Within the village is a drinking fountain erected in 1875 to the memory of James Bridley (also see Tunstead). This fountain is the scene of the village well-dressing each year, normally in late August or early September.

TUNSTEAD

3 miles E of Buxton off the A6

High in the hills above the valley of the River Wye, Tunstead is a small hamlet with a very famous son, James Brindley, born here in 1716. He became a civil engineer and the greatest canal builder of his time, he is known as the father of the canal system. And although Brindley never learned to read or write, his skills in engineering brought him to the attention of the Duke of Bridgewater, who commissioned Brindley to build the Bridgwater Canal to carry coal between Manchester and Worsley.

•

Tunstead Quarry, in Great Rocks Dale, is said to be the largest limestone quarry in Europe. Quarrying originally took place on the western slopes of the dale, but in 1978 quarrying also began on the eastern slopes.

•

The cosy Christ Church in King Sterndale was built in 1847 in Gothic style, to a design by Bonomi, though it looks much older. Inside the church there is a memorial to Miss Ellen Hawkins of the neighbouring village of Cowdale, founder of the church. Other memorials include those to the Pickford family, such as the one commemorating William Pickford, a judge who later became Lord Sterndale, Master of the Rolls.

Magpie Mine, to the south of the village of Sheldon, produced lead for over 300 years, only closing down in 1924. This important site of industrial archaeology has been preserved, from the Cornish-style chimney stack, engine house and dynamite cabin right down to the more recent corrugated iron-roofed buildings. Now owned by the Peak District Mines Historical Society, guided parties are taken round to see the techniques used by the miners.

KING STERNDALE

2 miles SE of Buxton off the A6

The regally named King Sterndale is a tiny hamlet, with a population of barely 30 souls, high above Ashwood Dale. Hundreds of wonderful beech trees were planted around King Sterndale by the Pickford family to transform the bleak and desolate moorland landscape into a more cultured and sheltered parkland.

SOUTH AND WEST OF BAKEWELL

SHELDON

3 miles W of Bakewell off the A6

Situated 1,000 feet up on the limestone plateau, Sheldon was mentioned in the *Domesday Book* as Scheldhaun. However, its heyday was in the 18th and 19th centuries, when black marble was mined here, as it was at nearby Ashford in the Water. However, due to a lack of water to power the many manufacturing processes, it was not as successful as its neighbour.

The village itself is chiefly a single row of mainly 18th century cottages lining the main street. The 19th century **Parish Church of St Michael and All Angels**, with some notable features, is well worth a visit. Prehistoric monuments litter the limestone plateau above the village and, from Sheldon numerous footpaths lead through the surrounding countryside to Monyash, Flagg and Monsal Dale.

FLAGG

5 miles W of Bakewell off the A515

Each year on Easter Tuesday, thousands of enthusiastic spectators enjoy **Flagg Races**, the thrilling spectacle of thoroughbreds racing across spectacular open countryside. Flagg Races is a unique event that reflects the early days of horse racing when riders rode from one point to another with no defined course. It's a great day out!

The Elizabethan manor house, **Flagg Hall**, now known as Flagg Hall Farm, is visible from the main road, and is well worth seeing, although it is not open to the public.

CHELMORTON

7 miles W of Bakewell off the A5270

This 'mountain village' – is the second highest village in the county, with the **Parish Church of St John the Baptist** standing at 1,209 feet above sea level. The layout of the village is unchanged since Saxon times. It is linear, with farms built on either side of the gently sloping main street, which runs downhill in a south westerly direction from the parish church to the Flagg Lane crossroads. The remains of the narrow strips of land that were allotted to each cottage in medieval times can still be seen.

MONYASH

5 miles W of Bakewell off the B5055

Monyash, which is situated at the head of **Lathkill Dale**, can really only be experienced by walking along the path by the banks of the quiet river, is noted for its solitude and, consequently, there is an abundance of wildlife in and around the riverbank meadows. The upper valley is a National Nature Reserve; those who are lucky enough may even spot a kingfisher or two. One of the country's purest rivers, the Lathkill is famed for the range of aquatic life that it supports as well as being a popular trout river. Renowned for many centuries, it was Izaak Walton who said of the Lathkill, back in 1676, 'the purest and most transparent stream that I ever yet saw, either at home or abroad; and breeds, 'tis said, the reddest and best Trouts in England.' The **River Lathkill**, like others in the limestone area of the Peak District, disappears underground for parts of its course. In this case the river rises, in winter, from a large cave above Monyash, known as Lathkill Head Cave. In summer, the river emerges further downstream at Over Haddon.

Farming and tourism are its main industries now but it was once at the centre of the Peak District's lead mining industry (from medieval times to the end of the 19th century) and had its own Barmote Court (one of the oldest industrial courts in the country). Its market charter was granted in 1340 and the old market cross still stands on the village green. Due to its isolated position, Monyash had, for many years, to support itself and this led to a great many

industries within the village. As far back as prehistoric times there was a flint-tool 'factory' here and, as well as mining, candle-making and rope-making, mere-building was a village speciality.

The **Parish Church of St Leonard** was founded in 1178, though it has been much altered and added to over the years. Its parish chest is still preserved as one of its greatest treasures. It is 10-feet long and thought to date from the 13th century, when it was used to store the silver vessels and the robes worn during mass. It was once a centre for the Quaker movement, and John Gratton, a prominent preacher, lived at One Ash Grange.

POMEROY

7 miles W of Bakewell on the A515

Pomeroy is a charming hamlet with lovely buildings, some dating back to medieval times. The alehouse, the Duke of York, was first opened in 1618 as part of the farmstead owned by John and Maria White. The chestnut tree in the car park was planted in the 1900s by the then Prince of Wales, later King Edward VIII, on an occasion when he was visiting the area with Sir Thomas Pomeroy.

EARL STERNDALE

7 miles W of Bakewell off the A515

At the less well-known northern end of Dove Valley, Earl Sterndale is close to the limestone peaks of Hitter Hill and High Wheeldon, where there is Fox Hole Cave, which has been a shelter for people

Monyash was recorded in the Domesday Book as Maneis, thought to derive from 'many ash trees'. It is a picturesque village clustered around the village green, probably founded because of its 'mere' or ponds which were so vital on the fast-draining limestone.

46 BULL I' TH' THORN

Hurdlow

The Bull I' th' Thorn with Rare Breed Farm is a traditional Robinsons Pub retaining the olde worlde atmosphere. Original flagstone floors, oak beams and lots of interesting militaries and old furniture.

see page 204

47 THE BLACK GROUSE

Longnor

The Black Grouse offers luxurious hotel rooms, an elegant and intimate dining experience and a warm and friendly bar.

 see page 205

48 YE OLDE CHESHIRE INN

Longnor

Good food, good accommodation and good prices makes Ye Olde Cheshire Cheese Inn a firm favourite with holidaymakers at any time of year.

 see page 206

since Stone Age times. Over 1,100 feet above sea level, it is surrounded by lovely farmland. A number of the farmsteads are called 'granges', a relic of the Middle Ages when the granges were where monks of the local Abbey lived. The **Parish Church of St Michael**, built in the early 19th century, was the only church in Derbyshire to suffer a direct hit from a Second World War bomb. It was refurbished and restored in 1952, and retains a Saxon font.

The village inn, the Quiet Woman, has a sign showing a headless woman, with the words 'Soft words turneth away wrath'. It is supposedly of a previous landlord's nagging wife, known as 'Chattering Charteris', whose husband cut off her head.

CROWDECOTE

8 miles W of Bakewell off the B5053

Viewed from the tiny hamlet of Crowdecote are the sharply pointed summits and knife-edge ridges of **Chrome Hill** and **Parkhouse Hill**. They dominate the dale with a fair impression of real Alpine giants, especially after a snowfall. Over 350 million years ago, these knolls were actually coral reefs within a shallow, warm sea - hard to believe, but perhaps not so puzzling when one remembers that much of this landscape has been formed by the action of water. Unlike the softer limestone, they retained their original structure and are richer in marine fossils than limestone, containing trilobites and corals.

The original Crowdy Coat Bridge over the river Dove was a wooden footbridge. In 1709 this was replaced by a stone packhorse bridge, which was constructed to enable the heavily laden packhorse ponies to cross. The nearby Packhorse Inn dating back to 1723 was used by traders when this was the main road to Leek and Buxton.

LONGNOR

8 miles W of Bakewell off the B5053

On a ridge between the River Manifold and the River Dove, Longnor, has one of the oldest cobbled **Market Squares** in Britain, dating back to medieval times. Its **Market Hall** was built in 1873 and now houses the **Longnor Craft Centre**; at present there are over thirty exhibitors, and an outlet for craftspeople, artists and publishers. The village also has some fascinating narrow flagged passages, which seem to go nowhere but suddenly emerge among some beautiful scenery.

Though the late 18th century **Church of St Bartholomew** is grim and plain, it sits on foundations at least 800 years old, and contains a Norman font. The churchyard has an interesting gravestone. The epitaph tells the tale of the life of William Billinge, who was born in 1679, and died in 1791. This means that he died at a grand old age of 112 years. As a soldier Billinge served under Rooke at Gibraltar and Marlborough at Ramilles. After being sent home wounded, he recovered to take part in defending the King in the Jacobite Uprisings of 1715 and 1745.

On the first Thursday after the first Sunday in September, the annual 'Wakes Races', or 'Longnor Sports', takes place in the village. They go back to 1904, and are held at Waterhouse Farm.

OVER HADDON

1½ miles SW of Bakewell off the B5055

Sitting at the top of a steep valley there are beautiful views south over the Lathkill Dale and river. Over Haddon is now visited by walkers as it lies on the **Lathkill Dale Trail** which follows the River Lathkill up the valley to beyond Monyash. For several centuries the valley was alive with the lead mining industry that was a mainstay of the economy of much of northern Derbyshire, and any walk along the riverbanks will reveal remains from those workings as well as from limestone quarries.

There is an old engine house at **Mandale Mine** that was built in 1847 and further upstream from the mine are the stone pillars of an aqueduct, built in 1840, which carried water down to the engine house. Downstream from the village is the first National Nature Reserve established in the Peak District in 1972. Set mainly in an ash and elm wood, the reserve is home to many varieties of shrubs.

Over Haddon enjoys several claims to fame: the Gold Rush of 1854, when iron pyrites ('fool's gold') was found, Martha Taylor, the 'Fasting damsel' - she didn't eat for almost two years! And Maurice

Oldfield, head of the MI6 from 1973 – 1978, who lived in the village and is buried in the churchyard.

BEELEY

3 miles SE of Bakewell off the B6012

Anyone compiling a list of the most picturesque villages in Derbyshire would have to include Beeley. It is a pretty, unspoilt village sheltered by Beeley Moor with wonderful views in all directions. What makes the village so beautiful is that almost all the farm and domestic buildings are built from the same honey coloured sandstone, quarried locally close to Fallinge Edge. The ancient **Parish Church of St Anne,** close to the gabled vicarage - now a private house, is one of the oldest in Derbyshire. Its considerably mutilated round-headed doorway dates back to the middle of the 12th century. However, the star attraction, at least as far as age is concerned, is a gnarled old yew - once a massive tree - said to be older than the church. There is a tradition that, when marriages take place, the bride and groom must not enter the churchyard by the west gate, and must pay a token sum, after the ceremony, to leave by the east gate.

To the west of Beeley a small road climbs up onto Beeley Moor and here, along a concessionary path from Hell Bank, can be found **Hob Hurst's House**. Local folklore tells that this was the home of a goblin but it is just one of 30 or so Bronze Age barrows to be found on the moor.

*Longnor was the location for the filming of the TV series **Peak Practice** and fans of the series will easily spot Dr Tom's House, The Beeches Surgery, The Black Swan (actually the real-life Horseshoe Inn, the oldest in the village) and other familiar buildings.*

49 THE WIND IN THE WILLOWS ATTRACTION

Rowsley

Every scene from the classic English countryside tale is brought to life in an award winning indoor re-creation.

 see page 207

ROWSLEY

4 miles SE of Bakewell off the A6

The river Derwent and the river Wye merge at this village, giving the impression of two separate settlements. Not surprisingly called Great Rowsley and Little Rowsley, but perhaps more unexpectedly it is the latter that has the larger population. The older part of this small village, Great Rowsley, lies between the two rivers, while to the east is the 'railway village' around the former Midland railway station. The two areas are quite distinct. The old part has gritstone cottages and farmhouses, while the newer part is clearly Victorian.

The oldest surviving structure in the village is the bridge over the Derwent which was originally a 15th century packhorse bridge, widened to carry increasingly motorised traffic in 1925. However, there are some architectural gems and the most prominent of these is undoubtedly the magnificent **Peacock Hotel** whose visitors' book includes the names of many famous guests, including royalty, who have enjoyed a brief sojourn in the luxuriant surroundings since it became a hostelry in 1828. The house was built in 1652 by John Stevenson of Elton, founder in 1636 of the Lady Manners School in Bakewell. It is aptly named as a carved Peacock stands over the porch and is actually part of the family crest of the Manners family, whose descendents live at nearby Haddon Hall. It lies to the west of

the village, and is reckoned to be the most perfect house to survive from the Middle Ages in England.

The **Parish Church of St Katherine** dates from 1855, and contains the fine chest tomb of Lady Catherine Manners, first wife of the 7th Duke of Rutland, who died in 1859.

On the banks of the River Wye lies **Caudwell's Mill**, a unique Grade II listed historic roller flour mill. A mill has stood on this site for at least 400 years. The present mill was built in 1874, powered by water from the River Wye, and was run as a family business for over a century up until 1978. Since then the Mill has undergone extensive restoration by a group of dedicated volunteers and, using machinery that was installed at the beginning of this century, the mill is once again producing wholemeal flour. Other mill buildings on the site have been converted to house a variety of craft workshops, shops and a restaurant.

On Chatsworth Road, **Peak Village** is an extensive shopping centre but aside from shops, it boasts a coffee house, restaurant and is home to the fascinating **Toys of Yesteryear** exhibition. The impressive displays feature over 6,000 toys dating from the early 1900s right up until the 1970s, including a model of the 'Herbie' and 'Chitty Chitty Bang Bang' cars. It is also the home of the award-winning Wind in the Willows Attraction, an enchanting re-creation of Kenneth Grahame's magical tale that brings Toad's adventures to life and delights young and old alike.

MATLOCK

Matlock and its surrounding townships are built on the banks of the River Derwent. There are actually eight Matlocks that make up the town, but most have simply been engulfed and have lost their identity as the town grew. Just downriver of the main town **Matlock Bath**, the site of the spa, still maintains some individuality and contains the main tourist attractions of the locality. The Matlocks are just outside the boundaries of the National Park, but for many visitors marks the southern entrance to the Peak District. The towns, villages and much of the surrounding countryside have plenty of the typical Peak District characteristics. There are also some fine views over the Lower Derwent Valley from its well planned vantage points.

Matlock lies right on the divide between the gritstone of the Dark Peak and the limestone of the White Peak. The whole area is dominated by the imposing cliffs of High Tor and the Heights of Abraham, which tower 120 metres above the gorge. Though the hilltops are often windswept and bleak, the numerous dales, cut deep into the limestone, provide a lush and green haven for all manner of wild and plant life. Several of the rivers are famous for their trout, particularly the

Lathkill, which was greatly favoured by the keen angler and writer Sir Izaak Walton. The attractive four-arched bridge across the Derwent was built in the 1400s. It was made famous by Joseph Turner's painting - 'The Bridge at Matlock'.

In many respects Matlock seems quite a new town, certainly when compared with Buxton or Bakewell for instance. This is because until relatively recently Matlock was a collection of insignificant hamlets, but then the thermal springs were discovered and harnessed to make Matlock's name as a fashionable Victorian retreat. In the early Matlock village, known as Old Matlock you will find most of the buildings that predate the town's spa heyday.

The **Parish Church of St Giles** is an attractive building with fragments of masonry dating from its foundation in the 13th century, and its tower, in the perpendicular style, dates from the 16th century. However, most of the medieval church was destroyed in the 18th century during alterations, and in 1859 the chancel was completely rebuilt. Inside the church can be seen a preserved funeral garland or 'virgin crantse', though the church has others in storage. These were once common all over Derbyshire, and were bell-shaped, decorated with rosettes and ribbons and usually containing a personal item. They were made in memory of a deceased young girl of the parish. At her funeral the garland was carried by the dead

50 STONES RESTAURANT

Matlock

Unquestionably, the best place to eat in Matlock! A cosy, eclectic restaurant with stylish interior and a superb modern British menu.

see page 207

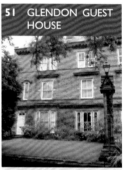

51 GLENDON GUEST HOUSE

Matlock

A cosy "home from home" feeling awaits you here, at this elegant, spacious Victorian home, that has been rightly awarded four stars by the AA.

see page 208

52 THE HORSESHOE

Matlock

A pub that is renowned for its great family-friendly atmosphere, its drink and fun entertainment evenings.

see page 208

53 THE SYCAMORE INN

Matlock

A honest decent pub with good food and well kept ale and service that is second to none!

see page 209

54 THE DUKE OF WELLINGTON RESIDENTIAL COUNTRY INN

Matlock

Delicious food and real ales are served at unbeatable prices, making it perfect for all!

see page 210

55 TAWNEY'S COFFEE SHOP

Matlock Green

A great place to relax, soak in the surroundings and enjoy a fine cup of coffee.

see page 209

girl's friends and, after the service, it would be suspended from the church rafters above the pew she had normally occupied.

Matlock is famed as, at one time, having the steepest gradient (a 1-in-5½) tramway in the world. It ran between the railway station and the hydro of John Smedley, and so steep was it that a cable beneath the road connected the two trams - one going uphill and one going downhill. It was also the only tram system in the Peak District. Opened in 1893, the tramcars ran until 1927 and the depot can still be seen at the top of Bank Road. The old ticket office and waiting room at Matlock station have been taken over by the **Peak Rail Society** and here can be found not only their shop, but also exhibitions explaining the history and aims of the society.

For train enthusiasts, the **Peak Rail** run regular steam and diesel hauled heritage passenger trains between Matlock Riverside station, through the charming rural station of Darley Dale to the terminus at Rowsley South. Run entirely by volunteers, this lovely old line operates on different days throughout the year. The full journey (one way) takes just 20 minutes, and passengers can alight to enjoy the picnic area at the entrance to Rowsley South Station, or the exhibition coach at Darley Dale platform to learn about the history of the reopening of the line. Special events are held throughout the year, and engine-

driving courses can be taken.

High up on the hill behind the town is the brooding ruin of **Riber Castle**, which sits 850 feet above sea level. The castle was built between 1862 and 1868 by John Smedley, as his residence. He was a local hosiery manufacturer who became interested in the hydropathic qualities of Matlock, and drew up the designs for the building himself. Lavishly decorated inside, Smedley constructed his own gas-producing plant to provide lighting for the castle and it even had its own well. The castle has been the former site of a boys' school, a food store during the Second World War, and later a nature reserve before it was left to become a ruined shell. It is currently privately owned, and not open to the public, with planning permission to convert it into luxury flats.

A popular attraction in the area is **Matlock Farm Park**, set in 600 acres of working farm and providing a great day out for all the family. The Park is home to a wide variety of animals including llamas, red deer, donkeys and peacocks, which children can feed. Two Dales Riding School and Trekking centre is part of the farm park. This offers riding lessons as well as pony trekking in the nearby forests (booking is essential).

To the west of Matlock, down a no-through road, can be found one of Derbyshire's few Grade I listed buildings, the secluded and well-hidden **Snitterton Hall**. The hall, built in the 1630s, is a rare surviving example of an Elizabethan manor house in a substantially original state. It was bought in 1996 for use as a private home and underwent a seven-year restoration project relying on authentic materials and traditional craftsmanship. The gardens were also restored in the late Elizabethan-Jacobean style with extensive terraces and lawns and formal box hedging. The main architect was quoted having said: "Snitterton was saved just in time. Another two or three years and it might have been too late".

NORTH OF MATLOCK

DARLEY DALE

2 miles NW of Matlock off the A6

This straggling village along the main road north from Matlock dates only from the 19th century, and was created out of several smaller settlements, three of them being Darley Bridge, Darley Hillside and South Darley. Indeed, Darley is mentioned in the *Domesday Book* as 'Derelie', showing that the name at least is ancient. The all-encompassing 'Darley Dale' was either devised by the commercially minded railway company at work in the area or by the romantically inclined vicar of the parish. Darley Dale makes up one of three stops on the Matlock-to-Rowsley South Peak Rail line.

One of the most unassuming heroines of this part of Derbyshire must be Lady Louisa Whitworth.

She was the second wife of Sir Joseph Whitworth, the famous Victorian engineer whose name is associated with the Great Exhibition of 1851 and who invented the screw thread. Sir Joseph made a fortune manufacturing, amongst other items, machine tools, munitions and nuts and bolts. Following his death in 1887, Lady Louisa brought sweeping changes to the lifestyle of the local poor and needy. She allowed the grounds of her home, Stancliffe Hall, to be used for school outings and events. In 1889, the Whitworth Cottage Hospital was opened under her auspices.

The **Whitworth Institute** was opened in 1890, bringing to the community a wide range of facilities including a swimming pool (the first heated pool in Britain), an assembly hall, a natural history museum and a library. At a time when a woman was required to take a secondary role in society, Lady Louisa was determined to credit her late husband with these changes, which so benefited Darley Dale. Lady Whitworth died in France in 1896, and is buried next to her husband at the **Parish Church of St Helen**, in the hamlet of Churchtown. The church as we see it today dates from at least the 12th century, and has the tomb of Sir John de Darley dating from 1322. It also contains two fine examples of Burne-Jones stained glass windows.

A tree that can be seen at the top of **Oker Hill** is a lobe

56 TALL TREES COFFEE SHOP AND RESTAURANT

Two Dales

A smart, stylish coffee shop and restaurant within a garden centre, the emphasis is good quality homemade food.

see page 211

●

The churchyard of the Church of St Helen in Darley Dale is home to the Darley Yew, reputed to be 2,000 years old, and one of the oldest living trees in Britain, with a girth of 33 feet. The yew predates the Norman origins of the church and may be older than the Saxon fragments found here during the last century.

●

At the centre of Stanton Moor is the best known monument, the Nine Ladies, the stone circle has a solitary boulder nearby called the King's Stone. Legend has it that one Sunday nine women and a fiddler came up onto the moor to dance and, for their act of sacrilege, they were turned to stone.

sycamore, and an unusual tale is attached to it. It seems that two brothers planted sycamore trees at the same time. One tree flourished, just as the brother who planted it did, while the other one died, just like the other brother, who died soon after. A different tale claims that a local man named Shore planted the twin trees to provide in due course of time, the wood for his coffin! William Wordsworth, passing through Darley in 1838 on his way to Dovedale was sufficiently inspired by the legend that he composed a sonnet about it called 'The Keepsake'.

Much of the stone used for local buildings came from nearby Stancliffe Quarry, which also supplied stone for the Thames Embankment and Hyde Park Corner in London, and the Walker Art Gallery in Liverpool. To the north of the 15th century **Darley Bridge**, which carries the road to Winster over the River Derwent, are the remains of **Mill Close Mine**. This was the largest and most productive lead mine in Derbyshire until 1938, when flooding caused it to be abandoned.

Darley Dale has an extensive park that is very pretty in all seasons. Another of this small village's attractions is **Red House Carriage Museum**, a working carriage museum featuring some fine examples of traditional horse-drawn vehicles and equipment. One of the finest collections in the country, it consists of nearly 40 carriages, including one of the very few surviving Hansom cabs, a stage coach, Royal Mail coach, Park Drag and many other private and commercial vehicles. Carriage rides are available, making regular trips through the countryside to places such as Chatsworth and Haddon Hall, and the carriages and horses can be hired for special occasions.

STANTON IN PEAK

5 miles NW of Matlock off the B5056

Stanton is a hillside village which climbs up the western flank of **Stanton Moor,** which rises to some 1,096 feet, one of the richest prehistoric sites in the Peak. The moor contains at least 70 barrows as well as stone circles, ancient enclosures and standing stones and is of such interest to archaeologists that the whole area is now protected. However, don't go expecting anything on the scale of Stonehenge, or even Arbor Low - most of the monuments and remains are very small-scale and overgrown with heather. There are interesting features on the moorland such as, the folly, **Earl Grey's Tower**, which was built in 1832 to commemorate the reform of Parliament.

This is a typical Peak District village, with numerous alleyways and courtyards off its main street. A quick glance at the village cottages and the visitor will soon notice the initials WPT that appear above most of the doorways. The initials are those of William Pole

Nine Ladies Stone Circle, Stanton in Peak

Thornhill, the owner of Stanton Hall, which stands near the church and is still home to his descendents. There are some fine 17th and 18th century cottages, one of which, Holly House, has some of its windows still blocked since the window tax of 1697.

The village pub, The Flying Childers, is named after one of the 4th Duke of Devonshire's most successful racehorses.

ALPORT

5½ miles NW of Matlock on a minor road off the B5056

Derbyshire has three such named places, the others being Alport Heights between Wirksworth and Ambergate, and Alport Moor in the High Peak. Better known is this charming village of Alport which stands at the confluence of the Bradford and Lathkill Rivers,

near Youlgreave. What connects the three Alports and indeed, is responsible for the place name, is the ancient track known as the Portway. This ancient way pre-dates the Roman occupation and runs roughly south-east to north-west through the county.

The cottages here mainly date from the 17th and 18th centuries, but the village itself is much older than these dwelling would suggest. Much its wealth was found, like so many other White Peak villages, on lead mining.

The surrounding countryside (its lead mining area) was owned by the Duke of Rutland and, by the end of the 18th century, the industry was struggling due to flooding. In order to prevent the mines filling up with water, the Duke had a 4 mile sough (underground drainage canal) built

Peak District National Park, Youlgreave

57 THE BULLS HEAD

Youlgreave

A warm welcome awaits you at the Bull's Head from Sharon and Mark Atkinson.

❘❙ ⊨ see page 211

to run the water off into the River Derwent. Begun in 1766, this project took 21 years to complete and, in an attempt to recover some of the construction costs, a levy was put on any ore being taken from below a certain level.

Sometime after completion of the project, in 1881, the **River Bradford** disappeared underground for several years. As with other rivers in this limestone landscape, it had channelled a route out underground, only this time it was taking the route of the sough to the River Derwent. After sealing the chasm through which the river had joined up with Hillcar Sough, it was restored to the above-ground landscape.

Among Alport's many fine houses, **Monk's Hall** (private) is one of the best, dating from the late 16th or early 17th century

and probably, at one time, was connected to a monastic grange. Another is **Harthill Hall Farm**, a gabled 17th century yeoman's farmhouse with stone mullioned and transomed windows.

YOULGREAVE

6 miles NW of Matlock on a minor road off the B5056

This straggling village can also be spelled Youlgrave, and to confuse matters further, it is known locally as Pommy. There have been over sixty variations of the name of this busy, one-street village recorded. The name is thought to mean 'the yellow grove' or 'Geola's grove' – an old name for a lead mine – and Youlgreave was certainly once at the centre of the Derbyshire lead mining industry. In fact, fluorspar and calcite are still extracted from some of the old mines.

The **Parish Church of All Saints,** one of the most beautiful churches in Derbyshire, contains some parts of the original Saxon building though its ancient font is, unfortunately, upturned and used as a sundial. Inside, the working font is Norman and still retains its stoup for holding the Holy Water. It is well worth taking the time to have a look at, as it is the only such font in England. The Church also contains a small tomb with an equally small alabaster effigy; dated 1488, it is a memorial to Thomas Cockayne, who was killed in a brawl when only in his teens. A fine alabaster panel in the north aisle, dated 1492, depicts the Virgin with Robert Gylbert, his wife and seventeen children. There is a glorious Burne-Jones stained-glass window, which was added in 1870, when Norman Shaw very sensitively restored the church.

Further up the village's main street is **Thimble Hall**, the smallest market hall in the Peak District. It dates from 1656 and there are also some rather grand Georgian houses to be found in the village. Nearby the old shop built in 1887 for the local Co-operative Society is now a youth hostel. It featured in the film of DH Lawrence's *The Virgin and the Gypsy*, much of which was filmed in the village. Standing opposite is the **Conduit Head**, a gritstone water tank that has the unofficial name of The Fountain. Built by the village's own water company in 1829, it supplied fresh soft water to all those who paid an annual fee of sixpence. In celebration of their new, clean water supply, the villagers held their first well-dressing in 1829. Today, Youlgreave dresses its wells for the Saturday nearest to St John the Baptist's Day (24th June). Such is the standard of the work that the villagers, all amateurs, are in great demand for advice and help.

Two or three miles to the west of the village is the Bronze Age **Arbor Low**, sometimes referred to as the 'Stonehenge of the Peak District'. About 250 feet in diameter, the central plateau is encircled by a ditch, which lies within a high circular bank. On the plateau is a stone circle of limestone blocks, with a group of

four stones in the centre cove. There are a total of 47 stones each weighing no less than eight tonnes, and a further three stones in the centre. Probably used as an observatory and also a religious site, it is not known whether the stones, which have been placed in pairs, ever stood upright. There is no archaeological evidence to suggest that they did. Gaps in the outer bank, to the northwest and southeast, could have been entrances and exits for religious ceremonies.

Arbor Low dates to the Early Bronze Age period, and there is much evidence in the dales along the River Lathkill that they were inhabited at that time. Nearby there is a large barrow known as **Gib Hill**, which stands at around 16 feet. When it was excavated a stone cist was discovered, containing a clay urn and burned human bones. This circular mound to the south of the stone circle, offers some protection against the weather and it is from this that Arbor Low got its name – 'sheltered heap'.

MIDDLETON BY YOULGREAVE

7 miles NW of Matlock on a minor road east of the A515

Thomas Bateman, the local squire, rebuilt the entire village in the 1820s, though more famous is his grandson. Thomas Bateman Jnr. (a pioneer archeologist) who, in the 19th century, excavated some 500 barrows in the Peak District, revealing many valuable Bronze

Age artefacts, many of which can be seen at Weston Park Museum in Sheffield. His book *Ten Years Digging* was published just two weeks before he died. Before his grandfather's death, he built **Lomberdale Hall** in 1844, which he enlarged in 1856 to house his growing collection of archeological artefacts. In the village is a small building with a signpost pointing to Thomas Batemans Jnr's grave. His tomb is surmounted with a replica of a Bronze Age urn.

WENSLEY

2½ miles W of Matlock off the B5057

Derbyshire, like Yorkshire, has a Wensley and a Wensleydale – yet there's not a cheese factory in sight! Its name derives from Woden, the Norse God of War, however the following rhyme suggests the village now has more romantic connotations.

*'At Winster Wakes there's ale and cakes
At Elton Wakes there's quenchers
At Bircher Wakes there's knives and forks
At Wensley Wakes there's wenches'.*

This is a modest village that often goes unnoticed as you drive through, but as a result provides a peaceful and pleasant alternative to many other villages.

BIRCHOVER

4 miles W of Matlock off the B5056

Birchover's name means 'the ridge where the birch trees grow'. Its main street meanders gently up from the unusual outcrops of **Rowtor Rocks** at the foot of the village, heading up towards neighbouring Stanton Moor. The village was once home to father-and-son amateur antiquarians J.C. and J.P. Heathcote, who excavated over seventy Bronze Age burial mounds. They kept a detailed and fascinating private museum in the old village post office in the main street and it is now in Sheffield's Weston Park Museum.

The strange Rocks of Rowtor, behind The Druid Inn, are said to have been used for Druidical rites. The Reverend Thomas Eyre, who died in 1717, was fascinated by these rocks and built the strange collection of steps, rooms and seats which have been carved out of the gritstone rocks on the summit of the outcrop. It is said that the reverend would take his friends there to admire the view across the valley below - a view, which nowadays is obscured by trees. Prehistoric cup-and-ring marks have been discovered on the rocks and several rocking stones can be moved by the application of a shoulder. One of these, weighing about 50 tons, could once be rocked easily by hand, but in 1799 fourteen young men decided to remove it for a bit of a lark. However when they put it back, they couldn't get the balance right.

Thomas Eyre lived at the Old Vicarage in the village below Rowtor Rocks, and also restored the lovely tiny church known as the Jesus Chapel or **Rowtor Chapel**. The chapel had been demoted to the village cheese shop, and it now features, among fragments of

Norman work, unusual carvings and some wonderful decorative features, including modern stained glass by the artist Brian Clarke, who lived at the vicarage for a time during the 1970s.

Nearby across the fields are two equally strange outcrops **Robin Hood's Stride** (also known as 'Mock beggar's Hall') and **Cratcliff Tor**. A medieval hermit's cave, complete with crucifix, can be seen at the foot of Cratcliff Tor, hidden behind an ancient yew tree.

WINSTER

4 miles W of Matlock off the B5056

This attractive gritstone village was once a lead mining centre and market town, the last mine at Mill Close, two miles to the northeast, closing down in 1938. Today it is a conservation village, with a pleasant high street and some fine late 18th century houses. Less splendid than the surrounding houses, but no less interesting, are the ginnels - little alleyways -

which run off the main street. The name 'Winster' is a corruption of 'Wysterne', the name under which it appears in the *Domesday Book*. It is thought to mean 'Wyn's thorn tree', though who Wyn is no one knows. The most impressive building here, however, must be the **Market House**, owned by the National Trust and found at the top of the main street. The Trust's first purchase in Derbyshire (in 1906) was the rugged, two-storey Market House. The lower portion, with its built-up arches, is over 500 years old, while the upper portion was added on in the 18th century, and rebuilt in 1905 using old materials. The house is open to the public and acts as an information centre and shop for the Trust.

Within the Burton Institute, Winster's village hall, is a more modern attraction, the **Winster Millennium Tapestry**. It took six years to make, and involved the whole village. For a payment of

•

The Ore House at Winster is the best preserved ore house left in the Peak District. Up to 50 years ago miners used it to lodge lead ore in safety over night. It had a chute at the back for depositing the lead ore and a vaulted roof for security. The ore house has been preserved by the Peak Park Authority.

•

Market House, Winster

The village of Elton overlooks Robin Hood's Stride - a spectacular tor of gritstone rocks. Legend has it that Robin strode between the tower-like stones at either end of the tor, but this is unlikely because they are 15 metres apart and the ascent of the towers is difficult - especially the southern one.

25p, villagers could get their name woven into it.

Winster Hall, built in 1628 by Francis Moore, a local businessman, has, like all good manor houses, its own ghost, which haunts the grounds. The ghost, in the form of a 'white lady', is said to be that of a daughter from the Hall, who fell in love with one of the coachmen. Her parents were horrified at her choice of husband and vowed to find a more suitable partner. However, before such a match could be made the girl and her lover climbed to the top of the Hall and jumped, together, to their deaths.

The **Bank House** is another building with a gruesome tale attached to it. It was built around 1580, and was occupied in the early 19th century by the local doctor, William Cuddie. The owner of nearby Oddo House, William Brittlebank, was visiting in 1821, and murdered Cuddie. He then fled, and a reward of £100 (a vast sum in those days) was offered for his capture, but he was never heard of again.

The **Parish Church of St John** stands on the site of an ancient chapel built by the Ferrers family, who was given the manor soon after the Conquest. The nave was built in 1833, tacked on to a tower of 1721, which itself was added to the original Norman building. It has a curfew bell which still rings at 8 pm every evening.

Finally, although Morris dancing is traditionally associated with the Cotswold area, two of the best known and most often played tunes, The Winster Gallop and Blue-eyed Stranger, originate from the village. Collected many years ago by Cecil Sharpe, a legend in the world of Morris dancing, they were rediscovered in the 1960s. The Winster Morris men traditionally dance through the village at the beginning of Wakes Week, in June, finishing, as all good Morris dances do, at one of the local pubs.

ELTON

5 miles W of Matlock off the B5056

One can't make reference to Elton without mentioning that it is one of the coldest places in Derbyshire. Not surprising given that it sits at an altitude of 900 feet, with no shelter from the cold north and east winds. This must raise the inevitable question as to why the village was built in such an exposed position. The facts that lead was in plentiful supply, as was water, were probably the major factors behind the location of the village.

Interestingly the village is set on a division in the underlying rocks, to the north is limestone and to the south is gritstone. This produces an unusual effect with gritstone vegetation on one side (i.e. oak trees) and limestone on the other (i.e. ash trees). The houses too reflect the division, some of limestone, some of gritstone, or a mixture of both. This is no more apparent than along the main street, where The Old Hall, which for many years acted as a Youth Hostel before being turned into a private residence, is built of girtstone. Whereas just across the road, Greenacres Farm, is built of pure limestone.

The surrounding area contains traces of barrows, Bronze or Iron Age enclosures and hut circles, but the most visible monument is the stone circle called the **Nine Stones** (though in fact only four are left standing) or **'Grey Ladies'**. It is another Bronze Age monument connected with the Portway, and is probably the most impressive in the area.

SOUTH OF MATLOCK

MATLOCK BATH

1 mile S of Matlock off the A6

Known as "Little Switzerland" to generations of tourists, Matlock Bath began its life as a craggy limestone gorge cut by the River Derwent. Developed as one of the country's first tourist destinations, it retains much of the character and interest that impressed early visitors. Matlock Bath was formed as a Spa Town, famous for its healing waters.

A turnpike road built in 1818, and the coming of the railways in 1849, brought Matlock Bath within easy reach, at small cost, to many more people and it became a popular destination for day excursions. Many famous people have visited the town such as the young Victoria before she succeeded to the throne. Lord Byron confirmed its romantic

character, comparing it with alpine Switzerland, hence its nickname "Little Switzerland".

Today, it is still essentially a holiday resort and manages to possess an air of Victorian charm left over from the days when many Victorians descended on the town looking for a 'cure'. Attractions in and around the village include High Tor, the Heights of Abraham including the cable cars, Gulliver's Kingdom, an Aquarium and the Peak District Mining Museum to name but a few. The town is also known as a meeting point for motorcyclists.

High Tor is a spectacular 390 feet high limestone cliff that towers

58 THE PRINCESS VICTORIA

Matlock Bath

For a novel and sensational dining experience...plus immaculately kept real ales...seek out The Princess Victoria.

🍴 *see page 212*

Cable Cars on Heights of Abraham, Matlock Bath

59 RIVERSIDE TEA ROOM AND OLD BANK CAFÉ BAR

Matlock Bath

Quaint tearoom and licensed Café bar offering a wide range of drinks and home cooked foods.

🍴 see page 213

60 HEIGHTS OF ABRAHAM

Matlock Bath

Overlooking the spa town, this country park with its spectacular views, makes an ideal day out .

 see page 212

above Matlock Bath, giving wonderful views of the town and its environs. Nothing beats a walk on High Tor Grounds, where there are 60 acres of nature trails to wander around, while, far below, the River Derwent appears like a silver thread through the gorge. A popular viewing point for Victorian visitors to the town, today rock climbers practice their skills on the precipitous crags. For those a little less energetic, a relatively steady walk to the top is amply rewarded by the magnificent views over the town and surrounding area.

On the opposite side of the valley are the beautiful wooded slopes of Masson Hill, the southern face of which has become known as the **Heights of Abraham**. This particular name was chosen after the inhabitants of Matlock had shown great enthusiasm for General Wolfe's victory in Quebec in 1759. This part of the Derwent valley was seen to resemble the gorge of the St Lawrence River and the original Heights of Abraham lying a mile north of Quebec. Today it is a well-known viewing point, reached on foot or, more easily, by cable car.

For a family 'fun' day out there is **Gulliver's Kingdom Theme Park** - nestled within breathtaking woodlands, all the rides are centred on family fun, so nothing too scary or unsettling. Just enough thrills to make your visit an unforgettable one!

One of the great attractions of the town is **The Aquarium**, which occupies what was once the old

Matlock Bath Hydro that was established in 1833. The original splendour of the Bath Hydro can still be seen, in the fine stone staircase and also in the thermal pool. The pool, maintained at a constant temperature of 68 degrees Fahrenheit, was where the rheumatic patients would come to immerse themselves in the waters and relieve their symptoms. Today the pool is home to a large collection of Common and Koi carp, while the upstairs consulting rooms now house tanks full of native, tropical and marine fish. Visitors are welcome to feed the fish with food obtainable from the Aquarium.

Down by the riverbank and housed in the old Pavilion can be found the **Peak District Mining Museum**. Opened in 1978, the Museum offers an enthralling insight into the many facets of mining from as far back as Roman times to the 20th century.

Life in a Lens, opened in 2001, is a museum of popular photography set in a beautiful renovated Victorian house. Displays include cameras of all ages, toy and novelty cameras, postcards and much more. The Victorian teashop is the latest attraction, opened in 2005. There is definitely an overriding ambiance of Victorian times.

Being a relatively new town, Matlock Bath has no ancient place of worship, but the **Parish Church of the Holy Trinity** is a fine early Victorian edifice which was built in 1842 and enlarged in 1873/74 to accommodate the growing congregation. Of greater architectural merit is, however, the **Chapel of St John the Baptist**, found on the road between Matlock and Matlock Bath and built into a cliff. Built in 1897, it was designed by architect Guy Dawber to be a chapel-of-ease for those finding it difficult to attend St Giles in Matlock, but it also became a place of worship for those who preferred a High Church service.

Matlock Bath is of course famous for its Illuminations and Venetian nights. In 1898 a Venetian Fete was conceived when a number of tradesmen in Matlock Bath decided to purchase 2,500 coloured-glass bucket lanterns to illuminate the gardens on the promenade and on Lover's Walk. They are now firmly part of the tourism year, and are held annually from the end of August to the end of October.

LEA

4 miles SE of Matlock off the A615

Lea is mentioned briefly in the *Domesday Book* when it was spelt 'Lede' and was owned by Ralph fitzHerbert. But it is better known now for its association with John Marsden-Smedley (1867-1959) who spent much of his life in the village. As well as being the local squire, he was the owner of John Smedley Ltd, a manufacturer of quality woollen garments.

Lea Gardens offer a rare collection of rhododendrons, azaleas, alpines and conifers in a superb woodland setting. This unique collection including kalmias and other plants of interest has been introduced from all over the world to this area in the heart of Derbyshire. The gardens provide a stunning visual display to enthral the whole family. Covering an area of some four acres, the site is set on the remains of a mediaeval millstone quarry and includes a lovely rock garden with dwarf conifers, alpines, heathers and spring bulbs. A mile of walks takes visitors through a blaze of spring colour. The house at Lea Gardens was a later addition, built in 1967.

HOLLOWAY

4½ miles SE of Matlock off the A6

In close proximity to Lea, this attractive village has one famous daughter, Florence Nightingale, who lived here at **Lea Hurst**, a 17th century gabled farmhouse. Although she was named after the city of her birth, Florence spent much of her childhood in the Derbyshire mansion. Florence was the second daughter of William Edward Shore, who had to adopt the name of a distant relative, in order to benefit from his inheritance, including the family seat of Lea Hurst.

Florence Nightingale is most remembered as a pioneer of nursing and a reformer of hospital sanitation methods. But perhaps the most interesting member of the early Nightingale family was Peter, born in 1736. His nickname was 'Mad Peter' on account of his lifestyle, which consisted of heavy

61 THE PEAK DISTRICT MINING MUSEUM

Matlock Bath

An exciting insight into the world of the Derbyshire Mines.

 see page 214

62 SCOTLAND NURSERIES GARDEN CENTRE, RESTAURANT & CHOCOLATE SHOP

Tansley

A wonderful garden centre –
an oasis for any gardener
and chocoholic alike!

 ¶ see page 215

63 THE GATE

Tansley

Along with top quality food,
drink and company you will
receive a friendly welcome
when visiting The Gate.

¶ see page 214

drinking, gambling and horse riding. However, he was an astute businessman and established a lead smelting business and extended an arm of the Cromford Canal.

Florence's father left Lea Hurst to her in his will and, after her courageous work in the dreadful conditions of the Crimean War, she retired to the house and spent the next 50 years writing, specifically on the subject of hospital organisation. Florence died in London in 1910 and the house remained in the family until 1940. Still in private hands, Lea Hurst is occasionally opened to the public.

TANSLEY

1 mile SE of Matlock on the A615

Around the village a network of footpaths lead through beautiful and varied countryside to Matlock, a lane to the left of The Gate Inn leads down to Oaksedge Lane which continues northward up a steep hill to a track below a magnificent pinewood. There are outstanding views towards Matlock and Masson Hill to be had from here and soon the track arrives at the head of the Lumsdale Valley.

This tiny and picturesque village has an 18th century mill, **Tansley Wood Mill** and some good 18th century houses including Knoll House with an impressive carved doorway. Today there are no more working mills and quarries but there are six garden centres within half a mile of the village. Making it well worth a visit by keen gardeners.

CROMFORD

2 miles S of Matlock off the A5012

Although at first sight not a 'pretty' village, it has a charm of its own, with much to surprise and please the visitor. It was here, in 1771, that Sir Richard Arkwright started to build **Cromford Mill**, the world's first successful water-powered spinning mill. Though some of the buildings predate Arkwright, he also built a new town round the mill, providing decent housing and other amenities for his workers, such as an inn, shops, a school and a village lock up for miscreants. In this respect, Cromford became possibly the first purpose-built industrial town in the world.

The area Arkwright had chosen for his mill was perfect. The River Derwent described by Daniel Defoe as 'a fury of a river', provided an ample power supply; there was an unorganised but very willing workforce, as the lead mining industry was experiencing a decline, and probably most importantly, Cromford was away from the prying eyes of Arkwright's competitors. In 1792, he commissioned the building of the village church, where he now lies. The mill proved to be a great success and became the model for others both in Britain and abroad, earning Arkwright the accolade 'Father of the Factory System'. His pioneering work and contributions to the great Industrial Age resulted in a knighthood in 1786, and one year later he became High Sheriff of Derbyshire. Cromford Mill was last in use as a Colour Works, but is now a Visitor Centre owned and run by the Arkwright Society, with a variety of shops and businesses occupying the old buildings. Tours of the mill and Cromford village are available throughout the year.

For lovers of waterways, there is an opportunity, at **Cromford Canal,** to wander along the five-mile stretch of towpath to Ambergate. At **Cromford Wharf** there is a warehouse dating back to 1794, a counting house from the same year and a couple of canal cottages. The old **Leawood Pumping Station**, which transferred water from the River Derwent to the Cromford Canal, has been fully restored. Inside, the engine house is a preserved Cornish-type beam engine and is occasionally steamed up. Close by the Pump House is the **Wigwell Aqueduct,** (also known as the Derwent Aqueduct) dating from 1793, which carries the canal high over the River Derwent. It had to be rebuilt when it partially collapsed during construction.

The **High Peak Trail**, which stretches some 17-and-a-half miles up to Dowlow near Buxton, starts at Cromford and follows the track bed of the Cromford and High Peak Railway. First opened in 1880, the railway was built to connect the Cromford Canal with the Peak Forest Canal. It is somewhat reminiscent of a canal as it has long level sections interspersed

Two Swans on The Mill Pool, Cromford

with sharp inclines (instead of locks) and many of the stations are known as wharfs. After walking the trail it is not surprising to learn that its chief engineer was really a canal builder! The railway was finally closed in 1967; the old stations are now car parks and picnic areas and there is an information office in the former Hartington station signal box. Surfaced with clinker rather than limestone, the trail is suitable for walkers, cyclists and horses.

The **Cromford Venture Centre** is an ideal base for study visits, holidays, training and self-development courses. It offers self-catering accommodation for parties of up to 24 young people and four staff. It is run by the Arkwright Society in association with the Prince's Trust, and is housed in a listed building.

"Celebrating Cromford", is a weekend festival celebrating the village and the talents of the

64 THE OLD BAKERY COFFEE SHOP & RESTAURANT

Cromford

Cosy coffee shop by day, and active restaurant by night – whatever time, food is prepared fresh with passion using local ingredients.

¶   see page 216

71

people who live there; it began in June 2005 and has become an annual event.

BONSALL

2 miles SW of Matlock off the A5012

In a steep-sided dale beneath Masson Hill, Bonsall has a long history of lead mining, possibly going back to Roman times, and is mentioned in the *Domesday Book*. Many of the fields and meadows around are still littered with the remains of the miners' work. Bonsall inhabitants have also been involved in the textile industry, pre- and post-Arkwright. The village was also at one time a centre of framework knitting, and east of the village cross is an old knitting workshop, with its large windows and outside staircase.

Bonsall owes its size and relative prosperity almost exclusively to the numerous industries which once flourished beside the **Bonsall Brook**. Indeed, the Bonsall Brook is responsible for the shape of the village which follows every twist of the stream from its rising at the highest point above Uppertown to its cascading plunge down the Clatterway.

It is also one of the Derbyshire villages which continues the tradition of well-dressing, usually on the last Saturday in July.

Beside the market square cross stands The King's Head inn, dating from the late 17th century and said to be haunted. Another pub in the village reflects the traditional occupations of its residents, as it is called the Barley Mow. Another was called the Pig of Lead but is now a private residence. Above the village centre stands the battlemented **Parish Church of St James**, with its pinnacled tower and spire. Dating originally from the 1200s, it has a wonderful clerestory lighting the nave, though the outer walls were substantially rebuilt in 1862-63. From one end of the main street, the road climbs up some 400 feet to the Uppertown which lies just below the rim of the limestone plateau. In order to cope with the steep hill, the village church is split-level.

A few years ago people in Bonsall produced an illustrated map of the village and, in summer 2002 completed the Village Design Statement.

MIDDLETON BY WIRKSWORTH

4 miles SW of Matlock off the A5012

From Middleton-by-Wirksworth there are lovely far-reaching views, despite the scars of the quarrying industry. Just north of the village, which is also known as Middleton, lies the **Good Luck Mine**, which is now a lead mining museum. Usually open the first Sunday in the month, this old mine, found on the Via Gellia, is typically narrow and, in places, the roof is low. Not a place for the claustrophobic, it does, however, give an excellent impression of a lead mine. The village also has another mine, where a particularly rare form of limestone is quarried. Hopton Wood marble from here has been used in Westminster

Abbey, York Minster and the Houses of Parliament.

The Cromford and High Peak Railway had many inclines, and no less than nine steam-powered winding engines to haul the wagons and engines up them. **Middleton Top Winding Engine**, to the west of the village, was built in 1829, and is the only survivor. On certain days of the year between April and October it can still be seen in action. At **Middleton Top** is a visitor centre that explains the Cromford and High Peak Railway.

A lead mining disaster occurred in 1797 close to Middleton-by-Wirksworth and involved two miners named Job Boden and Anthony Pearson. There was a huge fall of earth and a rush of water while these men were working 50 yards underground. It was thought that Job and Anthony had surely perished. Other miners rushed to clear the debris, and after three days they came across the body of Anthony Pearson who was found in an upright position. Eight days after the disaster Job was found and still alive. Although badly emaciated, he recovered from his ordeal, and lived for many years to tell the story of his rescue.

In Balleye Quarry between Matlock Bath and Middleton-by-Wirksworth there was an amazing discovery recorded in 1663. George Mower found the bones and molar teeth of an elephant! He also found a huge natural cavern large enough to contain a

great church, and there was also the skeleton of a man said to be of monster proportions.

WIRKSWORTH

4 miles S of Matlock off the B5023

Standing as it does virtually at the centre of Derbyshire, where north meets south, Wirksworth was once the leading lead-mining town in the Peak District when the industry was at its height.

Babington House dates back to Jacobean Wirksworth. Another former lead merchant's house, **Hopkinsons House**, was restored in 1980 as part of a number of restoration schemes initiated by the Civic Trust's 'Wirksworth Project'. The ancient **Parish Church of St Mary's** is a fine building dating originally from the 13th century and standing on a site previously occupied by a Saxon and then a Norman church. It sits in a tranquil close bounded by the former (Georgian) grammar school and the Elizabethan **Gell's Almshouses**, named after Sir Philip Gell who founded them in 1584. The church holds one of the oldest stone carvings in the country. Known as the Wirksworth Stone, it is a coffin lid dating from the 8th century, and was found beneath the chancel floor in the 1820s. There are also tombs of the Gell family, local lords of the manor in Tudor times and lead mine owners. The ancient ceremony of 'clypping the church' takes place here on the first Sunday after 8th September each year. It is thought to date from pre-Christian times, and consists of the people

65 THE NATIONAL STONE CENTRE

Wirksworth
A dramatic site in the heart of the Derbyshire Dales is where you will find this wonderful outdoor museum.

🏛 *see page 216*

Wirksworth

of the village circling the church and linking hands. Another ceremony is that of well-dressing, which takes place during the last few days of May/first week of June.

The **National Stone Centre** in Porter Lane tells 'the story of stone', with a wealth of exhibits, activities such as gem-panning and fossil-casting, and outdoor trails tailored to introduce topics such as the geology, ecology and history of the dramatic Peak District landscape.

At **North End Mills**, visitors are able to witness hosiery being made as it has been for over half a century; a special viewing area offers an insight into some of the items on sale in the factory shop.

The town has connections with Mary Ann Evans, the author who wrote under the pen name of George Eliot. At the southern end of the town is a cottage known as **Adam Bede Cottage**. This is where Samuel Evans and his wife Elizabeth lived, in real life Mary Ann's aunt and uncle. In the book *Adam Bede*, Wirksworth is called Snowfield, and Samuel and Elizabeth are portrayed as Adam Bede and Dinah Morris. Another literary connection is to be found at the Crown Inn, which Baroness Orczy featured in her novel *Beau Brocade*. Wirksworth was also where D.H. Lawrence's mother came from, and indeed Lawrence lived close to the town at Mountain Cottage for a year with his German born wife.

Carsington Water just outside Wirksworth is one of Britain's newest reservoirs. This 741-acre expanse of water is a beauty spot that has attracted well over a million visitors a year since it was opened by Queen Elizabeth in 1992. It can be reached on foot from Wirksworth along a series of footpaths, and aims to be disabled friendly with wheelchairs available and access to as many attractions as possible. Sailing, windsurfing, fishing and canoeing can be enjoyed here, as well as just quiet strolls or bike rides. The Visitor Centre on the west bank offers visitors the opportunity to learn about all aspects of Severn Trent Water, who own it, and water supplies in general. The reservoir is unusual in that it is not fed by streams and rivers, but by water pumped into it from the River Derwent when the water is high. It can hold up to 7.8 billion gallons of water at any one time.

An impressive exhibit in the courtyard is the Kugel Stone, a massive ball of granite weighing over one tonne, which revolves on a thin film of water under pressure. It can be moved with a touch of the hand! Some half a million trees and shrubs have been planted and are managed to attract wildlife and to enhance the landscape. There are two bird hides and a wildlife centre to help visitors understand the variety of wildlife and observe the birdlife that visits the reservoir. The reservoir is stocked for fishing either from the bank or from boats available for hire. There is a large adventure playground and numerous open spaces for families to relax.

For those wanting to know more about Wirksworth a visit to the highly acclaimed **Wirksworth Heritage Centre** is essential. Situated just off the market place in Crown Yard, where Crown Yard Kitchen offers snacks and delicious home cooked meals. The Heritage Centre is housed in a former Silk and Velvet Mill and takes visitors through time from when the bones of a Woolly Rhino were found, to the Romans in Wirksworth through to the present day, with all this being explained over three floors. Excellent views over the town are obtained from the windows. One of the town's most interesting sights is the jumble of cottages linked by a maze of tiny lanes on the hillside between The Dale and Greenhill, in particular the area known locally as 'The Puzzle Gardens'.

Wirksworth wells are dressed on spring bank holiday and there is also an annual arts and crafts festival in September.

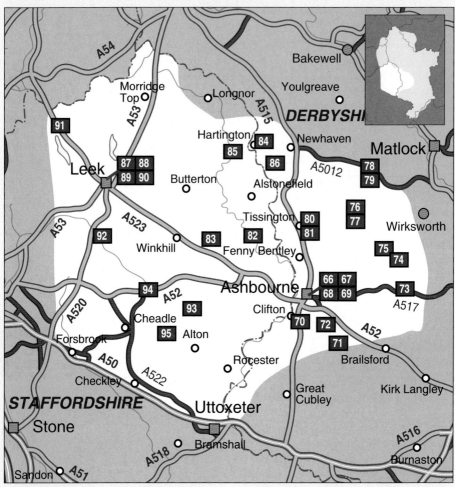

🛏 ACCOMMODATION

66	White Hart Hotel, Ashbourne	p 79, 216
69	Ye Olde Vaults, Ashbourne	p 81, 218
71	Saracens Head, Shirley, nr Ashbourne	p 82, 220
73	The Black Horse Inn, Hulland Ward, nr Ashbourne	p 83, 222
74	The Barley Mow Inn, Kirk Ireton, nr Ashbourne	p 83, 224
76	The Miners Arms, Brassington	p 85, 225
78	Middlehills Farm, Grangemill, nr Matlock	p 86, 226
79	The Hollybush Inn, Grangemill, nr Matlock	p 86, 226
85	Manifold Inn, Hartington, nr Buxton	p 97, 230

🛏 ACCOMMODATION

86	Biggin Hall Country House Hotel, Biggin-by-Hartington, nr Buxton	p 98, 231
87	The Swan, Leek	p 99, 232
94	The Railway Inn, Froghall	p 103, 239
95	Crowtrees Farm Bed & Breakfast, Oakamoor	p 103, 240

🍴 FOOD & DRINK

66	White Hart Hotel, Ashbourne	p 79, 216
67	Gallery Cafe, Ashbourne	p 79, 217
68	Bowling Green Inn, Ashbourne	p 80, 218

Dovedale and the Staffordshire Moorlands

This area of Derbyshire, which includes a southern section of the Peak District, is probably best known for the beautiful Dovedale. For the walker, the area holds mile after mile of paths, both alongside the River Dove and over the surrounding countryside, linking villages and hamlets. A walk in Dovedale – perhaps the most famous dale of all thanks to its connections with Izaak Walton, who published his famous book, *The Compleat Angler,* in 1653 – passes a whole collection of fancifully-named rock features and a dozen fascinating and beautiful villages.

Standing either side of the entrance to Dovedale are the shapely twin southern sentinels of Bunster Hill and Thorpe Cloud. They are followed in swift succession by features like the Twelve Apostles, Lover's Leap, Tissington Spires, Ilam Rock and Pickering Tor. All can be reached by car, but to discover the best of the dales or the hilltops it is advised to walk. Watch out for a wide variety of birdlife from kingfishers to dippers and the odd heron, grey wagtails and moor hens. Wild flora abounds with mosses, lichens and flowers such as Herb Robert everywhere. An aura of peaceful seclusion hangs over the valley, making a walk in Dovedale one of the highlights of a visit to the Peak District.

The Stepping Stones at the entrance to Dovedale appear on thousands of post cards and have delighted visitors for years. The footing in the river is uncertain to say the least, so be careful, and wear good footwear. Though for those who do not want to cross the river at this

🍴 FOOD & DRINK

69	Ye Olde Vaults, Ashbourne	p 81, 218
70	Cock Inn, Clifton, nr Ashbourne	p 82, 219
71	Saracens Head, Shirley, nr Ashbourne	p 82, 220
72	Shoulder of Mutton, Osmaston, nr Ashbourne	p 82, 221
73	The Black Horse Inn, Hulland Ward, nr Ashbourne	p 83, 222
74	The Barley Mow Inn, Kirk Ireton, nr Ashbourne	p 83, 224
75	Main Sail Restaurant, Carsington Water, nr Ashbourne	p 83, 223
76	The Miners Arms, Brassington	p 85, 225
77	Ye Olde Gate Inn, Brassington	p 85, 224
79	The Hollybush Inn, Grangemill, nr Matlock	p 86, 226
80	Bluebell Inn & Restaurant, Tissington, nr Ashbourne	p 88, 227
83	Red Lion Inn, Waterfall, nr Waterhouses	p 94, 229
84	Beresford Tea Rooms, Hartington, nr Buxton	p 97, 230

🍴 FOOD & DRINK

85	Manifold Inn, Hartington, nr Buxton	p 97, 230
86	Biggin Hall Country House Hotel, Biggin-by-Hartington, nr Buxton	p 98, 231
87	The Swan, Leek	p 99, 232
88	The Dyers Arms, Leek	p 99, 233
89	Blueberrys, Leek	p 100, 234
90	Den Engel Belgian Bar & Restaurant, Leek	p 100, 235
91	The Knot Inn, Rushton Spencer, nr Macclesfield	p 102, 236
92	Castro's Restaurant & Lounge, Cheddleton, nr Leek	p 102, 237
93	Ye Olde Star Inn, Cotton, nr Oakamoor	p 102, 238
94	The Railway Inn, Froghall	p 103, 239

🏛 PLACES OF INTEREST

81	Tissington Hall and Gardens, Tissington, nr Ashbourne	p 88, 228
82	The South Peak Estate, Ilam, nr Ashbourne	p 92, 228

Upper Dove Valley, nr Hartington

point there is a foot bridge closer to the car park, below Thorpe Cloud.

The River Dove meanders slowly through Dovedale and takes its name from the British Gaelic word 'dutho', meaning dark. It is 45 miles long from its source at Axe Edge to the River Derwent, and for much of its length it forms the boundary between Derbyshire and Staffordshire. It is a favourite place for fishermen, and is forever associated with the aforementioned Izaak Walton.

Izaak Walton was born in Stafford, and later moved to London, where he was an ironmonger. He later lived in Farnham, Surrey, but spent a lot of time with his poet friend Charles Cotton at the latter's fishing cottage on the Dove. An old farmhouse, at the head of the Dale, was converted, many years ago, into the well-known and much-loved Izaak Walton Hotel.

The spectacular scenery was perfect for the television and camera crews that were on location late in 2006 filming scenes for a BBC documentary, which celebrated the Centenary of the work of the National Trust in Derbyshire, and heralded the dawning of Dovedale as a National Nature Reserve.

Dovedale, however, is not the only dale worth exploring. The River Manifold offers some equally wonderful scenery, as does Ilam. A

beautifully preserved estate village, with a well-established youth hostel, Ilam is also a popular starting point from which to explore the Manifold Valley. But look out for the phantom Cromwell Coach riding along the lane from Ilam to Throwley. During the day it is heard but not seen, but its lights can be seen at night.

On the southern edge of the Peak District, the Staffordshire Moorlands certainly rival those of Derbyshire in terms of scenery and tranquil atmosphere. There are attractions for everyone from Britain's favourite theme park, Alton Towers, to steam railways, animal parks and gardens to stir the imagination. Plus undulating pastures of the moorlands, along with the fresh air and ancient weatherworn crags, make this the ideal place to walk, cycle or trek.

It is also an area full of character, with charming scattered villages, historic market towns and a wealth of history. Many of the farms and buildings date back hundreds of years, and the Industrial Revolution also left its mark. This region is also blessed with the two great reservoirs of Rudyard and Tittesworth, which make for pleasant and easy-to-navigate walks and cycle routes while offering peaceful havens for a wide variety of plants, animals and birds. There is a visitor centre, café and large car park, as well as recreational facilities such as fishing and boating at each site.

Most of this area is now used for dairy farming (for which calcium soil is essential). In the past it supported a number of creameries and the famous Hartington cheese factory survives today (see also Hartington).

Let us leave the last words with Lord Byron, who wrote with Dovedale in mind, to his friend, 'I can assure you there are things in Derbyshire as noble as Greece or Switzerland'.

ASHBOURNE

There can be no doubt left in the mind of the visitor who leaves the limestone plateau of the White Peak and travels south to the cobbled Market Place at Ashbourne that they have well and truly left the highlands behind.

Although just outside the National Peak boundary, Ashbourne proclaims itself as 'the Gateway to Dovedale'. But there is much more to this charming Georgian town than that, it is probably best known for its gingerbread and unique Shrovetide football match. It is one of Derbyshire's finest old towns having recently celebrated the 750th anniversary of its market charter in 2007. It is a pleasure to visit and the cobbled market place is still used twice weekly (Thursday and Saturday) – a popular haunt for bargain-hunters and local shoppers alike. It has an enviable reputation for its abundance of antique shops,

shopping facilities and modern leisure centre.

Mentioned in the *Domesday Book* as 'Essiburn', - derived from the local stream with its many ash trees - it was originally a small settlement lying on the northern bank of Henmore Brook, which already had a church. It was a 13th century lord of the manor who laid out the new town to the east, around its unusual shaped market place. Many of the town's traders, in order to continue to enjoy the benefits without paying the town's tolls, built themselves houses on the south side of the Brook. The area became known as Compton (or 'Campdene') and it was slowly absorbed into the town.

The triangular, sloping **Market Square**, in the heart of Ashbourne, was part of the new development begun in the 13th century that shifted the town to the east, away from the church. It was from this market place during the height of the Jacobite Rebellion in 1745, that

66 WHITE HART HOTEL

Ashbourne

A picturesque place offering fantastic real ales and old fashioned value-for-money. Four letting rooms are also available.

🍴 🛏 *see page 216*

67 GALLERY CAFE

Ashbourne

Award winning café, well known for the "best coffee in town" with contemporary art abound.

🍴 *see page 217*

Walker crossing the river, Dovedale

68 BOWLING GREEN INN

Ashbourne

A perfectly quintessential village pub, fine cask and draught ales and delicious home cooked food.

see page 218

Bonnie Prince Charlie proclaimed his father to be King James III.

Though the old bull ring no longer exists, the town boasts many fine examples of 18th century architecture as well as some older buildings. On the **Gingerbread Shop** can be seen the original wattle and daub and probably dates from the 15th century but for many years was covered by a mock Elizabethan front. Ashbourne Gingerbread has a fascinating history, and the recipe is said to have been acquired from French prisoners during the Napoleonic Wars. The personal chef of a captured French general reputedly made it in 1805, and his recipe was copied and used locally. You can buy it today at Spencers bakery in the Town centre.

Also worthy of a second glance is the unique double inn sign for the **Green Man and Black's Head Royal Hotel**. The inn sign stretches over St John's Street and was put up when the Blackamoor Inn joined with the Green Man in 1825. Though the Blackamoor is no more, the sign remains and it claims to be the longest hotel name in the country. If you look carefully, you will see that the blackamoor's head is smiling on one side and scowling on the other. Of Georgian origin, the amalgamated hotel has played host to James Boswell, Dr Johnson and the young Princess Victoria. Ashbourne was, in fact, one of Dr Johnson's favourite places; he came to the town on several occasions between 1737 and 1784 to visit Dr

John Taylor, an old friend. He also visited the hotel so often that he had his own chair with his name on it! The chair can still be seen at the Green Man. Today one of the two bars in named after him.

A stroll down Church Street, described by Pevsner as one of the finest streets in Derbyshire, takes the walker past many interesting Georgian houses - including the Grey House, which stands next to the **Grammar School**. Founded by Sir Thomas Cockayne on behalf of Elizabeth I in 1585, the school was visited on its 400th anniversary by the present Queen. Almost opposite the Grey House is **The Mansion**, the late 17th century home of the Reverend Dr John Taylor, oldest friend of Dr Johnson. In 1764, a domed, octagonal drawing room was added to the house, and a new brick façade built facing the street. Next to The Mansion are the **Owfield's Almshouses,** dating from the early 17th century. Next to them, at right angles to the street, are **Pegg's Almshouses**, founded in 1669. Ashbourne also retains many of its narrow alleyways and, in particular, there is Lovatt's Yard where the town lock-up can be seen.

The **Parish Church of St Oswald**, with its elegant 212 feet spire, was described by Victorian novelist George Eliot as 'the finest mere parish church in England'. The town was a regular haunt of George Eliot, who used it as a model for the fictional town of 'Oakbourne' in the novel *Adam Bede*. James Boswell said that the church was 'one of the largest and most luminous that I have seen in any town of the same size'. St Oswald's stands on the site of a Minster church mentioned in the *Domesday Book*, though most of what we see today dates from rebuilding work in the 13th century. There is a dedication brass in the south transept dated 1241. The south doorway, with its dog-toothed decoration and ribbed moulding, reflects the church's classic early English style. St Oswald's has chapels to its transepts, adding to the spacious feeling that is more reminiscent of a small cathedral than a parish church. To the southeast of the church are the **Spalden Almshouses**, built between 1723 and 1724.

Don't miss the monuments to the Bradbourne and Cockayne families in the north transept chapel or that of Penelope Boothby, who died in 1791 at the tender age of five. It is perhaps Thomas Banks, the sculptor's, most famous work, and is in white Carrara marble. The figure of the sleeping child is so life-like that it appears that she is only sleeping. Queen Charlotte, wife of George II, is supposed to have burst into tears when she saw the sculpture at the Royal Academy exhibition. The moving epitaph reads:

'She was in form and intellect most exquisite. The unfortunate parents ventured their all on this frail bark, and the wreck was total.'

It is said that Penelope's parents separated at the child's grave and never spoke to each other again.

More recently, it was the birthplace of Catherine Mumford, in 1829, who later married William Booth and helped her found the Salvation Army, Catherine became known as the 'Mother of the Army'. She was responsible for many of the changes in the new organization, designing the flag and bonnets for the ladies, and contributed to the Army's ideas on many important issues and matters of belief. There is a bust of her in the War Memorial Gardens.

Ashbourne is home, too, to the famous Royal Shrovetide football match, played on Shrove Tuesday and Ash Wednesday – an annual game of 'traditional' football, played with a leather ball stuffed with sawdust. Apart from the pubs the whole of the town closes for this event. The two teams, the 'Up'ards' (those born north of the Henmore Brook) and the 'Down'ards' (those born south of it) begin their match at 2pm behind the Green Man Hotel. The game continues until 10pm unless a goal is scored after 5pm. The two goals are situated three miles apart, along the Brook, on the site of the old mills at Clifton and Sturston. Despite there being hundreds of participants, it is rare for more than one goal to be scored in this slow-moving game. To describe it as boisterous would be an understatement, the violence involved has led to intermittent attempts to ban it, but the game has been played here for hundreds

69 YE OLDE VAULTS

Ashbourne

A small pub, but what it lacks in size it makes up for in hospitality, good ale, fine food and quality accommodation.

🍴 🛏 *see page 218*

70 COCK INN

Clifton

Unpretentious atmosphere, friendly landlords, good pub food and play area on site.

‖ see page 219

71 SARACEN'S HEAD

Shirley

Here you can expect a relaxing atmosphere, the finest wines, real beers and ales together with exceptionally prepared, home-cooked food.

‖ ⊨ see page 220

72 SHOULDER OF MUTTON

Osmaston

Fine pub in an attractive, sleepy village with great owners offering quality food and drink.

‖ see page 221

of years and fortunately it still continues.

AROUND ASHBOURNE

YELDERSLEY

3 miles SE of Ashbourne off the A52

Yeldersley has long been the home of gentlemen farmers and those who love the countryside. This picturesque village offers many scenic delights. **Yeldersley Hall** is a spacious country mansion, dating back to the 18th century and has a fascinating history. It also has a royal connection - the Duchess of York's grandfather was born here. Today the mansion is made up of luxury self-catering holiday apartments.

OSMASTON

2½ miles SE of Ashbourne off the A52

Five minutes drive from Ashbourne, the visitor must think they are in another world when they arrive at Osmaston. Formerly Osmaston-in-the-Wood, this sleepy, beautiful village, neither crowded nor bustling, offers the visitor a real haven of tranquillity. It is the archetypal English village, with thatched cottages, village green, duck pond, pub and church. Thatched cottages are rare in Derbyshire, but at Osmaston, even the village hall has a thatched roof.

However - not everything is as it seems - it was built in the 19th century as an estate village to house the workers at the Butterley Iron Works. The manor house,

Osmaston Manor, was built in 1849 for Francis Wright (his memorial stands in the market place at Ashbourne), the owner of the ironworks, and was demolished in 1964; the main staircase is now in Wooton Lodge, Staffordshire. The park, formerly the manor grounds, is open to the public and has an abundance of wildlife; as well it is the location for the internationally recognised annual Osmaston Horse Trials and the more local annual Ashbourne Shire Horse Show.

The Gothic **Parish Church of St Martin** dates from 1845, and replaced an earlier church whose register dates back to 1606.

BRADLEY

3 miles E of Ashbourne just off the A517

A regular visitor to the Georgian **Bradley Hall** (private) was Dr Johnson, who would visit the Meynell family here when he was staying in Ashbourne with his friend, Dr John Taylor. The Meynells had come to Bradley in 1655 and bought the hall from Sir Andrew Kniveton, who had been ruined by the Civil War.

Opposite the hall stands the rather squat **Parish Church of All Saints**, which is interesting in having a bell turret but no tower on its 14th century nave and chancel. The original wooden bell tower was struck by lightning. There are several memorials to the Meynell family in the church. The base and part of the shaft of a Saxon cross stand in the churchyard. The archway, crossing the formerly gated road between cottages at Moorend, is known locally as 'The Hole in the Wall'. The former village pub had the distinction, common in Derbyshire, of two official names, The Jinglers and the Fox and Hounds. Nearby **Bradley Wood** was given to the people of Ashbourne in 1935 by Captain Fitzherbert Wright.

KIRK IRETON

6 miles NE of Ashbourne off the B5023

Nestled in the hills near **Carsington Reservoir**, Kirk Ireton sits at 700 feet above sea level. Its name means 'church of the Irish enclosure', and at one time a Celtic monastery is supposed to have stood here. Much of the village is 17th century and one of the oldest buildings is the 15th century Barley Mow Inn. Tradition here was so strong that when decimal coinage was introduced in 1971, the 87-year-old landlady refused to accept the new currency. This caused regulars a great deal of amusement to watch the faces of visitors when asked for 'five shillings and eleven pence'. Customers had to pay in 'old money' up to the time of the owner's death in 1977. The Barley Mow was one of the last places in the country to go decimal.

The **Parish Church of the Holy Trinity** is partly Norman, with 14th century additions. There is an interesting custom observed here at weddings known as 'roping for weddings', when children would stretch a rope across the road as the bride and broom leave the

church. They can only pass if they pay a toll.

According to village records, on the 12th May 1811, the village and neighbourhood were visited by an awful tornado, accompanied by lightning and loud claps of thunder; large trees were twisted from their roots, most of the houses were unroofed, and the church was stripped of its lead, which was blown into the adjoining fields.

KNIVETON

3 miles NE of Ashbourne on the B5035

This tiny village of grey stone houses lies close to Carsington Reservoir, sheltered in a dip in the hills. Its beautiful little **Parish Church of St Michael** has a 13th century tower and font, a Norman doorway, small lancet windows, battlements and a short spire. The medieval glass in the chancel depicts the arms of the family of Kniveton. Sir Andrew Kniveton became so impoverished through his loyalty to Charles I that he had to sell most of the family estates. A huge sycamore tree and an ancient yew stand in the churchyard. The yew has grooves in its bark, said to have been made by archers sharpening their arrows.

Close by is the Bronze Age burial mound of **Wigber Low,** which has revealed some important remains from the villages past.

HOGNASTON

4 miles NE of Ashbourne off the B5035

In 1675, John Ogilby compiled the

73 THE BLACK HORSE INN

Hulland Ward, nr Ashbourne

Well-appointed traditional country inn, handy for Carsington Water.

🍽 🛏 *see page 222*

74 THE BARLEY MOW INN

Kirk Ireton

Fantastic food, chilled Real Ales and 5 en-suite bedrooms providing an ideal base to explore the local village.

🍽 🛏 *see page 224*

75 MAIN SAIL RESTAURANT

Carsington Water, nr Ashbourne

Watch over the water, the boats, the birds – or simply watch each other indulging in the fabulous food.

🍽 *see page 223*

83

first practical road map of England. On his map, the only road in Derbyshire is shown going through Hognaston, when it would have been little more than a cart track. People have lived on the site of the village for at least 1,000 years and it was entered in the *Domesday Book* as 'Ochenaueston': King's land. It used to be a busy place in coaching days when the London to Manchester coaches passed through, also the famous stagecoach 'The Devonshire' used to call here en route from Wirksworth to Ashbourne.

According to some of the old village records, Hognaston was not always as picturesque as it is today. One court order read, 'Every person who has a Dunghill Town Street to remove it out of town'. While another order required a villager to remove his 'Necessary House', to stop the fouling of a neighbour's water.

The **Parish Church of St Bartholomew**, dating back to the late 12th century, has some extraordinary Norman carvings over the doorway in the tympanum, and an early Norman font. Two of the bells date back to the 13th century. The clock was a gift from John Smith and Sons, the famous Derby clock-makers as a memorial to John Smith who lived in the village. John Smith and Sons maintain the clock each year.

HOPTON

8 miles NE of Ashbourne off the B5035

Hopton is the ancestral home of the famous Derbyshire family of the Gells. They are recorded as holding an estate at Hopton since at least the 14th century, until it was sold in 1989, their influence is apparent throughout both Hopton and neighbouring Carsington. The **Sir Philip Gell Almshouses** were built between 1719 and 1722 for two men and two women. The Gell family made their fortune in the nearby limestone quarries and they were also responsible for the construction of the **Via Gellia**, a road which runs along a valley to the west of Cromford.

This village, now by-passed by the main road, is dominated by the Carsington Water reservoir. The land rises to the north of Hopton and here can be found the **Hopton Incline**, once the steepest railway incline in the British Isles. Lying on the **High Peak Railway**, carriages

Walkers, Dovedale

were hauled up using fixed engines on their journey from Cromford to Whaley Bridge. It is now part of the High Peak Trail.

BRADBOURNE

4 miles NE of Ashbourne off the A5056

"I have travelled in many lands, but never seen a more beautiful place"; so wrote author Nat Gould of Bradbourne, which is indeed a 'beautiful place' set in sylvan surroundings just beyond the south eastern boundary of the Peak National Park. Nat was born in 1857, and was a journalist who emigrated to Australia. There he worked on the Brisbane Telegraph, where his first fiction appeared. Eventually he returned to England and by the time of his death in 1919 had written 130 horse racing novels. That Nat Gould chose this as his final resting place speaks volumes, his grave is in the **Parish Church of All Saints** churchyard.

The pastoral beauty of Bradbourne is enhanced by its elevated position on a ridge between the valleys of Bradbourne Brook and Havenhill Dale, and this hill-top village of just over 100 inhabitants enjoys some fine views over the surrounding countryside.

Bradbourne may be a small village but it has a large and straggling parish. Essentially Norman, but with some fragments of Saxon work - especially on the north side of the nave where typical long-and-short work is visible. The church's large, unbuttressed west tower is Norman and has an elegantly decorated

south door. Most of the rest of this appealing little church dates from the 14th century, but there are some fine modern furnishings which owe much to William Morris' Arts and Crafts movement. Some of the wall paintings date from the 17th and 18th centuries. The church is surrounded by its hilltop churchyard which contains not only the remains of a Saxon cross, dated approx AD 800, but also a scene of the crucifixion. The **Bradbourne Stone**, dating from ancient times, stands well north of the church.

While in the village it is also worth taking a look at the fine grey stone Elizabethan manor house **Bradbourne Hall** (private), with its three gables and beautiful terraced gardens. **The Old Parsonage**, which has a rather peculiar appearance as it was built in three completely different styles and materials, is also worthy of note.

BRASSINGTON

7 miles NE of Ashbourne off the B5056

According to the *Oxford Dictionary of English Place-Names*, Brassington derives from Old English and is said to mean 'the farm by the steep path'. At the time of the *Domesday Book*, the Manor of 'Branzincton' belonged to Henry de Ferrers and had a population of around 100, who were mostly farm workers. The men of 'Brass'on', as it is still known locally, have earned their daily bread for centuries by working either on the land or under it; in the limestone quarries

76 THE MINERS ARMS

Brassington
250+ year old traditional country pub offering a warm and friendly welcome.

‖ ⊨ see page 225

77 YE OLDE GATE INN

Brassington
Seventeenth century pub open evenings and lunchtimes with varied menus.

‖ see page 224

Brassington's oldest 'resident' is a relief carving depicting a man with one hand over his heart, which can be seen inside the Norman tower of the Parish Church of St James. It may date back to Saxon times, but most of the rest of the church is Norman, heavily restored by the Victorians. The north aisle dates from Victorian times, but the south aisle dates to about 1200.

78 MIDDLEHILLS FARM

Grangemill

Great for families and budget conscious backpackers, there is a caravan & campsite as well as B&B accommodation in a family run farmhouse.

 see page 226

79 THE HOLLYBUSH INN

Grangemill

Scrumptious food, quaffable ales and quality accommodation.

see page 226

or the lead mines. The hollows and bumps in the green meadows tell of 200 years of underground industry in pursuit of lead, and now lead-tolerant flowers such as mountain pansy, sandwort and orchids flourish here.

Protected from the wind by the limestone plateau that soars some 1,000 feet above sea level, the village sits by strange-shaped rocks, the result of weather erosion, with names like **Rainster Rocks** and **Harborough Rocks**. At Rainster Rocks there is evidence of a Roman British settlement, and at Harborough there are the remains of a chambered cairn. Stone Age man found snug dwellings amongst these dolomite limestone formations and there is evidence that animals like the sabre-toothed tiger, brown bear, wolf and hyena also found comfort here in the caves. As late as the 18th century, families were still living in the caves.

Nearby is the Wesleyan Reform Chapel, one of the so-called 'Smedley Chapels' built by local mill owner, Mr Smedley, in 1852. Smedley was a keen Revivalist and his two other chapels in the village are now the village hall and a private house.

In recent years television cameras have been on location in the village to film episodes of *Peak Practice*, but this was not a 'first', - for a sequence in the film, *The Virgin & The Gipsy* starring Derbyshire-born Alan Bates was also shot in Brassington some years ago.

BALLIDON

5 miles N of Ashbourne off the B5056

You can see a well-preserved deserted medieval village and open fields at Ballidon. According to the 2001 census it had a population of just 79 souls, but in medieval times, was a thriving community. It dates originally from the Norman period, but it was so heavily restored in 1882 that most Norman details have been obliterated. There are four rather grand 17th century farms and the **Chapel of All Saints** standing isolated in a field.

Overshadowed by its gigantic limestone quarry, the legacy of this tiny hamlet's days as a robust medieval village, remain in the numerous earthworks, lynchets and evidence of ridge-and-furrow cultivation in its fields. One-and-a-half miles north is **Minning Low**, one of the most impressive Bronze Age chambered tombs. It was the best discovery of its kind in Derbyshire at the time.

ALDWARK

9 miles NE of Ashbourne off the B5056

Close to the High Peak Trail, just inside the Peak Park boundary, Aldwark is one of the most unspoilt villages in Derbyshire. A quiet and tranquil backwater, its name comes from the Saxon for 'Old Fort', meaning that even then it was considered an ancient settlement. The highest recorded population was 97 in 1831, though at this time it was one of the staging posts on the coaching route between Derby and Buxton. A chambered tomb dating from 2000 BC was discovered at **Green Low**, just to the north of the village, which contained pottery, flints and animal bones.

FENNY BENTLEY

2 miles N of Ashbourne off the A515

Fenny Bentley is the first village of the Peak for visitors coming from the south, with a steep hill up into the Peak District and the old railway bridge where the Tissington Trail passes through the village (see also Tissington).

The **Parish Church of St Edmund's** has a dominant position in the village and dates back to the 13th century, although it has been heavily restored in later years. You can find some wonderful examples of the Arts and Crafts movement art works in many of the surrounding churches. At Fenny Bentley you can see angels lined up behind the altar and a stunningly painted aluminium ceiling in the northeast aisle. Also, inside the church can be found the tomb of Thomas Beresford, the local lord of the manor who fought, alongside eight of his 16 sons, at Agincourt. The effigies of Beresford and his wife are surrounded by those of their 21 children - each covered by a shroud as, by the time the tombs were built nobody could remember what they had looked like! It is said that everyone with the surname of Beresford is descended from Thomas and his

Fortified Manor, Fenny Bentley

wife, and the annual meeting of the Beresford Family Society takes place in the village each year.

The 15th century square tower of the Beresford's fortified manor house is now incorporated into **Cherry Orchard Farm**. It was also the home of poet Charles Cotton at one time, and is a local landmark that can be seen from the Buxton road.

TISSINGTON

4 miles N of Ashbourne off the A515

The 'modern' tradition of well-dressing is said to have been started at Tissington in 1350. But it is almost certain that the tradition goes back much further than that, to pagan times when the life-giving gift of water was so important to communities like this. Today the ceremony takes place on Ascension Day, the 40th day after Easter (usually the middle of May), and draws many crowds who come to see the spectacular folk art created by the local people. The

80 BLUEBELL INN & RESTAURANT

Tissington

A gem of a pub that is renowned throughout the area for its fine food and warm welcome.

 see page 227

81 TISSINGTON HALL & GARDENS

Tissington

Home to the FitzHerbert family, the hall and gardens are open to the public on selected dates during the year.

 see page 228

significance of the event in Tissington may have been to give thanks for their pure springs that had saved them from the ravages of the Black Death of 1348-49. During this time some 77 of the 100 clergy in Derbyshire died; the surviving villagers simply returned to the pagan custom of well-dressing. Another plausible theory dates back only as far as the great drought of 1615, when the Tissington wells kept flowing though water everywhere was in very short supply. Whichever theory is true, one thing is certain: in the last 50 years or so many villages that had not dressed a well for centuries, if ever, began to take part in this colourful tradition.

A total of six wells are dressed at Tissington - the Hall, the Town, the Yew Tree, the Hands, the Coffin and the Children's Wells. Each depicts a separate scene, usually from the Bible. Visitors should follow the signs in the village or ask at the Old Coach House.

Very much on the tourist route, particularly in the early summer, Tissington has plenty of tea rooms and ice cream shops to satisfy the hot and thirsty visitor, as well as that essential of any picturesque English village - a duck pond. The village itself, though often overlooked in favour of the colourful well-dressings, has some interesting buildings. The **Parish Church of St Mary**, situated on a rise overlooking Tissington, dates originally from Norman times, and is still essentially Norman, even though it was restored in 1854, with many mock Norman features being added. It has an unusual tub-shaped font, which dates back to the original Norman Church. The pulpit too is unusual. Converted from a double-decker type, it once had a set of steps leading out from the priest's stall below.

Home of the FitzHerbert family for 500 years, **Tissington Hall** is a distinguished and impressive stately home which was built by Francis FitzHerbert in 1609, though there may be fragments of an earlier building incorporated. During the Civil War, the Fitzherberts were for the king, and the then Fitzherbert was a colonel with the Royalist forces. He used the hall as a garrison for his troops.

The estate consists of 2,405 acres, and the Hall boasts a wealth of original pieces, artwork, furnishings and architectural features tracing the times and tastes of the FitzHerbert family over the centuries. The oak-panelled main hall has the original stone-flagged floor and is dominated by a stunning Gothic fireplace installed in 1757. Here visitors will also find a pair of late 18th century Chippendale bookcases, a rosewood piano and other fine pieces. The Dining Room, originally the old kitchen, is also panelled in oak and has an original Waring & Gillow table with a matching set of 13 chairs. The frieze work was added in the early 1900s. Paintings of country scenes and family portraits adorn the walls. The Library is a repository of over 3,000 books, and is adorned with a frieze depicting a woodland scene. Other fine pieces include a bracket clock made by Jasper Taylor of Holborn in about 1907. The East and West Drawing Rooms can also be visited.

Tissington Hall and Gardens are open to the public on certain afternoons throughout the summer. Please call the Estate Office for details. In addition, the gardens are open on several days for charity including the National Gardens Scheme. Private groups and societies are welcome by written appointment throughout the year.

Following the old Ashbourne to Parsley Hay railway line, the **Tissington Trail** is a popular walk which can be combined with other old railway trails in the area, or country lanes, to make an enjoyable circular country walk. The trail passes through some lovely countryside and, having a reasonable surface, it is also popular with cyclists. Along the route can also be found many of the old railway buildings and junction boxes and, in particular, Hartington station, which is now a picnic site with an information centre in the old signal box.

Yew Tree Well, Tissington

PARWICH

5 miles N of Ashbourne off the A515

The pronunciation of the name varies, some people say 'Par-rich' while others say 'Par-wich', - most locals seem to favour the latter, - but whichever way you say it, Parwich must rank as one of the most attractive villages in the southern part of the Peak District, and not being on the main route to anywhere, remains relatively undiscovered.

Conspicuous amongst the stone built houses is **Parwich Hall**, constructed of brick and finished in 1747. The wonderful gardens at the Hall were created at the turn of the 20th century and it remains

Parwich Moor

•

Parwich Moor, above the village, is home to many mysterious Bronze Age circles, which vary in size from 12 to 50 feet in diameter. Though their function is unknown, it is unlikely that they were used as burial chambers.

•

today a family home, though, over the years it has changed hands on several occasions. Parwich Hall is a grade II* listed building and is occasionally open to the public. The **Parish Church of St Peter** is Victorian, built between 1873 and 1874, though there are some Norman details.

Close to Parwich is Roystone Grange, an important archaeological site where, to the north of the present farmhouse, the remains of a Roman farmhouse have been excavated. To the south are an old engine house and the remains of the old medieval monastic grange. Both Roystone Grange and Parwich lie on the interesting and informative **Roystone Grange Archaeological Trail,** which starts at Minninglow car park. Some six miles long, the circular trail follows, in part, the old railway line that was built to connect the Cromford and the Peak Forest Canals in the 1820s

before taking in some of the Tissington Trail.

ALSOP-EN-LE-DALE

5 miles N of Ashbourne off the A515

The old station on the Ashbourne-Buxton line, which once served this tiny hamlet is today a car park on the Tissington Trail. The tranquil hamlet itself is on a narrow lane, east of the main road towards Parwich, just a mile from Dovedale. Alsop-en-le-Dale's **Parish Church of St Michael and all Angels** is Norman, though it was refurbished substantially during Victorian times, when the tower was completely rebuilt. The nave retains Norman features, with impressive double zigzag mouldings in the arches, but the west tower is only imitation Norman, and dates from 1883. One unusual feature, which dominates this small church is its extraordinary 19th century square mock-Gothic pulpit.

Opposite the church is the graceful and slender building known as **Alsop Hall**, constructed in the early 1600s for the Alsop family, who were lords of the manor. Though privately owned, it is worth seeing even for its exterior, as it is built in a handsome pre-classical style with stone-mullioned windows.

Alsop makes a good base for exploring the White Peak and is also convenient for Dovedale. The renowned **Viator's Bridge** at Milldale is a mile to the west, and was immortalised in a scene in Izaak Walton's *The Compleat Angler* in which the character Viator complains to another about the size of the tiny, two-arched packhorse bridge, deeming it 'not two fingers broad'.

Surrounding the village are many Bronze Age burial sites, including **Cross Low** (north of the village), **Nat Low** (north west of the village), **Moat Low** (southwest of the village) and **Green Low** on Alsop Moor.

NEWHAVEN

11 miles N of Ashbourne on the A515

The High Peak Trail crosses Newhaven to link up with the Tissington Trail. This charming village is also along the White Peak tourist route, though it retains a tranquil air. At Newhaven you can find Carriages Restaurant, which offers a taste of Scilly, and the meticulously maintained Newhaven Caravan Park.

MAPPLETON

2 miles NW of Ashbourne off the A515

Mappleton can also be spelled Mapleton, as the Ordnance Survey map of Derbyshire will testify. It is a village that has existed in some form or other since before 1086, when it is recorded in the *Domesday Book*. It is a pleasant and charming village that sits almost astride the River Dove, with attractive views and a wealth of exciting natural beauty. The spectacular scenery surrounding the village includes the aforementioned Thorpe Cloud and Bunster Hill, with the famous stepping stones across the River Dove just a mile or so upstream, all of which puts Mappleton well

within reach of the two million visitors each year who come to experience the natural delights of Dovedale.

The extremely small **Parish Church of St Mary** dates from 1751, and is unusual in that it has a dome rather than a tower or a steeple. There has been a church here since at least the reign of Edward I.

THORPE

3 miles NW of Ashbourne off the A515

Thorpe was mentioned in the *Domesday Book* and is one of the few villages in the Peak whose name has Norse origins, for the Danish settlers did not generally penetrate far into this area. It lies at the confluence of the Rivers Manifold and Dove, and is dominated by the conical hill of **Thorpe Cloud**, which guards the entrance to **Dovedale**. Out of interest the word 'cloud' is a corruption of the Old English word 'clud', meaning hill – a pity really as 'Thorpe Cloud' sounds like it should have a more romantic meaning than 'The hill by the Danish farm'. The summit is a short but stiff climb from any direction, but whichever way you go you are rewarded with panoramic views over Dovedale all the way to Alstonefield, Ilam and the lower Manifold valley. Although the Dale becomes over-crowded at times, there is always plenty of open space to explore on the hill as well as excellent walking. For much of its 45-mile course from Axe Edge to its confluence with the River Trent, the **River Dove** is a walker's

•

The beautiful little Parish Church of St Leonard in Thorpe, with its Norman tower and nave, was built about 1100, with some Saxon work still evident. It has walls of limestone rubble which give the curious impression that the building is leaning outwards. There is a fine tomb of the Millward family (1632) by the altar, showing John Milward, his two daughters and his two sons. The sundial of 1767 in the churchyard is curious, as it is too high to be read properly. In the porch of the church are some scratch marks, said to have been made by archers in the 14th and 15th centuries, sharpening their arrows before practicing archery in the churchyard.

•

View from Thorpe Cloud, Peak District

82 THE SOUTH PEAK ESTATE

Ilam

The estate centres around Ilam Hall and within its 4,000 acres are popular visitor attractions such as Dovedale.

 see page 228

river as it is mostly inaccessible by car. The steep sided valley, the fast-flowing water and the magnificent white rock formations all give Dovedale a special charm.

Dovedale, however, is only a short section of the valley; above Viator Bridge it becomes **Mill Dale** and further upstream again are **Wolfscote Dale** and **Beresford Dale**. The temptation to provide amenities for visitors, at the expense of the scenery, has been avoided, and the limestone village of Thorpe, clustered around its church, remains unspoilt and unsophisticated.

Further up the dale is the limestone crag known as **Dovedale Castle** and, on the opposite bank, is the higher promontory known as **Lover's Leap**. It's a view to gladden your hearts – not the sort

of place you'd think of throwing yourself from at all. However, it was named after a young woman, who, on hearing that her lover had been killed in the Napoleonic Wars, tried to commit suicide here by jumping. However, her skirts billowed out like a parachute and she survived. The poignant end to the story is that, soon after, she discovered that her lover was very much alive, and on his way home. Other interesting natural features with romantic names found along the way include the **Twelve Apostles**, a series of limestone crags, and the **Tissington Spires**, another limestone outcrop.

Thorpe village and its surrounding area plays host to the annual **Dovedale Dash** – a cross-country race of 4 -and-a-half miles run by about 1200 people of all abilities. One of the main excitements is crossing the river Dove at the well-known Stepping Stones. The event was first established in 1953, and takes place on the first Sunday of November, although previously it was held on the closest Sunday to Guy Fawkes Night.

ILAM

4 miles NW of Ashbourne off the A52

The village was inhabited in Saxon times and the ancient **Parish Church of the Holy Cross** still displays some Saxon stonework as well as the shrine of a much-loved Staffordshire saint and 8th century Mercian king, Bertelin, or Bertram. Ilam has been an English pilgrim destination for over 1,300 years –

ever since grief-stricken St Bertram arrived here to live as a hermit. Legend recalls that Bertram, the 'First Evangelist of the Moorlands', spent the remainder of his life here after wolves killed his wife and newborn baby, while he was out looking for food.

Now a model village of great charm on the Staffordshire side of the River Dove, Ilam was originally an important settlement belonging to Burton Abbey. Following the Reformation in the 16th century, the estate was broken up and Ilam came into the hands of the Port family. In the early 1800s the family sold the property to Jesse Watts Russell, a wealthy industrialist. He moved the village from its position near Ilam Hall and rebuilt it in its current location in 'Alpine style'. This explains both the Swiss style of the buildings and the surprising distance between them and the village church.

John Port originally built **Ilam Hall** in 1546, and while in the possession of the Ports, both Samuel Johnson and the playwright William Congreve stayed there. Watts Russell bought it in 1820 along with the estate and rebuilt it. As well as building a fine mansion, Watts Russell also spent a great deal of money refurbishing the village. Obviously devoted to his wife, he had the village hall rebuilt in a romantic Gothic style and, in the centre of the village; he had a cross erected in her memory. In the 1930s most of the hall had been demolished before being bought by Sir Robert McDougall, who

presented it to the Youth Hostelling Association in 1934. It remains a youth hostel to this day. The 158 acres of **Ilam Park**, on which the hall stands, is owned and managed by the National Trust.

In the valley of the River Manifold, a much-used starting point for walks along this beautiful stretch of river, the Manifold disappears underground north of the village in summer, to reappear

Cross Stone, Ilam Parish Church

below Ilam Hall. The village is also the place where the Rivers Manifold and Dove merge. Though Dovedale is, deservedly so, considered the most scenic of the Peak District valleys, the Manifold Valley is very similar and while being marginally less beautiful it is often much less crowded. The two

St Bertrams Well, Ilam

•

Waterfall was once the starting point of the Manifold Valley Light Railway, a narrow gauge railway from the main Leek-Ashbourne railway line, via Waterhouses to Hume End. The line has since been removed and now the track is the Hamps-Manifold Trail, a well used tourist trail for walkers and cyclists.

•

Waterfall, nr Waterhouses

A friendly and historic inn set in a scenic location in the picturesque village of Waterfall.

see page 229

rivers rise close together; on Axe Edge, and for much of their course follow a parallel path, so it is fitting that they should come together eventually.

Be sure not to leave without visiting Ilam Hall's visitor centre. Jackson's Geology is a new touchscreen exploration of Dovedale, explaining the geology of the White Peak through the eyes of celebrating the work of Dr Jackson. This pioneer geologist and cave archaeologist worked in Dovedale during the 1920s–1930s.

WATERHOUSES

6 miles NW of Ashbourne off the A523

Between here and Hulme End, is the Leek and Manifold Valley Light Railway, a piece of Indian engineering transplanted into Staffordshire. The Edwardian engineer who created it had recently come back from India, where he built narrow gauge railways. Sadly, it only ran from 1904 to 1934 but its track bed has been transformed into the **Hamps-Manifold Trail** – nine miles of gentle footpath and cycle way. The scenery of the Hamps and Manifold valleys should be enough to tempt anyone on to this trail, which takes you through limestone gorges, woodlands and picturesque villages. Highlights along the way include Thor's Cave, Ecton Copper mine and Throwley Old Hall. The terminus at Hulme End has an excellent visitor centre (also see Hulme End). The trail can be reached from car parks at Hulme End, Waterhouses, Weags Bridge near Grindon, and Wetton.

WATERFALL

7 miles NW of Ashbourne off the A523

The tiny village of Waterfall is on the Staffordshire moors. It gets its name from the way that the **River Hamps** disappears underground through crevices in the ground. In the case of the Hamps, it disappears at Waterhouses and reappears again near Ilam before merging with the River Manifold.

The **Parish Church of St James and St Bartholomew** is originally Norman but was largely rebuilt in the 19th century. However, the Norman chancel has been retained.

GRINDON

7 miles NW of Ashbourne off the B5053

This unique moorland hill village stands over 1,000 feet above sea level and overlooks the beautiful Manifold Valley. Recorded in the *Domesday Book* as 'Grendon', meaning green hill, 'an ancient manor in the 20th year of the reign of William the Conqueror', Grindon is reputed to have been visited by Bonnie Prince Charlie on his way to Derby. It was once a staging post on the packhorse route from Ecton Hill and had the most productive copper mine in the country, where many of the local people would have worked. The local pub, the Cavalier, was possibly named after Bonny Prince Charlie.

The splendid isolation in which this village stands is confirmed by a look around the churchyard. The names on the epitaphs and graves reflect the close-knit nature of the communities. The Salt family, for instance, are to be seen everywhere, followed closely by the Stubbs, Cantrells, Hambletons and, to a lesser extent, the Mycocks.

WETTON

7 miles NW of Ashbourne between the B5053 and the A515

The village gives its name to Wetton Hill, a 'reef knoll' formed from the ancient remains of a coral reef, and Wetton Mill, on the River Manifold, both are in the care of the National Trust. **Wetton Mill**, which closed down in the mid 19th century, is being sympathetically restored by the National Trust as a museum piece. There is a café on site, a very welcome sight for those walking the **Manifold Valley Trail**. There is also a car park, campsite and a picnic area for those who would rather cater for themselves.

There are many burial chambers or mounds in the area, including those on Wetton Hill itself, at Wetton Low, and at Long Low, some 2 km south east of the village. On **Wetton Low,** 1 km south of the village, some of the burial mounds, contained bones dating back at least to 1600 BC. **Ecton Hill** is covered in the remains of old lead mines worked by the Duke of Devonshire. His profits from the mine were used to build the Crescent at Buxton.

Easily accessible from Wetton is the ominous-sounding **Thor's Cave**, situated some 360 feet above the River Manifold. Though the cave is not deep, the entrance is huge, some 60 feet high, a sight which is clearly visible for several miles. The stiff climb up is well worth the effort for the spectacular views, all framed by the great natural stone arch. The acoustics, too, are interesting, and conversations can easily be carried out with people far below. Ancient bones and implements have been found here dating back 10,000 years. The openings at the bottom of the crag on which the cave sits are known as **Radcliffe Stables** and are said to have been used by a Jacobite as a hiding place after Bonnie Prince Charlie had retreated from Derby.

The **Parish Church of St Margaret** is partly 14th century, though most of it dates from around 1820. In the churchyard is the grave of Samuel Carrington, who, along with Thomas Bateman of Youlgreave, found evidence that Thor's Cave was occupied in ancient times. Carrington also excavated the fields close to Wetton, where he was schoolmaster in the mid 1800s, and found an abandoned village, though neither he nor his friend Bateman could put an age to the settlement.

ALSTONEFIELD

7 miles NW of Ashbourne off the A515

This ancient village, situated between the Manifold and the Dove valleys, lies at the crossroads of several old packhorse routes and even had its own market charter granted in 1308. The market ceased in 1500 but the annual cattle sales continued right up until the beginning of the 20th century. The

•

Peter Riley's magically imaginative poem Alstonefield is named after the small limestone village. He shares an intimate love of the area in language to rejoice in. It is a poem about passage, transformation, and the resources of the imagination in quest of a sense of justice.

•

hamlet was also the site of England's first co-operative cheese factory, which produced a variety of Derby cheese.

Its geographical location has helped to maintain the charm of Alstonefield. There has been no invasion by the canal or railway builders (it lies at 900 feet above sea level) and it is still two miles from the nearest classified road. One hundred and fifty years ago Alstonefield was at the centre of a huge parish which covered all the land between the two rivers. There has been a church here since at least AD 892, when a visit by St Oswald is recorded, but the earliest known parts of the large **Parish Church of St Peter** are the Norman doorway and chancel arch. It was added to in the 15th century and restored in Victorian times. There is also plenty of 17th century woodwork and a double-decker pulpit dated 1637. Izaak Walton's friend, Charles Cotton, and his family, lived at nearby Beresford Hall, now unfortunately no more, but their elaborate pew, with the Cotton coat-of-arms, is still in the church.

The village also retains its ancient **Tithe Barn**, found behind the late 16th century rectory. The internal exposed wattle and daub wall and the spiral stone staircase may, however, have been part of an earlier building.

Nearby Alstonefield you will find **Hanson Grange**, an old farmstead, and the site of an ancient burial ground. The numerous reported sounds of

violent fighting and cries of anguish are thought to stem back to the murder, in 1467, of a man named John Mycock. Four people participated in his death; John de la Pole of Hartington hit him on the side of his head. Henry Vigers of Monyash stabbed him in the chest. John Harrison shot him in the back with a bow and arrow, and Matthew Bland of Hartington struck him on the head with a club staff. Witnesses were too scared to testify, so the murderers never went to trial before the king. Maybe this is why the sounds of that fateful night can still be heard as this murder most foul has gone unavenged for centuries.

ECTON
9½ miles NW of Ashbourne off the B5054

If not *'gold in them thar hills'*, there was certainly plenty of copper. In the late 1750s Deep Ecton Mine was, at nearly 1,400 feet, the richest and deepest copper mine in Europe. The copper mines here were owned by the Duke of Devonshire and it is generally accepted that the profits from the ore extraction paid for his building of The Crescent at Buxton. Work had ceased in the mines by 1900 but so impervious was the surrounding limestone that the workings took several years to flood, though now they are under water.

WARSLOW
9 miles NW of Ashbourne off the B5054

Situated opposite Wetton on the other side of the River Manifold, the village is one of the main access points to this dramatic section of the Manifold Valley. Lying below the gritstone moorlands, this was an estate village for the eccentric Crewe family, who lived at Calke Abbey in south Derbyshire. The **Parish Church of St Lawrence** is a handsome building of 1820, and was formerly dedicated to St James. The village also has some pleasant 18th and 19th century cottages and a welcoming pub called the Greyhound, a 250 year old coaching inn, once known as the Greyhound and Hare.

HULME END

9 miles NW of Ashbourne on the B5054

From here to Ilam, the River Manifold runs southwards through a deep, twisting limestone cleft, between steep and wooded banks. For much of its dramatic course the Manifold disappears underground in dry weather through swallow holes, which is typical of a river in a limestone area.

The village also lies at the terminus of the narrow gauge **Leek and Manifold Valley Light Railway**, which opened in 1904. Already aware of the tourism possibilities of the Peak District by the beginning of the 20th century, the other reason for constructing the railway was to transport coal and other raw materials to the surrounding settlements. The line, however, was unable to pay its way, particularly after the creamery at Ecton, just a mile south of Hulme End, closed in 1933. The following

year the railway ceased operation. The tracks were taken up and, if it had not been turned into a semi-long distance footpath, the route of the railway might have been lost forever. The old station building at the western end of the hamlet has been beautifully restored and is now an excellent visitor centre, with public toilets and a car park.

HARTINGTON

10 miles NW of Ashbourne on the B5054

People come to Hartington to buy the world renown blue-veined Stilton – *'the King of English Chesses'*. The Duke of Devonshire opened the creamery in 1876 so that his tenant farmers could better utilise their milk but the venture failed and the business was closed in 1895. Thomas Nuttall then bought the site in 1900 and reopened it as a Stilton creamery, processing 50 gallons of milk a day. It is the only remaining cheese factory in Derbyshire and now produces no less than a quarter of the world's supply of Stilton. However, at the time of writing this, the future of the creamery is in doubt after its rival Long Clawson Dairy announced it had bought Dairy Crest's Stilton, so production could be moved to a site in Leicestershire.

The village is very much on the tourist route and, though popular, has retained much of its village appeal. As well as the famous Old Cheese Shop, there are two old coaching inns left over from the days when this was an important market centre. One of these goes by the rather unusual name of The

Hartington

Open seven days a week from Easter, this busy little Tea Room provides a good selection of light meals and teas. It also houses the village Post Office.

‖ see page 230

Hartington

The Manifold Inn is a 200-year-old coaching inn that offers a warm welcome and fresh home cooked food and accommodation. It's an ideal base for a holiday in the Peak District.

‖ ⊨ see page 230

86 BIGGIN HALL COUNTRY HOUSE HOTEL

Biggin-by-Hartington

It's decadent, it's cosseting, and it doesn't get much finer than The Biggin Hall - a country house with a difference.

 see page 231

Upper Dove Valley, nr Hartington

Charles Cotton, named after the friend of Izaak Walton. Situated in the valley of the River Dove, Hartington is an excellent place from which to explore both the Dove and the Manifold valleys. To the south lies **Beresford Dale**, the upper valley of the River Dove and every bit as pretty as its more famous neighbour, Dovedale. It was immortalised by Izaak Walton and Charles Cotton when *The Compleat Angler* was published in 1653.

Venturing back into the annals of history, Hartington is noted at the time of the *Domesday Book* as being called 'Hortedvn'. This charming limestone village was granted a market charter in 1203 and it is likely that its spacious market place was once the village green.

Hartington Hall, built in the 17th century and enlarged in the 19th century, is typical of many Peak District manor houses and a fine example of a Derbyshire

yeoman's house and farm. It is thought that Bonny Prince Charlie stayed there on his way to Derby. It became a youth hostel in 1934, and is the oldest such youth hostel in the Peak District.

MAYFIELD

2½ miles SW of Ashbourne on the A5032

Mayfield is a large village on the edge of Ashbourne, divided into Upper Mayfield and Middle Mayfield. Though it is so close to Ashbourne, it actually lies in Stafforshire, as the border runs west of the village. Mayfield was originally a Saxon village, dating back over a thousand years and listed in the *Domesday Book* as Mavreveldt. The first Norman church was probably built about 1125 during the reign of Henry I, and the present **Parish Church of St John the Baptist** illustrates the progressive styles of architecture since that date, with a 14th century chancel and a 16th century tower.

In the churchyard there is an original Saxon cross. The ballad writer, Thomas Moore, lived at Moore Cottage, formerly Stancliffe Farm. His young daughter, Olivia, is buried in the local churchyard, her slate tombstone reading 'Olivia Byron Moore, died March 18, 1815'. Moore was friendly with Lord Byron, who visited him here.

On 7th December 1745 Bonnie Prince Charlie and his army passed through Mayfield on their retreat from Derby, terrorising the local populace. They shot the innkeeper at Hanging Bridge as well as a Mr Humphrey Brown, who refused to hand over his horse to them. Many of the terrified villagers locked themselves in the church. The soldiers fired shots through the door and the bullet holes can still be seen in the woodwork of the west door. Legend has it that many of the rebels were caught and hung from gibbets on the old packhorse bridge, whose 500-year-old grey stone arches can still be seen, even though the bridge has been rebuilt.

There is however a road out of the village, leading to the main Leek highway, marked on the Ordnance Survey map as "Gallowstree Lane", suggesting that those to be hung went their way via the bridge and Gallowstree Lane to Gallowstree Hill. Today it is a pleasant walk rewarded by a lovely view down the Dove Valley.

Mayfield Mill has been producing textiles for 200 years. The first mention of a mill occurs in 1291, when Mayfield, including its mill, belonged to the Priory of Tutbury. By 1793 there had been various owners of the site, which now included two corn mills, a leather mill and two fulling mills. Textiles were first produced in 1795. In 1806 the interior of the building and all its machinery was destroyed in a fire. The mill was eventually rebuilt with a cast iron framework and brick vaulted ceilings, as can still be seen today.

The spinning of cotton continued in Mayfield until 1934 when it was sold to William Tatton and Company who used the mill to process silk.

LEEK

Leek advertises itself as the 'Queen of the Moorlands', and is just becoming recognised as a historical jewel in the old silk mills and Arts and Crafts heritage. Until the 19th century, this was a domestic industry with the workshops on the top storeys of the houses. Many examples of these 'top shops' have survived to this day. Leek also became an important dyeing town, particularly after the death of Prince Albert, when 'Raven Black' was popularised by Queen Victoria, who remained in mourning for her beloved husband for many years.

Leek has strong connections with the Arts and Crafts Movement because in 1873, William Morris (founder of this movement) came to Leek to investigate new techniques of dyeing and printing, staying with the Wardle family who were silk manufacturers. Lady Elizabeth Wardle founded the Leek

The Parish Church of St Giles stands above the Mayfield market square, and has a fine perpendicular tower. Up until 1848, it was divided into two churches, as the south transept was used for worship by the people of the nearby hamlet of Biggin.

87 THE SWAN

Leek

The town's oldest hostelry offering a courtyard and garden in which to enjoy Real Ales and homemade food in the warmer months.

🍴 🛏 see page 232

88 THE DYERS ARMS

Leek

Come in and relax in homely surroundings, you can be sure of a friendly welcome.

🍴 see page 233

89 BLUEBERRYS

Leek

Popular and customer-friendly town centre tearoom/café serving wholesome and appetising fare.

🍴 *see page 234*

90 DEN ENGLE BELGIAN BAR AND RESTAURANT

Leek

A stylish and well-known Belgian bar serving not only Belgian beers, but good food with a Belgian twist as well.

🍴 *see page 235*

School of Embroidery in 1879. Elizabeth Wardle, along with thirty-five members of the school and other embroiderers from the surrounding area created a full size replica of the Bayeux Tapestry in just over a year. Each embroiderer stitched her name beneath her completed panel. The tapestry toured the nation and even went to Germany and North America! It is now on display in the Museum of Reading and was first displayed here in 1886. The imposing brick-built **Nicholson Institute** holds exhibitions on the wonderful and intricate work of the famous Leek School of Embroidery.

These days Leek is an antiques lovers' paradise with indoor and outdoor markets. Leek's first market was established by Royal Charter in 1208, and was a thriving market centre, rivaling Macclesfield and Congleton. It still runs every Wednesday in the cobbled Market Place. Leek also has a craft and antiques market on Saturday and an indoor 'butter market' on Wednesday, Friday and Saturday. Every road coming into the town seems to converge on the old cobbled Market Place and the road to the west leads down to the church. Dedicated to Edward the Confessor (the full name is the **Parish Church of St Edward's and All Saints**), the original church was burnt down in 1297 and rebuilt some 20 years later, though the building is now largely 17th century. The timber roof of the nave is well worth a second look and is the church's pride and joy. It

is boasted that each of the cross beams was hewn from a separate oak tree and, in the west part of the nave, an enormous 18th century gallery rises up, tier on tier, giving the impression of a theatre's dress circle.

Although much has been altered inside the church, most notably in 1865 when G.E. Street rebuilt the chancel, reredos, sanctuary, pulpit and stalls, there still remains one interesting original artefact to see - a wooden chair. Traditionally this is believed to have been a ducking stool for scolds, which was used in the nearby River Churnet. Outside, in the churchyard, can be found a curious inscription on a gravestone: 'James Robinson interred February the 28th 1788 Aged 438'!

Another building worthy of a second glance is the imposing **Nicholson Institute**, mentioned earlier, with its copper dome. Completed in 1884 and funded by the local industrialist Joshua Nicholson, the Institute offered the people of Leek an opportunity to learn and expand their cultural horizons. The Nicholson has seen many famous people pass through its doors including the likes of Oscar Wilde, John Betjeman and D.H Lawrence. It is currently being restored, (due for completion start of 2009), so that this beautiful old building will be preserved for the enjoyment of future generations. The town's **War Memorial**, built in Portland stone and with a clock tower, has a dedication to the youngest Nicholson son, who was killed in the First World War.

Leek has a famous son; it was the home of James Brindley, the 18th-century engineer who built much of the early canal network. A water-powered corn mill built by him in 1752 (on the site of an earlier mill) in Mill Street has been restored and now houses the **Brindley Water Museum** (known as Brindley Mill), which is devoted to his life and work. Visitors can see corn being ground and see displays of millwrighting skills.

The **River Churnet**, though little known outside Staffordshire, has a wealth of scenery and industrial archaeology. It is easily accessible to walkers and its valley deserves better recognition. The river rises to the west of Leek in rugged gritstone country, but for most of its length it flows through softer, red sandstone countryside in a valley that was carved out during the Ice Age. Though there are few footpaths directly adjacent to the riverbank, most of the valley can be walked close to the river using a combination of canal towpaths and former railway tracks.

Four miles to the north of the town on the A53 rise the dark, jagged gritstone outcrops of **The Roaches**, **Ramshaw Rocks** and **Hen Cloud**. 'Roaches' is a corruption of the French word 'roches' or rocks. 'Cloud' is a local word used for high hills. Just below The Roaches there is a delightful stretch of water, **Tittesworth Reservoir**, which is extremely popular with trout fishermen.

Saxon Cross, Leek

At Winkhill is the **Blackbrook Zoological Park**, which is open all year, and which has rare birds, insects, reptiles and unusual animals. **Kiddies Kingdom,** in Cross Mill Street, is an indoor play area for children, just right for children's parties and days out.

Leeks calendar of events include annual Arts Festival, showcasing the wealth and range of artistic talent within Leek and, Agricultural show on the last Saturday of July.

91 KNOT INN

Rushton Spencer

The Knot Inn is set in the beautiful location of Rushton Spencer where proprietors, Vin and Gina run a family friendly pub and offer you good old fashioned hospitality.

see page 236

92 CASTRO'S RESTAURANT AND LOUNGE

Cheddleton

A friendly and historic English Inn, boasting an extensive menu of locally sourced food, within a beautiful countryside setting.

see page 237

93 YE OLDE STAR INN

Cotton

A family-run free house which has a great reputation for its food and drink among locals and visitors alike.

see page 238

AROUND LEEK

RUDYARD

2 miles NW of Leek off the A523

In fond memory of the place where they first met in 1863, Mr and Mrs Kipling named their famous son, born in 1865, after this village. The nearby two-mile-long **Rudyard Lake** was built in 1831 by John Rennie to feed the Cauldon canal. With steeply wooded banks, the lake is now a leisure centre with facilities for picnicking, walking, fishing and sailing. Along the west shore is also a section of the **Staffordshire Way**, the long distance footpath which runs from Mow Cop to **Kinver Edge**, near Stourbridge. This is a sandstone ridge covered in woodland and heath, and with several famous rock houses which were inhabited until the 1950s.

Back in Victorian days, Rudyard was a popular lakeside resort which developed after the construction of the North Staffordshire Railway in 1845. The **Rudyard Lake Steam Railway** uses miniature narrow gauge steam trains to give a three-mile return trip along the side of the reservoir. Its popularity became so great that, on one particular day in 1877, over 20,000 people came here to see Captain Webb, the first man to swim the English Channel, swim in the reservoir.

RUSHTON SPENCER

5 miles NW of Leek on the A523

This pleasant, moorland village nestles under the distinctive hill called **The Cloud** (from the Old English 'clud', meaning hill or mountain) and is the ideal starting point for a walk to the summit. The church for Rushton Spencer is not in the village but up the hill to the west. It is also well known for its appealing mix of styles, the **'Chapel in the Wilderness'**, dedicated to St Lawrence was originally of wood in the 14th century and later in stone. It served both Rushton Spencer and neighbouring Rushton James. There has been a church on this site from 1206.

Trains once stopped at the magnificent Gothic station, now a private house. Near here is a car park that is ideally placed for those wishing to walk to nearby Lake Rudyard.

FLASH

7 miles N of Leek off the A53

At over 1,518 feet above sea level, Flash is said to be the highest village in England. The village has historical connections with cock fighting and counterfeiting money. The area around is also notable for the weirdly shaped outcrops of gritstone that occur - Ball Stones, Gib Torr and Ball Stone Rock, for example.

Cock fighting was so popular here, that it continued long after it had been made illegal.

The men of Flash, or Flashmen, were notorious for counterfeiting coins and they found a novel way to escape punishment. The **Three Shires**

Head is a local beauty spot where the three counties of Derbyshire, Cheshire and Staffordshire meet, this meant then that the police in one county could not arrest wrongdoers in another county. So, at the Three Shires Head Flashmen escaped capture by hopping from Shire to Shire.

CAULDON

8 miles SE of Leek off the A52

Cauldon Lowe, a lofty hill in this village, is valuable for its extensive quarries of excellent Limestone, used as a building material and in iron smelting. Formerly carried to the Caldon Canal and to the station at Froghall for transport across the country.

94 RAILWAY INN

Froghall

Romantic bedrooms with four poster beds, family rooms, excellent food and stunning scenery are just a few good reasons to stay at The Railway Inn

❚ ➤ see *page 239*

95 CROWTREES FARM

Oakamoor

Friendly hosts provide a warm welcome at this delightfully traditional B & B.

➤ see *page 240*

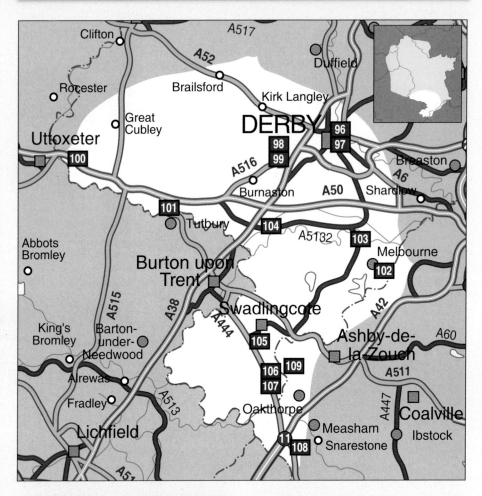

🛏 ACCOMMODATION

100	Cavendish Arms, Doveridge, nr Ashbourne	p 114, 242
101	The Castle Hotel, Hatton	p 116, 241
103	Ivy House Farm B&B and Woodland Hills Court Self Catering, Stanton-by-Bridge	p 120, 244
106	Overseale House, Overseal, nr Swadlincote	p 124, 246
107	Robin Hood Inn, Overseal, nr Swadlincote	p 124, 247

🍴 FOOD & DRINK

98	The Honeycomb, Mickleover	p 109, 241
99	The Great Northern, Mickleover	p 109, 241
100	Cavendish Arms, Doveridge, nr Ashbourne	p 114, 242
101	The Castle Hotel, Hatton	p 116, 241
102	Bay Tree Restaurant, Melbourne	p 119, 243
104	Rising Sun, Willington	p 122, 245
105	Traveller's Rest, Church Gresley, nr Swadlincote	p 123, 245
107	Robin Hood Inn, Overseal, nr Swadlincote	p 124, 247

The Trent Valley

Mention the Dark or White Peak and most people will have in mind the areas within the boundaries of the Peak District National Park. However that boundary is a man-made line and there are some fine villages and architecture to be had outside these areas. This chapter will focus upon Derby and The Trent Valley plus the surrounding villages.

Derbyshire was at the forefront of modern thinking at the beginning of the Industrial Revolution. The chief inheritor of this legacy was Derby, and the city is still a busy industrial centre,

Church and Hall across a Frozen Lake, Melbourne

home to engineering companies as well as a university and a cathedral. It is one of England's more recent cities, having been granted city status as late as 1977. However, it is an historic place, with a great choice of attractions. And though the county is called Derbyshire, the city is not the county town. This honour goes to Matlock, where the city council meets.

If you are interested in stately homes, it is worth leaving the peak and heading to the lowlands of the Trent Valley, where there are many splendid stately homes, including

Kedleston Hall and the eccentric Calke Abbey. The scenery affords ample opportunities to enjoy pleasant walks. Truly an area of hidden places, the Trent Valley has many gems worth visiting, such as the picturesque villages of Church Gresley and Castle Gresley, the welcoming centres of Melbourne and Hartshorne, quiet Repton on the River Trent itself and the 'border' town of Swadlincote. The Trent Valley is a historically interesting area and has been a focus of human activity since early prehistory.

🍴 FOOD & DRINK

108	The Black Horse, Appleby Magna, nr Swadlincote	p 125, 246
109	Moira Tea Room, Moira, nr Swadlincote	p 125, 248

🏛 PLACES OF INTEREST

96	Pickford's House Museum, Derby	p 107, 240
97	Derby Museums and Art Gallery, Derby	p 108, 240

DERBY

A city that literally changed the world - Derby was the birthplace of the industrial revolution. Derby's position, historically and geographically, has ensured that it has remained one of the most important and interesting cities in the East Midlands. Consequently, there is much for the visitor to see, whether from an architectural or historical point of view. The city's rich heritage can be seen all around - from the magnificent Cathedral with imposing tower that can be seen for miles around, to artistic treasures at the Derby Museum and Art Gallery. There are, however, two things that most people, whether they have been to the city before or not, know of Derby: **Rolls-Royce** and Royal Crown Derby Porcelain.

When, in 1904, Sir Henry Royce and the Hon C S Rolls joined forces, and subsequently built the first Rolls-Royce (a Silver Ghost) at Derby in 1906, they built much more than just a motor car - they built a legend. Considered by many to be the best cars in the world, it is often said that the noisiest moving part in any Rolls-Royce is the dashboard clock! It is now owned by BMW of Germany, though the aircraft engine division (also based in Derby, but an entirely separate company), is a joint venture between BMW and Rolls Royce itself.

The home of **Royal Crown Derby Porcelain**, any visit to the city would not be complete without a trip to the factory and its museum and shop on Ormaston Road. The guided tours offer an intriguing insight into the high level of skill required to create the delicate flower petals, hand-gild the plates and hand paint the Derby Dwarves. You can ask questions and even try your hand at some of the skills. There are examples of some early Derby pottery preserved at the works museum, and another extensive collection is maintained in a special Ceramics Gallery at the Derby Museum. The factory shop sells both seconds and items currently in production.

There has been a church on the site of the city's **Cathedral of All Saints** since at least AD 943. It possesses a fine 16th century tower, the second highest perpendicular tower in England, and the oldest ring of ten bells in the country. Before 1927 it was the Parish Church of All Saints, the main church for Derby, but in that year was raised to cathedral status. In the early 18th century the nave and chancel was in a ruinous state, so they were rebuilt between 1723 and 1725 to the designs of James Gibbs. Inside is a beautiful wrought-iron screen by Robert Bakewell and, among the splendid monuments, is the tomb of Bess of Hardwick Hall, who died in 1607. In the late 1960s and early 1970s the building was extended eastwards and the retrochoir, baldacchino and sacristy were added, along with the screen. Only five minutes walk from the cathedral, the beautifully restored medieval **St Mary's Chapel on the Bridge** is one of only six surviving bridge chapels still in use. There is some medieval stained glass in one of the windows. In 1588 three Catholic priests, Nicholas Garlick, Richard Simpson and Robert Ludlum (the 'Padley Martyrs') were hung, drawn and quartered, and their remains hung from the chapel entrance. The bridge itself is 18th century, and straddles the River Derwent.

One of Derby's most interesting attractions is **Pickford's House Museum**, situated on the city's finest Georgian street, Friar Gate, at number 41. This Grade I listed building was erected in 1770 by the architect Joseph Pickford as a combined family home and place of work. Pickford House differs from the majority of grand stately homes in that it does not have a wealth of priceless furniture or works of art. Instead, visitors are able to gain a true insight into everyday upper middle-class life – it's a time capsule of Georgian life and costume. The kitchen and servants' quarters have been re-created showing the conditions they worked under during the 1830s. Pickford House is the epitome of a late-Georgian professional man's residence. There is an exciting programme of temporary exhibitions, as well as other displays that deal with the history of the Friar's Gate area and the importance of Joseph Pickford as a Midlands architect. One special feature of Pickford House is the excellent collection of costumes,

Derby Cathedral, Derby

some dating back to the mid-1700s. A period 18th century garden is also laid out at the rear of the house, and there are toy theatres from the Frank Bradley collection.

Just a short walk from Pickford House is the **Derby Industrial Museum**, which is on the site of the world's oldest factories, the Silk Mills built by George Sorocold in 1702 and 1717. The foundations and parts of the tower from the 1717 mill are still visible. The displays tell the story of the industrial heritage and achievement of Derby and its people. Since 1915 Derby has been involved with the manufacture of engines, and the whole of the ground floor

96 PICKFORD'S HOUSE MUSEUM

Derby

Pickford's House Museum, in the historic Friar Gate area, is a beautifully restored Georgian house, and was the home of Derby industrialist Joseph Pickford

🏛 *see page 240*

107

•

Derbyshire has been named "Ghost capital of Britain" with over 1,000 paranormal sightings recorded in recent years.

•

97 DERBY MUSEUMS AND ART GALLERY

Derby

A fascinating museum and art gallery, housing collections of porcelain, paintings, archaelogy, geology and wildlife.

 see page 240

galleries are devoted to the Rolls-Royce aircraft engine collection, illustrating the importance played by the aero industry in the city's history. On the first floor of the building there is an introduction to other Derbyshire industries, with displays on lead and coal mining, iron founding, limestone quarrying, ceramics and brick making. There is also a Railway Research Gallery with displays covering the history of the Midland Railway since the 1840's and children will enjoy the life sized replica of an engine driver's cab. The railway industry played a large part in the life of the city, and along with Rolls Royce, British Rail Engineering Ltd (BREL) is one of its largest employers.

The **City Museum and Art Gallery** in the Strand is also well worth visiting. Opened in 1879, it is the oldest of Derby's museums and the displays relate to the social, military, and natural history of the city and county, as well as paintings by the celebrated 18th Century Derby artist Joseph Wright. This is the largest collection of the artist's work in any public gallery in the world.

The Archaeology Gallery contains local material from the Stone Age to the Middle Ages, with several fine Anglo-Saxon crosses and a splendid sarcophagus. There are also two Egyptian mummies. Derbyshire wildlife and geology feature in an exciting series of natural settings and hands-on exhibits. One section of the museum is devoted to a Military

Gallery, which tells of Derby's regiments over the years. The walk-in First World War trench scene captures the experience of a night at the front. The Bonnie Prince Charlie Room tells the story of Derby's role in the 1745 Jacobite uprising, and a life-sized figure of the prince relates the sad events that led to his defeat.

The ground floor gallery houses an award-winning Ceramics Gallery, with samples of Royal Crown Derby porcelain dating to the 1750s. It is the most comprehensive collection of Derby Porcelain to be seen anywhere in the world, including 18th century figurines, many interpretations of the Japanese designs for which the company is famous, the delicate 'Eggshell' China by French Art Director Desire Leroy, and examples of the Crown Derby ware commissioned for the restaurants of the *Titanic*. On the second floor of the Museum are temporary exhibition galleries. These change every three or four weeks and cover not only the museum's own collection but also travelling exhibitions

TV's 'Most Haunted' programme brought the **Derby Gaol** to the nation's attention in 2002. The Derby Gaol is situated in the depths of the original dungeons of the Derbyshire County Gaol, dating back to 1756. It offers a reminder of the city's grisly past. It includes a debtor's cell and a condemned cell, and was the site of the last hanging, drawing and quartering in the country, which took place after England's last revolution, the Pentrich Rebellion, in 1817. Three men were sentenced to the grisly form of execution, while thirteen others were sent to a penal colony in Australia. The Gaol has rapidly become a popular destination for ghost hunters, serious investigators, or just the curious. Whatever your interest, this site is here to represent one of Derby's most famous places. Open on Tuesday, Thursday and Sunday, with conducted tours.

Surely one of the finest buildings in Derby is St Helen's House, a Grade I listed building situated in King Street. This hidden attraction has been described by the Georgian Group, of London, as "one of the finest and largest eighteenth century townhouses to survive in any provincial city". Originally built about 1726 by Joseph Pickford for John Gisborne, at one time Derby School, and for a few years home to The Joseph Wright School of Art, the building unfortunately is currently disused, but it is planned to reopen the building as a hotel.

A much more modern attraction within the city's Market Place was opened in September 2008, and is called the **Quad**. Quad is a visual arts and media centre, cinema, café bar and workshop that anyone can use. Many believe this will herald a period when the city can really shine as a leading hub of creativity within Britain.

Derby also has the first public recreational park in the country, the **Arboretum**, is to the south of the city centre. The arboretum was set up by philanthropic land owner and industrialist Joseph Strutt in 1840. The arboretum's web site states that the arboretum's design was the inspiration for the vision of great urban parks in the USA, notably Central Park in New York City. Other major parks in the city include **Allestree Park** to the north and **Markeaton Park** to the west. The Markeaton Park Light Railway operates within Markeaton Park, which is located next to what remains of Markeaton Village. The trains are owned by a charitable trust and are driven and maintained by volunteers. Trains run every twenty minutes to the Mundy Play Centre; the journey is about three quarters of a mile long.

Further treasures including Chatsworth, Kedleston Hall and many National Trust properties are a short scenic drive away throughout Derbyshire and the Peak District.

Derby and its surrounding area host an array of annual events, whether it's the CAMRA Beer Festival, the classical music at the annual Darley Park concert or the beauty of the traditional well dressing displays.

AROUND DERBY

DARLEY ABBEY

2 miles N of Derby off the A6

Within walking distance of Derby City Centre is the tranquil village of Darley Abbey, featuring delightfully restored mill cottages.

98 THE HONEYCOMB

Mickleover

A great place to meet, drink and eat in Mickleover, near by the popular Radbourne Walk.

see page 241

99 THE GREAT NORTHERN

Mickleover

Great reputation for exceptional food and drink with a warm welcome offered to all.

see page 241

The Parish Church of All Saints in Breadsall possesses one of the most elegant steeples in the country, dating from the early 1400s. The south doorway is Norman and the tower and chancel date back to the 1200s. The church was burnt down by suffragettes in 1914 and carefully restored over the next two years. Inside there is a touching pieta from the late 1300s. This beautiful alabaster depiction of the Virgin Mary with the crucified Christ lying across her knees, was found under the floor of the church after another fire, and was restored to its present position by W D Caroe.

The Augustinian **Abbey of St Mary** was founded by Robert Ferrers, second Earl of Derby, around 1140 and grew to become the most powerful abbey in Derbyshire and possibly in the whole of the East Midlands. In 1538 the Abbey was surrendered to the crown as part of the Dissolution of the Monasteries. Sadly, few monasteries could have been so completely obliterated, and what is now known as The Abbey pub is the only building remaining. The layout is of a simple medieval hall house and is thought to have been used as the Abbey's guest house for travellers and pilgrims during the 13th century. During renovation, 12th century pottery was unearthed.

Darley Park, on the River Derwent, was landscaped by William Evans and has attractive flower beds, shrubberies and lawns. It once had a hall, built in 1727 but now demolished, that for 120 years was the home of the Evans family who built the cotton mill by the river in 1783.

Pause beside the River Derwent, within sight of one of the most complete early textile mill complexes. The mill area is quite a large complex. The oldest parts, east mill, middle mill and west mill, are five-storeyed and brick built. There is also a finishing house which has three storeys and sash windows, and an octagonal toll house in the mill yard. The Evans family built the red brick houses, still evident in the village, for the

mill workers. They were typical paternalistic employers, providing subsidised rents, coal, blankets in cold weather and even arranging burials and memorials for their workers.

The **Parish Church of St Matthew** was built in the early 19th century, with a chancel added between 1885 and 1901. It is an elegant building in Gothic style, and contains monuments to the Evans family.

In the 21st century, the old village of Darley Abbey is regarded as a desirable place to live.

BREADSALL

3 miles N of Derby off the A6

Breadsall began life as a small hamlet clustered around its Norman church. It is now known primarily as a residential suburb of Derby, with new estates around the original centre.

Opposite the west end of the church can be found **The Old Hall**, which has been part of village life for over 600 years. It was originally the manor house when the village was divided into the wards of Overhall and Netherhall. In later years it has been employed as a school, farmhouse, hunting box, public house, shop, joiner's shop and post office. It currently serves as a parish hall and is used by various village organisations.

Close by is Breadsall Priory. This was originally a small 13th Augustinian Priory and was later converted to a large Elizabethan house. Successive owners have all left their mark on the building which is now a luxurious hotel and leisure complex. The most famous resident of Breadsall Priory was Erasmus Darwin, a respected physician, well-known poet, philosopher, botanist, and naturalist, who lived there for a short time until his death in 1802. Erasmus is one of the most remarkable and internationally important figures of the 18th century and is buried in the church graveyard. It is probably no coincidence that Charles Darwin, the grandson of such a progressive thinker, produced some of the most important work in the history of biological and social thought.

MACKWORTH

2 miles NW of Derby off the A52

Mackworth village is situated in a quiet lane and consists of a few cottages, farms, and a church, which stands alone in a field to the east of the village. The **Parish Church of All Saints**, dates mainly from the 14th century and although its position is unusual, it is well worth taking a look inside to see the wealth of ancient and modern alabaster carving that it holds. Interestingly, it has no outside door which probably suggests it was built for defence.

A ruined 15th century gatehouse in the village is sometimes referred to as **Mackworth Castle**, but it may have been the gatehouse of Mackworth Hall, a mansion which was never built.

KIRK LANGLEY

4 miles NW of Derby on the A52

Just a five minute drive from the city of Derby, yet the setting is truly rural and peaceful, with delightful views towards the National Trust's Kedleston Estate. Kirk Langley is bisected by the main road from Derby to Ashbourne, and actually consists of two villages: Kirk Langley and Meynell Langley, centred on the Victorian brick mansion of Langley Park, site of the Meynell Family for 800 years, since the reign of Henry I. The Poles of Radbourne have also had landed interests in this area for many years.

The **Parish Church of St Michael** is early 14th century, built on the site of an older Saxon church. There are monuments to the Meynell and Pole families, including a memorial to Hugo Frances Meynell, 'who was deprived of his life in a collision of carriages' in Clay Cross tunnel. Another one commemorates William Meynell, who was killed in the 19th century when leading the Turks against the Russians on the river Danube. The only pub is the Bluebell at Langley Common.

KEDLESTON

4 miles NW of Derby off the A52

Kedleston Hall has been the family seat of the Curzon family since the 12th century and, until it was taken over by the National Trust, it had the longest continuous male line in Derbyshire and one of the longest in the country. Nothing

---

• *Kedleston Hall was built between 1759 and 1765 to designs by Robert Adam and it remains one of the finest examples of his work. The façade represents an impressive Roman temple with six tall columns supporting a portico, and a double-armed stone stairway leading to the entrance. Inside, the elegant and extravagant Marble Hall is a massive open space, dominated by 20 pink alabaster Corinthian columns around a white marble inlaid floor, with an intricate plasterwork ceiling above. As well as the design for the house and the three-arched bridge across the lake, it is likely that Robert Adam had a hand in designing the 820-acre parkland in the Serpentine style. The three-mile Long Walk was created in 1776. Edwin Lutyens designed the sunken rose garden.*

•

111

remains of the original medieval structure and little is known about it other than details recorded in a survey of 1657 which state that one of the doorways was over 500 years old and that there was also a large hall and a buttery.

Since taking over the property, the National Trust has embarked on a major restoration programme and many of the stately home's rooms have been beautifully furnished with contemporary pieces; modern photographs of the family can be seen mingled with priceless paintings and other treasures such as Blue John vases. Along with the house itself and the park with its lakes, there are the boat house and fishing pavilion to explore.

One member of the family, George Nathaniel Curzon, was the Viceroy of India from 1899 to 1905. When he returned to England he brought back numerous works of art, carvings and ivories that can be seen on display in the **Indian Museum**. Though he was out in India for some time, George would not have missed his family home, as Government House in Calcutta is a copy of Kedleston Hall. Once back in England, George did not have much time to enjoy his lands: he became a member of Lloyd George's inner War Cabinet, which met over 500 times during the First World War.

The nearby **All Saints Church**, in the ownership of the Churches Conservation Trust, is the only part of the old village that was allowed to remain when the rest was moved in 1765 to make way for the landscaped park around the Hall. It dates from the 12th century, and is of an unusual design for Derbyshire in that it is cruciform in shape and the tower is placed in the centre. Inside are Curzon monuments dating from 1275 to the present day, some designed by Adam. The only brass in the church is to Richard Curzon, who died in 1496. Perhaps the most magnificent tomb is of Mary, wife of George Curzon, Viceroy of India. It was built within a magnificent memorial chapel by her husband between 1907 and 1913, and is of white marble. The church has an unusual east-facing sundial. Because of its orientation, the dial only catches the sun between the hours of 6am and 11am. The hour lines are parallel with each other, with half hour lines in between. The gnomon is in the form of a letter "T", the top bar of which casts a shadow across the dial. The inscription above the dial is "Wee Shall", which cryptically links to sundial (soon die all) to make a sombre message. This is reinforced by the carvings on top of the dial, showing a skull between two hour glasses.

BRAILSFORD

8 miles NW of Derby on the A52

Brailsford is a pretty, red-brick village bisected by the A52. It is mentioned in the *Domesday Book* as having a priest and 'half a church', this curious tale refers to the shared ownership of its church with Ednaston, to the north. The **Parish Church of All Saints** is set in a delightful location, about half a mile from the village, down a long country lane. The carved Saxon cross in the churchyard dates from the 11th century. Though the church itself is an interesting mix of the 11th and 12th centuries, with much Norman work and an ashlar-faced diagonally buttressed tower.

There are many fine houses in the district, which includes two 20th century country homes, Brailsford Hall, built in 1905 in Jacobean style, and Culland Hall. Also on the first Wednesday in October, an annual ploughing match takes place in Brailsford.

EDNASTON

7 miles NW of Derby off the A52

This is a small ancient manor and was recorded, in the *Domesday Book* of 1086, as being in the ownership of Henry de Ferrers of Duffield Castle. The present manor house, **Ednaston Manor** on Brailsford Brook was built in a Queen Anne style by Sir Edwin Lutyens between 1912 and 1914. It is a Grade I listed building, unfortunately, though the house, grounds and plant nursery used to be open to the public, now it is a private house and access is not permitted.

LONG LANE

6 miles NW of Derby off the A52

You won't find Long Lane village on most maps – it is truly a hidden place! But it can be reached by heading for the village of Lees and then following the sign for Long Lane. It is set on the old Roman road bearing the same name and is not much more than a cluster of cottages, a school, a church and a pub. The **Parish Church of Christ Church** dates from the 1860s along with the school. The church is a plain structure of brick and consists of chancel, nave, south porch and a belfry containing 3 bells.

LONGFORD

8 miles W of Derby well south of the A515

Longford lies very much off the beaten track, but it is well worth finding as the village has the distinction of being the home of the first cheese factory in England. Opened on the 4th May in 1870, its first manager bore the memorable name Cornelius Schermerhorn. Derbyshire, with its excellent rail and canal links, made the county an ideal centre for the mass production of cheeses for foreign markets.

The ancient and spacious mansion of **Longford Hall**, with its pleasant grounds are ornaments to the scenery. Longford Hall was the family seat, first of the Longford family and then the Cokes. The Longfords settled here in the 12th century and the church, which is close to the hall, was built then. The **Parish Church of St Chad,** surrounded by magnificent lime trees, still retains many Norman parts, though the tower was added in the 15th century. There are some fine monuments to both the Cokes and the Longfords.

The Three Horseshoes in Long Lane dates back to 1750, when it was a grain store where ale was brewed for the adjacent blacksmith's. Unusually, the village owns the property, this is because when it was threatened with closure a few years ago, a group of customers averted the danger by clubbing together and buying it.

113

100 CAVENDISH ARMS

Doveridge

A traditional inn offering fine food, Real Ales, entertainment and genuine hospitality.

see page 242

NORBURY

14 miles W of Derby off the B5033

Norbury lies on the River Dove and was recorded in the *Domesday Book* as Norberre or Nordberie, the 'norther' defence on the Dove. The 14th and 15th century **Parish Church of St Mary and St Barlok** is one of the most significant churches to be found in Derbyshire, because of the outstanding quality of the stained glass in the chancel. This dates from 1305 and was restored by Holywell Glass in 2004. Much of the original expense of the current church building was met by Nicholas Fitzherbert, who died in 1473. You will find his magnificent tomb in the chancel. Like many churches in Derbyshire, this is another church with literary connections. Those familiar with the works of George Eliot will feel much at home in this part of the county. Eliot's real name was Mary Anne Evans. The characters Adam and Seth from her famous novel *Adam Bede* were based on her father, Robert Evans, and his brother, and many scenes from the book are set in this village. Members of Eliot's family are buried in the churchyard. The church is generally kept open. Unfortunately though, there are no tourist facilities in the village.

DOVERIDGE

15 miles W of Derby off the A50

As its name suggests, this village is situated on the banks of the River Dove, more specifically its name stems from having a bridge over the River Dove (i.e. Dove[B]rigde). Although there is a fair amount of modern housing, Doveridge still retains a rural atmosphere and like many of Derbyshire's old villages was mentioned in the *Domesday Book* as having a parish church and a water mill. Today the church remains, but the mill was demolished in the 1970's after being left in disrepair for many years. The **Parish Church of St Cuthbert**, dating essentially from the 13th century, contains memorials to the Canvendish family. Approaching St Cuthbert's by the main path you enter a 'tunnel' of branches formed by an ancient yew tree, reputed to be some 1,200 years old. According to legend, Robin Hood was betrothed to his lady under its boughs.

BOYLESTONE

10 miles W of Derby off the A515

The church at Boylestone, dedicated to **St John the Baptist** is famous for an incident during the Civil War. Two hundred Royalist troops spent the night in the local church on their way to Wingfield Manor. Rather foolishly they set no watch, and in the morning found themselves surrounded by Cromwell's men. The Royalists surrendered, were disarmed, and quietly filed out of the building. This later became known as the bloodless battle of Boylestone. The priest's doorway through which the Royalist troops emerged is still there. The church itself is mainly 14th century, and has an unusual pyramidal roof. The unusual tower dates from 1846, and was added after a fire. Today the heart of the village is based around the Rose & Crown, a welcoming 17th Century pub with real ales.

CHURCH BROUGHTON

10 miles W of Derby off the A50

Church Broughton is a quiet village which was, until the early part of the 20th century, part of the Duke of Devonshire's Derbyshire estates. The **Parish Church of St Michael**, built in the 14th century is a handsome building benefiting from a sturdy west tower topped with a small spire and Victorian pinnacles. Interestingly there are also gargoyles and a long 14th century chancel.

One of the first police houses in the country, now called Peel House, was established here in 1855 due to the amount of rowdy locals. The **Old Hall** (private) in Hall Lane is a 16th century timber framed building. The Holly Bush is the only pub in the village and together with the village shop and tennis club, it forms the main daily focus of activity in the village.

SUTTON-ON-THE-HILL

8 miles W of Derby off the A516

Despite its name, this is a sheltered spot, with only the church standing on the hill. The **Parish Church of St Michael** has a 14th century tower with a spire that was rebuilt in 1841. A few other parts are 14th century, but mostly the church was rebuilt in 1863. It contains an unusual monument to Judith Sleigh,

who died in 1634. It is a standing coffin with handles carved in black stone.

A cheese factory was built here in 1875, as in other local villages, but closed down due to competition and the building is now private housing. There was also a water mill, again now private housing.

Cricket fans will take special pleasure in visiting Sutton-on-the-Hill, as it was the family home of G. M. and R. H. R. Buckston, both of whom captained the Derbyshire cricket team.

SUDBURY

12 miles W of Derby off the A50

This is the estate village to **Sudbury Hall**, home of a branch of the Vernon family who lived at Haddon Hall. It was built in the late 17th century by George Vernon in red brick and gifted to the National Trust in 1967. The house and gardens are open to visitors and the hall offers many specialised tours too. The lavish interiors boast elaborate decorative plasterwork, woodcarving by Grinling Gibbons, murals throughout, including painted ceilings by Louis Laguerre. The long gallery and staircase are among the grandest in any English country house. Perhaps you will recognize it from the BBC's *Pride and Prejudice.*

Of particular interest is the **Museum of Childhood,** which is situated in the servants' wing and provides fascinating displays telling the story of what it was like to be a

•

The Parish Church of All Saints in Sudbury was recorded in the Domesday Book, and has been extensively restored in later years. The east window, made in Germany in 1850, was donated by Queen Victoria and Prince Albert.

•

101 THE CASTLE HOTEL

Hatton

A wonderful retreat offering a great place to enjoy top quality food and comfortable accommodation.

 see page 241

child in England from the 18th century to the present. Displays range from a wealthy family's nursery and an Edwardian schoolroom to a 'chimney climb' and coal tunnel for the adventurous. The formal gardens and meadows lead to the tree-fringed lake. Wildlife abounds, including kestrels, grey herons, grass snakes, dragonflies, newts, frogs, toads, little and tawny owls and woodpeckers. Special events are held throughout the year.

ETWALL

5 miles SW of Derby off the A516

This charming place has a fine range of Georgian buildings including some almshouses known as the **Port Hospital Almshouses,** built by Sir John Port, the founder of nearby Repton College. The almshouses, fronted by wrought iron gates made by Robert Bakewell of Derby, were rebuilt in 1681 and recently restored again. Until the 1960s, almsmen and women wore special hats or bonnets and a dark blue cloak with a silver clasp.

The original site of **Etwall Hall**, where Sir John lived, is now the site of a large comprehensive school, which bears his name. For a village that derived its name from 'Eata's Well', it seems strange that Etwall only took up the custom of well-dressing recently and by chance. To mark the centenary of the village primary school, the teachers dressed a token well while the Women's Institute, with the help of people from two villages within the Peak District, dressed

the only true well in Etwall, Town Well. This was in 1970 and the event, in mid May, was so successful that it is now an annual occasion and a total of eight wells are decorated.

As there is no long-standing tradition of well-dressing in the village, the themes for the dressings are not the more usual Biblical subjects but have covered a wide range of stories and ideas, including racial unity and the life and times of Sir John Port. Etwall is also the most southerly village to take part in the custom of well-dressing and its position, well below the harsh uplands of Derbyshire's Peak District, has ensured that there is always a good supply of flowers, even though the dressing takes place late in spring. Etwall Well Dressings is a popular event, there are eight well dressing sites around the village to visit plus a 'Have-a-go' tent, where visitors can try their hand at making a well dressing. The event also includes a variety of family entertainment like traditional dancing, musical entertainment, puppet shows, a dog show competition, a scarecrow competition, a hog roast, 'village fete' stalls, an owls display and much more...

The **Parish Church of St Helen** has some stonework of the 13th century and earlier, though the building was largely rebuilt in the mid-16th century after a great storm damaged it. It was restored in 1881, and has a monument to Sir Arthur Cochrane, who died in 1954 and was the Clarenceux King of

Arms, an officer of the College of Arms who looked after the armorial bearings for the south of England.

HILTON

8 miles SW of Derby off the A5132

As with other ancient settlements, Hilton, like Breaston and Borrowash, have undergone rapid expansion during the 20th century with the construction of new housing estates to serve the city of Derby. Though most of the buildings are new, it has a few points of interest; the Old Talbot Inn, the Wesleyan Chapel and Wakelyn Hall. The Old Talbot Inn dates back to the 15th century. The old gravel works are now a bird sanctuary and a nature reserve. **Wakelyn Hall** is an unusual half-timbered house dating from the 17th century. When the Wakelyn family left in 1621, the building became The Bull's Head Inn. Supposedly Mary, Queen of Scots stopped here briefly on her way to imprisonment at Tutbury Castle.

SWADLINCOTE

Here at the extreme edge of Derbyshire, well south of the River Trent, Swadlincote is known to its inhabitants simply as, "Swad", and shares many characteristics with Staffordshire. It is South Derbyshire's largest town; the population at the beginning of the 21st century was around 30,000 people. Historically more a collection of villages, though officially an urban district, it retains a rural feel that is charming and worth exploring. The **Parish Church of Emmanuelle** was built in 1846: the year Swadlincote became a parish in its own right. Modern attractions in Swadlincote include, Swadlincote Ski Slope and Conkers.

NORTH OF SWADLINCOTE

HARTSHORNE

1 mile NE of Swadlincote off the A514

One of this lovely village's most renowned sons was George Stanhope, who grew up to be a famous preacher, a bold critic and a brave writer during the reign of Queen Anne.

Like many villages there are certain buildings in Hartshorne that are very old, have unique historical value or just have distinctive character. The **Parish Church of St Peter** was rebuilt in 1835, only the tower remains of the original church, although the font is believed to be 14th century and two of the five bells pre-date the Reformation. A fine altar tomb shows the alabaster figures of Sir Humphry Dethick of 1599 and his wife, along with relief carvings of their six children. The Dethicks paid long and loyal service to the Royal family of their day - one of the Dethicks went to Cleves to find a fourth wife for Henry VIII. His son Sir William is said to have laid a pall of rich velvet on the coffin of Mary, Queen of Scots.

•

Among Swadlincote's thriving industries, based on the clay and coal on which it stands, are brickworks and large potteries. The best known was Sharpe's founded in 1821 by Thomas Sharpe for the manufacture of sanitary ware. Sharpe's Pottery Centre is an award winning visitor experience, telling the story of the South Derbyshire Pottery industry from the 16th to the 21st century. Located within Sharpe's Pottery Centre is Swadlincote's Tourist Information Centre, they can help visitors make the most of their visit to the area.

•

CALKE

5 miles NE of Swadlincote off the B587

Calke village barely exists but the main focus of interest here is the hall known as Calke Abbey. In 1985 the National Trust bought **Calke Abbey**, a large Baroque-style mansion built between 1701 and 1704 on the site of an Augustinian priory founded in 1133. However, it was not until 1989 that the Trust was able to open the house to the public, for this was no ordinary building. Dubbed 'the house that time forgot', since the death of the owner, Sir Vauncy Harpur-Crewe, in 1924, nothing had been altered in the mansion. In fact, the seclusion of the house and also the rather bizarre lifestyle of its inhabitants, had left many rooms and objects untouched for over 100 years. There was even a spectacular 18th century Chinese silk state bed that had never been unpacked.

Today, the Trust has repaired the house and returned all 13,000 items to their original positions so that the Abbey now looks just as it did when it was bought in 1981. The attention to detail has been so great that none of the rooms have been redecorated. Visitors can enjoy the display of silver and trace the route of 18th century servants along the brew house tunnel to the house cellars. The house stands in its own large park with gardens, a chapel and stables that are also open to the public. There are three walled gardens with their glasshouses, a restored orangery, vegetable garden, pheasant aviaries and the summer flower display within the unusual 'auricular' theatre. Calke is home to lots of wildlife including fallow deer, weasels, stoats, barn, little and tawny owls, woodpeckers, common toads, butterflies and beetles.

MELBOURNE

6 miles NE of Swadlincote off the B587

This small town, which gave its name to the rather better-known city in Australia, is a fascinating little town. A famous son of Melbourne, who started his working life in one of the market gardens, was Thomas Cook, who was born here in 1808. He went on to pioneer personally conducted tours and gave his name to the famous travel company.

Full of Georgian charm, Melbourne has a wealth of historic buildings which includes one of the finest examples of Norman ecclesiastical architecture

Church and Hall across a Frozen Lake, Melbourne

in the country, the **Parish Church of St Michael and St Mary**. It sits on the site of an earlier Saxon church, and seems rather a grand church for this modest place. It is a large, very lavish mid 12th century cruciform building, often described as a "miniature cathedral". In the 12th century, when the Bishopric of Carlisle was formed, the bishops needed a place of safety for the clergy when Carlisle was being raided by the Scots. So this church was built many miles south at Melbourne and, while Carlisle was subjected to raids and violence, the Bishop retired to Melbourne and continued to carry out his duties. The church was built between 1133 and 1229 and, in 1299, the then Bishop built a palace on land that is now home to **Melbourne Hall**, which is another fine building in this area. Originally a rectory for the Norman Parish Church, it became the home of Sir John Coke in 1628 and has been inherited by subsequent members of the family to the present day and is now home to Lord and Lady Ralph Kerr and their young family. Melbourne Hall gardens are the place to visit if you are seeking a relaxing thoughtful stroll. The walks, vistas and statuary, much favoured in the early 18th century, have been restored in the influential, Dutch / French formal style of the time. The most notable feature is a beautiful wrought-iron birdcage pergola, built in the early 1700s by Robert Bakewell, a local blacksmith from

War Memorial, Melbourne

Derby. Bakewell lived in Melbourne for a time at the house of a widow named Fisher and her daughters. However when one daughter became pregnant, he moved hurriedly to Derby. Unfortunately the house is only open to the public in August, but the splendid and famous formal gardens are open April through to September, and are well worth a visit.

There was also once a substantial castle in the town, but it fell into disrepair in the 17th century. **Melbourne Castle**, located in the village centre, was built by the Earl of Lancaster in the early 14th century, and later became a royal castle when it came into the possession of Henry IV. The castle was bought from the crown by the Earl of Huntingdon, who demolished it in 1637. Remnants of it can be seen in Castle Farm by prior appointment.

102 BAY TREE RESTAURANT

Melbourne
Warm and contemporary – with an enviable reputation for offering 'new world cuisine at its best'.

see page 243

103 IVY HOUSE FARM
B&B AND
WOODLANDS
HILLS COURT SELF
CATERING

Stanton-by-Bridge

The perfect place to escape
the humdrum routine and
stresses of everyday working
life.

 see page 244

•

*Legend has it that the
original bridge at
Swarkestone was built
by two daughters of the
Harpur family in the
early 13th century. The
girls were celebrating
their joint betrothals
when their fiancés were
summoned to a barons'
meeting across the river.
While they were away
torrential rain fell,
flooding the river, and
the two young men
drowned as they
attempted to ford the
raging torrent on their
return. The girls built
the bridge as a memorial
to their lovers. Both girls
later died impoverished
and unmarried.*

•

SWARKESTONE

9 miles NE of Swadlincote off the A5132

The ancient village of Swarkestone
originated at a crossing point of
the River Trent. This small village
has also been, quite literally, a
turning point in history. The
Swarkestone Bridge, with its
seven arches and three-quarter-mile
long causeway, is the longest stone
bridge in England and holds Grade
I listed building status. In 1745,
during the second Jacobite
Rebellion, Bonnie Prince Charlie
and his army reached Derby and
made arrangements for the capture
of the strategically important
Swarkestone Bridge. It was the only
bridge on the River Trent, between
Burton and Nottingham. Had they
managed to cross it at this point,
they would have faced no other
natural barriers on their 120-mile
march to London. As it transpired,
the army retreated and fled north,
if the march had continued, it
would probably have been

successful and the whole course of
British history could have changed.
In memory of this important
event, a cairn has been erected at
Swarkestone Bridge, to mark the
southern most point reached by
Bonnie Prince Charlie's army.

The tiny **Parish Church of St
James** was so heavily restored
between 1874 and 1876 that little
now remains of the original
church, apart form the southwest
tower and the Harpur Chapel. The
chapel contains tomb chests of
Richard Harpur (1573), who was
one of Queen Elizabeth's judges,
and Sir John Harpur, who died in
1627. Close to the parish church
are the scanty remains of old
Harpur Hall (the precursor of
Calke Abbey) which includes a
Jacobean grandstand (now a
Landmark Trust property) to a
bowling green or bull-baiting ring.
Most of the Hall remains date to
about 1630.

Excavations in the village of
Swarkestone, at Lowes Farm, led to

Swarkestone Causeway, Swarkestone

the discovery that the district was occupied in the Bronze Age and also in Saxon times. Iron Age remains were found here when the A50 was constructed.

BARROW-ON-TRENT

8 miles NE of Swadlincote off the A514

Barrow-on-Trent, as its name tells us, stands between the River Trent and the Trent & Mersey Canal. An interesting feature of this attractive village is that during the 18th century a row of parish cottages were built by parish levy, and first rented for £1.50 a year, and the parish council still maintains them.

The **Parish Church of St Wilfrid's** is a beautiful medieval building overlooking the Trent valley, and dates mainly from the 13th century. The Church, at one time, was an outpost for the Knights Hospitallers of St John and has many interesting features, old and new. The north arcade, with its original columns, is a notable feature. The plain glass windows lend the church a light and airy atmosphere. The base of the square tower and the north aisle date from the 1300s; there is also a Georgian east window.

The Derbyshire-born artist George Turner (1841-1910) was such an accomplished landscape painter that he has been dubbed 'Derbyshire's John Constable'. George's favourite painting haunt was around this village, and it is where he met his first wife, Eliza Lakin of Walnut Farm. They were married in the village in 1865 and took up residence at The Walnuts.

MILTON

5 miles N of Swadlincote off the A514

Milton is a small village, established over 1,500 years ago. It was once owned by the Burdett family, who built the nearby church of St Saviour. Although the village has seen many changes in the last century, it still has a very rural character with its one main street and the many paths, initially used for the movement of cattle and sheep, have become public footpaths and bridle paths to provide pleasant walks for residents and visitors. The village has an original classic red phone box on main street which was given a Grade II listing in January 2005.

BRETBY

2 miles N of Swadlincote off the A50

Now a leafy rural backwater, Bretby was first mentioned in the *Domesday Book* as an agricultural settlement around a green. The name means *"dwelling place of Britons"*. There was once a castle in this quiet village until it was demolished during the reign of James l, and the stones used to build a mansion house. In the 18th century, that too was demolished and **Bretby Hall** was built in 1813 by Sir Jeffrey Wyatville, the designer of the 19th century extension at Chatsworth House. Only the Hall and lakes remain.

One of the owners of the estate was Lord Carnarvon, the Egyptologist, who sold the property to finance the famous

Sat snugly in the Milton countryside is the 230-acre Foremark Water - a reservoir and wildlife habitat offering many outdoor and leisure activities, such as adventure playgrounds, fishing, bird watching, sailing and cycling, as well as countryside walks for those who want to explore and discover the magic of the growing National Forest.

104 RISING SUN

Willington

A typical village 'local' offering delicious food, tip-top condition ales and with quality entertainment from the 'The Real Music Club'.

see page 245

expedition in search of the tomb of Tutankhamun, the boy king. The present Bretby Hall has been sold to developers to provide private residential units.

REPTON

5 miles N of Swadlincote off the B5008

This village, by the tranquil waters of the River Trent, is steeped in history. The main core of Repton village was designated as a Conservation Area in 1969, and extended in 1982. There are some forty buildings listed as being of historical and architectural interest. However, the village is not just about its historical past, it is a vibrant community with many clubs, societies, shops and pubs.

The first mention of Repton came in the 7th century when it was established as the capital of the Saxon Kingdom of Mercia. A monastery, housing both monks and nuns, was founded here sometime after AD 653 but the building was sacked by the Danes in AD 874. Three Mercian kings were buried

here - Merewahl in AD 686, Aethelbald in AD 757 and Wiglaf in AD 839, as well as St Wystan, who was Wiglaf's grandson. He is supposed to have been interred alongside his grandfather. A battle-axe, now on display in the school museum, was excavated a little distance from the church. It had apparently lain undisturbed for well over 1,000 years.

The **Parish Church of St Wystan** is famous for its distinctive Anglo-Saxon stonework, which can be admired from both inside and outside the church. Sir Nikolaus Pevsner wrote: "...the chancel....and the crypt form one of the most precious survivals of Anglo-Saxon architecture in England." When the chancel and part of the nave were enlarged in 1854, the original Anglo-Saxon columns were moved to the 14th century porch. The crypt claims to be one of the oldest intact Anglo-Saxon buildings in England and was rediscovered by chance in 1779 by a workman who was digging a hole for a grave in the chancel floor.

To read an interesting tale, before you reach the south porch, turn right and go up to the stone wall and look at the headstones against it. One slate memorial is dedicated to a Samuel Marshall, aged 21, he was murdered in 1786, and his killer was caught but acquitted at trial for the lack of witnesses. If you examine the headstone, you will see it depicts a tree with five branches, one of

Repton Priory Gateway, Repton

which has been cut off with an axe, representing the dead man, and the others his surviving brothers.

The ancient but restored **Cross**, still at the central crossroads in the village, has been the focal point of life here for centuries and it has also stood at the heart of the Wednesday market. Right up until the late 19th century a Statutes Fair, for the hiring of farm labourers and domestics, was also held here at Michaelmas.

Parts of an Augustinian priory, founded in 1170, are incorporated in the buildings of **Repton College**, itself founded in 1557. Sir John Port had specifically intended the college to be a grammar school for the local poor children of Etwall, Repton and Burnaston. These intentions have somewhat deviated over the passing years and now Repton is one of the foremost public schools in the country. Interestingly, two of its headmasters, Dr Temple and Dr Fisher, went on to become Archbishops of Canterbury, while Dr Ramsey was a pupil at the school under Dr Fisher's guiding light. Film buffs will recognise the 14th century gatehouse and causeway, as they featured in both film versions of the popular story *Goodbye, Mr Chips*.

Just to the west of the village is **Foremark Hall**, built by Robert Adam in 1762 for the Burdett family. It is now a preparatory school for Repton College.

SOUTH OF SWADLINCOTE

CHURCH GRESLEY

2 miles SW of Swadlincote off the A514

This former mining village has a distinguished history dating back to the time of the Augustinian monks who settled here in the 12th century and founded a priory. The village's name, like that of nearby Castle Gresley, recalls the great Gresley family, said to have been the only Derbyshire family to have retained their lands from the time of the *Domesday Book* up until the 20th century.

The **Parish Church of St Mary and St George** has a link with this illustrious past, as the tower and two internal arches are all that remain of the priory church. It became run-down after the Dissolution of the Monasteries, and remained in a sad state of disrepair up until 1872, when a new chancel was built. Remains of the priory have been found, including fragments of painted glass, stone coffins and medieval tiles. An impressive alabaster monument of 1699 depicts Sir Thomas Gresley, surrounded by arms showing the marriages of his ancestors dating back to the time of William the Conqueror. The church's treasures, though, are the ten large and wonderfully carved 17th century stalls.

In around 1800 the pottery Mason Cash was established here. Mason Cash has become a much-loved English pottery, producing

105 TRAVELLERS REST

Church Gresley

A village pub with a strong sense of community spirit! Regular charity events and themed evenings are held here.

see page 245

123

traditional ceramic mixing and baking ware.

CASTLE GRESLEY

3 miles SW of Swadlincote on the A444

Just like Church Gresley, Castle Gresley, unsurprisingly, is also named after the Derbyshire family of Gresley, which has owned land in the area since before the *Domesday Book*. But where is the castle? Unfortunately, nothing is left of the castle built by William de Gresley in the mid 14th century - apart from the grassy mound, or motte, on which it stood, still known as **Castle Knob**.

LINTON

2 miles SW of Swadlincote off the A444

Linton is a charming and restful village, within the National Forest, which is mainly agricultural since the closure of the Coton Park colliery. This place is celebrated for its cheese and cattle.

ROSLISTON

5 miles SW of Swadlincote off the A444

Rosliston was recorded in the *Domesday Book* as Redlauseton, an Anglo-Saxon name meaning 'farm of Hrolf', this Hrolf probably being a Norseman. Rosliston is part of the National Forest and in the **Rosliston Forestry Centre** there are way-marked walks, a wildlife hide and children's play equipment. On summer evenings bats may be seen at dusk - several different species make this area their home.

The **Parish Church of St Mary the Virgin** is mainly 19th century but the 14th century tower with its broach spire still remains. Except for the later Victorian furnishings the interior is quite unaltered and well worth a visit.

COTON-IN-THE-ELMS

6 miles SW of Swadlincote off the A444

Until around 60 years ago, Coton-in-the-elms had elm trees bordering every road into the village, but they all succumbed to Dutch Elm disease. The **Parish Church of St Mary** dates from 1846. It replaced an earlier church which stood behind the Shoulder of Mutton pub in the village. The bells from this older church were removed when it was pulled down and hung in the nearby church at Lullington. It is said that when the wind is in the right direction, the villagers of Coton-in-the-Elms can still hear their original bells.

Nearby is Grangewood Farm Forestry, which has 100 acres of new woodland adjoining the ancient woodland of Grange Wood. The site includes laid out trails, camping facilities, horse riding and fishing.

NETHERSEAL

6 miles S of Swadlincote off the A444

Netherseal is a picturesque village on the banks of the river Mease, overlooking Leicestershire. The village was once part of the district of Seal, which included quite a few settlements, many of which form Netherseal and Overseal in modern times. 'Seal' suggests the area was once heavily forested and Netherseal was recorded in the *Domesday Book* as a wooded area on the edge of the Ashby Woulds. It was once a mining community with a two-shaft colliery and several related industries. The mining industry has long gone and the centre of Netherseal village is now a conservation area with many listed buildings, including the 17th century almshouses.

The **Parish Church of St Peter** was built in the 19th century, though it looks much older, and has some medieval fragments, including the tower. It stands on the site of an earlier church dating from the 13th century. The churchyard is the final resting place of Sir Nigel Gresley, who designed the famous Mallard locomotive.

DONISTHORPE

3 miles SE of Swadlincote off the A444

Donisthorpe is a famous old mining village right on the Derbyshire-Leicestershire border. The River Mease, which marks the border, runs right through it. Its inhabitants are justly proud of the village's industrial and historical heritage. The old colliery, the pit railway and the old British Rail line closed down by the

1960s. Left behind is a proud history and a tranquillity unknown in the days of the mines.

MOIRA

6 miles SE of Swadlincote off the A444

Moira is actually just over the border in Leicestershire, and close by is the award winning attraction called **Conkers**, at the heart of the National Forest. It is a mix of indoor and outdoor experiences where you can watch the effect the four seasons have on a forest. There are over 1,000 interactive exhibits.

Another legacy of the area's industrial heritage is the Moira Furnace, a restored 19th century blast furnace. Today it is a museum with interactive displays and information on how the furnace worked, and its influence on the local economy and the lives of the workers. There is also a restored section of Ashby Canal near the site so you may wish to enjoy a boat trip. The furnace adjoins a 50 acre newly planted Woodland Park. The furnace site also includes craft workshops and a small nature reserve.

108 THE BLACK HORSE

Appleby Magna

Appleby Magna – cute in name, cute in nature – offers a thoroughly appropriate pub and restaurant.

🍴 *see page 246*

109 MOIRA TEA ROOM

Moira

The Moira Tea Room is a great place to take a break from history and eat a modern sandwich.

🍴 *see page 248*

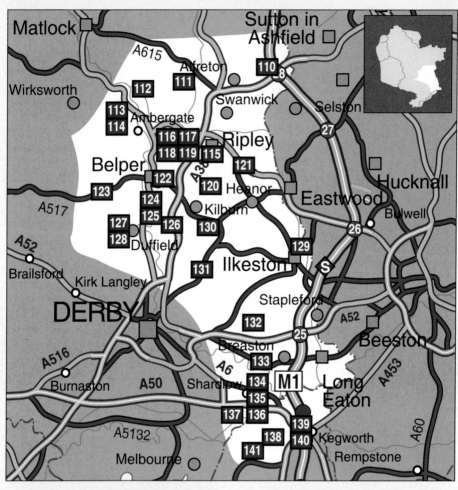

🛏 ACCOMMODATION

113	The Bear Inn, Alderwasley, nr Belper	p 132, 251
124	The Strutt Arms Hotel, Milford	p 140, 258
125	King William IV, Milford	p 140, 258
126	Spotted Cow, Holbrook	p 141, 259
128	The Kings Head Inn, Duffield	p 141, 260
140	The Anchor Inn, Kegworth	p 152, 267
141	Donington Park Farmhouse, Isley Walton,	
	nr Castle Donington	p 152, 269

🍴 FOOD & DRINK

110	The Devonshire Arms, South Normanton	p 129, 249
111	Old Yew Tree Inn, South Wingfield	p 130, 250

🍴 FOOD & DRINK

113	The Bear Inn, Alderwasley, nr Belper	p 132, 251
114	The Greyhound Hotel, Alderwasley,	
	nr Belper	p 132, 252
115	Brocks Café & Bistro, Ripley	p 134, 253
116	Black Boy Inn, Heage	p 135, 254
117	The White Hart Inn, Heage	p 136, 254
118	Eagle Tavern, Heage	p 136, 254
119	Spanker Inn, Nether Heage, nr Belper	p 136, 255
121	The Poet & Castle, Codnor, nr Ripley	p 137, 256
122	The Thorn Tree Inn, Belper	p 139, 256
123	The Railway, Cowers Lane, nr Belper	p 140, 257
124	The Strutt Arms Hotel, Milford	p 140, 258
125	King William IV, Milford	p 140, 258

The Amber Valley and Erewash

This area encompasses the Amber Valley and the eastern part of the area known as Erewash. These two regions cover the eastern and south eastern parts of Derbyshire respectively. The Rivers Amber, Derwent and Trent run through this part of the county. With such spectacular scenery, it's no surprise that the area abounds with excellent walks and trails, many of which are drawn together in the annual Amber Valley and Erewash Walking Festival. Taking place each September, the festival attracts walkers from around the area and includes guided walks by experienced guides as well as numerous self-guided trails. The festival is in its fourth year and is proving to be a great success.

There's plenty to discover in the towns, villages and landscapes of the Amber Valley and Erewash - whether you're exploring the area's rich industrial heritage and historical connections, visiting one of the areas numerous attractions or simply absorbing the views by foot, wheels or hooves, there's something for everyone.

The landscape of the area is one shaped both by nature and by entrepreneurs, it's a landscape rich in history and nostalgia. Originally small farming communities, many of the villages expanded at the time of the Industrial Revolution and they can, in many cases, be characterised by unflattering rows of workers' cottages. And while a lot of the area did not escape from the growth of Derby and Nottingham, there are still some interesting and unique buildings to be found in this corner of the county. The grade II listed Heage Windmill, built in 1797, is the only stone-towered, multi-sailed windmill in England and many of its original wooden mechanisms are still in place – offering a nostalgic glimpse back to the past. Crich Tramway Village is home to a superb collection of running trams, set in a beautifully restored period townscape, the buildings of which have been brought in from around the UK, restored and reconstructed brick by brick! Or get all steamed up on a seven-mile steam train ride through the countryside at the Midland Railway. The ruined Dale Abbey is another of the region's attractions, founded here by Augustinian monks in the 13th century. However, unlike the area to the west, there are no great stately mansions, except for one, Elvaston Castle, which, along with its extensive grounds, is an interesting and delightful place to explore.

The area's villages and towns like Belper and Alfreton (said by legend to have been named after King Alfred, who once occupied a house in King Street) also provide great places to explore and offer regular markets.

🍴 FOOD & DRINK

126	Spotted Cow, Holbrook	p 141, 259
127	The Pattenmakers Arms, Duffield	p 141, 259
128	The Kings Head Inn, Duffield	p 141, 260
129	Finn M'Couls, Ilkeston	p 142, 260
130	The Sitwell Arms, Horsley Woodhouse	p 144, 261
131	Three Horseshoes, Morley	p 144, 260
132	Royal Oak, Ockbrook, nr Derby	p 147, 262
133	The Olympic Hotel, Draycott	p 148, 262
134	The New Inn, Shardlow	p 150, 263
135	The Old Marina Bar & Restaurant, Shardlow	p 150, 264

🍴 FOOD & DRINK

136	Shakespeare Inn & Restaurant, Shardlow	p 150, 265
137	Malt Shovel Inn, Aston-on-Trent	p 151, 267
138	The Cross Keys, Castle Donnington	p 151, 266
139	Ye Olde Flying Horse, Kegworth	p 152, 268
140	The Anchor Inn, Kegworth	p 152, 267

🏛 PLACES OF INTEREST

| 112 | Crich Tramway Village, Crich, nr Matlock | p 131, 248 |
| 120 | Denby Visitor Centre, Denby | p 137, 255 |

127

ALFRETON

This historic town dates back to Saxon times and, despite local legends to the contrary, Alfred the Great was not immortalised in the naming of the place, nor, as legend tells us, did he live in a house on what is now King Street. Instead the town belonged to a Saxon nobleman called Alfred, and was named 'Aelfredingtune', which, in the *Domesday Book*, is recorded as 'Elstretune'.

This attractive former coal mining town stands on a hill close to the Nottinghamshire border, and benefited from the philanthropy of Robert Watchorn, a local pit boy made good, who emigrated to America and became Commissioner of Immigration in the early 19th century. This highly respected man never forgot his roots and gave the town a substantial amount of money. Several buildings including the Watchorn Memorial Church, a school, a manse, cottages, sports ground, pavillion and the Lincoln Library were built by him.

Along the charming High Street can be found the George Hotel, a fine Georgian building that looks down the length of the street. Also on the High Street you can find plenty of shops, and there are a great many restaurants, pubs and other places to visit, including a number of splendid 18th century stone built houses that add real character to a stroll along this High Street.

Further historical points of interest in Alfreton include the **Parish Church of St Martin** that contains monuments to the Morewood family, and dates from the 13th century. The south arcade is 14th century, and the north arcade was rebuilt in 1868. Its impressive fine western tower dates from the 15th century, and rises from an earlier base. Also of interest is an old lock-up, known as a 'house of confinement' dating from 1820, which can be found at the bottom of King Street. It was built to house lawbreakers and drunkards. The close confines of the prison, with its two cells, minute windows and thick outer walls, must have been a very effective deterrent.

The market at Alfreton was granted, in 1251, to Robert de Latham and Thomas de Chaworth, to be held on a Monday, together with a fair for three days at the Feast of St Margaret. There is still a bustling market and Alfreton attracts visitors from a wide radius to its busy town centre. The **Alfreton Heritage Centre** in Rodgers Lane is housed in an old chapel with the municipal cemetery, and contains a collection of material relating to Alfreton and its hinterland including photographs, maps, etc. **Alfreton Park** on the edge of the town was once part of the Palmer-Morewood estate, their home, Alfreton Hall, is now an adult education centre and the surrounding land is an attractive public park.

AROUND ALFRETON

SOUTH NORMANTON

2 miles east of Alfreton off the B6109

The origin of South Normanton is uncertain. Early evidence suggests that the first settlement was Celtic although other evidence points to the name Normanton having an Anglo Saxon derivation, meaning 'the farm of the north men' or 'Northwegans'. However, it is certain that following the Norman Conquest of 1066, South Normanton was granted by William the Conqueror to his bastard son William Peveril. In common with much of the rest of the country the main activity of the village in medieval times was that of agriculture though by 1881 the county had been overtaken by 'coal fever'.

The village was transformed after the opening of 'A Winning' colliery in 1871 and 'B Winning' in 1875, by the Blackwell Colliery Company. By the 1880s 'A Winning' had the largest output of coal in Derbyshire, but with the pits came the insatiable demand for miners. Many people came to South Normanton from depressed agricultural areas and this migration was helped by the Erewash Valley railway extension, which reached Alfreton in 1865. Terraced houses were built to accommodate the growing population, which doubled in the ten years from 1871 to 1881. Like many Victorian industrialists, the Blackwell Colliery Company took a paternalistic attitude to its workforce, providing a reading room, library, tennis courts and playing fields, as well as a cottage hospital. In February 1937 the South Normanton Mining Disaster killed eight miners due to an underground explosion. South Normanton Colliery closed in 1952, B Winning in 1964 and A Winning in 1969.

Today South Normanton is a large, busy, industrial village, but it has definitely cleaned up it's act since the early part of the 20th century when it was known as the dirtiest village in Derbyshire. The **Parish Church of St Michael** dates from around the 13th century but most of the present building is 19th century. It contains a monument to a Robert Ravel who lived at the nearby Carnfield Hall, an early 17th century stone mansion built by the Revell family.

The most famous person to come out of South Normanton was Jedediah Strutt, who, along with Rickard Arkwright, founded the Derbyshire cotton industry; he was born in the village in 1726. Its former centre, around the old market place has moved to a new market area and a mass of housing covers the site of Jedediah Strutt's birthplace next to the Shoulder of Mutton pub.

OAKERTHORPE

1 mile W of Alfreton off the B6013

Tucked away in a narrow valley lies **Oakerthorpe Nature Reserve**. Its size and location make it easy to miss, yet this patch of land supports a variety of species and habitats. There is a short circular

110 THE DEVONSHIRE ARMS

South Normanton
Good company, good food, good times!

¶ *see page 249*

III OLD YEW TREE INN

South Wingfield

Cask beers, nice food, friendly hosts and a cosy if haunted atmosphere.

see page 250

walk around the reserve, with a pond dipping platform which is an ideal location to spot frogs, toads and common newt - and you may be lucky enough to come across a grass snake. These reptiles are now rare in Derbyshire, and Oakerthorpe is one place where they are still seen regularly.

SOUTH WINGFIELD

2 miles W of Alfreton on the B5053

As Derbyshire emerged from the Dark Ages and towns with markets like Chesterfield began to attract a population of artisans and traders during the early Middle Ages, prosperous merchants and churchmen became attracted to the county. One of the most eminent of these was Thomas Cromwell, at one time the richest and most powerful man in England, who built **Wingfield Manor**.

The evocative and hauntingly beautiful ruins of Wingfield Manor stand proudly atop a rocky hill above the village of South Wingfield, with the tall chimneys and gaunt towers rising resolutely to two hundred feet above the valley floor, and dominating the surrounding pastoral landscape. High up in the tower can also be seen a single archer's slit, built the opposite way round so that only one archer was needed to defend the whole tower. A wander around the remains reveals the large banqueting hall with its unusual oriel window and a crypt which was probably used to store food and wine. Whatever its use, it is a particularly fine example and rivals a similar structure at Fountains Abbey.

This was the romantic setting for scenes from the films, *The Virgin & the Gypsy* and Zefferelli's adaptation of *Jane Eyre*, also the ruins have been featured in the TV series, *Peak Practice* - but most famously, the manor house was used as Mary, Queen of Scots' prison on two separate occasions in 1569 and 1584 when she was held under the care of the Earl of Shrewsbury. The local squire, Anthony Babington, attempted to rescue the queen and lead her to safety but the plot failed and, instead, led to them both being

Wingfield Manor, South Wingfield

beheaded. Though still a ruin, the house is now owned by English Heritage and open to the public at certain times of the year. It can be reached by a farm track half a mile to the south of the village.

East of the village is the **Parish Church of All Saints,** which dates originally from the 13th century. At the same time as building Wingfield Manor, Cromwell refurbished the church and built a new tower, while at the same time preserving the arcades on both sides of the nave.

CRICH

6 miles W of Alfreton off the A6

Probably better known as the village of Cardale in the TV series *Peak Practice*, Crich (pronounced 'Cry-ch' and meaning 'hilltop'), with its church and market cross, is also the home of the **Crich Tramway Village**. Referring to itself intriguingly as 'the museum that's a mile long', it offers a wonderful opportunity to enjoy a tram ride along a Victorian street. The signposts, stone flags and gas lamps are all original and come from such diverse places as Liverpool, Oldham and Leeds. Today, in many towns and cities, trams are making a come-back, but here the museum gives visitors the opportunity to view tramways of the past. As well as those shuttling up and down the mile-long scenic route, there is an exhibition, which contains not only trams but also much more besides, including some wonderfully colourful fairground organs. Throughout the year the

museum holds many special events and, with their policy of no hidden extras, this is a great place to take all the family for a fun day out. Started in 1959, it now has over 50 trams, with a third of them being in full working order. It stands on the site of a quarry that was owned by the great engineer, George Stephenson, who also owned the railway that carried the stone down the steep incline to his lime kilns alongside the Cromford Canal.

This large, straggling village was also a flourishing knitting centre at one time, and the telltale 18th century cottages with their long upper windows can still be seen. The **Parish Church of St Mary**, with its tall spire, dates back to around 1135, but is now mostly 14th century. Although there is evidence of 'Norman' influence inside the Church. It sits on a hilltop, and contains a built-in stone lectern, which, though common in Derbyshire, is rare elsewhere in the country.

Also situated on a hilltop, 1,100 feet above sea level is **Crich Stand**, an operational lighthouse and memorial tower, complete with flashing beacon. Built in 1923 and dedicated to the memory of 11,409 men of the Sherwood Foresters who died during the First World War. The memorial also honours those who died in the Second World War and other conflicts, up to the year 1970. There is another part to the Memorial, which is not generally known. This was the provision of two books in which are inscribed the names of all the

112 CRICH TRAMWAY VILLAGE

Crich, nr Matlock

Crich Tramway Village offers a family day out in the relaxing atmosphere of a bygone era.

 see page 248

131

115 BROCKS CAFÉ AND BISTRO

Ripley

A home from home experience where locals and visitors alike get together to enjoy good local food at very reasonable prices.

🍴 see page 253

worldwide search for petroleum began.

RIPLEY

Ripley may not be the largest tourist Mecca in the world but, acre for acre, it probably has more to offer the curious and the casual caller than most other towns in the county. This old industrial town is mentioned in the *Domesday Book*. Ripley was originally called Ripelie. Once a typical small market town, Ripley expanded dramatically during the Industrial Revolution when great use was made of the iron, clay and coal deposits found nearby. The town's Butterley ironworks, founded in 1792 by a group of men which included renowned engineer Benjamin Outram, created the arched roof for London's St Pancras station. Outram's even more famous son Sir James enjoyed an illustrious

career that saw him claimed Bayard of India, and earned him a resting place in Westminster Abbey. Butterley Hall, which was built in the 18th century, is the headquarters for the Derbyshire Constabulary.

Interestingly, according to a study of people's names, the town of Ripley is the most English. The research, which classified the ethnic background of Britain's 42.2 million adult voters according to the origin of their names, found that 88.5 per cent of Ripley's inhabitants were ethnically English. The study, carried out by Professor Richard Webber, of University College London, was on behalf of OriginsInfo marketing.

AROUND RIPLEY

PENTRICH

1 mile NW of Ripley off the A38

Mentioned in the *Domesday Book* as Pentric, this hilltop village with its brownstone gabled houses is very charming. Some Pentrich houses still stand exactly where medieval cottages were shown in maps of the 16th and 17th centuries. Its sturdy **Parish Church of St Matthew** is approached via a picturesque flight of 48 steps. It dates back to the 12th century, with much rebuilding and alterations being carried out in the 15th century. A striking stained-glass War Memorial window created in 1916 depicts the warrior saints of England and France and a figure of St Michael.

Pentrich is probably most famous for the **Pentrich**

Butterley Railway Centre, Ripley

Revolution of 1817. A small band of half-starved weavers, labourers and stockingers - no more than 200 or 300 men - met and marched towards Nottingham, where they expected to meet up with more men before marching on London. However, the uprising was soon quelled, with a resultant trial of 50 of the insurgents in Derby that lasted 10 days. The men were accused of high treason, and a few were pardoned, 11 sent to Australia for life and three to Australia for 14 years. Three of the men, however, were executed at Derby Gaol. The poet Shelley witnessed the scene and described the despair of the relatives and the disturbance of the crowd as the men were beheaded. So restless and angry was the crowd watching the executions that the executioners were masked and their names kept secret. The execution block is still to be seen in Derby Prison.

The history of Pentrich almost stopped with the revolution. The 1821 census recorded a decrease of a third in the population of the parish because the Duke of Devonshire's agents destroyed many of the houses after the insurrection. Wives and children were put out of their tenancies and years later can be traced in other parts of the country, still scraping a livelihood after their disgrace. The village became smaller and less important in succeeding years.

LOWER HARTSHAY

2 miles W of Ripley off the A610

Lower Hartshay sits on what was Ryknield Street, an important Roman military and trade route from the Fosse Way in Gloucestershire to the north. The line of Ryknield Street through Ripley, Pentrich and Lower Hartshay can still be seen and makes a pleasant walk with splendid views. Lower Hartshay was still on a main route for traffic until the 1970s. Now by-passed by the major trunk roads, it is a pleasant and tranquil backwater.

HEAGE

1 mile W of Ripley on the B6013

Heage, from the Anglo-Saxon word 'heegge', meaning 'high', was on the ancient packhorse route from Derby to Chesterfield, and the old turnpike road passed through here. The village has no obvious centre and is scattered along the roads and lanes. The village is still split into two main parts, High Heage and Low or Nether Heage. The main occupation for centuries was farming and coal mining. In fact, Morley Park has been worked for coal and ironstone since 1372, and the remains of bell-pits were discovered during recent open cast mining. On Morley Park are the remains of two cold blast coke iron furnaces built by Francis Hurt in 1780 and the Mold Brothers in 1818. The older furnace was probably the first of its kind in Derbyshire. Other local industries included framework knitting and weaving.

The oldest domestic building in the village is Heage Hall Farm, once the home of a branch of the Pole family. Crowtrees Farm was

In 1842 three men from Heage were involved in criminal activities which must have caused quite a stir at the time and gave rise to local sayings such as "They 'ang 'em in bunches in Heage", and "You can tell a man from Heage by the rope mark on his neck". The three men Samuel Bonsall, William Bland and John Hulme went to rob a house at Stanley Common one September night. The dwelling was owned and lived in by spinsters Martha and Sarah Goddard. Both were beaten by the robbers, Sarah survived but Martha died. More than 50,000 people attended Derby Gaol to witness the hanging of these men.

116 BLACK BOY INN

Heage

A visit to the Black Boy Inn is time and money well spent.

🍴 *see page 254*

117 THE WHITE HART INN

Heage

An historic country pub with plenty to offer! Enjoy, open fires through the winter or the pleasant beer garden in the summer.

📍 see page 254

118 EAGLE TAVERN

Heage

A warm, family run establishment offering exceptional food and quality ales. If you pay a visit, you're sure to come back!

📍 see page 254

119 SPANKER INN

Nether Heage

This is a pub which has everything - a cosy, welcoming atmosphere, good food, great drink and good old-fashioned value for money!

📍 see page 255

Hot air balloons over village, Heage

built in 1450 with three good cruck beams and was refurbished in 1712. An interesting feature of the village is its postbox, in the wall of the post office. It is one of the few in the country bearing the name of Edward VII, who abdicated in 1936.

The **Parish Church of St Luke** was originally constructed of wood, and during a great storm in June 1545 it was destroyed. It was then rebuilt in stone in 1661, and subsequently enlarged in 1836.

Heage Windmill is situated west of the village between High Heage and Nether Heage. It is a grade II listed tower mill and the only one in Derbyshire to retain its six sails, fan tail and machinery. Standing on the brow of a hill, overlooking Nether Heage, it is built of local sandstone and is over two hundred years old. It has been restored to full working order and

is open to the public at weekends and bank holidays. There was a small stone building, built some years after the mill itself, alongside the mill which was used as the kiln. This kiln has been rebuilt and provides the Visitor Centre & shop selling souvenirs, flour and light refreshments.

DENBY

2 miles S of Ripley off the A38

Denby was mentioned in the *Domesday Book* as Denebi, which means village of the Danes. Ryknield Street, a Roman road, runs through the village.

Denby Pottery, to the north of the village, is one of the biggest attractions in Derbyshire, and has a fascinating history. Derbyshire has a long tradition of stoneware pottery, closely associated with the natural clay deposits of the county. When a seam of clay was discovered in Denby in 1806 while constructing a road, a local man, William Borne, recognised its quality, and thus Denby Pottery was born. Production of salt-glazed pottery began in 1809, with Bourne's son Joseph in charge. Soon the company was known world-wide for its containers and stoneware bottles. Soon the company diversified into kitchen and tableware. By the 1930s, classic ranges such as Imperial Blue orient ware, which was brown, had established the company as one of the premier stoneware potteries in the world, introducing its 'oven to tableware' in the 1970s.

Open all year, Denby Visitor Centre is next to the working pottery, set in a cobbled courtyard with award winning home, garden, cookery and gift shops. There are two Pottery Tours to choose from: both include a video presentation, and the opportunity to have fun! A factory shop for Dartington Crystal can also be found at this superb attraction.

A mile from the pottery visitor centre, in Denby's oldest part, is the little **Parish Church of St Mary**, set amid a lovely churchyard filled with trees. The church's round arches and pillars date from the late 12th century, while the chancel with its sedilia, piscina and aumbry is from the 14th century. The altar table is 17th century, while the tower, spire, porch and eight-sided font are from the 20th century.

As well as clay, tarmacadam was also founded here by accident

at the start of the 20th century and it revolutionized road building. The history of Tarmac is itself interesting. As if by chance, the county surveyor of Nottingham - Edgar Purnell Hooley noticed a barrel of tar had fallen from a dray and burst open. To avoid a nuisance, someone from the ironworks had thoughtfully covered the sticky black mess with waste slag from nearby furnaces - and the world's first tarmacadam surface was born by accident. Hooley noticed that the patch of road, which had been unintentionally re-surfaced, was dust-free and hadn't been rutted by traffic. So he set to work and by the following year, 1902, Hooley obtained a British patent for a method of mixing slag with tar, naming the material Tarmac.

CODNOR

2 miles SE of Ripley on the A610

The village of Codnor has been a major crossroads for over a thousand years. Roads meet on the market place from Ripley, Alfreton, Langley Mill and Heanor. The village itself probably dates back to Saxon times, and is mentioned in the *Domesday Book* of 1086 as Cotenovre. Following the Norman Conquest, the land around Codnor fell under the jurisdiction of William Peveril.

The surrounding fields and woods make it easy to forget the coal and iron which made this part of Derbyshire famous. Once it was a great park of nearly 2,000 acres, the centrepiece being the mighty

•

One of Denby's most famous sons was John Flamsteed, born here in 1646. A poor boy, he went on to become the first Astronomer-Royal at the then new observatory at Greenwich. Benjamin Outram, the railway engineer was also born here.

•

120 DENBY VISITOR CENTRE

Denby

An interesting day out can be found here with tours of the factory and a selection of retail options.

 see page 255

121 THE POET AND CASTLE

Codnor

A Friendly and welcoming Free House boasting an impressive range of Real Ale and Cider, with sensible food and great entertainment.

see page 256

Although it is called Codnor Castle, access to it is not easy from Codnor itself (though it is a pleasant walk on a summer's day). You can't get all the way to the castle by car. The easiest route is to go via Aldercar and Aldercar Lane, parking near the Boat Inn at Stoneyford, and then walk the rest of the way.

Codnor Castle, the scant ruins of which still stand. The castle itself was a stone 'keep and bailey' fortress, with a three storey keep and a strong curtain wall and ditch, flanked by round towers. It was the home of the influential de Grey family, the most famous member being Richard de Grey, who was one of Henry III's loyal barons. Edward II visited another Richard de Grey here after fighting the rebels at Burton-on-Trent. All that survives today is a length of the boundary wall from the upper court, parts of the dividing wall and the defending towers, as well as the odd doorway, window and fireplace.

HEANOR

3 miles SE of Ripley off the A608

Heanor sits facing across the valley of Eastwood in Nottinghamshire, the town made famous by writer D.H. Lawrence and so this area is often described in his novels. The River Erewash passes through the area at Langley Mill and visitors are able to enjoy the restored boats, which travel to and from the 200-year-old canal basin.

Heanor's hub is the market place, where the annual fair is held, as well as a twice-weekly market, which takes place on Fridays and Saturdays. To the south of Heanor is the **Shipley Country Park**, on the estate of the now-demolished Shipley Hall. In addition to its magnificent lake, the country park boasts over 600 acres of beautiful countryside, which should keep even the most enthusiastic walker

busy. Shipley Country Park visitors centre, in October 2008, went 'green' and is now being powered by the wind after the installation of a wind turbine. Well known as both an educational and holiday centre, there are facilities for horse riding, cycling and fishing. Near the park is **Shanakiel House**, built in the early 1900s for Dr E.V. Eaves.

This medieval estate was mentioned in the *Domesday Book* and, under the Miller-Mundy family it became a centre for farming and coal mining production during the 18th century. Restoration over the years has transformed former railways into wooded paths, reservoirs into peaceful lakes, and has re-established the once-flowering meadows and rolling hills, which had been destroyed by the colliery pits.

The ancient **Parish Church of St Lawrence** dates back to the 12th century, though little of the old church remains after rebuilding in 1868. The 15th century tower is still intact.

BELPER

Belper is a small, attractive market town eight miles north of Derby. Until Jedediah Strutt came to Belper in 1776, it was a small town well known for producing nails. These quality nails were used throughout the world. If your surname is Naylor then it is most probable that your family originate from Belper. The town grew rapidly at the beginning of the 19th century due to the industrial development of cotton mills. However the origins of the town go back much further than the Industrial Revolution. It was mentioned in the *Domesday Book* as 'Beau Repaire', the beautiful retreat; in 1964 the remains of a Roman kiln were found here.

Now famous for its cotton mills, the town is situated alongside the **River Derwent** on the floor of the valley. In 1776, Jedediah Strutt, the wheelwright son of a South Normanton farmer, set up one of the earliest water-powered cotton mills here to harness the natural powers of the river. With the river providing power and fuel coming from the nearby South Derbyshire coalfield, the valley has a good claim to be one of the cradles of the Industrial Revolution. Earlier, in 1771, Strutt had gone into profitable partnership with Richard Arkwright to establish the world's first water-powered cotton mill at Cromford. In 1780 another mill was built at Milford. Over a period of almost 30 years, a collection of six mills were built. Great benefactors of the town for 150 years, the Strutt family provided housing, work, education and even food from the model farms they established in the surrounding countryside.

Today only the North and East Mills remain, the historic **North Mill** on the River Derwent, is one of the oldest surviving examples of industrialised water powered cotton spinning mills in the world. The original North Mill was destroyed in a fire in 1803 and was rebuilt by

Strutt's son William, this time he built it out of Iron and bricks so it was fire proof. The North Mill is open to the public and well worth a visit. The massive **East Mill** was built by the English Sewing Cotton Company in 1912. It closed as a mill in the late 20th century and now houses a number of small industrial units, but remains largely empty.

The **Derwent Valley Visitor Centre** tells the story of the cotton industry and the great influence the Strutt family had on the town. It also tells of Samuel Slater, Strutt's apprentice, who emigrated to America in 1789, built a mill, and became the father of the American cotton industry. The centre is housed in the oldest surviving mill, the two-storey North Mill at Bridgefoot, near the magnificent crescent-shaped weir in the Derwent and the town's main bridge.

Less than two minutes stroll away from North Mill, are **The River Gardens** offering a wonderful place for a picnic, play or simply a sit-down. Rowing boats can be hired for a trip along the Derwent. The gardens are a favourite with the film industry, having been used in Ken Russell's *Women in Love*, as well as television's *Sounding Brass* and *In the Shadow of the Noose*. The riverside walk through the meadows is particularly rich in bird life.

The **Chapel of St John the Baptist** in The Butts was the chapel of the original village of Belper. It consists of nave and

Belper

Renowned throughout Belper and beyond, this fine inn offers a fantastic venue to enjoy one of many Real Ales.

see *page 256*

•

Between 1838 and 1840 the North Midland Railway was built through Belper, and train travellers today can still admire George Stephenson's mile-long cutting. The unusual feature about the path of the railway through Belper is the fact that Strutt did not want to see the trains, because of this fact the railway lines run in a cutting. This means no level crossings or footbridges were required. On long row you can see where some houses were demolished to make way for this cutting. When completed in 1840 it was considered an engineering wonder of its day. The passenger station on King Street was opened on 10th March 1878, unfortunately the original train station is now covered by the supermarket.

•

123 THE RAILWAY

Cowers Lane, nr Belper
A real gem of a village pub offering a fantastic menu and the service to match!

🍴 see page 257

124 THE STRUTT ARMS HOTEL

Milford
The Strutt Arms Hotel is a warm, welcoming ex-coaching Inn offering fine food, good ales and comfortable accommodation.

🛏 🍴 see page 258

125 KING WILLIAM IV

Milford
A superb Olde Worlde inn with a cosy atmosphere, real ales and affordable accommodation. Be sure to visit in April and September during the Beer Festival!

🍴 🛏 see page 258

140

chancel only, and dates from 1250. The **Parish Church of St Peter** with its pinnacled west tower dates from 1824. It contains a monument to George Brettle, who built **George Brettle's Warehouse** in Chapel Street, a distinctive and elegant building in the classical style.

AROUND BELPER

FARNAH GREEN

1 mile W of Belper on the A517

Farnah Green is a charming hamlet on the outskirts of Belper, near to the village of Hazelwood. It has no shops but has a pleasant old country pub which serves food.

SHOTTLE

2 miles W of Belper off the A517

Shottle is a picturesque hamlet of a few farms, houses, the **Parish Church of St Lawrence**, and a chapel, surrounded by little lanes and footpaths. Unlike most of the surrounding villages it appears little changed since the 19th century. Shottle was the birthplace of Samuel Slater, the apprentice to Jedediah Strutt, who left Belper for the USA and built the first water powered cotton mill there; his original Slater Mill at Pawtucket is now a museum. American President Andrew Jackson called him the 'Father of American Manufactures'. His technological contribution and unique management style made him one of the most successful New England entrepreneurs of his era.

IDRIDGEHAY

10 miles NW of Derby off the B5023

This pleasant village is called 'Ithersee' by the locals and it lies in the valley of the River Ecclesbourne. Formerly a working rural village, it is now purely residential. The area is also part of a conservation scheme including the half-timbered building, **South Sitch**. The date above the door, 1621, may refer to alterations carried out to a much older building. The apparent Elizabethan mansion, **Alton Manor**, was in fact built by Sir George Gilbert Scott in 1846, when he moved from Darley Dale because of the coming of the railway.

Idridgehay's most prominent building is the **Parish Church of St James,** built in the early 1840s and consecrated in 1845. George Turner the Victorian landscape painter from Barrow on Trent is buried here, as is Sir Peter Hilton, a former incumbent of the manor house.

MILFORD

1 mile S of Belper off the A6

Milford was a quiet hamlet until the cotton mills came. The power of the River Derwent brought Jedediah Strutt and Richard Arkwright to Milford, where he built the mill which gave the village its name around 1780. It was only a year later that their partnership dissolved and both industrialists went their separate ways to forge individual empires. The majority of the mill was demolished around the middle of the last century. What does remain of the mill is now filled with a shop and small business.

HOLBROOK

2 miles S of Belper off the A6

The Saxon name for Holbrook was Hale Broc meaning 'badger hill'. The ancient Roman Portway (which the Romans surfaced with coal) runs through the village and one of the toll houses for the turnpike road still stands in the village. In the early 1960s two Roman kilns were discovered here. Holbrook was once a busy industrial village well known for framework knitters, who supplied stockings for royalty. It is now a pleasant place, with some attractive old houses, serving mainly as a commuter area for the nearby towns of Belper and Derby.

The **Parish Church of St Michael** was built in 1761 as a private chapel to Holbrook Hall. It was rebuilt as the parish church in 1841, but still retains the elegant classical lines of its predecessor. Holbrook Hall was built in 1681 although it looks later, it is grade II* listed and is now a residential home for the elderly.

DUFFIELD

2 miles S of Belper off the A6

This ancient village is a charming place, with Georgian houses and cottages lining the banks of the River Ecclesbourne. For such a cosy place, it seems odd that the **Parish Church of St Alkmund** is situated in isolation down by the river. However, as it stands on the

site of a Saxon one, it is thought that the river was used to baptise converts. The saint to whom it is dedicated was a Northumbrian prince who was murdered in AD 800 at nearby Derby by bodyguards supposed to be protecting him. They were sent by King Eardulf, who was trying to claim the Northumbrian throne. Alkmund's sarcophagus is now in a Derby museum.

The church has a 14th century east tower with a recessed spire. It was much restored in the 19th century. Inside the Church there is an impressive monument dating from 1600, dedicated to Anthony Bradshaw, his two wives and their 20 children. He had 23 children in all, with the 22nd being called 'Penultima'. Bradshaw was a barrister and the deputy steward of Duffield Firth, a former hunting forest between Duffield and Wirksworth. His great nephew went on to officiate over the court, which called for the execution of Charles I.

Located in the centre of Duffield, **Duffield Castle** is an 11th century stone motte and bailey fortress, founded by Henry de Ferrers, Earl of Derby. In 1886 and 1957, excavations on the large low motte and wide bailey ditch, uncovered the foundations of a magnificent square Norman keep, with a forebuilding and a deep well. Sadly the keep, one of the largest in England, is only five courses of sandstone ashlar high, after being taken and destroyed in 1266, by the Royalist forces of Henry III. The site

126 SPOTTED COW

Holbrook

Come along to the Spotted Cow and enjoy luxurious accommodation, outstanding food and the best in English hospitality!

see page 259

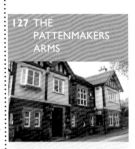

127 THE PATTENMAKERS ARMS

Duffield

Visitors can expect to enjoy warm hospitality, well kept ales and fine food in a relaxed atmosphere.

see page 259

128 THE KINGS HEAD INN

Duffield

A comfortable pub/B&B that has a rather varied and interesting history. Call in to learn more!

see page 260

129 FINN M'COULS

Ilkeston

A popular and friendly public house providing a good choice of excellent value food and weekend entertainment.

see page 260

●

Ilkeston commands fine, wide views from the hillside above the valley of the Erewash, which here bounds the county. The town has been used as a filming location for the BBC's TV series **Playing The Field.** *Ilkeston is also the birthplace of actor Robert Lindsay, well known for his part in* **Me and My Girl, My Family** *and* **Horatio Hornblower.**

●

Shipley Country Park, nr Ilkeston

is owned by The National Trust and is freely accessible in daylight hours, by steep steps from Milford Road.

Duffield Hall is situated at the southern edge of the village. It is an Elizabethan building, enlarged in 1870 and once used as a girls boarding school. It is now the head quarters of the Derbyshire Building Society.

ILKESTON

With a population of just over 37,000, Ilkeston is the third largest town in Derbyshire. It received its royal charter for a market and fair in 1252, the market and fair continue to flourish to this day. The market place is brought to life every Thursday and Saturday offering an excellent range of goods, from toys, confectionery and greeting cards to electrical goods, books and clothes. The **Charter Fair**, held in October each year, is one of the oldest and largest in Europe – it's an event not to be missed! The history of the town, however, goes back to when it was an Anglo Saxon hilltop settlement known as Tilchestune.

Once a mining and lace-making centre, a history of the town's industrial past is told in the **Erewash Museum**, housed in a fine Georgian house with Victorian extensions on the High Street. It was a family home and then part of a school before becoming a Museum in the 1980s. Many original features survive including a restored Edwardian kitchen and wash house. The garden has unrivalled views across the Erewash Valley. Other fine examples of elegant 18th century houses can be found in East Street while, in Wharncliffe Road, there are period houses with art nouveau features. Despite the towns industrial outlook, parks, trees and flower beds are a feature of the community and there is some pleasant countryside around the town.

The **Parish Church of St Mary** has undergone many changes since it was first erected in the 1200s. It is particularly notable for its window tracery, especially in the six windows in the older part of the church. A former tower and elegant spire were destroyed by storm in 1714. The tower only was rebuilt, to be succeeded by another on the old foundations in 1855. This tower was then moved westwards in 1907, at which time the nave was doubled in length. One intriguing feature it has retained throughout all these changes is its 13th century archway. The organ is also distinguished, in that it originally came from a London church and is known to have been played by the great Mendelssohn himself.

AROUND ILKESTON

MAPPERLEY

2 miles NW of Ilkeston off the A609

Although Mapperley is an agricultural village with half a dozen working farms, any stroll from the village centre will take the walker past industrial remains. To the south of Mapperley is the former branch line of the Midland Railway, which served Mapperley Colliery, as well as the old raised track which is all that remains of an old tramway, and ran from the Blue Fly Shaft of West Hallam Pit to the **Nutbrook Canal** further east. The canal, which opened in 1796, carried coal from the pits at Shipley to the ironworks at Stanton and beyond. Only just over four miles long, the canal had some 13 locks but it fell into disuse after the Second World War and much of it has now been filled in.

This historic village was first granted a market charter in 1267 and, though its old church was demolished due to mining subsidence, the modern church has some interesting stained glass windows. Opposite the church, are the village stocks.

WEST HALLAM

2 miles W of Ilkeston off the A609

West Hallam stands on a hilltop. Its **Parish Church of St Wilfrid**, set between the great expanse of **West Hallam Hall** and the rectory, is approached via a lovely avenue of limes. The church is over 700 years old and has a very handsome tower, with a blue clock with gilt hands and figures. The rector's garden has a glorious lime tree, and looks out over the valley to a great windmill with its arms still working as they have done since Georgian times.

One of the premier attractions in the area, **The Bottle Kiln** is a handsome and impressive brick built former working pottery, now home to a fine art gallery with a new exhibition every month. Visitors can take a leisurely look at both British studio ceramics and contemporary painting in the European tradition. Two shops filled with jewellery, cards, gifts, objects d'art, soft furnishings and house wares with an accent on style, design and originality can also be found here. At the Buttery Café, visitors can enjoy a wide choice of freshly prepared and hearty food, along with a tasty selection of teas, coffees and cakes. All this is in an attractive landscaped setting with a Japanese style tea garden and a unique renovated bottle-necked kiln.

West Hallam has a well-dressing ceremony each year, normally held during the second week of July.

•

The Powtrell family were historically important to the village of West Hallam, and their former home was offered as a hiding place for fugitive priests during the 16th century. One priest taken at the house was condemned to death, but after long imprisonment his sentence was commuted to banishment. Another priest, sentenced for celebrating mass at West Hallam Hall, was sent to prison and later died there. On a stone on the chancel floor of the village church is an engraved portrait of Thomas Powtrell in armour, dating from the 15th century. A magnificent canopied tomb depicts Walter Powtrell, who died in 1598, and his wife Cassandra. He wears richly decorated armour, she a gown of many folds. Around them are depicted their seven children.

•

143

130 THE SITWELL ARMS

Horsley Woodhouse

A picture postcard premises offering fine food and drink at affordable prices.

see page 261

131 THREE HORSESHOES

Morley

This traditional, friendly, whitewashed inn epitomises all that is good about England's village pubs.

see page 260

HORSLEY

6 miles W of Ilkeston on the A609

Horsley is a charming little village, complete with traditional village green and spreading chestnut tree. Walking is a popular activity for locals thanks to the beautiful surrounding countryside. Horsley boasts one of the most attractive village churches in the county, sitting on a hill, set amongst flowers and trees. The **Parish Church of St Clement and St James** is a real gem dating back to the 13th century with later additions. It has a broach spire and mid-15th century battlements and a pretty porch with a medieval crucifix. The interior is much restored but there are some scraps of ancient glass in one window.

The village pillar box is one of the most unusual in England, as it is made of stone. The village also has three wells, called Blanche, Sophie and Rosamund. They were given to the village in 1824 by the local vicar, Reverend Sitwell.

There once was a castle, but few traces of it remain today. Horsley Castle, also known as Horston or Horeston Castle was a Norman earthwork motte and bailey fortress, built in the 12th century with a rectangular great tower which was in ruins from the late 16th century. It was owned by the Crown from 1268 to 1514. The site has a dense cover of trees and is best viewed in winter.

MORLEY

4 miles SW of Ilkeston off the A608

Morley is essentially a rural village with working farms around it. There

are four parts to the village, Brackley Gate and the Croft, the Smithy and Brick Kiln Lane, Almshouse Lane and Church Lane.

Brackley Gates has some disused quarries and marvellous views to the north. It is now a wildlife reserve owned by the Derbyshire Wildlife Trust. The Croft has a cluster of 17th and 18th century cottages. The 17th century **Almshouses** in Almshouse Lane were originally provided by Jacinth Sitwell, then Lord of the Manor of Morley for 'six poor, lame or impotent men'.

The **Parish Church of St Matthew** has a Norman nave, with the tower, chancel and north chapel being late 14th/early 15th century. It is perhaps best known for its magnificent stained glass windows dating from medieval times. Originally in the Abbey Refectory at Dale, the windows were acquired by Sir Henry Sacheverell in 1539. There are monuments and brasses to important local families like the Sacheverell's and the Sitwell's, including one to John Sacheverell, who died at Bosworth Field in 1485, and the beautifully carved tomb chest of Henry Sacheverell, who died in 1558 and his beautiful wife Katherine Babington, who died in 1553.

DALE ABBEY

3 miles SW of Ilkeston off the A6096

The village takes its name from the now-ruined abbey that was founded here by Augustinian monks in the 13th century. Beginning life in a very humble manner, local legend has it that a Derbyshire baker had a vision of the Virgin Mary, which told him to come to Dale Abbey and live the life of a hermit. He accordingly came to the area in 1130, carved himself a niche in the sandstone and devoted himself to the way of the hermit. The owner of the land, Ralph FitzGeremunde, discovered the baker and was so impressed by the man's devotion that he bestowed on him the land and tithe rights to his mill in Borrowash. In about 1200 the Augustinian canons founded **Dale Abbey** on the site, which lasted until the Dissolution of the monasteries in 1538.

The sandstone cave and the romantic ruined 40-feet-high window archway (all that now remains of the original Dale Abbey) are popular attractions locally and a walk around the village is both an interesting and pleasurable experience. Nearby **Hermit's Wood** is an ancient area of woodland with beech, ash, oak and lime trees. It is wonderful at any time of year, but particularly in the spring when the woodland floor is covered with a carpet of bluebells.

Evening view, Dale Abbey

though all that remains of this Norman building nowadays is the south door. Some of the buttresses and a small lancet date from the mid 1200s. The font dates back to the 1300s, and the pulpit from the 17th century. A brass tablet on the floor by the pulpit is dedicated to Sir John Bentley of Breadsall, who was buried here 20 years before the Civil War.

STANTON BY DALE

2 miles S of Ilkeston off the A6096

The village of Stanton by Dale retains its unspoilt charm and peace and quiet of days gone by, and is mentioned in the *Domesday Book* having derived its name from the nearby stone quarries. The houses in the village are mainly

STANLEY

3 miles SW of Ilkeston off the A609

Stanley is a pleasant little rural village, whose main industry was coal mining until the closure of Stanley colliery in 1959. The remains of the pits can still be seen on the outskirts of the village. Stanley's church, the **Parish Church of St Andrew**, dates originally from the 12th century,

• *The Parish Church of All Saints in Dale Abbey, which dates back to the mid-12th century, must be the only church in England, which shares its roof with a farm. The church has a pulpit that dates from 1634 and the whole interior appears rather crammed with its box pews and open benches. The farmhouse was once possibly used as an infirmary for the Abbey and then as an inn. The adjoining door was blocked up in the 1820s to prevent swift transition from salvation to damnation.*

•

Village, Stanton-by-Dale

Sandiacre is usually thought to refer to a sandy acre, though another interpretation, based on Saint Diacre, is sometimes advanced. Although it has been all but incorporated into the ever-expanding Nottingham conurbation, it maintains many village features including the picturesque 14th century **Parish Church of St Giles**, situated up a narrow lane at the top of a hill. In the churchyard, four stones commemorate the remarkable Charlton family. One was an MP as far back as 1318. Sir Richard was slain on Bosworth field. Sir Thomas was Speaker in 1453. Edward was a commissioner in the Civil War.

The Erewash Canal passes through the centre of Sandiacre and situated next to the canal is Springfield Mills, built in 1888, it acts as a reminder of Sandiacre's industrial heritage. Examples of lace making, engineering and furniture making can still be found today.

RISLEY

4 miles S of Ilkeston on the B5010

Risley consists of no more than a small group of old buildings, but they are unique and well worth a visit. **Risley Hall** is a gorgeous manor house dating back to the 15th century. However, nothing now remains of the original Risley Hall, home of the Willoughbys, except an Elizabethan gateway. The present one dates from the late 17th century.

The 12-acre **Risley Hall**

18th and 19th century brick or stone. The village pump, erected in 1897 to commemorate Queen Victoria's jubilee, had fallen into a sad state of dilapidation. It is now repaired, completely renovated and returned to its original green and gold.

The **Parish Church of St Michael and All Angels** is 13th century in origin but there is a fine modern stained glass window depicting Stanton Ironworks. At the bottom of the path leading to the church, on the right are the **Middlemore Almshouses**; the row is named after Mrs Winifred Middlemore, who gave the four houses nearest the church for occupation by 'eight poor people'.

SANDIACRE

4 miles S of Ilkeston off the B5010

Sandiacre is situated on the border with Nottinghamshire. The name

Gardens are open to the public. In 1593, Sir Michael Willoughby started to rebuild the **Parish Church of All Saints**. Although small, even by the standards of the day, it is charming and essentially Gothic in style.

OCKBROOK

4 miles SW of Ilkeston off the A52

This attractive village close to, but hidden from, the busy main road between Derby and Nottingham, has managed to retain much of its charm and at least a reasonable level of peace and quiet. There is evidence of human activity in Ockbrook as far back as 10,000 BC (the Mesolithic) in the form of two bifacial cores of flint. A small greenstone axe head attests to Neolithic activity. There are two distinct parts to the village. The old part of Ockbrook was established by Occa, an Anglo-Saxon, around the 6th century. Alongside it is the Moravian settlement, a product of the 18th century, with its delightful terrace of red brick Georgian buildings and handsome **Moravian Chapel.**

This is farming country and many of the ancient hedgerows remain, sustaining all manner of wildlife that has disappeared from many other areas. Several old farm buildings also remain, including an impressive 17th century timber-framed building at Church Farm. Little but the ground floor however, remains of **Ockbrook Windmill**, one of only 10 windmill sites extant in Derbyshire.

BORROWASH

6 miles SW of Ilkeston off the A6005

Pronounced 'borrow-ash', this now quiet village has lost its railway station and canal, which was filled in during the early 1960s. However thanks to the efforts of the Derby and Sandiacre Canal Society, the Derby canal is currently undergoing restoration. The Borrowash Bottom lock is beginning to look like a canal lock again.

P H Currey designed the small redbrick **Parish Church of St Stephen** in 1899. The interior features a low, 18th century ironwork chancel screen, believed to be the work of Robert Bakewell of Derby.

SPONDON

5 miles SW of Ilkeston on the A6096

This village, with many Georgian brick houses, is now almost engulfed by Derby, but the older parts can still be picked out. The **Parish Church of St Werburgh**, damaged by fire in 1340, was completely rebuilt and has also undergone restoration work in 1826 and again in the 1890s. Nearby is **Locko Park**, the privately owned ancestral home of the Drury-Lowe family since 1747, when it was purchased from the Gilberts by John Lowe. In 1790 it passed to William Drury, who changed his name to Drury-Lowe. The present hall was built by Francis Smith in the mid 1700s, and since then it has been given an Italian appearance. Today, the hall houses one of the largest private

132 ROYAL OAK

Ockbrook

Welcoming hostelry in picturesque village serving excellent home-made foods and well-kept real ales.

🍴 *see page 262*

collections of Italian paintings in Britain. The chapel is earlier than the hall, having been built in 1669. Way back in medieval times a leper hospital stood here, and indeed the word 'Locko' comes from the Old French 'loques', meaning rags.

BREASTON

5 miles S of Ilkeston on the A6005

On the southern borders of the county, close to Nottinghamshire and Leicestershire, Breaston occupies the flat countryside near the point where the River Derwent joins the River Trent. Of particular note in the village is the 13th century **Parish Church of St Michael**, with its recently restored soaring spire, spotted for miles around and which tops a short square clock-face tower. This ancient building occupies a peaceful setting and has many treasures from the past that are well worth seeing.

The church also boasts the 'Boy of Breaston' - a small, chubby-faced child, immortalised in the 13th century by the mason of the nave arches. He has smiled down on worshippers and visitors for the past seven centuries. The story has it that this boy would come in and watch the masons at work while the church was being built. The master mason decided to make the child part of the church, so that he could always have a good view of it.

For visitors who chance to be this way Breaston's fine **Millennium Sensory Garden** is worth spending time in, also the delightful Butterfly garden.

DRAYCOTT

7 miles S of Ilkeston on the A6005

The uninformed visitor might at first sight be forgiven for believing that this village, nestling on the banks of the River Derwent, has little to offer historically and that there is little of interest for the casual visitor. Well he would be wrong on both counts. The best known land mark in Draycott is **Victoria Mill**, built in 1888 and established as one of the most important lace factories in the world. When it was completed in 1907, it was the largest manufacturing mill in Europe. The four-storey building, with its green-capped ornamental clock tower, still dominates the Draycott skyline though it is now the home of an electrical component manufacturer. **Draycott House**, designed by Joseph Pickford, was built in 1781. It remains a private residence.

Draycott also boast the beautiful St Chad's Water, a 12 acre Nature Reserve sitting peacefully beside St Chad's Church (records of which go back to the 7th century).

ELVASTON

8 miles SW of Ilkeston on the B5010

Elvaston Castle Country Park opened to the public in 1970. It was the first of it's kind in Britain and spans more than 200 acres of woodland, parkland and fascinating formal gardens. At the heart of the park is the **Elvaston Castle**, which despite its name, is really a country house. Today, due to its need for restoration, the castle is only occasionally open to the public. The magnificent Gothic castle seen today was designed by James Wyatt and built about 1817 for the 3rd Earl of Harrington. It is now owned by Derbyshire County Council.

Though the building itself is strikingly handsome, it is, perhaps, the grounds, which make Elvaston Castle famous. They were originally laid out and designed for the 4th Earl by William Barron. Barron, who was born in Berwickshire in 1805, started work in 1830 on what, at first, appeared to be an impossible task. The 4th Earl wanted a garden 'second to none', but the land available, which had never been landscaped, was flat, water-logged and uninspiring with just two avenues of trees and a walled kitchen garden (but no greenhouses or hot houses). First draining the land, Barron then planted trees to offer shelter to more tender plants. From there the project grew.

In order to stock the gardens, Barron began a programme of propagation of rarer tree species and, along with the tree-planting methods he developed specially to deal with Elvaston's problems, his fame spread. The gardens became a showcase of rare and interesting trees, many to be found nowhere else in Britain. Barron continued to work for the 5th Earl, but resigned in 1865 to live in nearby Borrowash and set up his own nursery. Now owned by Derby County Council, the gardens, after years of neglect,

have been completely restored and the delights of the formal gardens, with their fine topiary, the avenues and the kitchen garden can be enjoyed by all visitors to the grounds, which are now a Country Park.

As well as fine formal gardens and the walled kitchen garden, there are gentle woodland walks and, of course, the man-made lake. However, no visit to Elvaston would be complete without a walk down to the **Golden Gates**. Erected in 1819 at the southern end of the formal gardens, the gates were brought from the Palace of Versailles by the 3rd Earl of Harrington. Little is known of the gates' history, but they remain a fine monument and are the symbol of Elvaston. Around the courtyard of the castle can be found a restaurant as well as an information centre and well-stocked gift shop. All manner of activities take place from the castle, which can provide details. Elvaston Country Park is open to the public from dawn to dusk. Admission is free though a small car parking fee applies.

SHARDLOW

9 miles SW of Ilkeston off the A6

Shardlow is located just within the Derbyshire border. There was a settlement here at the time of the *Domesday Book*, when the area belonged to the Abbey of Chester and the village was known as Serdelov. Shardlow was once an important port on the River Trent and a horse drawn ferry was used

• *The Parish Church of St Bartholomew in Elvaston dates from the 13th century, with later additions. There is a monument to the 3rd Earl of Harrington, who brought the Golden Gates to Elvaston, dating from 1829. It was the work of the Venetian Antonio Canova, and one of only three in England.*

•

134 THE NEW INN

Shardlow

Truly a hidden gem, the New Inn is popular with people near and far for its location, fine food and hospitality.

see page 263

135 THE OLD MARINA BAR AND RESTAURANT

Shardlow

Wine, Dine, Relax... and watch the world drift by...

see page 264

136 SHAKESPEARE INN & RESTAURANT

Shardlow

Drop in for a drink, a snack or a great meal and enjoy yourself.

see page 265

to cross the river. This was replaced in 1760 by a toll bridge and the stone giving the toll charges can still be seen on the roadside approaching the modern Cavendish Bridge. This replaced the old bridge, which collapsed in 1947.

After 1777, when the **Trent and Mersey Canal** was opened, Shardlow became a canal port, one of only a few in the country. With Liverpool, Hull and Bristol now linked by water, the warehouses here were quickly filled with heavy goods of all descriptions that could be carried at half the cost of road transport and with greater safety. Many of the homes of the canal carriers and their warehouses survive to this day and the port is now a modern marina, linked to the River Trent, and filled with all manner of pleasure barges.

Many of the old cottages in Shardlow were swept away by 1960s development but some were saved when much of the canal side was designated a conservation area in 1978. There are still some fine houses remaining that were built by the wealthy canal merchants. **Broughton House**, built in the early part of the 19th century is just one example. The **Shardlow Heritage Centre** is housed in the earliest of the old canal warehouses, the Old Salt Warehouse, and has exhibitions and displays about Shardlow's heyday as a canal port. The outstanding **Shardlow Marina** covers 46 acres, of which the Marina itself covers 12 acres, set in beautiful rolling countryside. The marina has moorings for up to 365 boats, with berths available for up to 70-feet narrow and wide-beam boats.

The **Parish Church of St**

Canal Boat on Trent & Mersey Canal, Shardlow

James, though it looks much older, dates only from 1838, and sits on land given to the village by the Sutton Family of Shardlow hall.

ASTON-ON-TRENT

9 miles S of Ilkeston off the A50

It won't come as a suprise to learn that Aston-on-Trent stands on the River Trent, marking the border between Derbyshire and Leicestershire. Aston's **Parish Church of All Saints** is mainly Norman, though there is plenty of evidence of Saxon masonry, notably in the northeast corner of the nave. There is an octagonal font dating from the 1200s inside the church, and a moving, early 15th century alabaster tomb chest of a husband and wife holding hands, she with a small dog at her feet.

Aston Hall dates from 1753; much enlarged over the centuries, it was originally a fine Georgian mansion with no fewer than five bays and central Venetian windows. Ashton Lodge stands close to the heart of the village and was once the home of the Bowden family, who were lace makers. The main part of the house was dismantled and transported to the United States, while the rest was converted into flats.

CASTLE DONINGTON

10 miles S of Ilkeston off the A50

Castle Donington (pronounced Dunington) is just over the Leicestershire border on a hill above the Trent River. As the name suggests, there was once a Castle in the area built in the 11th or 12th century, demolished in 1216, rebuilt later that century and was finally demolished in 1595. All that is left of the castle is a mound in the actual location.

Today the village is a pleasant blend of the old and new, with modern shops standing alongside dignified Georgian and Regency houses. Several timber framed houses dating from the 17th century and earlier, survive along the main road. The oldest part of the **Parish Church of St Edward, King and Martyr**, dates back to 1200 but it was probably built on the site of an older Saxon church. The spire, rising to a height of 160 feet, is a landmark for miles around.

Donington Hall with its park was the home of members of the Hastings family from 1595 until the death of Lord Donington in 1895. The old hall was replaced by the present building in 1793 by Earl Moira, later 1st Marquis Hastings. The Hall is of the 'Strawberry Hill Gothic' style, first made fashionable by Walpole. The hall and park were developed between the wars into what would today be known as a Country Club with accommodation, golf, boating and other amusements, the most notable of which was the racetrack, which developed from humble beginnings using the park driveways to a Grand Prix circuit. Today the racetrack is open again and it is possible to see something of its pre-war glories in the **Donington**

137 MALT SHOVEL INN

Aston-on-Trent

The watchword here is good, old-fashioned English hospitality, and you'll be assured of a warm welcome if you visit!

see page 267

138 THE CROSS KEYS

Castle Donington

A friendly village pub close to Donington Park Racetrack and East Midlands Airport that is noted for its real ales and filling snacks.

see page 266

139 YE OLDE FLYING HORSE

Kegworth

Good food, great ale and fun entertainment can all be found in abundance here at Ye Olde Flying Horse.

🍴 see page 268

140 THE ANCHOR INN

Kegworth

Ideal for walkers, cyclists or those touring the area, who need refreshments and simple room only accommodation.

🍴 🛏 see page 267

141 DONINGTON PARK FARMHOUSE

Isley Walton

Charming 17th century farmhouse hotel with adjacent deer park offering outstanding food and quality en suite rooms.

🛏 see page 269

Park Museum. Vehicles on show include Ascari's Ferrari, Jim Clark's Lotus 23 and Nigel Mansell's Williams. The Hall is now the headquarters of British Midland Airways who have carefully restored it to much of its former glory. The medieval Deer Park survives and is designated a Site of Special Scientific Interest.

Close to the village stands **Nottingham East Midlands Airport**, originally a Royal Air Force base. It was purchased in the 1960s and soon became the main airport for the nearby conurbations of Derby, Nottingham and Leicester.

LONG EATON

7 miles SE of Ilkeston off the A52

Long Eaton, straddling the Derbyshire and Nottinghamshire border, has a history that goes back earlier than the 7th century. Lying close by the River Trent, the name came from the Anglo-Saxon 'Aitone' meaning town by the water. Visited by the Romans and settled by the Danes, the medieval village remained undisturbed for centuries. A national census of 1801 recorded that only some 504 people lived here.

The **Parish Church of St Lawrence**, according to local legend, dates from the time of King Canute, though it is more likely to be Norman in origin. At one time it was only a 'chapel of ease' for the main parish church in Sawley, but in 1868, when the church was largely rebuilt, it became a parish church in its own right.

It was not until the Industrial Revolution and the 19th century that Long Eaton awoke from its long slumbers to become a centre for quarrying, lace making and other industries, all boosted by the coming of railways and canals. The arrival of the railway in 1847 triggered the expansion, and the hosiery and lace making factories, escaping the restrictive practices in nearby Nottingham, brought employment for many and wealth for some. By the 1870s the population was recorded at over 3,000, doubling over the following 10 years. In 1915 construction began on the National Shell Filling Factory sited just over a mile away from Long Eaton's ancient market place. A staggering 19 million large shells were filled to aid the war effort, and it was not until there had been some 19 explosions at the plant, the worst with a death toll of 140, that the operation ceased.

The lace industry, forever associated with this area, gave way to furniture, narrow fabrics and electrical wiring manufacture which reflected the interests and activities of a stream of entrepreneurs drawn to the town. The most famous of these men was Ernest Tehra Hooley - lace maker, property dealer, builder, benefactor and company director. Hooley was responsible for the flotation of such well-known names as Dunlop, Raleigh, Humber and Bovril before he went bankrupt.

Trent Lock, an easy stroll from the town, is a centre for sailing and boating and there are plenty of other sporting facilities available.

SAWLEY

8 miles SE of Ilkeston off the B6540

Up until the 19th century, Sawley was the most important village in the area, an extensive ecclesiastical parish, which included Breaston, Draycott, Hopwell, Long Eaton, Risley, Wilne and Wilsthorpe. The old English name for Sawley village was Sallé, meaning 'hill where willow trees grow' and the early development of the village was due to its command of a river crossing.

Over 1,000 years ago a small collective of monks boated down the Trent from Repton to the green meadows of Sawley, where they built the **Parish Church of All Saints**. Much of the church we see today is 14th century, with a 15th century tower and spire and much 15th century timbering. The chancel arch is Saxon. The interior boasts an impressive group of monuments, a 600-year-old font, a 500-year-old screen, a Jacobean pulpit and 17th century altar table.

In the late 1400s the Bothes (or Booths) settled at Sawley in a house of which some of the timbers remain in the cellars of **Bothe Hall**, near the church. Sawley's most noted son was John Clifford. Born here in 1836, he became one of the most powerful voices of nonconformity, known as 'the greatest Free Churchman of his day'.

Sawley Marina, with over 600 moorings, has been described as the 'most sophisticated ' marina on the inland waterways network, sitting as it does at the junction of four cruising routes. You can cruise from here all the way to the North Sea.

For the canal enthusiast, the Trent & Mersey Canal starts just two miles from Sawley near the historic canal village of Shardlow. Less well known, but some argue the better for it, is the quiet and intriguing Erewash Canal, providing a mixed cruising experience for those who love industrial heritage and exploring the 'out of the way'

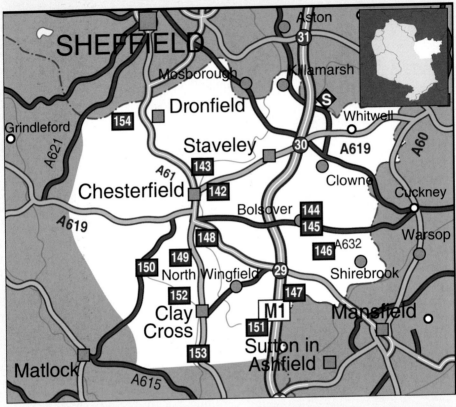

ACCOMMODATION

142	The Lockoford Inn, Tapton, nr Chesterfield	p 157, 270
146	Horse & Groom, Scarcliffe, nr Chesterfield	p 163, 274
151	King Edward VII, Tibshelf	p 168, 279
152	Batemans Mill Country Hotel & Restaurant, Old Tupton, nr Chesterfield	p 168, 280
153	The Crown Inn, Old Higham	p 169, 281

FOOD & DRINK

142	The Lockoford Inn, Tapton, nr Chesterfield	p 157, 270
143	Cock & Magpie, Old Whittington, nr Chesterfield	p 158, 271
144	Whyld About Food, Bolsover	p 162, 272

FOOD & DRINK

146	Horse & Groom, Scarcliffe, nr Chesterfield	p 163, 274
147	Hardwick Inn, Hardwick Park, nr Chesterfield	p 165, 275
148	Telmere Lodge, Hasland, nr Chesterfield	p 166, 276
149	Hunloke Arms, Wingerworth	p 167, 277
150	Three Horseshoes, Spitewinter, nr Ashover	p 167, 278
151	King Edward VII, Tibshelf	p 168, 279
152	Batemans Mill Country Hotel & Restaurant, Old Tupton, nr Chesterfield	p 168, 280
153	The Crown Inn, Old Higham	p 169, 281
154	The Miners Arms, Dronfield Woodhouse	p 172, 282

PLACES OF INTEREST

145	Bolsover Castle, Bolsover	p 163, 273

The Derbyshire Coalmines

A landscape of rolling hills, meadows and moorland, rippling river valleys and sleepy villages, North East Derbyshire is a varied area that's still surprisingly unspoilt. While the urban crowds escape en-masse to the Peak District and the Derbyshire Dales, the north eastern corner of the county centred on the coal mining town of Chesterfield, remains a largely undiscovered jewel - boasting some of Derbyshire's best views within easy reach of the M1 motorway.

Snow Scene, Ashover

The clang of pick and shovel have echoed down through the centuries, as this was heart of the county's coal mining area, and many of the towns and villages reflect the prosperity the mines brought in Victorian times. It was George Stephenson, a pioneering railway engineer, who discovered the important coal reserves under the hamlet of Clay Cross during the building of the North Midlands Railway between Derby and Chesterfield in the early 1840s. Sadly, the traditional industries have waned in recent years and an era finally came to an end with the closure of the last colliery at Renishaw in 1989.

Despite the fact that many of the places in and around Chesterfield only date from the Industrial Revolution, the area is rich in history. From medieval times this has been an area of trade, and the weekly markets were an important part of the local economy. Though some have been lost over the years, most of these traditional centres and meeting-places remain.

There are also many new and interesting sights and attractions to discover, as well as many superb walks and specially designed trails throughout the area. But there's nothing like a carnival and, between Spring and Autumn, most villages in the area have either a carnival, gala or fair – Barlow, Dronfield, Grassmoor and Wingerworth, to name but a few. For a real country experience, the Ashover Show is held every August and is a great day out for all the family.

The ancient custom of well-dressing is just as popular and well-executed here as elsewhere in the county, plus there are curiosities such as a 'castle that isn't a castle despite its battlements, a church clock that has sixty-three minutes in an hour and an Italian-style garden in the grounds owned by a famous English family'. The area boasts several exceptional Norman churches, most notably, at Steetley (near Creswell) and Ault Hucknall.

155

CHESTERFIELD

Situated just three miles from the eastern boundary of the Peak District National Park, Chesterfield is a medieval market town with a history and treasures of its own. It is Derbyshire's largest town (Derby itself being a city), although the county town of Derbyshire is Matlock in the Derbyshire Dales. The *Domesday Book* calls the town 'Cestrefield', meaning open field which points towards its success as a market town. The market, established over 800 years ago and claims to be England's largest, still remains a bustling area of the town itself, running on a Monday, Friday and Saturday, with an antique/bric-a-brac market on Thursday. More than 250 stalls crowd into the town centre, enabling the visitor to purchase almost anything.

The town centre has been conserved for future generations by a far-sighted council, and many buildings have been saved, including the Victorian **Market Hall** built in 1857. The traditional cobbled paving was restored in the Market Place, and New Square was given a complete facelift. It's worth taking a walk down the narrow streets off the Market Place into the **Shambles**, an area of old, narrow streets featuring the Royal Oak, one of Chesterfields oldest public houses, first mentioned as an inn in 1722 formerly being a rest house for the Knights Templar band of Crusaders.

Visitors to the town are drawn to a peculiarly graceful spire on top of the **Parish Church of St Mary and All Saints**. Twisting and leaning, it is totally confusing to the eye, and gives Chesterfield its identity. Built, along with much of the rest of the church in the 14th century, it was straight for several centuries before it began to twist. Its 228 feet spire stands on the skyline like a question mark: how did it happen? Superstition surrounds it and, sadly, the real story of its unusual appearance has been lost over the years. The truth probably lies in the wake of

Crooked Spire, St Mary & All Angels, Chesterfield

the Black Death during the 14th century, many must have fallen to the plague and, among them, skilled craftsmen who knew how to correctly cross-brace and season wood. However, legends say a magician persuaded the Bolsover blacksmith to shoe the Devil. Shaking with fear, he drove a nail into the Devil's food. Howling in pain, the Devil took flight towards Chesterfield. Skimming over the church he lashed out in agony, caught the spire and twisted it out of shape. It now leans over 9 feet to the south, twisting 45 degrees from its true centre and is still moving. It is eight-sided, but the herringbone pattern of the lead slates trick the eye into seeing 16 sides from the ground. The spire is open most Bank Holidays and at advertised times; the church, the largest in Derbyshire, is open all year, Monday to Saturday 9am to 5pm (9am to 3pm January and February), and Sundays at service times only.

The church itself is also impressive since it is the largest in Derbyshire and has seen Civil War, fire, revolution and World Wars, but it still survives as a symbol of Chesterfield.

If this has peaked your interest in Chesterfield's past, opposite the church is **Chesterfield Museum and Art Gallery**, there's no better place to start investigating it than here. The museum is home to exhibitions depicting the story of the town, from the arrival of the Romans to the first days of the

market town, the industry of the 18th century and the coming of the 'father of the railways', George Stephenson. Take a look round the Art Gallery as well, where the works of local artist, Joesph Syddall, are on show (Syddall lived at nearby Whittington).

Perhaps surprisingly, Chesterfield is home to one of the earliest canals in the country, the **Chesterfield Canal**. The canal was surveyed by James Brindley and linked the town to the River Trent. At the cutting edge of technology in its day, it had the longest tunnel in the country at Norwood, and one of the first multiple staircase lock flights. It was 2,884 yards long, 9 feet 3 inches wide and 12 feet high. The entire canal was officially opened in 1777.

All the working boats on the Chesterfield Canal were horse-drawn until, by 1962, virtually all the boat traffic had gone. The whole length of the canal is in the process of restoration and is open to walkers and, though some sections border onto busy roads, much of the waterway runs through quiet and secluded countryside. The Chesterfield Canal Trust runs boat trips on the canal, and one of the boats has wheelchair access.

Apart from the famous Crooked Spire and medieval market, Chesterfield is also worthy of note for its, Queen's Park, Tapton Lock – where you can go for a ride on a narrow boat, Pomegrante Theatre, the Winding Wheel and The Revolution House

142 THE LOCKOFORD INN

Tapton

Close to popular Derbyshire attractions, the Lockoford inn is in a prime location for those looking for a night's sleep or just a warm and friendly atmosphere in which to enjoy a drink.

‖ ⊨ see *page 270*

•

The most famous item carried on Chesterfield canal was stone to rebuild the Houses of Parliament in the 1840s. The stone was loaded into canal boats at Dog Kennels Bridge, carried to West Stockwith, and transferred to Trent sloops for the journey to Westminster, via the Humber, North Sea and the Thames. In October 1907 the roof of Norwood Tunnel collapsed, cutting the canal in two. Coal cargoes from Shireoaks colliery continued until the Second World War, but after that there was little boat traffic apart from brick cargoes from the kilns at Walkeringham.

•

157

Old Whittington

Warm friendly atmosphere - quality foods, ales and wines. All occasions catered for.

see page 271

(see Whittington). The fine **Queen's Park** has delighted locals and visitors alike since it was opened to celebrate Queen Victoria's Golden Jubilee, in 1893. There are gardens, a boating lake, children's play area, Victorian Bandstand and occasionally it is used for county cricket. The Pomegranate is a grade II listed Victorian 546 seated proscenium arch theatre offering a wide range of professional touring and local amateur productions. The Winding Wheel is a grade II listed building situated on the edge of the town centre; a former cinema it was restored in the late 1980s by Chesterfield Borough Council to provide a much needed multi purpose venue. The venue plays host to many of Chesterfield's popular exhibitions and shows such as, the annual fashion show put together by students from Chesterfield College. To find out more about the attractions in and around Chesterfield, The Tourist Information Centre can be found in a new building, beside the church in Rykneld Way. It moved from the old Peacock Centre, now a coffee bar, several years ago. It is open all year Monday to Saturday.

Finally, although the custom of tap-dressing took place in Chesterfield in the 19th century, it was not until 1991 that the tradition, this time of well-dressing, was revived. Initially with help from local experts from Holymoorside, the Chesterfield dressers are developing their own styles and customs.

AROUND CHESTERFIELD

SHEEPBRIDGE

3 miles N of Chesterfield off the A61

Dunstan Hall, below Newbold Moor, was built in the 17th century and extended in the 18th century. In an excellent parkland setting, the Gothic style park railings mirror the Gothic revival details that were added to the hall in 1826.

WHITTINGTON

3 miles NE of Chesterfield off the B6052/A61

The village is one to which many note, is attached, to the Glorious Revolution, which changed the face of English history. Travel back to the 17th century, James II is on the throne, but rumour and unrest mutter up and down the country. It was here, in 1688, that three local noblemen - the Earl of Devonshire, the Earl of Danby and John D'Arcy - met to plan the downfall of James II in favour of his daughter Mary and her husband, William of Orange. As planned, the North and Midlands rose in support and James fled to France. The Glorious Revolution was over.

More specifically the men met in an alehouse called the 'Cock and Pynot' ('pynot' being the local dialect word for magpie) and on the 250th anniversary of the Glorious Revolution this modest house was turned into a museum, and named **Revolution House**. The national importance of the 16th century former 'Cock & Pynot

Inn' is signified by its designation by English Heritage as a Grade I listed building. Both the 100th and the 200th anniversary of the revolution were keenly celebrated here.

Revolution House is now open to the public and features period furnishings and a changing programme of exhibitions on local themes. A video relates the story of the revolution and the role which the house played in those fraught and dangerous days.

ECKINGTON
6 miles NE of Chesterfield off the A616

This large, sprawling village built of local Derbyshire stone, lies close to the Yorkshire county border. The name Eckington is of Saxon origin, meaning the township of Ecca. Eckington was once an agricultural settlement, but as a result of coal beneath and around it was transformed into a village dependent on the collieries. Since the decline of coal mining in the late 20th century, several light industries have become established and much farmland has been lost.

The village has a fascinating church, the **Parish Church of St Peter and St Paul** dates from 1100 and still retains the original Norman doorway. In a field at the back of the church, near the river, stands the Priest's Well where the parish priest used to draw water, as did the travelling people who used the field as a camp until the 1930s.

D.H. Lawrence is said to have used the village of Eckington and Renishaw Hall as inspiration for his most famous novel *Lady Chatterley's Lover*.

The area to the west of Eckington, once known for its sickle and scythe industry, is today a sanctuary for wildlife. A two-mile circular walk, 'Old Eckington Explored', highlights the history of this delightful Derbyshire town. Other circular walks of varying length take in all aspects of the Moss Valley.

RENISHAW
6 miles NE of Chesterfield off the A616

A large industrial village, whose industry long pre-dates the Industrial Revolution, the Sitwell family founded an ironworks here in about 1640. To the east lies **Renishaw Hall and Gardens** overlooking the pleasantly situated Renishaw Park Golf Club. Renishaw Hall was for four centuries the home of the idiosyncratic Sitwells and in our own century famed for the unmatchable four-acre Italianate garden laid out by the eccentric Sir George Sitwell, and in the grounds can be found the world's most

Renishaw Hall and Gardens

159

The historic canal designed by James Brindley and built between 1771 and 1777 is now navigable from Staveley to Chesterfield. The towpath is part of a long distance footpath called the 'Cuckoo Way'. It acts as a linear nature reserve and makes an excellent walk or cycle ride.

northerly vineyard. The Sitwell family and, in particular, Dame Edith, Sir Sacheverell and Sir Osbert, have, over the years, become famous for their literary leanings - perhaps there is something in the wine that promotes success in this field.

The Hall is also said to be haunted by a number of ghosts. In particular there is the little boy in pink, known as the kissing ghost because it seems that this is just what he likes to do to any guests at the Hall. The grounds of the village rectory, a handsome late-Georgian building, are also worth a second glance. Though not laid out by the Reverend Christopher Alderson, he set about improving them in the late 18th century. A magazine of the time said that the Reverend 'was so renowned as a garden improver that he was employed at Windsor aswell'.

Renishaw village also marked the end of an era, for the traditional industries of the area, when the last colliery closed here in 1989.

STAVELEY

4 miles NE of Chesterfield off the A619

Staveley lies to the south of the great **Staveley Iron Works** and has its fair share of large 20th century housing estates. However, this is not altogether a modern village and has some fine earlier structures, including the **Parish Church of St John the Baptist**, dating originally from the 13th century. In the north aisle is a rare example of a medieval Easter Sepulchre. The

name of Frecheville is one that crops up from time to time in this part of Derbyshire, and the church has a selection of tombs and monuments to the family. As well as the tomb-chest of Peter Frecheville, dating from around 1480, there is also an early 16th century monument to Piers Frecheville. In the Frecheville Chapel is a memorial to Christina Frecheville, who died in childbirth in 1653. Another fine building in the village is **Staveley Hall**, built in 1604 and now the District Council Offices.

BARLBOROUGH

7 miles NE of Chesterfield off the A619

Lying close to the county borders with both Nottinghamshire and Yorkshire, this village still retains its manor house. Lying just north of the village centre, **Barlborough Hall** (private) was built in 1584 by Lord Justice Francis Rodes to plans drawn up by the designer of Hardwick Hall, Robert Smythson. Those who visit both houses will notice the strong resemblance. As well as building houses, Rodes was also one of the judges at the trial of Mary, Queen of Scots. The Hall is supposed to be haunted by a grey lady, said to be the ghost of a bride who received the news of her groom's death as she was on her way to the village church. Barlborough Hall should not be confused with **Barlborough Old Hall**: this is an easy mistake to make as Barlborough Old Hall is actually the younger of the two! Built in 1618, as the date stone over the front door states, the Old Hall is of a large H-plan design and has mullioned windows.

Although there is a lot of new development, particularly around Barlborough Links, the village also boasts some fine old stone houses with pantile roofs. The **Parish Church of St James** dates from the beginning of the 13th century, though it was heavily restored in 1899. Among the medieval work extant is the four-bay north arcade. The church contains the effigy of a grieving woman, said to be Lady Furnival, who died in 1395. The monument was probably brought here from Worksop, where she is buried.

The **Market Cross**, which stands in the High Street, bears testimony to the fact that this was an important place at one time - a centre of trade for the surrounding area.

CLOWNE

7½ miles NE of Chesterfield off the A616

The village derives is name from 'Clun', a Celtic river name. This small village started off as an ancient settlement but grew up around the county's coal mining industry. The **Parish Church of St John the Baptist** in Clowne is nearly a mile away from the centre and one explanation for its location is that the church stands close to an ancient ridgeway, once the site of a monastery. The church is believed to have been built in 1130, with the two side chapels not added until 1955, one of them dedicated to the memory of those lives lost

in the Creswell Colliery disaster and in other coal mines (see also Creswell). The village is now mainly residential, but retains its own identity and sense of community. It is well known locally for its dazzling Christmas lights display.

Clowne is only a few minutes away from Creswell Crags, the UK's only verified example of Palaeolithic cave art.

CRESWELL

9 miles E of Chesterfield on the A616

Once a sleepy hamlet nestling amid peaceful farming country, the character of Creswell was

Clowne Cross, Clowne

●

Creswell Colliery was also the site of a tragic mining disaster. On the night of September 26th 1950, 80 men were overcome by smoke and fumes and perished underground, with 23 bodies remaining underground for a year until it was safe to remove them.

●

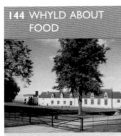

144 WHYLD ABOUT FOOD

Bolsover Castle

Situated on the grounds inside the castle, this café is the perfect place to pause and recharge after a days sightseeing.

¶ see page 272

irreversibly changed at the end of the 19th century. It was then that Creswell Colliery was opened, and now the village is one of the biggest in the county. There is also a village within a village here as, between 1896 and 1900 a model village of houses and cottages was built around an open space called Creswell Green, part of which is now known as Fox Green. The **Model Village** was built by the Bolsover and Creswell Colliery Company in 1896 to house the workforce at the Creswell Colliery, and everybody who lived on the Model worked in the coal mine. It remained as housing for miners until the mid 1980s when they were let on the open market. The houses were neglected, repairs were not done and the area became run down. Now with the help of a lottery grant, the central park has been almost restored to its original Victorian state with newly planted trees and shrubs, seating and play areas. The restored Model Village is an excellent example of Victorian social housing for working families.

Lying close to the Derbyshire-Nottinghamshire border, the limestone gorge of the **Creswell Crags** is well worth seeing. Here are caves, some of the oldest once inhabited caves in the world, certainly the furthest north that have been discovered. Used by Neanderthal man as shelters while out hunting, tours can be taken from the visitor centre, where there is also a display of artefacts found in the area. The largest cavern,

Church Hole Cave, extends some 170 feet into the side of the gorge; it was here that hand tools were found.

WHALEY

8 miles E of Chesterfield off the A632

The **Whaley Thorns Heritage Centre**, situated in a disused school, tells the story of human activity in the area from the Stone Age to the present day. In particular there are displays illustrating the history of coal mining in this region of Derbyshire and, since the decline of the industry, the efforts that have been made to restore the area to its natural state.

BOLSOVER

7 miles E of Chesterfield off the A632

The approach to Bolsover from the north and east is surrounded by some splendid dramatic scenery, and the town has a significant amount of historical importance, with the main tourist attraction being **Bolsover Castle**. A castle has stood here since the 12th century, though the present building is a fairytale 'folly' built for Sir Charles Cavendish during the early 1600s on the site of a ruined castle. By the mid-18th century much of the building had been reduced to the ruins seen today, though thankfully the splendid keep has withstood the test of time.

Pevsner remarked that not many large houses in England occupy such an impressive position as Bolsover Castle, as it stands on the brow of a hill overlooking the valley of the River Rother and Doe Lea. The first castle at Bolsover was built by William Peveril, illegitimate son of William the Conqueror, as part of his vast Derbyshire estates. Nothing remains of that Norman building. Now owned by English Heritage, visitors can explore the Little Castle, or Keep, which is decorated in an elaborate Jacobean celebration with wonderful fireplaces, panelling and wall paintings. The series of remarkable rooms includes the Vaulted Hall, the Pillar Room, the Star Chamber, the Elysium and the Heaven Room. Sir Charles' son, William, was responsible for the eastern range of buildings known as the Riding School, an impressive indoor area built in the 17th century, and the roofless but still impressive western terrace. The ruins of the state apartments are also here to be discovered. The whole building later descended to the Dukes of Portland, and it remains a strangely impressive place. However it is threatened by its industrial surroundings. The legacy of centuries of coal mining beneath its walls is subsidence. Bolsover Castle regularly hosts historic and cultural events throughout the year and the site is ideal for family picnics.

One building in Derbyshire no longer in need of restoration is Bolsover's Cundy House. It's recently been restored using money from English Heritage. Hundreds of years ago, Cundy House was built to provide water for Bolsover Castle.

Naturally, the **Parish Church of St Mary's** in Bolsover holds many monuments to the Cavendish family, but it seems amazing that the church has survived when its recent history is revealed. Dating from the 13th century, the church's monuments include two magnificent tombs to Charles Cavendish, who died in 1617, and Henry Cavendish, who died in 1727. Destroyed by fire in 1897, except for the Cavendish Chapel, St Mary's was rebuilt, only to be damaged again by fire in 1960. It has since been restored. Buried in the churchyard are John Smythson and Huntingdon Smythson, the 17th century architects probably responsible for the design of the rebuilt Bolsover Castle.

SCARCLIFFE

8 miles E of Chesterfield off the B6417

Scarcliffe, recorded as Scardeclif in the *Domesday Book*, takes its name from the escarpment of magnesium limestone on which the village stands. It was settled in Roman times evidenced by the collection of Roman coins found near the village in 1876. The skyline of this tiny village is dominated by the **Parish Church of St Leonard**. This Norman church contains a magnificent monument of a woman holding a child in her arms, which roughly dates from the 12th or 13th century, the effigy is probably that of Constantia de Frecheville, who died in 1175. Known in Scarcliffe as Lady Constantia, a bell is tolled in her memory around Christmas. During the industrial revolution, coal mining

145 BOLSOVER CASTLE

Bolsover

'By an unlikely miracle,' wrote the architectural historian Mark Girouard, 'the keep at Bolsover has survived into this century as an almost untouched expression in stone of the lost world of Elizabethan chivalry and romance.'

 see page 273

146 HORSE & GROOM

Scarcliffe

This spectacular pub is perfect for short term accommodation or the connoisseur of ales.

see page 274

was the main industry and the Lancashire, Derbyshire and East Coast Railway cut through the previously agricultural land. It included a tunnel between Scarcliffe and Bolsover. The Langwith Colliery closed in 1978 and the railway has long gone.

Poulter Country Park, created from the old colliery spoil heaps, provides scenic walks with excellent views of the surrounding countryside. Also to the east of the village are two large wooded areas, Langwith Wood and Roseland Wood.

HEATH

5 miles SE of Chesterfield off the A617

In the *Domesday Book* of 1086, two settlements are recorded around the present location of the village of Heath; they were called 'Lunt' and 'Le Hethe'. The two villages probably combined during the 12/13th century. However, relatively little change has taken place since then, maps from around 1609 show the village in almost its present layout.

There many places of interest close to Heath, to the north there are the ruins of what was one of the grandest mansions in Derbyshire, **Sutton Scarsdale Hall**. Built in 1724 for the 4th Earl of Scarsdale, to the designs of Francis Smith, the stonework of the previous Tudor manor house was completely hidden behind the Baroque splendour of the new hall. At the beginning of the 20th century Sutton Scarsdale was owned by a descendent of Sir Richard Arkwright, the famous industrialist. It is this gentleman that D.H. Lawrence is supposed to have chosen as the inspiration for his character of Sir Clifford Chatterley in the controversial novel *Lady Chatterley's Lover*. The hall is said to have many ghosts.

Stainsby Mill is also a short distance away as is Hardwick Hall. With its machinery now restored to illustrate the workings of a 19th century water-powered corn mill, Stainsby is well worth a visit. Open between March and 21st December, however the particular days vary, please check opening times. Details can be found online at www.nationaltrust.org.uk.

AULT HUCKNALL

6 miles SE of Chesterfield off the A617

Known locally as the 'smallest village in England', a claim which can't be proved, Ault Hucknall was much larger in the Middle Ages than it is today. It's most significant building is the magnificent Tudor house, **Hardwick Hall**. 'More glass than wall', it is one of Derbyshire's Big Three stately homes alongside Chatsworth and Haddon, all three glorious monuments to the great land-owning families who played so

Old Churb Ruins, Heath

great a role in shaping the history of the county. Set in rolling parkland, the house, with its glittering tiers of windows and crowned turrets, offers quite a spellbinding sight. Inside, the silence of the chambers strewn with rush matting, combined with the simplicity of the white-washed walls, gives a feeling of almost overwhelming peace. The letters E S can be seen carved in stone on the outside of the house: E S, or Elizabeth of Shrewsbury, was perhaps better known as Bess of Hardwick. This larger-than-life figure had attachments with many places in Derbyshire, and the story of her life makes fascinating reading.

She was born in the manor house at Hardwick in 1520. The house stood only a little distance from the present-day hall and was then not much more than a farmhouse. The young Bess married her neighbour's son, Robert Barlow, when she was only 12. When her young husband, himself only 14, died a few months later she naturally inherited a great deal of property. Some 15 years later she married Sir William Cavendish and, when he died in 1557, she was bequeathed his entire fortune. By this time she was the richest woman in England, save for one, Queen Elizabeth.

The Gallery at Hardwick Hall, with its gorgeous lavender-hued tapestries, has, in pride of place, a portrait of this formidable woman. It depicts a personage who could be mistaken for Queen Elizabeth, and indeed they were both forceful, independently-minded women. Bess began the building of the house in 1590, towards the end of her life and after her fourth lucrative marriage to George Talbot, sixth Earl of Shrewsbury. It stands as a monument to her wealth and good taste, and is justly famous for its magnificent needlework and tapestries, carved fireplaces and friezes, which are considered as among the finest in Britain. She died in 1608, and now lies within Derby Cathedral.

Though Bess is the first person that springs to mind with regard to Hardwick Hall, it was the 6th Duke of Devonshire who was responsible for the hall's antiquarian atmosphere. He inherited the property in 1811 and, as well as promoting the legend that Mary, Queen of Scots stayed here, he filled the house with furniture, paintings and tapestries from his other houses and from Chatsworth in particular.

As well as viewing the hall, there are some wonderful grounds to explore. To the south are the formal gardens, laid out in the 19th century and separated by long walks lined with yew. One area has been planted as a Tudor herb garden and is stocked with both culinary and medicinal plants used at that time. Down in the southeast corner of the garden is the small Elizabethan banqueting hall, used as a smoking room by the 6th Duke's orchestra, as they were not allowed to smoke in the hall itself. There is also, to the back of the

147 HARDWICK INN

Hardwick Park

Set in glorious historical surroundings, the Hardwick Inn has a well deserved reputation for fine dining and drinking, not to be missed.

see page 275

148 TELMERE LODGE

Hasland

Andy, Helen and Mary offer a warm welcome, delicious home-cooked food and a dining experience not to be forgotton.

🍴 see page 276

house, a lake and lime avenue. Owned by the National Trust, Hardwick Hall is a must for any visitor to Derbyshire and is certainly a place not to be missed. The parkland, which overlooks the valley of the Doe Lea as well as the M1, is home to an impressive herd of Longhorn cattle among the stag-headed oaks. The ruins of Hardwick Old Hall (English Heritage) also stand in the grounds, and are the remains of Bess's former Tudor mansion.

Another interesting building here is the **Parish Church of St John the Baptist**, it is Grade I listed and dates back to Saxon times. The Yew Tree in the churchyard is variously aged between 2,000 and 4,000 years old but, again, this can't be proved. Overlooking Hardwick Hall's beautiful parklands, with the square towers of Bess of Hardwick's great house in the distance, the battlemented church exterior does not prepare visitors for its dark, mysterious interior, which reveals the church's much earlier origins. Though dating originally from Saxon times, there are many Norman features, including the north arcade, nave and the narrow arches holding up the rare crossing tower. There is more Norman work in the plain capitals of the north arcade.

There are several interesting tombs in the church, such as the large and detailed wall monument just below the east window to the first Countess of Devonshire, dating from 1627. On the floor in

front is a simple black slab commemorating the influential and renowned philosopher, Thomas Hobbes - author of *The Leviathan* and *De Mirabilibus Pecci: Concerning the Wonders of the Peak* (the latter being one of the first accounts of the Seven Wonders of the Peak) - who died at Hardwick. A much simpler table in the north aisle commemorates Robert Hackett, a keeper of Hardwick Park who died n 1703. It reads: 'Long has he chas'd/The red and fallow deer/ But death's cold dart/At last has fix'd him here.'

WINSICK

2 miles S of Chesterfield off the A617

This charming hamlet is just a short drive from the centre of Chesterfield but retains a tranquil rural feel.

GRASSMOOR

3 miles S of Chesterfield on the B6038

Whilst Grassmoor is mentioned in the *Domesday Book*, as 'Grey Copse', there is little else worthy of historic note. The present village of Grassmoor owes its existence to the seams of coal upon which it stands but has since expanded and developed, now having a golf course, driving range and country park. The country park is on the site of the old Grassmoor Colliery and marks the start of a pleasant walk called the **Five Pits Trail**, a popular trail running between Grassmoor and Tibshelf, with miles of traffic free walking and cycling. Originally created in 1971, the paths have been recently re-surfaced. There are many picnic sites along the way past the sites of the old pits, along the line of some of the old railways.

WINGERWORTH

3 miles S of Chesterfield off the A61

The village was settled in Anglo-Saxon times, and is recorded in the *Domesday Book*, as a community of fourteen households. It is today an attractive residential area set amidst undulating wooded countryside providing pleasant walks. Smithy Pond is a pleasant area for visitors to relax.

The Hunlokes were the dominant family in Wingerworth from the reign of Queen Elizabeth I until 1920, acquiring nine-tenths of the land in the parish and becoming lords of the manor. The grand mansion of Wingerworth Hall, which they built in the early 18th century, was demolished in the 1920s. Olave, Lady Baden-Powell, first Chief Guide, was born here in 1889.

Standing at one of the highest points of the village is the **Parish Church of all Saints**, although it retains some Norman and 13th century work, it has had many additions over the centuries. A tower was added around 1500 and a substantial extension in 1963.

PILSLEY

5 miles S of Chesterfield off the B6014

As mentioned earlier in Chapter

Two, there are two Pilsleys in Derbyshire, this one in North East Derbyshire and the other near the Chatsworth Estate Village. This Pilsley is actually comprised of two smaller villages, Lower Pilsley and (Upper) Pilsley, but most locals class the two as just one, fairly large village. Mary Queen of Scots whilst in captivity in Derbyshire is said to have enjoyed riding through the leafy lanes of the village.

The Herb Garden in Pilsley, featured on the BBC TV programme *Country Gardens*, is one of the foremost herb gardens in the country. Consisting of four display gardens, the largest is the Mixed Herb Garden, boasting an impressive established parterre. The remaining three gardens are the Physic, the Lavender and the Pot Pourri, each with its own special theme and housing many rare and unusual species. Areas of native flowers and wild spring bulbs can be enjoyed from March to September. On the grounds there is also a lovely tea room serving such delicacies as lavender cake, rosemary fruit slice and cheese and herb scones.

TIBSHELF

6 miles S of Chesterfield on the B6014

Stretching from here north, to Grassmoor, the **Five Pits Trail** follows an undulating off-road route between former coal mines, at Tibshelf, Pilsley, Alameda, Williamthorpe and Grassmoor, transformed into peaceful lakes and parks. Suitable for walkers, cyclists and horse riders, the trail is lovely,

151 KING EDWARD VII

Tibshelf

Why pay hotel prices when you can enjoy the hospitality of a traditional British Pub at better rates?

see page 279

152 BATEMAN'S MILL COUNTRY HOTEL AND RESTAURANT

Old Tupton, nr Chesterfield

Here you can enjoy excellent food and quality accommodation in friendly, informal surroundings.

see page 280

and offers some splendid views. The **Tibshelf Ponds picnic site**, a popular place with locals and fishermen, is a picturesque mix of wooded glades, meadows and ponds where Tibshelf Colliery stood. And also provides several opportunities for short walks.

The village stretches for about a mile along a main street that was once part of the Mansfield-Matlock turnpike road. There are fine views all round. Westwards you look across to the hills around Ashover with Crich Stand on the horizon. Eastwards, to what is left of Sherwood Forest and a couple miles northwards, Hardwick Hall sits grandly on its own hilltop. Within the village, the **Parish Church of St John the Baptist** has been extensively restored over the centuries but it still retains an impressive 14th century tower.

CLAY CROSS

5 miles S of Chesterfield off the A61

At the beginning of the 19th century Clay Cross was mainly a rural area, but George Stephenson the railway pioneer changed that. During the building of the North Midlands Railway between Derby and Chesterfield, he found massive deposits of coal and iron ore that persuaded Stephenson to stay in North East Derbyshire and launch the Clay Cross Company in 1840. Subsequently, the hamlet grew from a small farming community into an industrial town dominated by the Clay Cross Company. The Company also provided schools, churches and housing. An

impressive monument consisting of two large wheels with the inscription "In memory of all North East Derbyshire miners who lost their lives working to keep the home fires burning and the wheels of industry turning", takes pride of place in the High Street.

The **Parish Church of St Bartholomew** dates from 1851, though it looks much older. The land on which it stands was gifted to the church by George Stephenson and Company.

The **Clay Cross Countryside Centre** is one of three bases for the Countryside Service working throughout the north east of the county. Regular exhibitions are held and there is a shop stocking many free leaflets, local maps, guides, gifts, educational toys and a variety of books including walking, cycling, local and natural history. The Five Pits Trail is managed from Clay Cross Countryside Centre. The Trail is all that remains of an old mineral railway. To discover more about Clay Cross you can follow the Heritage Trail on a one-hour walk around the area's industrial heritage.

In 1972 the town earned the title "the Republic of Clay Cross", when left wing councillors, including David and Graham Skinner, both related to Dennis Skinner, MP for Bolsover, would not implement the terms of the Tory Housing Finance Act. The Clay Cross Rebels, as they became known, refused to put up council house rents by £1 a week. After a bitter dispute with the

Government, which divided the community, they were surcharged, bankrupted and disqualified from office.

STRETTON

6 miles S of Chesterfield on the A61

First mentioned in 1002, Stretton is situated on the old Roman road known as Ryknield Street. Stretton village lies close to **Ogston Reservoir**, which covers an area of over 200 acres and is a favourite place for sailing. An old railway line lies at the bottom of the reservoir, as well as a pub that were lost in 1964. The man-made lake is overlooked by the romantic **Ogston Hall**, which dates from the 16th century and was the ancestral home of the Turbutt and Revell families. The house was altered extensively in 1768, and then modernised and 'medievalised' during Victorian times.

BRACKENFIELD

7 miles S of Chesterfield off the A615

This village was known as Brackenthwaite in the Middle Ages, a name that means 'clearing in the bracken'. Like Clay Cross, Brackenfield is known today primarily for its proximity to the Ogston Reservoir, created in 1960 by damming the River Amber at the south end of the valley. The site of the former Ogston Mill was submerged under the rising waters.

Hidden in the surrounding trees is the ruin of the former **Trinity Chapel**, built around 1500. A pilgrimage from the village to this chapel is still held on Trinity Sunday to commemorate its historic place in the community. This church was abandoned when the new **Parish Church of the Holy Trinity** was built in 1856. It contains the 15th century screen from the ruined church.

ASHOVER

6 miles SW of Chesterfield off the B6036

Ashover contains plenty of historical connections, including the site of a Druid temple on one of the surrounding hills. There is plenty of evidence of its past heritage of local industries, which include lead mining and nail making amongst many others. For visitors who chance to be this way Ashover's splendid **Parish Church of All Saints** dating in parts from the 13th century is worth a visit.

Viewed from the southern rocky ridge known as **The Fabric**

153 THE CROWN INN

Old Higham

Serving quality food and drink and providing quality accommodation, the Crown Inn caters for all customers.

🍴 🛏 see page 281

Snow Scene, Ashover

169

Ashover is said to be home to a couple of ghosts - the Laughing Cavalier who haunts the Black Swan pub and the Headless Woman who roams the Churchyard. Ashover also hosts a vintage car rally and auto jumble in July.

(apparently because it provided the fabric for much of the local building stone) and with the monolith of **Cocking Tor** in the foreground, Ashover can be seen as a scattered village filling the pleasantly wooded valley of the River Amber. The name of this village means 'ash tree slope' and though there are, indeed, many ash trees in the area, other varieties, including oak and birch, also flourish. Ashover was a flourishing industrial town in the past. As well as lead mining, which dated back to Roman times, there was nail making, lace, ropes, stocking weaving and malting. The ropes were said to be the longest and strongest in the country.

One part of the village is called the Rattle because of the sound of the looms rattling in the making of stockings. The industries, with the exception of quarrying and fluorspar have all died out and the work is now chiefly farming. Ashover lies just outside the boundary of the Peak District National Park but it still captures the typical character of a Peak village. At the heart of the largest parish in northeast Derbyshire, the village is chiefly constructed from limestone and gritstone, which were both quarried locally. The ruined shell of **Eastwood Hall**, once a large fortified Elizabethan manor house, also lies in the village. Owned, over the years, by several prominent Derbyshire families, including the Willoughbys, the house was blown up by the

Roundheads during the Civil War.

The **Parish Church of All Saints**, with its 15th century tower, is a prominent landmark in the valley. It houses the alabaster tomb of Thomas Babington and his wife, said by many to be the best in Derbyshire. There are also some handsome brasses. What is surprising is the lead-lined Norman font, described by Pevsner as 'the most important Norman font in the country'. It is the only lead-lined font in an area that is so well known for its mining. The Crispin Inn, next to the church, claims to date from the time of Agincourt, 1415. However, it is far more likely that, like many other buildings in the parish, it dates from the 17th century. The inn's name reflects one of Ashover's traditional trades: St Crispin is the patron saint of shoemakers and cobblers.

HOLYMOORSIDE

3 miles SW of Chesterfield off the A619

Holymoorside was once a thriving industrial centre, with three cotton thread mills dominating the village. Nothing remains now except The Dam and the mill pond, which is now a popular recreation spot. Surrounded by the attractive moorland of Beeley Moor and Eastmoor, and lying in the picturesque valley of the River Hipper, this scattered village has now become a much-sought-after place to live in the 21st century.

Hipper Hall, an early 17th century farmhouse with an even older tithe barn, is probably the oldest building in the village. It contains later additions and has some interesting internal features including an oak partition.

The **Stone Edge Cupola**, in a remote spot beside the B5057, is Britain's oldest free-standing chimney. Dating from 1770, it is a testimony to the lead mining industry that survived here until the 19th century.

OLD BRAMPTON

3½ miles W of Chesterfield off the A619

Situated on a quiet road above a wooded valley, Old Brampton is well know locally for its most unusual church clock that actually has sixty three minutes in the hour! Just over the road from the Norman church is the George and Dragon pub, where the painter of the clock might have spent too long since he painted only four minutes between twelve and one, then six minutes between one and two. The mainly 13th century **Parish Church of Saints Peter and Paul** is also of interest for its battlemented walls, short octagonal spire and Norman doorway and window. Opposite the Norman church is **Brampton Hall**, a 12th century building of immense historical interest with cruck oak beams reputed to have come from the earlier village. Also worthy of note is the large cruck barn, probably the largest in Derbyshire, to be found at **Frith Hall Farmhouse**.

CUTTHORPE

4 miles W of Chesterfield off the B6050

Cutthorpe does not have its own parish church, it forms part of the parish of Old Brampton, but the village does have two historic halls. These include: The Old Manor House, 1625, once the property of the Sitwell family, and Cutthorpe Hall, 1675, a former residence of the Heathcote family.

The land of Walter de Linacre is listed in the *Domesday Book*. Linacre Hall was situated at Cutthorpe on land which now contains the three **Linacre Reservoirs**. Built between 1855 and 1904, until recently they supplied water to Chesterfield. Today the area is home to many species of fish, waterfowl, mammals and plant life, and is considered one of the most important ecological sites in the area. There are very pleasant walks, nature trails and fishing, and a scenic picnic area.

Before the Second World War the well-dressings in this village, which take place on the third Friday in July, had no religious links. After the war the custom died out, but was revived again by three people from nearby Barlow, in 1978. The three dressed wells are blessed during a service of thanksgiving for the pure water.

BARLOW

3 miles NW of Chesterfield on the B6051

Over a century ago, there were at least 14 coal mines and as many open cast sites in and around Barlow. Now the mining industry has gone completely, though it helped, over the years, to shape the village. It is mentioned in the

The custom of well-dressing in the village of Holymoorside was revived in 1979 after a gap of about 80 years. Two wells are dressed, a large one and a smaller one for children, on the Wednesday before the late summer Bank Holiday in August. The dressers follow the tradition of Barlow, where only flowers and leaves are used and not wool, seed and shells, though they do not stick to biblical themes. In 1990 the well-dressing depicted a scene commemorating the 50th anniversary of the Battle of Britain, one of their most spectacular dressings to date which resulted in photographs in the national press.

For those interested in Norman churches, the Parish Church of St Lawrence in Barlow will prove fascinating. It may appear to be Victorian, but this was the work of enthusiastic remodelling in the 1860s. The interior reveals the true Norman features - the doorways leading from the nave and the short chancel - and there is also a fine alabaster slab in memory of Robert Barley, who died in 1467, and his wife. (The village was originally known as Barley, and the family took their name from it, later changing it to Barlow.)

154 THE MINERS ARMS

Dronfield Woodhouse

The pubs family friendly atmosphere has created the perfect environment in which everyone can come and enjoy a fabulous traditional meal.

🍴 see page 282

Domesday Book, and was the home of Robert Barlow, the first of Bess of Hardwick's four husbands. Although situated outside the limestone area, Barlow has been dressing its main well for longer than most. It is not known for certain when the custom began in the village, though it is known that, like Tissington, the well here provided water throughout the drought of 1615, this may have marked the start of this colourful practice.

Another theory suggests that the tradition in Barlow could date back to the days of Elizabeth I's reign, as the church register of 1572 states that the festival of St Lawrence was celebrated. Whatever the origins of the well-dressings in the village, it is known that they have continued, unbroken even through two World Wars, throughout living memory. The wells are dressed during the second week of August every year.

HOLMESFIELD

4 miles NW of Chesterfield off the B6054

An ancient manor with the **Parish Church of St Swithin** standing on the highest point of the village, overlooking fine moorland scenery with spectacular views both north and south. Well-dressings are held in July.

DRONFIELD

5 miles NW of Chesterfield off the A61

Possessing an interesting blend of old and new buildings within a town centre Conservation Area, Dronfield hosts a bustling weekly market that has since developed industrially. The prosperity of Dronfield in the early years of the Industrial Revolution was such that an unexpectedly large number of mansions were built in and around the town, leaving a legacy of many beautiful 17th and 18th century listed buildings. **Chiverton House**, built in 1712, and **Rose Hill**, dating from 1719, are fine examples.

In the town centre, in front of the early 18th century **Manor House** (now the home of the town library), the **Peel Monument**, dating from 1854, stands on the site of the former town cross and stocks, as a tribute to Sir Robert Peel's efforts in repealing the Corn Law in 1846. **The Cottage**, close to the monument, dates from the 16th century, and is reputed to have been owned by Lord Byron, though he never visited it. The **Parish Church of St John the Baptist** has a fine perpendicular tower, though much of it is 14th century. South of the church is a fine **Cruck Barn. The Hall** is also worthy of a second glance as it has an attractive balustrade and a fine Queen Anne façade.

Accommodation, Food & Drink and Places of Interest

The establishments featured in this section includes hotels, inns, guest houses, bed & breakfasts, restaurants, cafes, tea and coffee shops, tourist attractions and places to visit. Each establishment has an entry number which can be used to identify its location at the beginning of the relevant chapter or its position in this section.

In addition full details of all these establishments and many others can be found on the Travel Publishing website - www.travelpublishing.co.uk. This website has a comprehensive database covering the whole of Britain and Ireland.

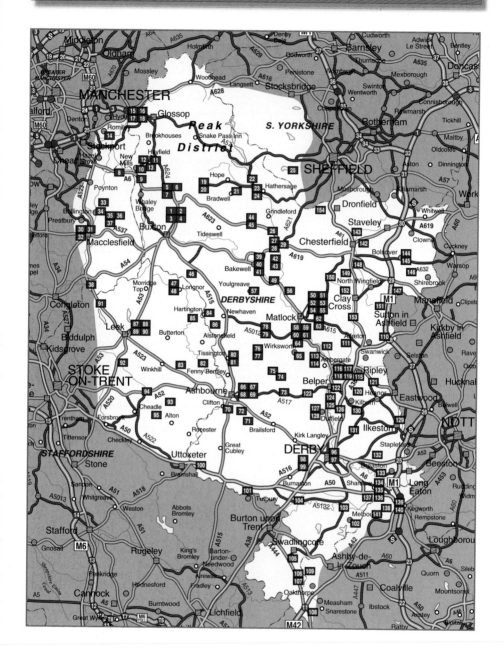

⊟ ACCOMMODATION

6	The Roebuck Inn, Chapel-en-le-Frith
10	The Torrs, New Mills
11	The Royal Hotel, Hayfield, High Peak
12	The Printers Arms, Thornsett
13	Sycamore Inn, Birch Vale, High Peak
17	The Star Inn, Glossop
19	Causeway House, Castleton
21	Bowling Green Inn, Bradwell
22	Ladybower Inn, Bamford, Hope Valley
24	The Little John Inn, Hathersage
28	Rutland Arms, Baslow
29	Devonshire Arms Hotel, Nether End
35	The Robin Hood, Rainow
37	Common Barn Farm, Rainow
40	The Manners Hotel, Bakewell
43	Ball Cross Farm Cottages, Chatsworth Estate, nr Bakewell
44	The Miners Arms, Eyam, Hope Valley
46	Bull I' th' Thorn, Hurdlow, nr Buxton
47	The Black Grouse, Longnor, nr Buxton
48	Ye Olde Cheshire Inn, Longnor
51	Glendon Guest House, Matlock
54	The Duke of Wellington Residential Country Inn, Matlock
57	The Bulls Head, Youlgreave
66	White Hart Hotel, Ashbourne
69	Ye Olde Vaults, Ashbourne
71	Saracens Head, Shirley, nr Ashbourne
73	The Black Horse Inn, Hulland Ward
74	The Barley Mow Inn, Kirk Ireton
76	The Miners Arms, Brassington
78	Middlehills Farm, Grangemill
79	The Hollybush Inn, Grangemill
85	Manifold Inn, Hartington, nr Buxton
86	Biggin Hall Hotel, Biggin-by-Hartington
87	The Swan, Leek
94	The Railway Inn, Froghall
95	Crowtrees Farm B&B, Oakamoor
100	Cavendish Arms, Doveridge
101	The Castle Hotel, Hatton
103	Ivy House Farm, Stanton-by-Bridge
106	Overseale House, Overseal
107	Robin Hood Inn, Overseal
113	The Bear Inn, Alderwasley, nr Belper
124	The Strutt Arms Hotel, Milford
125	King William IV, Milford
126	Spotted Cow, Holbrook
128	The Kings Head Inn, Duffield
140	The Anchor Inn, Kegworth
141	Donington Park Farmhouse, Isley Walton
142	The Lockoford Inn, Tapton
146	Horse & Groom, Scarcliffe
151	King Edward VII, Tibshelf
152	Batemans Mill Country Hotel & Restaurant, Old Tupton
153	The Crown Inn, Old Higham

❚ FOOD & DRINK

1	Eagle Public House & Restaurant, Buxton
2	Cafe @ The Green Pavilion, Buxton
3	The Old Sun Inn, Buxton
5	In a Pickle, Chapel-en-le-Frith
6	The Roebuck Inn, Chapel-en-le-Frith
8	Dandy Cock Inn, Disley, nr Stockport
9	The Crossings, Furness Vale,
10	The Torrs, New Mills
11	The Royal Hotel, Hayfield, High Peak
12	The Printers Arms, Thornsett

13	Sycamore Inn, Birch Vale, High Peak
14	Duke of York, Romiley, nr Stockport
16	Hare & Hounds, Simmondley Village
17	The Star Inn, Glossop
18	The Beehive & Hague Bistro, Glossop
21	Bowling Green Inn, Bradwell
22	Ladybower Inn, Bamford, Hope Valley
23	Pool Cafe, Hathersage, Hope Valley
24	The Little John Inn, Hathersage
25	The Three Merry Lads, Lodge Moor
26	The Eating House, Calver Bridge
28	Rutland Arms, Baslow
29	Devonshire Arms Hotel, Nether End
30	The Jolly Sailor, Macclesfield
31	Dolphin Inn, Macclesfield
32	Puss in Boots, Macclesfield
33	Coffee Tavern, Pott Shrigley
34	The Holly Bush, Bollington
35	The Robin Hood, Rainow
36	Rising Sun Inn, Rainow
38	Boars Leigh Restaurant, Bosley
39	The Bean & Bag, Bakewell
40	The Manners Hotel, Bakewell
44	The Miners Arms, Eyam, Hope Valley
46	Bull I' th' Thorn, Hurdlow, nr Buxton
47	The Black Grouse, Longnor, nr Buxton
48	Ye Olde Cheshire Inn, Longnor
50	Stones Restaurant, Matlock
52	The Horseshoe, Matlock
53	The Sycamore Inn, Matlock
54	The Duke of Wellington Residential Country Inn, Matlock
55	Tawney's Coffee Shop, Matlock
56	Tall Trees Coffee Shop, Two Dales
57	The Bulls Head, Youlgreave
58	The Princess Victoria, Matlock Bath
59	Riverside Tea Rooms, Matlock Bath
60	Heights of Abraham, Matlock Bath
61	The Peak District Mining Museum, Matlock Bath
62	Scotland Nurseries Garden Centre, Tansley, nr Matlock
63	The Gate, Tansley, nr Matlock
64	Old Bakery Coffee Shop, Cromford
66	White Hart Hotel, Ashbourne
67	Gallery Cafe, Ashbourne
68	Bowling Green Inn, Ashbourne
69	Ye Olde Vaults, Ashbourne
70	Cock Inn, Clifton, nr Ashbourne
71	Saracens Head, Shirley, nr Ashbourne
72	Shoulder of Mutton, Osmaston
73	The Black Horse Inn, Hulland Ward
74	The Barley Mow Inn, Kirk Ireton
75	Main Sail Restaurant, Carsington Water
76	The Miners Arms, Brassington
77	Ye Olde Gate Inn, Brassington
79	The Hollybush Inn, Grangemill
80	Bluebell Inn & Restaurant, Tissington
83	Red Lion Inn, Waterfall
84	Beresford Tea Rooms, Hartington
85	Manifold Inn, Hartington, nr Buxton
86	Biggin Hall Hotel, Biggin-by-Hartington
87	The Swan, Leek
88	The Dyers Arms, Leek
89	Blueberrys, Leek
90	Den Engel Belgian Bar, Leek
91	The Knot Inn, Rushton Spencer
92	Castro's Restaurant , Cheddleton
93	Ye Olde Star Inn, Cotton
94	The Railway Inn, Froghall
98	The Honeycomb, Mickleover
99	The Great Northern, Mickleover
100	Cavendish Arms, Doveridge
101	The Castle Hotel, Hatton
102	Bay Tree Restaurant, Melbourne

104	Rising Sun, Willington
105	Traveller's Rest, Church Gresley
107	Robin Hood Inn, Overseal
108	The Black Horse, Appleby Magna
109	Moira Tea Room, Moira
110	Devonshire Arms, South Normanton
111	Old Yew Tree Inn, South Wingfield
113	The Bear Inn, Alderwasley, nr Belper
114	The Greyhound Hotel, Alderwasley
115	Brocks Café & Bistro, Ripley
116	Black Boy Inn, Heage
117	The White Hart Inn, Heage
118	Eagle Tavern, Heage
119	Spanker Inn, Nether Heage, nr Belper
121	The Poet & Castle, Codnor, nr Ripley
122	The Thorn Tree Inn, Belper
123	The Railway, Cowers Lane, nr Belper
124	The Strutt Arms Hotel, Milford
125	King William IV, Milford
126	Spotted Cow, Holbrook
127	The Pattenmakers Arms, Duffield
128	The Kings Head Inn, Duffield
129	Finn M'Couls, Ilkeston
130	The Sitwell Arms, Horsley Woodhouse
131	Three Horseshoes, Morley
132	Royal Oak, Ockbrook, nr Derby
133	The Olympic Hotel, Draycott
134	The New Inn, Shardlow
135	The Old Marina Bar, Shardlow
136	Shakespeare Inn, Shardlow
137	Malt Shovel Inn, Aston-on-Trent
138	The Cross Keys, Castle Donnington
139	Ye Olde Flying Horse, Kegworth
140	The Anchor Inn, Kegworth
142	The Lockoford Inn, Tapton
143	Cock & Magpie, Old Whittington
144	Whyld About Food, Bolsover
146	Horse & Groom, Scarcliffe
147	Hardwick Inn, Hardwick Park
148	Telmere Lodge, Hasland
149	Hunloke Arms, Wingerworth
150	Three Horseshoes, Spitewinter
151	King Edward VII, Tibshelf
152	Batemans Mill Country Hotel & Restaurant, Old Tupton
153	The Crown Inn, Old Higham
154	Miners Arms, Dronfield Woodhouse

🏛 PLACES OF INTEREST

4	Buxton Museum and Art Gallery, Buxton
7	Chestnut Centre, Chapel-en-le-Frith
15	Glossop Heritage Centre, Glossop
20	Treak Cliff Cavern, Castleton,
27	Avant Garde of Baslow, Baslow
41	Haddon Hall, Bakewell
42	Chatsworth House, Edensor
45	Eyam Museum, Eyam, Hope Valley
49	The Wind in the Willows Attraction, Rowsley
62	Scotland Nurseries Garden Centre, Tansley, nr Matlock
65	National Stone Centre, Wirksworth
81	Tissington Hall and Gardens, Tissington, nr Ashbourne
82	The South Peak Estate, Ilam
96	Pickford's House Museum, Derby
97	Derby Museums and Art Gallery, Derby
112	Crich Tramway Village, Crich
120	Denby Visitor Centre, Denby
145	Bolsover Castle, Bolsover

EAGLE PUBLIC HOUSE AND RESTAURANT

10 Eagle Parade, Market Place, Buxton,
Derbyshire SK17 6EQ
Tel: 01298 73505 Fax: 01298 24115

As you'd expect, a historical town like Buxton is not without a wide selection of pubs, many of which also provide meals. Real ales, lagers and a good selection of wines can also be drunk amidst Victorian spleandour throughout the town. But, for all of the above plus a warm welcome and the greatest entertainment…there is only one place to go – **The Eagle Public House and Restaurant**.

The Eagle Public House & Restaurant, once an overnight stopping off point included in your fayre when travelling the London to Glasgow stagecoach is now the central venue for live music. Club Acoustic Sessions - mainly folk and folk rock - are held here every Wednesday. Public-i's Thursday Eagle provide the masses with live bands offering tributes, originals and cutting edge music from around the North and Midlands every Thursday.

But it isn't just music here. For the past three years, on the last Thursday of each month, a literacy club has met here. 'Telling Tales' provides a creative venue for writers, through poetry readings, open-mike events and story telling the club has proven itself an invaluable forum for the writing community and an asset to Buxton.

Experience licensee's Craig and Sharon have lived in Buxton for 16years now and have spent the last four as tenants, so there's not much they don't know about running a quality licensed premises or about this popular area.

Open all day every day for ale, there are two real ales to choose from, Hydes Original is a permanent fixture plus a rotating guest ale. The food here is of an excellent standard for your typical pub grub. Choose from a printed menu which features classics like succulent 8oz gammon

steak served with a fried egg on top & chips, sausage & mash and the gastronomically intimidating "Colossal Breakfast' – not for the faint hearted! Or for a smaller appetite they offer all the main meals at a reduced size and price, there are also baguettes, sandwiches and baked potatoes, all with a range of fillings to choose from. Food times are 11.30am – 2.30pm Monday through to Saturday, and 12noon – 3pm on Sunday – when you can also enjoy a traditional Sunday roast dinner. Although to avoid disappointment it's a good idea to book on Sundays.

2 CAFÉ @ THE GREEN PAVILION

4 Terrace Road, Buxton,
Derbyshire SK17 6AW
Tel: 01298 77480

Situated right in the heart of Buxton, the **Café @ The Green Pavilion**, with its modern, stylish and vibrant menu plus its relaxed atmosphere have made it a popular spot for lunches, snacks, teas and speciality coffee. It is open seven days a week from 8am to 5pm (4pm in winter months) throughout the year for anything from black pudding with Derbyshire Oatcakes to lamb curry, Spanish tortilla, frittatas and salads. Socialise with friends over breakfast or take a break from the rigours of the working day with a coffee or light meal such as New York Style Meatballs or Homity Pie.

Enjoy watching Buxton life pass you by while sitting at the café's outdoor tables when the weather is fine. All food, including the meals, snacks and baking, is home made from local ingredients, ensuring freshness and flavour. Sweet tooth indulgence is incredibly popular at The Café @ Green Pavilion, with sumptuous homemade cakes and delicious Italian Illy Coffee. The staff are very accommodating and friendly and will prepare food to conform to your dietary requirements, you could opt for a sandwich, made with local produce and prepared as you wait.

3 THE OLD SUN INN

33 High Street, Buxton,
Derbyshire SK17 6HA
Tel: 01298 23452

The warmth and character of the traditional English pub is epitomised at the **Old Sun Inn,** which stands close to Buxton's market place. It dates back some 400 years, and the promise of the whitewashed outer walls and window boxes is amply fulfilled within. Open fires, cosy corners, bare boards or slate floors, stripped wood screens and period pictures make a perfect setting for a drink and meeting the regulars.

The bar offers an impressive choice of cask ales, with two from Marston's Brewery - Bitter and Pedigree. and up to 4 other brews. The inn, which since 2000 has been run by Rachel Cresswell, is not only a fine place for a drink, it also serves an enticing range of great-value dishes prepared and cooked on the premises. The printed menu

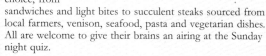

and specials board provide abundant choice, from

sandwiches and light bites to succulent steaks sourced from local farmers, venison, seafood, pasta and vegetarian dishes. All are welcome to give their brains an airing at the Sunday night quiz.

There's lots of local history in the pictures on the walls of the inn, and plenty more out and about in the town, the highest market town in Britain and the largest community in the Peak District National Park.

177

4 BUXTON MUSEUM AND ART GALLERY

Terrace Road, Buxton,
Derbyshire SK17 6DA
Tel: 01298 24658 Fax: 01298 79394
e-mail: buxton.museum@derbyshire.gov.uk
website: www.derbyshire.gov.uk

Explore the Wonders of the Peak through seven time zones. Discover when sharks swam in warm 'Derbyshire' seas; when lions and sabre tooth cats terrorised mastodons. Meet the Roman Legionaries, and the scientists unravelling the history of Earth. An audio tour, 'Time Moves On', helps to enhance your visit. For art lovers, enjoy intricate Ashford Black Marble inlay and Blue John ornaments, and a regular programme of exhibitions, featuring work by national and local artists, photographers and craftworkers. Activities for all the family accompany the exhibitions.

5 IN A PICKLE

31 Market St, Chapel-en-le-Frith,
High Peak, Derbyshire SK23 0HP
Tel: 01298 816555

Are you 'in a pickle' over your lunch routine? Sick of the same old offerings? **'In A Pickle'** is the new buzz word in Chapel-en-le-frith, opened in April 2008 by Mother and Daughter team, Dorothy and Sara, it provides a fresh new alternative. Sandwiches are custom-made to order with a great range of fillings. Almost all of the

delightful cakes are homemade. Favourites include the quiche and full English breakfast.

6 THE ROEBUCK INN

9 Market Place, Chapel-en-le-Frith,
Derbyshire SK23 0EN
Tel: 01298 812274
e-mail: info@roebuck-inn.co.uk
website: www.roebuck-inn.co.uk

The Roebuck Inn welcomes you for great company, an exceptional menu, wonderful accommodation and an incredible location. Situated 1, 100 feet above sea level in the heart of the Peak District with far reaching views towards Buxton spa town, The Roebuck Inn is well known for the warm and genuine welcome extended to locals and travellers alike. Recently refurbished to high standards, the inn still maintains its original 17th century character, open fires and original features. Open every day from 10am for morning coffee and breakfast. With a traditional menu of country delights, available Monday – Saturday 11.30am – 8pm, and Sunday 11.30am – 6pm, you will be spoilt for choice. They take the freshest local ingredients and create mouth-watering dishes for every appetite, including half-portions for children. Sunday Roasts are very popular here too, offering a choice of succulent meats with homemade 'Yorkies'

and real gravy for that good-old-fashioned flavour.

Angie Thomas (tenant) provides the perfect place for food and drink during a visit or to base yourself for a holiday; particularly if you are a walker, cyclist, horse rider, all of which are well catered for in this beautiful area of the Peak District. The B&B accommodation is exceptional. All 5 rooms are en-suite and have crisp white linen, Egyptian cotton towels, colour TV's, tea/coffee making facilities and bathroom condiments. The tariff also includes a hearty breakfast to ensure a pleasant stay.

7 THE CHESTNUT CENTRE

Castleton Road, Chapel-En-Le-Frith,
High Peak, Derbyshire SK23 0QS
Tel: 01298 814099

Set in 50 acres of stunning, unspoilt conservation park-land, **The Chestnut Centre** houses Europe's largest collection of otters and owls, a beautiful herd of fallow and seika deer, foxes, Scottish wildcats, pine marten and many many more. Through wildlife conservation the Centre makes a difference, taking care of and protecting over 70 individual animals from 30 species around the world, many endangered.

A fantastic day out for all the family, with enclosures situated on an extensive circular nature trail, meandering through historic woods and meadowland surrounding Ford Hall. Experience the close exciting proximity of this world and take time out to enjoy the animals in a very natural setting.

8 DANDY COCK INN

15 Market St, Disley, Stockport,
Cheshire SK12 2DT
Tel: 01663 763712

Nestling in the foothills of the Peak District, yet only a 15-minute drive from Stockport, the village of Disley combines rural charm with eminent commutability. It's most famed for Lyme Park, comprising thousands of acres of moorland plus Lyme Hall, where the BBC filmed Pride and Prejudice 10 years ago. It really is fabulous walking country around here, and it's also a lovely spot to stop for lunch or dinner. Food tends to be of the hearty rather than haute cuisine variety, though.

And if you don't mind a very traditional pub atmosphere the **Dandy Cock Inn** just might do it for the tastebuds. This venue is well known for its excellent hospitality, well kept ales and it has, as you'd expect, lots

of great stodgy foodstuffs like chilli, curry, gammon and chips with

plenty on your plate. Food is served 12-2pm Monday-Saturday and 12-4pm Sundays. But, more interestingly, you can try one of their real ales, Unicorn Bitter, Hatters Mild and seasonally brewed ale from Robinsons Brewery. The Dandy Cock Inn is one of several public houses that existed in the 19th century; it's a friendly bar in the centre of town with regular entertainment.

179

Station Road, Furness Vale, High Peak,
Derbyshire SK23 7QS
Tel: 01663 743642
e-mail: peter@thecrossingspub.com
website: www.thecrossingspub.com
blog: www.thecrossingspub.blogspot.com

You've probably heard a pint of Guinness referred to as a liquid meal. Maybe you've downed one yourself and called it dinner. But without a doubt, there are times when you'd like to drink a beer and eat an actual meal. At times like those, head to the **Crossings** in Furness Vale, for that perfect combination.

The Crossings is a warm, cosy village local, run with the community at its heart where you can enjoy the finest cask conditioned ales from Robinsons Brewery as well as a selection of keg beers, lager and cider, and also the finest wines from Spain.

The food is good, honest pub grub fodder! A highlight is the venerable dish, bangers and mash – splendid sausages with mash and onion gravy. On Friday and Saturday, you can enjoy freshly baked "Archers of Marple" pies, a local favourite. All food is locally sourced and it doesn't get more domestic than this - meat comes from Bryans Family butchers in New Mills with vegetables supplied by Darren on the Market Places again in New Mills. Food can be enjoyed within the bar area or al-fresco since there is a secluded courtyard beer garden with a contemporary design which is a sun trap on the odd sunny day!

Tenants David and Peter, have created a real hub for the community, they even host a Blog page on-line keeping you up-to-date with all the Crossing's/village gossip! It's a great testament to community spirit and neighbourliness – you couldn't find a friendlier place.

In the way of entertainment - all major sporting events are screened on LCD flat panel TV's including those on SKY, SKY HD and Setanta. There is a pool table and darts board and on Wednesday evening David and Peter hold a Fun Quiz with free sandwiches.

You can also surf the net via their free Wi-Fi access simply ask for the access code.

34 Market Street, New Mills,
Derbyshire SK22 4AE
Tel: 01663 744244

A quite outstanding inn located in the heart of the High Peak, **The Torrs** has been known in its time as The Crown and The Bee's Knees, but took on its new name at the time it was completely refurbished in 2001. The sensitive and tasteful conversion then has helped the inn become a popular and welcome retreat where you can enjoy great food, drink and accommodation, all year round. Leaseholders Lesley and Matthew took over here in December 2007 and have made the place come to life, it's a popular haunt for locals and visitors alike.

Dating back to 1884, the inn's refurbishment left intact lovely original features such as the wood-panelled walls, open fire and warm ambience. It is cosy and comfortable, and the friendly staff offer a high standard of service.

Open all day every day, the bar stocks a good selection of keg draught bitters, two real ales (Olde Specklend Hen and Greene King), lager, cider, stout, wines, spirits and soft drinks –something to quench every thirst. Food is served from breakfast at 9am until 3pm. Guests choose off the printed menu from a selection of traditional favourites. Spoil yourself and find calorific comfort in bacon, sausage, beans, tomato, egg, mushrooms and toast that make up a good old English fry up! At lunchtimes you can enjoy sandwiches/ jacket potatoes with a choice of fillings, soups or salads.

This fine inn also offers bed & breakfast accommodation and, having only three bedrooms, gives you the feeling you are staying with friends.

The inn makes an ideal base from which to explore the many sights and attractions of the region, which include Buxton, many picturesque villages and some great walking. Many, who have only driven through New Mills before, will not be prepared for the dramatic start and finish to the New Mills inspiring walk..

181

11 THE ROYAL HOTEL

Market Street, Hayfield, High Peak,
Derbyshire SK22 2EP
Tel: 01663 742721
e-mail: enquiries@theroyalhayfield.co.uk
website: www.theroyalhayfield.co.uk

Renowned for its character and comfort, **The Royal Hotel** dates from 1755 and has been brought up to date without losing its original charm. Located in Hayfield at the Gateway to Kinder in the High Peak, the Royal is ideally situated for walking trips on Kinder Scout or sightseeing some of the loveliest stately homes in the country. Hayfield is one of the oldest villages in the High Peak and has retained much of its old fashioned character. Within the mellow Derbyshire walls of this listed building, lies the perfect balance of traditional allure and comfort with all the modern amenities demanded by today's visitor.

All rooms are well appointed and fully equipped with television, tea and coffee making facilities and radio alarm clock. The spacious rooms are all en-suite, with hairdryers, irons and ironing boards available. Extra beds, cots, towels and shoe cleaning materials are also available.

For celebrating honeymoon couples there is a choice of the Buckingham Room with four poster bed or the Balmoral Room with king-sized bed and Jacuzzi spa bath. Bar snacks, traditional cask ales and a restaurant menu are served every day. Ample car parking is available in our private car park and is naturally free of charge.

15 GLOSSOP HERITAGE CENTRE

Henry Street, Glossop,
Derbyshire SK13 8BW
Tel: 01457 869176
e-mail: info@glossopheritage.co.uk
website: www.glossopheritage.co.uk

Nestling at the bottom of the spectacular Snake Pass is the market town of Glossop in North West Derbyshire. Once a cotton town, the mills have gone and Glossop is now a commuter town for Manchester.

The Heritage Centre, in the town's central square, houses a permanent exhibition illustrating the rich history of Glossop from pre-history to the present day. It includes an authentic Victorian Kitchen and a variety of historical costumes. A range of maps, plans, old photographs and newspapers help to give a better understanding of how the town and its people have developed.

There is also an Art Gallery with original paintings and prints by local artists for sale.

182

Thornsett, Birch Vale, High Peak,
Derbyshire SK22 1AZ
Tel: 01633 740 030

Once part of a large farm, **The Printers Arms** is an 18th century building found midway along the Sett Valley Trail, in the picturesque and quiet village of Thornsett, a real hidden gem, offering a warm and friendly welcome to all. Taken over in August 2007 by Jason and Julie, a hospitable and hard-working couple, the Printers Arms provides facilities for all visitors: locals, walkers, cyclists or tourists. Ideal for walkers exploring the Sett Valley trail, the pub is a good stop off point for food and drink, the bar hosting two superb real ales: Robinsons Unicorn and Halters Mild.

Food is available every evening and most lunchtimes throughout the year. The menu consists of well prepared pub classics, Fish & Chips, Scampi, burgers and steaks to name a few; alternatively for a lighter snack, there are various sandwiches, jacket potatoes and all day breakfasts. A very popular dinner choice is the Sunday roast, choose from Roast Beef, Chicken or Lamb and enjoy. The food is cooked by Julie, who is a superb cook, using local produce wherever possible to create daily specials.

As well as good food and drink, there is also accommodation available all year round, two upstairs rooms with good bathroom facilities. The rooms are comfortable and cosy, one double bedroom and one family room and the price includes a bonus of a hearty breakfast. The rooms are reasonably priced as well; they start from £30 a night. The accommodation is perfect for use as a base, with so many local attractions, including Peveril Castle, Werneth Low Country Park and Lyme Hall: a glorious mansion set in stunning grounds. The pub is a very popular venue, there is some form of entertainment every Saturday evening, usually a live band or a karaoke/disco night! The pub is open on Tuesday and Wednesday from 5pm – Close, Monday, Thursday and Friday between 12pm – 2.30 and 5 – Close and from 12pm – Close on Saturday and Sunday. There are full disabled facilities for eating and drinking but not for the accommodation.

13 SYCAMORE INN

Sycamore Rd, Birch Vale, High Peak,
Derbyshire SK22 1AB
Tel/Fax: 01663 742715
e-mail: info@thesycamoreinn.co.uk
website: www.thesycamoreinn.co.uk

The Sycamore Inn brings city style and luxury to the heart of England's countryside. Nestled in the beautiful Peak District, it fuses warm, traditional hospitality with fine dining and contemporary elegance.

No expense has been spared during the extensive refurbishment process, in order to create the ultimate gastronomic experience in a laid-back, pleasurable environment. The Sycamore Inn is unlike anything else in the area - a true gem.

Within its rugged stonewalls is a 65-seat a la carte restaurant, offering a mouth-watering menu, full of tasty creations which use the finest local ingredients, that are delivered fresh each day. A meal here is truly momentous, you could begin with The Sycamore's signature fishcakes topped with a fried egg and caper butter, followed by Crusted rack of lamb – oven roasted and served with a shoats cheese and blueberry sauce and round off with a dish of true indulgence by the name of Black forest baked alsaka – chocolate sponge soaked in kursh, vanilla pod ice cream, light Italian meringue, and served with a warm black cherry sauce! Minimalist Italian slate flooring and cream furnishings provide a quality setting in which to enjoy this perfect meal.

Alongside the restaurant there is a gastro pub and cocktail reception area, complete with comfy furniture and a roaring fire - the perfect place to sit and unwind after a day's work. There is a delicious bar menu catering for all tastes and appetites, whether you fancy a country platter to share or a light lunchtime bite. A bar favourite dish is the 'Moby Dick and chips' – prime code fillets in the pub's own beer batter with thick chips, mushy peas and homemade tartare sauce. The Sycamore carries an extensive wine and champagne list, and a fine selection of cask ales and bottled beers. Downstairs, the romantic Jazz Lounge is ideal for relaxing 'a deux', or in company, while you enjoy your evening with an expertly-mixed cocktail or two. Keep an eye out for the live music performances and wine-tasting evenings.

The Sycamore extends its welcome to overnight guests, with 5 en-suite bedrooms fitted with flat-screen TVs, Internet access, chic modern furniture and the best Egyptian cotton bedding. Outside, visitors will find a huge terrace ideal for al-fresco dining, where outdoor heaters and ambient lighting provide a calm haven away from it all. Acres of grounds incorporate two patio areas, an outside bar, beer garden, barbecue terrace and an outdoor stage for live events and music. This establishment offers you a unique experience and is fast becoming one of the places to be in the north-west. Its friendly and professional team look forward to welcoming you time and time again.

14 DUKE OF YORK

Stockport Road, Romiley, Stockport,
Cheshire SK6 3AN
Tel: 0161 430 2806
e-mail: mail@dukeofyorkromiley.co.uk
website: www.dukeofyorkromiley.co.uk

The Duke of York is a fine inn just two minutes walk from the Peak Forest Canal. It dates back to 1786 and was originally a coaching inn, now it's a traditional pub serving some of the best food and drink in the area. Landlord Jim Grindrod is also the chef, and is proud of the inn's traditional cuisine and Mediterranean menu, which attracts people from the whole area and tempts the most discerning of taste buds. It gets busy so booking is advisable, especially at the weekends. Jim is also proud of the six real ales he serves, John Smiths, Sharp's Doombar, Bombardier, Deuchars IPA, Adnam's Explorer and a regularly changing 'guest' ale, all beautifully kept. And in recognition of his passion for the perfect pint, Jim has been given a Cask Marque award – so it's official, The

Duke of York pours the best pint in Romiley! Open all day, every day, with food being served in the restaurant from 12 noon to 10pm, alternatively food is also available in the bar – or al fresco in summer!

The Duke of York and Mediterranean Restaurant is conveniently located ½ mile from junction 27 on the M60 motorway and 2 minutes walk from bridge 14 on the Peak Forest Canal (mooring available).

16 THE HARE & HOUNDS

High Lane, Simmondley Village, Glossop,
Derbyshire SK13 6LS
Tel: 01457 852028

At **The Hare & Hounds** or "Hairy Dog" as the locals like to call it, you will find great pub food, a selection of real ales, and a warm welcome from your hosts Ray and Annette. Whether you want to try one of the traditional ales or treat yourself to a freshly prepared meal they promise to make your visit as enjoyable and relaxing as possible. The pub is situated on the edge of the town of Glossop, and only 30minutes from Manchester City Centre. With commanding views over the Longdendale Valley, this is a great watering-hole after a hike or ramble in the Peak District National Park.

17 THE STAR INN

2 Howard Street, Glossop,
Derbyshire SK13 7DD
Tel: 01457 853072

Hosts Paul and Vivien invite you to **The Star Inn**. Located in Glossop, in Derbyshire's High Peak this traditional street-corner inn is situated close to the town centre. It's the ideal place to replenish your energy for the rest of the day and to stop if passing through the area. Renowned for its warm hospitality, The Star welcomes thirsty travellers as well as a regular local clientele. This is a friendly local pub, with the accent on measured chat not loud music! The bar features up to 5 real ales,

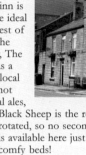

Black Sheep is the regular and the others are continually rotated, so no second visit is the same. Regrettably no food is available here just good ale, quiet contemplation and comfy beds!

Accommodation is available year round and is offered on a room only or B&B basis. There is 1 double and 1 twin en-suite and a single room with shared bathroom.

It is the perfect place for communications between Manchester and Sheffield, yet only a 30 minute drive from charming 'Last of the Summer Wine' country.

18 THE BEEHIVE AND HAGUE BISTRO

Hague Street, Glossop,
Derbyshire SK13 8NR
Tel: 01457 852 108

The Beehive and Hague Bistro is probably Glossop's best kept secret, just a short walk from the centre of Glossop, this establishment offers high class dining in traditional pub surroundings.

Stewart Hilton has held the lease since January '08 and boasts an impressive C.V of working in the trade; his local reputation is already very good and is spreading far and wide.

By far the biggest draw is the food available. Stewart has ensured that only the finest locally sourced ingredients are used and that all the dishes are created to order. Leaping off the menu are such choices as Fresh Whitby Cod with Best Bitter batter, the price set by the fishmongers that morning, or

Rack of Lamb, served on a bed of Herby Potato with

fresh vegetables. Even if a snack is all that's required, guests can create their own sandwich or choose from an extensive bar snacks menu, featuring hits like Greek style chicken kebabs, crevettes and locally made pork sausages with creamy mashed potato. The bar is open all day every day and is not short of choices, the wine list is well stocked and there are always two regular ales plus a rotating guest ale.

19 CAUSEWAY HOUSE

Back Street, Castleton, Hope Valley,
Derbyshire S33 8WE
Tel: 01433 623291
e-mail: steynberg@btinternet.com
website: www.causewayhouse.co.uk

Causeway House offers outstanding Bed & Breakfast accommodation in an area of the Peak District National Park renowned for its beautiful scenery. A real gem this house has all the conveniences of the 21st century in a 15th century 'cruck' cottage with huge original oak timbers that exude history. The little garden at the front is a cheerful, colourful spot in spring and summer. The accommodation comprises five comfortably appointed rooms, three luxurious en-suites and two with shared facilities. The stunning four-postered room just oozes history and character and the double room is a perfect place to relax. Each room has been tastefully decorated and comes complete with a hospitality tray, a colour TV, clock radio and hair-dryer.

A hearty English breakfast, with a lighter Continental and vegetarian alternatives, is included in the tariff and is sure to put a spring in the step for a day's exploring. The family-friendly house has been owned and run since May 2006 by Janet and Nick Steynberg, who are already attracting repeat visits with their amiable, welcoming style and excellent value for money. They also have a wealth of information about places in the area to visit and explore. Castleton, at the head of the Hope Valley, is overlooked by the ruins of Peveril Castle, built in 1080 by Willam Peveril, the King's bailiff for the Royal Manor of the Peak. Equally dominant is Mam Tor, where a walk to the summit (1700 feet) is rewarded with spectacular views.

20 TREAK CLIFF CAVERN

Castleton, Hope valley
Derbyshire S33 8WP
Tel: 01433 620571
e-mail: treakcliff@bluejohnstone.com
website: www.bluejohnstone.com

Treak Cliff Cavern is an underground wonderland of stalactites, stalagmites, rocks, minerals and fossils. It is also home to Blue John Stone, a rare form of fluorite with beautiful colours. Popular as an ornamental stone and mined for 300 years, one of the largest pieces ever found, called The Pillar, is still in situ. The Blue John Stone in Treak Cliff Cavern can be seen all around the walls and roof of the Witch's Cave. The guided tour takes you deeper underground to see multi coloured flowstone adorning the walls of Aladdin's Cave, and further on you can experience the wonder of the stalactites and stalagmites in Fairyland and the Dream Cave. The most famous formation is 'The Stork', standing on one leg.

People of all ages can enjoy a visit to Treak Cliff Cavern (guided tours take about 40 minutes), and also experience special events held at certain times during the year. 'Polish your own' Blue John Stone is an activity usually available during most of the school holidays. Other events include an Easter Egg Hunt and. prior to Christmas. 'Carols By Candlelight' in the cavern.

21 BOWLING GREEN INN

Smalldale, Bradwell, Hope Valley,
Derbyshire S33 9JQ
Tel: 01433 620450
e-mail: matthewwilde@yahoo.co.uk

The **Bowling Green Inn** is one of the most delightful inns in Derbyshire. Tucked away in the picturesque surroundings of Smalldale, it has whitewashed walls, bow windows and hanging baskets of colourful flowers. It is also a historic place, as it is a former coaching inn dating from 1577. The interior is everything that an English pub interior should be - warm, cosy and traditional, with many original features, such as exposed stone walls, low-beamed ceilings, dark wood and open fireplaces. Just the place to enjoy a quiet, relaxing drink as you explore this beautiful part of Derbyshire!

And yet the standards of service are firmly rooted in modern times. It is popular with tourists and visitors alike, and Jackie and Matthew, who are mine hosts, are justly proud of the value-for-money-prices they have set. There is a fine range of real ales,

including Tetleys and Black Sheep, and weekly changing guest beers all are immaculately kept. Plus, of course, there are beers, lagers, cider, spirits, wines, liqueurs and soft drinks for those driving.

The Bowling Green Inn also sells good pub food, and the platefuls are always hearty and filling. Serving times are 12 noon to 2.30pm and 6.30pm to 9pm seven days a week. There are two restaurants and if you wish to eat on Friday and Saturday evenings or Sunday lunchtime, you are well advised to book. There is a printed menu and a changing specials board that always has tempting dishes such as Thai red chicken curry, pork chops with orange and ginger, lamb chops (using the finest Derbyshire lamb) and juicy fillet steaks cooked to order. Fresh fish delivered daily includes monkfish, seabream, seabass and a popular favourite is the large fresh cod fillet cooked in beer batter.

The inn also offers six fully en suite rooms in a converted barn on a B&B basis, and each one is furnished and decorated to a high standard. They have been given a four star rating by the Automobile Association, so you know you are getting the very best!

All major credit cards are taken, and there is a pool table indoors and a patio and beer garden outside with stunning views.

22 LADYBOWER INN

Bamford, Hope Valley, Derbyshire S33 0AX
Tel: 01433 651241
e-mail: info@ladybower-inn.co.uk
website: www.ladybower-inn.co.uk

The **Ladybower Inn** is a charming old inn that overlooks the still waters of the Ladybower Reservoir, built during the Second World War. Under the expert ownership of Deborah and Stephen, it offers a warm, Derbyshire welcome to old friends and new visitors. It sits on the A57 Sheffield to Manchester road, and is a free house, serving great food and drink, and offering comfortable accommodation. It has seven en suite rooms and all are spacious, well furnished and beautifully decorated. The surrounding countryside is stunningly beautiful, and the inn makes the perfect base from which to explore it.

The cosy, friendly bar offers four real ales: these are Bradfield Blonde (from a local micro brewery), Barnsley Bitter and two rotating guest ales. The award-winning Barnsley bitter from the nearby Acorn brewery is always available with its nutty taste giving a deep, full flavour. The bar prides itself on its range of wines, so there is sure to be something to your taste.

Good, home-cooked food is served daily 12noon to 9pm and the produce is sourced locally wherever possible, making the dishes tasty and full of flavour. The ever changing menu of home made dishes can be enjoyed in the spacious and comfortable 30-seat restaurant, for which bookings are essential, or alternatively meals can be taken in the bar, or outside.

The bar and dining areas are disabled friendly, though you should phone about your accommodation requirements.

23 POOL CAFÉ

Oddfellows Road, Hathersage, Hope Valley,
Derbyshire S32 1DU
Tel: 01433 651159
e-mail: kevinasmith41@hotmail.com

The **Pool Café** is located in the picturesque Hope Valley and part of an outdoor swimming pool area. In the summer, there's no better way to round off a swimming session, than to enjoy a drink, or snack, on the cafe's patio. This child-friendly café offers food that is beautifully cooked and presented, using fresh, local produce wherever possible. You can choose from a printed menu or a specials board, with favourites being the full English breakfast, liver and onions, vegetable chilli and a host of other dishes that will satisfy the largest appetite. A highlight is 'Hikers Hash'; served in a giant Yorkshire pudding it's especially popular with hungry outdoor types. Portions are generous and prices represent value for money. And take note - the café's fish and chips are reputed to be the best for miles around! An addition to the menu is the popular Sunday lunches, for which you are well advised to book.

Kevin Smith has owned and managed the café for over four years, and in that time has built a reputation that is second to none. The premise comprises one light, open main room with ten glass-topped tables. The patio seats a futher 40 people. There is a takeaway service and the café can also be booked for private functions. Though it isn't licensed, you can BYOB (bring your own bottle!) The cafe opens at 8.00am all year round.

189

24 THE LITTLE JOHN INN

Station Road, Hathersage, Hope Valley,
Derbyshire S32 1DD
Tel: 01433 650225 Fax: 01433 659831

As its name tells us, **The Little John Inn** – and the idyllic village of Hathersage in which it is found – has associations with the legend of Robin Hood. Owner Stephanie Bushell has been the hand on the pump at this traditional inn for 18 years and has ensured it retains a real flavour of days gone by and a relaxed, friendly atmosphere that is sure to refresh visitors however long their stay. It is a handsome stone building which dates from the 19th century, and today has a bar, lounge and an excellent, roomy restaurant. The inn also has extensive accommodation available, comprising six en-suite rooms and one charming cottage – which sleeps four.

Enjoy a convivial pint and hearty meal after a day walking on the high moors. The varied and comprehensive menu makes use of only the finest, freshest ingredients for each dish. And if you have a real hunger, try the Little John mix grill – a platter not for the faint hearted – it is every bit as much a legend in these parts as Robin himself.

The inn has also won awards for its ale, and serves a wide selection of locally-brewed

traditional hand pulled ales and is constantly rotating between them – including their very own exclusive Little John Ale. The bar also has a good selection of draught bitter, stout, lager, cider, wines, spirits and soft drinks – a drink to quench any thirst is available here.

Food is served Monday to Thursday at lunch (12 till 2) and dinner (6 till10), Fridays and Saturday s 12 till10 and Sundays 12 till 8.30.

Stephanie offers all her guests a very warm welcome – and she'll dare you to order and finish that mixed grill!

610 Redmires Road, Lodge Moor,
Sheffield S10 4LJ
Tel: 01142 302 824

The subject of a charming poem by the celebrated author C. P. Cotterill, **The Three Merry Lads** dates back to the 17th Century and looks out over the stunning Bradfield Moor and the Rivelin valley. These spectacular surroundings and the welcoming look of the pub have helped make the Three Merry Lads a popular venue for walkers, cyclists and lovers of the countryside.

Offering five real ales at any one time; Marston's Pedigree, Greene King IPA and Abbot plus 2 rotating guest ales, usually from one of two local breweries: Kelham Island or Abbeydale Breweries, the pub caters for the ale connoisseur and anyone just popping in for a decent pint. For a slightly more substantial visit, the menu is impossible to fault, featuring a host of pub favourites: Fish & Chips, Chef's Pie of the Day and a variety of steaks from the grill. It is no wonder that the menu is well thought out and delicious, Peter has been a chef here for 10 years and became the Head Chef and landlord in the summer. Other sumptuous choices from the menu include the Olde English Fish Crumble; with haddock, salmon, cod & prawns, Hunter's Chicken and the Speciality Sausage of the day served with mashed potato and onion gravy. The puddings are mouth-watering, from Sticky Toffee Pudding with

toffee sauce to the luxury local ice-cream in many flavours, catering for every kind of sweet tooth. For a lighter meal, the pub has a bar snacks menu which has a variety of Panini, tortilla wraps, sandwiches, jacket potatoes, salads, and a delicious looking Indian platter: made up of onion bhajis, samosas and pakora. Food is available Monday to Friday between 12pm – 2.30pm and 5pm - 9pm, Saturday from 12pm – 9pm and Sundays and Bank Holidays between 12pm – 8pm. Due to high levels of custom, it is best to reserve a table on Sundays. Live entertainment is also available once a month and every Tuesday night is Curry night.

Away out west on an upland road, where heaven's clear baulk appears, a roman causeway once this road, a gone a thousand years. There stands aside an old world inn, it boasts no modern fads. A real old country calling place, it's called Three Merry Lads. – C. P. Cotterill, 1920.

191

26 THE EATING HOUSE

The Derbyshire Craft Centre,
Calver Bridge, Hope Valley,
Derbyshire S32 3XA
Tel: 01433 631583

The Eating House situated within the Derbyshire Craft Centre is a popular destination for both tourists and locals alike. The Craft Centre is located adjacent to the A623 and is open every day of the year except Christmas Day, Boxing Day and New Years Day. It is housed in a building of warm, old stone, and the interior has a traditional feel combined with contemporary designs and fittings. It is the perfect place to have a delicious meal, snack or cup of coffee if you're visiting the Craft Centre or just passing by. Homemade soups and fresh quiche, baked to their own recipe, help to reflect the very best of English cuisine. Ham and poached eggs, bubble and squeak

– they're all here! The old-fashioned puddings and desserts are very popular, especially the lemon meringue pie.

The Eating House is self-service, and the daily dishes are listed on the blackboard. Open 10am – 5.30pm it has seating for 35 inside and a further 15 outside. Children are very welcome, and the establishment is disabled-friendly but does not have disabled toilet facilities. There is plenty of off-road parking for customers, and all credit cards are taken with the exception of American Express and Diners.

HIDDEN PLACES GUIDES

Explore Britain and Ireland with *Hidden Places* guides - a fascinating series of national and local travel guides.

Packed with easy to read information on hundreds of places of interest as well as places to stay, eat and drink.

Available from both high street and internet booksellers

For more information on the full range of *Hidden Places* guides and other titles published by Travel Publishing visit our website on

www.travelpublishing.co.uk
or ask for our leaflet by phoning **01752 276660** or
emailing **info@travelpublishing.co.uk**

27 AVANT GARDE OF BASLOW

Holingworth House, Calver Road, Baslow,
Derbyshire DE45 1RD
Tel: 01246 583888
e-mail: avant.garde@btopenworld.com
website: www.avantgarde-of-baslow.co.uk

Avant Garde sells a stylish range of goods for the home and garden, and can be found a short drive from Chatsworth House. Great attention is paid by the owners, Linda and John Lowen, to design, colour, texture and fitness-for-purpose of the many items in the shop. So committed are they that they scour the UK and Europe looking for the latest trends. Attention to detail is king at Avant Garde.

Whether it's mirrors, cushions and throws from Sweden, wicker baskets, vases, silk flowers, books or gift wraps, there is sure to be something that will catch your eye. So well designed and crafted are the objects that the shop has featured many times in National magazines. All the items are displayed on various pieces of furniture such as painted housekeepers' cupboards, painted dressers and old pine chests, accentuating that country look that is so admired nowadays.

Plus there are many charming items for the garden, for not only do people like to personalise their interiors, they like to do the same to their gardens. French garden

furniture, brightly painted bird houses, galvanised planters, sweet pea baskets, metal obelisks - Avant Garde has got them all. Another section is called "Planted", where seasonal plants, bulbs and herbs are set in beautiful containers.

Just two doors away from Avant Garde, Linda has acquired the premises to sell a selection of beautifully crafted furniture, including many original pieces that cannot be found anywhere else. There are glass fronted cupboards, painted tables and chairs, wardrobes, small occasional tables plus many more pieces that would add grace and elegance to any house interior. There will also be bespoke pieces using original materials. In addition, Linda is also featuring an extension to her existing ranges of mirrors, lamps and pictures. Everything on display is designed and crafted with style in mind, and you are invited to browse to your heart's content. Those that visit this store just can't get enough, and their testimonials say it all:

"I could furnish my whole house from this shop" - Claire

"It's a lovely shop, with a great feel" - Jenny

Avant Garde of Baslow is a must-visit place for all your gift needs, and you can even buy Christmas gifts and decorations. It is open seven days a week from 10am to 5pm. Enjoy!

Calver Rod, Baslow,
Derbyshire DE45 1RP
Tel: 01246 582276
website: www.therutlandarmsbaslow.com

The Rutland Arms is a charming village pub situated in the heart of the delightful village of Baslow, on the edge of the Chatsworth Estate. Sitting on the river Derwent the Rutland has one of Derbyshire's most hidden secrets! A unique picturesque riverside beer garden with its 15th century Toll Bridge and Old Toll House as a feature.

The pub is an ideal base for exploring the beautiful countryside, attractions and historic houses of The Peak District whether on foot or by car. Chatsworth House, Buxton and Castleton Caverns are all within easy distance.

The Rutland Arms was very recently taken over in September 2008 by new tenants Tim & Alicia; it is their first venture into this trade, although Alicia does have over 10 years experience running bars and hotels in her homeland, Australia. Already word is spreading about the change of tenancy and the couples hospitality and charm – but as they say –

they've still got a lot of work ahead of them to bring the place up to their high standards.

None-the-less they have everything covered, to stop all the pubs guests from going hungry, they serve a mouth-watering traditional pub grub menu everyday: Lunch is served 12 - 2.30pm, Dinner 5.30 - 8.30pm and Sundays 12 - 7pm. During the summer month's customers can relax in the stunning beer garden, whilst enjoying a light bite to eat and a refreshing drink from the bar. All the food is fresh and it is derived from local produce wherever possible.

The pub serves a full selection of draught beers, wines and spirits for your enjoyment along with a range of soft drinks for those non-drinkers and drivers.

For all those customers who feel they have had a bit too much to drink and cannot drive home or for those on holiday the Rutland has three letting bedrooms, two doubles and one twin, each equipped with colour TV, tea and coffee facilities and hand wash basin. There are two shared bathrooms and the excellent tariff is popular with walkers. Children and dogs are very welcome and all major credit cards are accepted. The spacious off road car park makes it easily accessible for everyone.

So why not come and visit this pub next time your passing and see what the friendly staff and welcoming pub has to offer you.

Nether End, Baslow,
Derbyshire DE45 1SR
Tel: 01246 582551
e-mail: paul@devonshirearmsbaslow.com
website: www.devonshirearmsbaslow.com

Built on the site of an old coaching inn, the **Devonshire Arms Hotel** has recently been refurbished to provide twelve en-suite rooms to discerning guests. Each room is individually furnished and decorated to an extremely high standard, and represents outstanding value for money. It is set in the Peak District, so is the ideal base from which to explore a beautiful area that is rich in history and heritage. Chatsworth Park, Eyam and Haddon Hall are only a short distance away, as are the picturesque towns of Matlock, Buxton and Ashbourne.

Managed by Joanne and Paul Kaczmarek, who, between them, have many years experience in the licensing trade, they have created a hotel that combines charm, friendliness and high standards of service, with great food and drink. The hotel is open all day every day, and sells four real ales, all beautifully kept. These are Greene King Abbot, Greene King IPA, Directors plus a rotating guest ale. And there is a wide selection of beers, spirits, wines and soft drinks should you be driving.

Superb food is part of the magic of The Devonshire Arms and no less than four chefs are employed in the kitchen. All food is exquisitely and freshly prepared, using the best quality produce, sourced locally wherever possible. You can choose from the daily specials board or the printed menu, which contains such favourites as barbequed chicken wings, Highfield House Farm steaks, homemade steak onion & ale pie, deep fried whole tail scampi and so much more. If you would rather have a light bite or a snack, you can have Greek salad, a traditional Ploughman's platter or simply an age old favourite, a baked potato with choice of toppings. There is a daily carvery, which is very popular with visitors and locals alike.

You can dine in the spacious main lounge, which seats up to 68 people, or in the beautiful, circular Chatsworth Suite, which seats 90 in absolute comfort.

The Chatsworth Suite, with its own bar, is the ideal place for a wedding, party or anniversary celebration. All credit cards are taken with the exception of Diners and American Express, and children are most welcome. Dogs may stay in some rooms for an extra charge, and are welcome in some parts of the bar/restaurant area.

**63 Sunderland Street, Macclesfield,
Cheshire SK11 6HN
Tel: 01625 422015
e-mail:
glenandsarahthejollysailor@btinternet.com**

Close to all the amenities in Macclesfield, such as the bus and railway stations, you will find a gem of a pub, **The Jolly Sailor**. It is a real find, with mine hosts Sarah and Glen having been here since July 2006. They have made something special out of the pub. It dates from the 19th century, and has a well-proportioned exterior in red brick, with hanging baskets that bring a lot of colour to an already colourful and delightful building.

But being the landlord of the Jolly Sailor is a sort of return home for Glen, whose great-great grandfather was once licensee here almost 150 years ago. The interior is as delightful as the exterior with a relaxed, cosy atmosphere. Here you can enjoy a quiet drink or a delicious home-cooked meal, with the locals offering a real welcome. In fact, it's one of the most popular pubs in the area, and much visited by visitors and locals alike.

It is open all day, every day for a great range of drinks. It serves four real ales, permanent fixtures being Bass and Youngs while there's always one traditional hand pulled Scrumpy available. This classic boozer also has a wide selection of beers, lager, cider, spirits, wines, liqueurs and if you're driving, soft drinks. The pub also sells good, honest pub food that is tasty and always

beautifully cooked from local produce where possible. There is a fine selection of hot and cold dishes in the winter months, such as hot pot, beef stew and dumplings and so on.

Children are very welcome, and there are no smoking areas to the rear of the premises. Sarah and Glen regret, however, that they only take cash - they do not accept credit or debit cards or cheques. There are also five guest rooms (all twin) available, and these can be taken on a bed and breakfast or dinner, bed and breakfast basis. Each room is comfortable, well furnished and pleasantly decorated. The rooms are located on the first floor.

There is live music on the first Thursday of each month and regular entertainment every Fri/Sat/Sun (Ring for details.) Plus, a fun theme night once a month, on Saturdays, either Blues or Elvis etc...great for a good night out. Parking is next to the pub, and it has CCTV coverage. The dining and drinking areas downstairs are disabled friendly, though you should ring beforehand about the accommodation.

The Jolly Sailor in Macclesfield is a real find - a cosy town pub that has lost none of its character and warmth while at the same time offering up to date facilities, high standards of service and real value for money. Make it your first stop in Macclesfield!

31 DOLPHIN INN

76 Windmill Street, Macclesfield,
Cheshire SK11 7HS
Tel: 01625 616179

For good food and well-kept ales, you can't beat the **Dolphin Inn** in Windmill Street, a ten-minute walk from the town centre. Here, in this pub which dates to the 19th century, your hosts, Bev and John Lythaby, will make you most welcome. They've been here six years and during that time have turned the inn into one of the best and most popular in town. The exterior is whitewashed and picturesque, and the interior is cosy, warm and trim, as every pub should be, with comfortable seating and carpeted floors.

Food is served at lunchtimes only here, with Beth being the cook. Serving times are 12 noon to 2pm from Monday to Saturday. There is an across the board menu, with most of the produce being sourced locally, so you are assured of freshness and flavour at

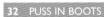

all times. The speciality of the house is steak pie, which is always piping hot and delicious.

The pub is open every session and all day Sunday with three real ales on offer, Robinson's Unicorn, Hatters and seasonally brewed brewery ale. This is usually Old Tom 8 per cent in the winter months. Plus there is a good range of beers, wines, spirits and soft drinks. The Dolphin is a real English local, though visitors are always made especially welcome. Children are welcome if eating.

32 PUSS IN BOOTS

198 Buxton Road, Macclesfield,
Cheshire SK10 1NF
Tel: 01625 423261

Only a short walk from the centre of Macclesfield, and on the borders of the Peak District National Park, you will find a superb small inn called the **Puss in Boots**. It has a fine, well-proportioned exterior of local stone, and dates from the 18th century, when it was a coaching inn. Inside it boasts comfortable seating, warm carpeting and dark, polished wood. Behind the pub is a canal, with alongside it, a beer garden where you can sit and enjoy a pint. Hosts Julie and Stephen Stokes, have the warmest of welcomes for their patrons. They serve good beer and equally good food, and take a great pride in the popularity of the inn.

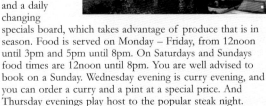

Open all day, every day, its sells three real ales, Boddington's, Bombadier plus a rotating guest ale. There is a printed menu and a daily changing specials board, which takes advantage of produce that is in season. Food is served on Monday – Friday, from 12noon until 3pm and 5pm until 8pm. On Saturdays and Sundays food times are 12noon until 8pm. You are well advised to book on a Sunday. Wednesday evening is curry evening, and you can order a curry and a pint at a special price. And Thursday evenings play host to the popular steak night.

33 COFFEE TAVERN

Shrigley Road, Pott Shrigley,
Cheshire SK10 5SE
Tel: 01625 576370

Pott Shrigley is a small village north of Macclesfield, on a minor road between the A523 and the B5470 that stands right on the edge of the Peak District National Park. Here you will find the excellent **Coffee Tavern**, housed in what was a reading room and library built in 1887 for workers on the nearby Lowther Estate. This quaint building is like taking a step back in time! It's an establishment that is renowned for serving some of the best food in the area - from home-baked cakes and scones to full three course meals. The tavern is licensed, and it has such a fine reputation that you are well advised to book a table at weekends.

All the food is cooked on the premises by Andrew Buffey, son of the owners (who have been here since 1992), and he uses the finest of local produce in the kitchen wherever possible. The new and exciting breakfast menu is available each day from 10am to 11.45pm and features the gastronomically intimidating Full Coffee Tavern Fry: local sausage, bacon, grilled tomato, fried mushrooms, black pudding, baked beans, local eggs (any which way), fried bread and handmade potato cake.

The Coffee Tavern is popular with walkers and cyclists, who enjoy not only the food, but also the excellent tea and coffee that is served as well. Not only that - people come from all over the area to sample the delicious cuisine and then pay a visit to the small craft shop upstairs. Here you will find a fascinating collection of craft items, from paintings and jewellery to pottery and cards, all made by local artists and craftspeople.

34 THE HOLLY BUSH

75 Palmerston Street, Bollington,
Cheshire SK10 5PW
Tel: 01625 573073
e-mail: adechef@hotmail.co.uk
website: www.thehollybush.uk.com

Located in the main street of old Bollington, by the bridge at the bottom of the slope, **The Holly Bush** is a pleasant old building in mock Tudor style. Inside you'll find an inviting traditional hostelry where customers relish the real fires, real ales and the genuine welcome from mine hosts Danielle and Adrian. A major attraction here is the quality of the food on offer - they have even had to dispense with the pool table to provide space for more tables. Adrian is an experienced and imaginative chef who makes good use of fresh ingredients from local suppliers - all the meat, for example, is farmed in Cheshire. The menu changes weekly but, typically, amongst the starters you'll

find dishes such as crab meat on toasted white bread topped with Welsh rarebit, or a black pudding and haggis tower with green peppercorn sauce. Main courses include a roast of the day, chicken roulade, and a wonderful fish pie topped with cheesy mashed potatoes. Real ale lovers have the choice of three brews from Robinsons Brewery. Food is served from noon until 3pm, and from 6pm to 9.30pm, Friday and Saturday; and from 10am to 4pm on Sunday.

Hawkins Lane, Rainow, Macclesfield,
Cheshire SK10 5TL
Tel: 01625 424235

The **Rising Sun Inn** is one of the most picturesque inns in the area, and is adjacent to the B5470 Macclesfield to Whaley Bridge Road, within the Peak District National Park. Just off the beaten track it is a haven of neighbourhood feeling. Dating back over 300 years, and under the management of Kathleen Jackson, it has regained all of its former popularity with the locals.

It is open all day Friday - Sunday, Monday - Thursday 12 - 2.30pm and 5pm - 11pm for the sale of a wide range of beers, lagers, cider, wines, spirits and soft drinks. It also offers three real ales, which are immaculately kept. These are Black Sheep and two rotating guest ales. Great food is served daily from 12 noon to 2.30pm and 6pm to 9pm and from 12 noon to 7pm on Sundays. Here the Sunday Carvery is unadulterated coma-inducing no-two-ways-about-it gluttony, indulge in 1, 2 or 3

courses. Dickie is the culinary whiz in the kitchen and does all the cooking, using only the finest and freshest local produce wherever possible. You can choose from a printed menu or a daily changing specials board. Dickie's specialities are Lamb's liver and bacon with mashed potato and vegetables perfectly followed by 'Death by Chocolate served with ice-cream', and as you can imagine they are all very popular with the locals!

All credit cards are accepted with the exception of American Express and Diners. Children are most welcome and there is also occasional entertainment and themed food nights, i.e. Wednesday night is Steak Night, choose from 8oz Rump Steak, Gammon Steak, Venison Steak or Pork Steak all served with chips and peas for a very reasonable £6 or 2 for £10! Please ring for details. Off road parking is available and there is a beer garden to the rear.

A great time to visit Rainow is during the annual Fete held in July, many visitors come to the village from far and wide to view the event, and are treated to a whole host of original ideas, which are all brought to life in ingenious ways. The whole village plays a part and its rows of cottages, winding lanes and nooks and crannies always bring a surprise at every turn!

35 THE ROBIN HOOD

Chapel Brow, Rainow, Macclesfield,
Cheshire SK10 5XE
Tel: 01625 574060
e-mail: info@robinhood-rainow.co.uk
website: www.robinhood-rainow.co.uk

Nestled on a hillside in the Cheshire village of Rainow, **The Robin Hood** is a charming rural pub on the outskirts of the Peak District National Park. Open all day every day, the beamed restaurant provides a home-cooked menu of British favourites amidst cosy, traditional surroundings. To whet your appetite, here you can enjoy a Cheshire Beef & Real Ale Pie with homemade chips and seasonal vegetables or Deep Fried Cod Fillet, mushy peas, tartare sauce & homemade chips and much more. For the best opportunity to enjoy the local region The Robin Hood offers Bed & Breakfast in quality en-suite accommodation.

37 COMMON BARN FARM

Smith Lane, Rainow, Macclesfield,
Cheshire SK10 5XJ
Tel: 01625 574878
e-mail: g_greengrass@hotmail.com
website: www.commonbarnfarm.co.uk

In the hills of the Peak District National Park, on a traditional working sheep farm, farmers Rona and Geoff Cooper run **Common Barn Farm** with five Bed and Breakfast rooms, plus two beautiful self-catering holiday cottages. The cottages are of upside-down construction with fabulous beams and galleried landings. Walks straight from the door take you to the Lamaload Reservoir with far-reaching views over the Cheshire Plain to the Welsh mountains. Ideally placed for visiting the Peak District. Homemade scones, muffins and teacakes are also available in the farm teashop. Ramblers, campers, horse riders and bikers, all are welcome!

38 BOARS LEIGH RESTAURANT

Leek Rd, Bosley, Cheshire SK11 0PN
Tel: 01260 223221
Fax: 01260 223500
e-mail: manxgirl@btconnect.com

You will be hard pressed to find a restaurant in Bosley which oozes as much class and sophistication as **Boars Leigh Restaurant**. Highly professional and attentive staff will greet you upon arrival but you will be immediately aware that it does not have a stiff or formal feel to it, instead you can look forward to a cosy and relaxing lunch or dinner in its warm and welcoming environment. The restaurant owned by Sandra and Lello Ingargiola enjoys a celebrated reputation as one of the finest in the area and 2008 marks there 30th year in business thanks to a dedicated team headed by Ian Moody in the kitchen. The Boars Leigh Restaurant is particularly popular due to its beautiful country setting.

40 THE MANNERS HOTEL

Haddon Road, Bakewell,
Derbyshire DE45 1EP
Tel: 01629 812756

The Manners Hotel is a lovely little pub situated in the heart of Bakewell. It attracts an impressive base of clientele along with all the local regulars. They serve a full selection of draught beers, wines and spirits for your enjoyment. To stop all the pubs guests from going hungry, the pub serves a  mouth-watering traditional pub grub menu every afternoon and evening. And for all those customers who feel they have had a bit too much to drink and cannot drive home there is cosy en-suite accommodation available. Please call for more information or to make a booking.

39 THE BEAN & BAG

Water Lane, Bakewell,
Derbyshire DE45 1EU
Tel: 01629 814404

Whether you are just looking for a cup of tea or coffee or light snack or a warm meal you will find something here to meet your need. **The Bean and Bag** is a superb coffee shop, tearoom and much more! Named by the staff, the Bean and Bag signifies the coffee *bean* and tea *bag*.

Set in the beautiful 'picture postcard' village of Bakewell, in the heart of the Peak District National Park. Bakewell dates back to Saxon times and of course is home to the famous Bakewell pudding. Visit the Bean and Bag for a lovely fresh coffee and indulge in an original Bakewell pudding, enjoy it with ice cream, cream or custard!

This is a quality establishment much loved by locals and visitors alike, the warm hospitality, quality homemade produce and great selection of teas and coffee make this a magnet for clients who visit time and time again!

Whether you are hiking, biking, or having a wander around the beautiful town of Bakewell, visit the Bean and Bag.

41 HADDON HALL

nr Bakewell, Derbyshire DE45 1LA
Tel: 01629 812855 Fax: 01629 814379
e-mail: info@haddonhall.co.uk
website: www.haddonhall.co.uk

Only a mile to the south of Bakewell down the Matlock Road, on a bluff overlooking the Wye, the romantic **Haddon Hall** stands hidden from the road by a beech hedge. The Hall is thought by many to have been the first fortified house in the country, although the turrets and battlements were actually put on purely for show. The home of the Dukes of Rutland for over 800 years, the Hall has enjoyed a fairly peaceful existence, in part no doubt because it stood empty and neglected for nearly 300 years after 1640, when the family chose Belvoir Castle in Leicestershire as their main home. Examples of work from every century from the 12th to the 17th are here in this treasure trove.

As with all good ancestral homes, it has a family legend. In this case the story dates from the 16th century when Lady Dorothy Vernon eloped with Sir John Manners. Many feel this legend was invented by the Victorians, partly because there is no historical evidence to back the claim that the two eloped together during a ball and also because neither the steps nor the pretty little packhorse bridge across the Wye, over which Dorothy is supposed to have escaped, existed during her time. However the small museum by the gatehouse tells of their romantic journey, as well as the history of the Hall.

42 CHATSWORTH HOUSE

nr Edensor, Derbyshire DE45 1PP
Tel: 01246 565300 Fax: 01246 583536
e-mail: visit@chatsworth.org
website: www.chatsworth.org

On the Outskirts of the village lies the home of the Dukes of Devonshire, **Chatsworth House**, known as the "Palace of the Peak", is without doubt one of the finest of the great houses in Britain. The origins of the House as a great showpiece must be attributable to the redoubtable Bess of Hardwick, whose marriage into the Cavendish family helped to secure the future of the palace.

Bess's husband, Sir William Cavendish, bought the estate for £600 in 1549. It was Bess who completed the new House after his death. Over the years, the Cavendish fortune continued to pour into Chatsworth, making it an almost unparalleled showcase for art treasures. Every aspect of the fine arts is here, ranging from old masterpieces, furniture, tapestries, porcelain and some magnificent alabaster carvings.

The gardens of this stately home also have some marvellous features, including the Emperor Fountain, which dominates the Canal Pond and is said to reach a height of 290 feet. There is a maze and a Laburnum Tunnel and, behind the house, the famous Cascades. The overall appearance of the park as it is seen today is chiefly due to the talents of "Capability" Brown, who was first consulted in 1761. However, the name perhaps most strongly associated with Chatsworth is Joseph Paxton. His experiments in glasshouse design led him eventually to his masterpiece, the Crystal Palace, built to house the Great Exhibition of 1851.

43 BALL CROSS FARM COTTAGES

Chatsworth Estate, Bakewell,
Derbyshire DE45 1PE
Tel: 01629 815215
e-mail: info@ballcrossfarm.com
website: www.ballcrossfarm.com

In a prime location on the historic Chatsworth Estate, **Ball Cross Farm Cottages** are superbly located for experiencing the spectacular beauty of the Peak District; Britain's best loved National Park. Dating back to 1668, the beautifully restored cottages bearing the Estate village names

of 'Edensor', 'Pilsley', 'Rowsley' and 'Beeley', offer unique holiday accommodation. Each cottage is individually designed and decorated combining an eclectic mixture of antique and contemporary furnishings to provide the ultimate in style and comfort.

Water Lane, Eyam, Hope Valley,
Derbyshire S32 5RG
Tel: 01433 630853

The Miners Arms is a fine Inn & Restaurant, that can trace its origins back over the centuries and has stood as a silent witness through changing times and historic events, built in 1630 just before the great plague found its way to Eyam. The story of how the villagers isolated themselves to save the lives of those in the surrounding areas is legendary.

There are many documented parts of the inns history around the pub, and as you would expect, the inn is also haunted. Reputedly by two young girls who died in a fire on the site before it was built, and by an ex-landlady who was murdered by her husband who is said to roam the corridors at night with her old fashioned dress making a loud rustling noise.

Today you will find 7 well presented guest bedrooms all with elegant and classic décor, some having original features. Most of the rooms are on the first floor but there is a ground floor room with one step, which may suit the less mobile. All rooms are en-suite and have a television, tea/coffee making facilities and a hairdryer if required.

The inn offers a creative Restaurant dinner menu as well as simpler food during lunchtimes and evenings all prepared by the resident chefs. A typical meal could begin with grilled black pudding with a honey & mustard sauce, followed by a main course of slow roasted lamb shank with lavender mash & rich redcurrant gravy. Most of the food is prepared from fresh local ingredients sourced from local suppliers.

The beautiful scenery of the Peak district remains unspoiled and unrivalled by any other county. Its combination of lush green river valleys and moorland with many miles of well-marked

footpaths makes this, a walkers' paradise. Other amenities in the area include horse riding, gliding and climbing. Places to visit include: Eyam's Village Museum, Tours of the Plague Saga and the many tearooms, shops and craft centres. A little further afield, visit Alton Towers, Blue John Mines, Buxton and Speedwell Cavern to name a few.

Open all day, everyday for ale! Of which you have three to choose from, Theakstons Best is the regular plus two rotating guest ales. Food is served most days 12 noon – 2pm and 6pm-9pm, please call to confirm certain days.

45 EYAM MUSEUM

Hawkhill Road, Eyam,
Derbyshire S32 5QP
Tel: 01433 631371
website: www.eyam.org

Bubonic plague has been described as the 'most dangerous disease known to mankind' and has killed more souls than all the wars ever fought between all the nations of the world. Known as the Black death, the Great Plague entered London in the 17th Century and came to Eyam by the most unfortunate of mishaps - carried by fleas festering in a box of cloth brought from the capital for the village tailor. When the box was opened plague fleas were released. Between September 1665 and October 1666 260 people - perhaps a third of the population - met an awful, pained death. Only the intervention of two clergymen ensured that the village survived through the next terrible months. William Mompesson was newly appointed rector of Eyam - and he and his predecessor Thomas Stanley, persuaded the village to enter voluntary quarantine, to bury their own dead and even change their pattern of worship. Some had sent their children away, but most folk stayed in Eyam.

People in the surrounding area, especially the Earl of Devonshire, sent provisions to the people of Eyam so they would not starve, though careful precautions were taken to avoid infection. When the plague finally loosed its terrible grip on the village, it left a population of more than 400 people who, needing to make a living, returned to their traditional task of mining lead in the hills above the village. Smallholdings were tended again, a few sheep and cows helping provide some of the necessities of life. Cottages in the village, emptied by the plague, were filled again, often by growm-up sons and daughters who had once moved away. In this way Eyam prospered again. Visit **Eyam Museum** to experience the full story.

46 BULL I' TH' THORN

Ashbourne Road, Hurdlow, nr Buxton,
Derbyshire SK17 9QQ
Tel: 01298 83348
e-mail: amaltby-baker@tiscali.co.uk
website: www.bulliththorn.co.uk

The former coaching inn of **Bull I' th' Thorn** dates back to 1472, with parts that may even date back to the 12th century, making it one of the most historic inns in Derbyshire. Today it still retains many of its original features such as flagstone floors and oak beams, though it now combines them with modern standards of service and outstanding value for money. It has three double en suite rooms and these are beautifully furnished and decorated. The whole inn has a warmth that is due in no small part to host Graeme, who has created a place that is renowned throughout the area for its food and drink. It is open every day with the exception of Mondays, though it opens on bank holiday Mondays. It offers one real ale at the bar - Robinsons Unicorn, as well as a wide array of beers, lagers, wines and spirits.

Food is served 12 noon - 2.30pm and 5.30pm - 8.45pm

and all day weekends. Graeme is the chef, and he uses locally sourced, fresh produce wherever possible. There is a menu and a daily specials board. You are well advised to book at weekends. Children are most welcome, and all credit and debit cards, with the exception of American Express and Diners, are accepted. To the rear is a rare breeds farm, which opens in the summer months. There is also a caravanning and camping site (with showers) and occasional medieval evenings are held within the inn itself.

47 THE BLACK GROUSE

The Market Square, Longnor, nr Buxton,
Derbyshire SK17 0NS
Tel: 01298 832 205
e-mail: theblackgrouse@btconnect.com
website: www.theblackgrouse.co.uk

Set within a traditional Georgian coaching inn, the property has been fully refurbished and modernised to offer stylish 4 Star accommodation in the heart of the Peak District National Park. **The Black Grouse** offers luxurious hotel rooms with modern comforts set in traditional period style, an elegant restaurant promoting intimacy and class and a warm and friendly bar, stocked with popular ales. The Black Grouse was awarded 1st place in the Pub of the Year competition by Taste of Staffordshire 2008, which gives an idea of the high level of hospitality and service offered.

The 8 hotel rooms all have a minimum specification; 30" wall mounted flat-screen TV with Free-View, telephone, Wi-Fi internet access, designer fabrics and tea & coffee making facilities. All of the rooms have en-suite bathrooms, decorated in an Italian style, with travertine basins and under-floor heated tiles. In addition to the main hotel, there are three self catering cottages for families and groups; Calke Cottage with 4 beds, Abbey Cottage with 5 and Etwell Cottage with 8 beds for the larger family! This hotel is the

ideal base for people wishing to explore the beauty of the Peak District, visit Buxton Opera House or go wild at Alton Towers. The elegant restaurant, which has been awarded an AA Rosette, bestows intimacy and elegance on guests with the help of Todd Carroll, the chef/proprietor, who prepares exquisite dishes from local produce. The seasonally varied menu includes mouth watering dishes, such as the Baked Artichoke, Asparagus, Baby Onion and Colsten Bassett Stilton Pithivier. The bar menu offers the same level of food quality, taking a traditional English menu and given a creative twist, for example Linguine with a morel and cream sauce and Dark chocolate tart with a hazelnut tuille & mint sorbet. The bar supplies a warm and friendly atmosphere to go with the cask conditioned Marston's Bitter, Pedigree and rotating guest ales. Live music features regularly in the bar, which is kept cool in the summer and warm and cosy in the winter, thanks to a roaring fire. The restaurant is available Monday to Friday between 12pm – 2pm & 6pm – 9.30pm, between 12pm – 3pm & 6pm – 10pm on Saturday and between 1pm – 4pm & 6pm – 9pm on Sunday. It is recommended that a reservation for a table is made to avoid disappointment.

High Street, Longnor, Buxton,
Derbyshire SK17 0NS
Tel: 01298 83218
e-mail: cheshire_cheese@btinternet.com
website: www.yeoldecheshirecheeseinn.com

A short drive from Buxton via the A515 and B5053 will take you to one of the quaintest and oldest inns in the Peak District - **Ye Olde Cheshire Cheese Inn**. Built in 1621, the building was a former farmhouse before being opened as an inn in 1706 by the Milward family. It got its name because the family dealt in Cheshire cheeses which it sold all over Derbyshire and Yorkshire.

It is a mellow building in old stone, with hanging baskets and window boxes adding colour in the summer months to an already charming exterior. Inside, it is equally appealing, with low, beamed rooms, warm wood and comfortable furniture. Many prints and nick-nacks hang on the walls. Look out for a photograph of Mrs Thirza Robinson, who was landlady here from 1909 until 1947. She is now reputed to haunt the building!

Hosts, Lynn and Chris, have created a place that is popular with visitors and locals alike. It offers two real ales - Robinsons Unicorn and a seasonally changing brewery guest ale, as well as a great selection of beers, wines, spirits and soft drinks if you're driving.

The inn is closed on Mondays, excluding bank holidays when they are open all day. Also open all day on Sunday. Great food is served in the Olde Cheshire Cheese, and you can choose from a specials board or a menu. Everything is home-cooked on the premises, and Lynn, who is a superb cook, sources the produce used in the kitchen locally, wherever possible. The homemade steak and ale pie is a popular dish, and on Saturday evenings and Sunday lunchtimes you are well advised to book in advance. Sunday lunch is a carvery - usually pork, beef or gammon, plus as many vegetables and potatoes as you can eat.

You can extend your visit, stay and be pampered in the elegantly converted stable block, extensively refurbished in 2007. Lynn and Chris spared no expense to provide comfort, quality, style and peaceful privacy for their guests. All rooms are beautifully decorated, have en-suite facilities and wall mounted colour TV's. The Dovedale Suite has been specially adapted for guests with reduced mobility. One will be specially adapted for the disabled, and you should ring for details.

Children are very welcome, and all credit cards, with the exception of American Express and Diners, are accepted. Chris is a professional magician, and can often be seen in the bar up to his tricks, if you ask he will visit your table and astound you with his sleight of hand!

49 THE WIND IN THE WILLOWS ATTRACTION

Peak Village, Rowsley, Derbyshire DE4 2NP
Tel 01629 733433
website: www.windinthewillows.info

The Wind in the Willows Attraction is between Chatsworth and Matlock. Every scene from the classic English countryside tale is brought to life in an award winning indoor re-creation. After a short introductory film walk along the River Bank, through the Wild Wood, into Badger's house and so on through all twelve chapters of this delightful adventure story, all faithfully recreated in 3D from the original Shepard drawings. You will be magically transported into the world of Ratty, Mole, Badger and of course the irrepressible Toad. Rediscover the child within, enthral your children, amaze your grandchildren.

"Beyond the Wild Wood comes the **Wide World**" said the Rat. Here you experience and learn about the real life of the creatures from the tale along with our own film "Toad's Tale" which takes you on a journey of real animals.

We have many souvenirs, toys and games in our exclusive gift shop **"Heroes"** along with lots of other famous characters from children's fiction.

50 STONES RESTAURANT

1c Dale Road, Matlock, Derbyshire DE4 3LT
Tel: 01629 56061
e-mail: info@stones-restaurant.co.uk
website: www.stones-restaurant.co.uk

Tucked away in the heart of Matlock, **Stones Restaurant** is a delightfully cosy and eclectic restaurant with stylish interior and a superb modern British menu. New owners took over here in May 2008; their philosophy is to provide a fantastic dining experience in a relaxed setting. And that's just what they've done – the intimate dining room at Stones (which is popular with couples, locals and visitors from out of town) is decorated in a warm palette of creams and browns, and features upholstered vintage church pews and abstract canvases - creating the perfect place for romantic meals, leisurely lunches and dinner parties. Alternatively you can relax in the courtyard overlooking the river as you enjoy lunch, dinner and a glass of wine from the extensive wine list.

In the evenings, a 2 or 3 course set menu is available Tuesday to Friday in addition to a stunning A La Carte menu,

and they also offer a superb 3 course Sunday lunch. For the indulgent amongst you, why not treat yourself to a glimpse of the extensive dessert menu. We highly recommend the ham hock, chicken and confit shallot terrine; slow braised lamb neck fillet with fondant potato and a sauce raz el hanout; and the warm Bakewell tart with a raspberry compote and vanilla ice cream. Please note that the menus change regularly as they source the best seasonal ingredients. If you require current menus, please visit the website or call for details.

51 GLENDON GUEST HOUSE

Knowleston Place, Matlock,
Derbyshire DE4 3BU
Tel: 01629 584732

A short tree lined walk from the centre of Matlock, is the **Glendon Guest House**, owned and run by husband and wife team, Sylvia and Dennis Elliott. They have been providing top quality bed and breakfast accommodation in these premises for over 30 years, and during that time have created a superb establishment that attracts people back again and again.

Situated in Matlock, the guest house is an ideal base for those wishing to explore the idyllic and stunning Peak District and its National Park. There are four wonderfully cosy rooms, two of which are fully en suite, and one being a family room. All rooms are well furnished with colour TVs, shaver points and tea/coffee making facilities, and the whole B&B has a real "home from home" feel to it. The building is a grade two listed dwelling house built in 1857, and retains many original features. It has been awarded four stars from the AA, so good is the hospitality.

The breakfasts here are legendary. Sylvia only uses eggs from her own hens, home-cured bacon, sausages and home-grown tomatoes in season. Breakfast times are flexible, but are usually between 8am and 9am. There is plenty of off road parking, and Sylvia and Dennis will offer you a real Derbyshire welcome should you choose to stay here!

52 THE HORSESHOE

81 Matlock Green, Matlock,
Derbyshire DE4 3BX
Tel: 01629 592911

The Horseshoe is a family-friendly pub, and one of the best of its kind in the whole of Derbyshire. Here, in this erstwhile coaching inn, you and your family can relax in warm, welcoming surroundings, know that you are safe and well looked after. It is popular with locals and visitors alike, and people from all over the globe have visited on a regular basis.

Matlock born and bred, Elaine Swindell took over licensee just over a year ago, and maintains the highest standards of service, the keenest prices as well as introducing a little fun to the place. The entertainment is what people flock here for. The comprehensive live pub entertainment system provides everything from

bingo nights, sports and general

knowledge quizzes, video juke box and karaoke – and much much more. Great for cold winter nights in particular.

The well proportioned building itself is of local stone, and makes a welcoming sight for anyone seeking out a quick snifter. Regularly stocked brews include the local favourites John Smiths Smooth and Carling whilst one further pump offers a real ale, usually, Tiger.

53   THE SYCAMORE INN

9 Sycamore Road, Matlock,
Derbyshire DE4 3HZ
Tel: 01629 584882

This beautiful 18th century former 'coaching inn' now finds itself a cosy, traditional country inn. **The Sycamore Inn** has recently turned a corner since the new leaseholder; Rebecca took over here a year ago. Rebecca has revived the place and seems to have got many of the pubs regulars back, through having a friendly team, well kept

beer and good food which you can enjoy in the bar or in the lovely beer garden on those warm evenings and summer afternoons. You can even place your order over the phone and it will be ready for when you arrive.

Placed in the heart of Matlock a short stroll from the centre, the Sycamore Inn is the ideal place to relax and enjoy a pint or bite to eat amongst friendly locals.

55   TAWNEY'S COFFEE SHOP

Matlock Green, Matlock,
Derbyshire DE4 3BT
Tel: 01629 760991

A visit to **Tawney's Coffee Shop** is an experience for all the senses. Proud owner Jill Gratton not only loves good coffee, she is also passionate about good food. That's why all dishes are freshly prepared to order including, soups, salads, baked potatoes, paninis and toasties. So whether cappuccino, espresso, latte or a slice of homemade carrot cake is your thing, come in, relax, soak in the surroundings and share Jill's passion for coffee and freshly cooked food.

HIDDEN PLACES GUIDES

Explore Britain and Ireland with *Hidden Places* guides - a fascinating series of national and local travel guides.

Packed with easy to read information on hundreds of places of interest as well as places to stay, eat and drink.

Available from both high street and internet booksellers

For more information on the full range of *Hidden Places* guides and other titles published by Travel Publishing visit our website on

www.travelpublishing.co.uk
or ask for our leaflet by phoning
01752 276660   or emailing
info@travelpublishing.co.uk

15 Wellington Street, Matlock,
Derbyshire DE4 3GX
Tel: 01629 582299
e-mail: info@thedukeatmatlock.co.uk
website: www.thedukeatmatlock.co.uk

Situated on the A632, a short distance from the centre of Matlock, the **Duke of Wellington Residential Country Inn** is one of the finest pubs in Derbyshire. Built in 1866 the 'Duke' has all the character and charm of a traditional country inn, built of Derbyshire limestone with slate roofs, roaring log fires and extensive gardens. Yet the key features of this very pleasant establishment are the friendly staff, the 5 real ales (regulars, Green King IPA and Abbot Ale), wholesome fresh food & the wonderful accommodation.

The inn serves superb food, and you can choose from the printed menu or the specials board. All the dishes are cooked on the premises from only the finest and freshest local produce wherever possible. Choose from a range of dishes to suit all palettes and all ages.

The speciality of the house is the sizzling skillet of steak. Roast dinners are available Monday, Wednesday and Sunday, on Thursday and Saturday you can enjoy Steak Night, two for just £10, choose from Rump, Sirloin, Pork, Gammon and Lamb. Food is served from 12 noon to 2pm and from 5pm to 8pm from Monday to Saturday, and Sunday 12 noon to 4pm (evening times can vary slightly so please call for further details).

Finally for any customer looking to spend the night, the 'Duke' would be more than happy to accommodate you in one of there twelve guest rooms. The old 'heards mans' cottage and 'stable block' have been painstakingly converted into nine en-suite rooms which offer our guests the very highest standards in comfort and privacy. These rooms are set away from the main building and 'The Stables' has its own flag stone courtyard and bespoke parking. All rooms come with T.V & Tea & Coffee making facilities, five of which are on the ground floor. There are a further three bedrooms available in the main building. The tariff is usually room only, but breakfasts are available at a small extra charge by prior arrangement. They are available all year round, and have a three-star rating.

The Duke of Wellington makes the ideal base from which to explore Derbyshire and the Peak District. Matlock is close by, as are Buxton, Chesterfield, Ashbourne and Bakewell, and the cities of Sheffield, Derby and Nottingham are no more than half an hour's drive away.

56 TALL TREES COFFEE SHOP AND RESTAURANT

Oddford Lane, Two Dales, Matlock,
Derbyshire DE4 2EX
Tel: 01629 732932

Housed within the Forest Garden Centre, off the A6 in Two Dales, the **Tall Trees Coffee Shop and Restaurant** is the ideal place for that welcoming cup of tea or coffee, or a hearty, filling lunch. It is a smart and delightful establishment with friendly, efficient staff and down to earth prices that are sure to please. All the produce used in the

kitchen is sourced locally wherever possible, and everything is home-cooked to perfection.

The freshly made meals (prepared daily), snacks and yummy cakes entice customers to return again and again. The relaxed and easy atmosphere makes Tall Trees Coffee Shop a favourite place to visit with friends when you want to treat them to a meal but still have time to enjoy their company, instead of running to and from the kitchen. If you're in the area, you just can't afford to miss it!

57 THE BULLS HEAD

Fountain Square, Youlgrave, nr Bakewell,
Derbyshire DE45 1UR
Tel: 01629 636307
e-mail: bookings@bullsheadyoulgrave.co.uk
website: www.bullsheadyoulgrave.co.uk

Riddled with character **The Bull's Head** provides the perfect place to unwind and enjoy a drink. The Atkinson family has run the pub for 28 years, with Mark and Sharon Atkinson at the helm for the last sixteen years. The pub enjoys leisurely pace of life, catering for its loyal locals as well as its passing tourists. They serve a full selection of draught beers, wines and spirits for your enjoyment. Also, at the Bull's Head you will find a wide choice of good value, traditional pub food including vegetarian options. Customers can choose from a large selection of meals, which are squeezed onto the blackboard or from the printed menus. All dishes are prepared using the freshest produce, which is sourced locally whenever possible. Together, the Atkinson's have

built up a well-deserved reputation for their superb food.

The Bull's Head has four bedrooms and a ground floor flat all

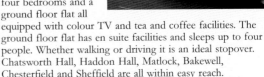

equipped with colour TV and tea and coffee facilities. The ground floor flat has en suite facilities and sleeps up to four people. Whether walking or driving it is an ideal stopover. Chatsworth Hall, Haddon Hall, Matlock, Bakewell, Chesterfield and Sheffield are all within easy reach.

58 THE PRINCESS VICTORIA

174/176 South Parade, Matlock Bath,
Derbyshire DE4 3NR
Tel: 01629 57462

Housed in a building that dates from the 18th century, **The Princess Victoria** is one of Matlock Bath's finest inns. Along with the arrival of a new tenant The Princess Victoria underwent a six-week refurbishment and opened refreshed and rejuvenated in August 2007. Since reopening it has been an undisputed hit with locals and visitors alike who are looking for good locally sourced food, local beers and a great selection of wine. It has a cosy, welcoming atmosphere and serves four real ales, Batemans XB, Batemans XXX, Abbot Ale plus a rotating guest ale.

There is a choice of two dining areas both serving the same menus – the atmospheric bar in the original part of the inn and the upstairs restaurant which seats 40 in spacious comfort. The Princess Victoria offers a novel and sensational dining experience, with the "Steak Stone" you are able to cook your

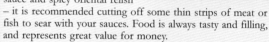

meat or fish exactly as you like. A highlight is the 8oz Oriental Sirloin Steak with noodles and shitaki mushrooms, served with sweet chilli sauce, wasabi sauce and spicy oriental relish – it is recommended cutting off some thin strips of meat or fish to sear with your sauces. Food is always tasty and filling, and represents great value for money.

60 HEIGHTS OF ABRAHAM

Matlock Bath, Derbyshire DE4 3PD
Tel: 01629 582365 Fax 01629 580279
e-mail: office@heightsofabraham.com
website: www.heightsofabraham.com

Featuring steep rocky gorges, vast caverns, fast running rivers, wide panoramic views and a cable car, it is easy to understand why the Victorian's called Matlock Bath "Little Switzerland"; however, the **Heights of Abraham Country Park and Caverns** overlooks the famous spa town, and provides a unique aspect to a day out or holiday in the Derbyshire Dales and Peak District.

The journey to the summit of the country park is easily made by taking the cable car, adjacent to Matlock Bath railway station and car park. The cable car ticket includes all the attractions in the grounds, as well as the two spectacular underground caverns. Tours throughout the day allow you to experience the exciting underground world within the hillside, with the "miner's tale' in the Great Rutland Cavern Nestus Mine, and the multivision presentation of the "story in the rock" at the Masson Cavern Pavilion.

The sixty-acre country park also features woodland walks, the Owl Maze, the Explorers Challenge, play and picnic areas, Victoria Prospect Tower, plus the High Falls Rocks & Fossils Shop featuring Ichthyosaur remains. When you have worked up an appetite, why not relax with a drink on the terrace and take in the views, or enjoy a snack in the Coffee Shop or a meal in the Woodlanders Restaurant. So next time you are planning a trip to the mountains, remember The Heights of Abraham at Matlock Bath "Little Switzerland" is nearer than you think.

59 RIVERSIDE TEA ROOM AND OLD BANK CAFÉ BAR

44-48 North Parade, Matlock Bath,
Derbyshire DE4 3NS
Tel: 01629 55550

The **Riverside Tea Room and Old Bank Café Bar** in Matlock Bath offer visitors to this wonderful, historic village the chance to enjoy a moment of unique atmosphere. Matlock Bath can be very busy or very calm, but either way, The Riverside Tea Room and Old Bank Café Bar have an ambience all of their own – a sanctuary from the busy, bustling weekend days of the summer, and warm and friendly when Matlock Bath seems to have fallen asleep.

A visit to Matlock Bath can be very rewarding – whatever time of year you choose and whatever the weather. It lies in a beautiful gorge, running alongside the Derwent River. The Derwent River runs by the Riverside Tea Room and Old Bank Café Bar. Beyond the river is the rising tree-covered cliff-face of the gorge. Simply gorgeous! Its spectacular views are what are most admired, as anyone who has gazed at the view from a good vantage point on either side of the narrow gorge can confirm

At the Riverside Tea Room they don't just serve tea, either – you can enjoy cakes, snacks and lots in between – plus a full range of drinks.

Next door in the licensed Old Bank Café you can indulge in a full meal with a glass of wine. The menus feature a range of homemade treats, everything including starters, soups, mains, roast dinners, steaks, fresh fish, omelettes, sandwiches, paninis, jacket potatoes, salads and side dishes are available. The roast dinners and full breakfasts are particular favourites. Both establishments offer alfresco dining in the summer months with tables out the front. Children are more than welcome.

Matlock Bath Illuminations and Venetian Nights are events that should not be missed!

61 THE PEAK DISTRICT MINING MUSEUM

The Pavilion, Matlock Bath,
Derbyshire DE4 3NR
Tel: 01629 583 834
e-mail: mail@peakmines.co.uk
website: www.peakmines.co.uk

Visit a hands-on museum where you can experience and wonder at the almost forgotten world of a Derbyshire lead miner. For centuries men have toiled underground in cramped and hazardous conditions to earn a meagre living by extracting the mineral *galena,* lead ore.

See the tools they used and the clothes they wore and encounter the problems that the miner overcame - flooding, explosions and roof falls. Experience the maze of twisting tunnels and shafts and observe the advances in technology and the great importance of lead in our modern day lives. Refresh yourself in the café and browse in the well-stocked shop. See the magnificent water pressure engine that was rescued from deep down in a local lead mine.

You can find out what "nicking" means and discover for yourself the amazing network of tunnels that exist under your feet and wonder at the crystals glistening in the walls. This two-man, working lead and fluorspar mine will give you an authentic insight into life underground and the tools and equipment involved. Gold! Gold! Gold! The magic word in mining. Stand in a real gold strike, then try your hand at panning for "gold" - but you won't get rich quick with the sort of gold that you recover! Don't think that the museum is a dry-as-dust, wet weather activity. The average family will be enthralled by the many hands-on, interactive and novel opportunities.

63 THE GATE

The Knoll, Tansley, Matlock,
Derbyshire DE4 5FN
Tel: 01629 583838
e-mail: bayfortytwo@gmail.com
website: www.thegateinntansley.co.uk

The Gate, a large and impressive establishment that dates back to the 17th century with old cobblestones on the forecourt still bearing signs of the route cows took to be milked.

With a good mix of customers, you can come along to enjoy a drink in a relaxed atmosphere or sample the delicious food from one of the many menus. From home style cooked food to food with a difference, The Gate offers a wide range of menus including: a bar menu, vegetarian menu, senior citizen menu, children's menu and specials board for both lunchtime and evening.

Lunches are served Monday to Saturday from 12 noon to 3pm and evening meals are served from 6 to

9pm. Big steak night is on a Wednesday and on Sunday there is a carvery with a choice of three roasts and all the trimmings. The Gate is quickly gaining a reputation for having the best food and service in the area. In warmer weather, you can unwind and benefit from the sunshine in the large beer garden whilst enjoying a thirst-quenching drink and BBQ. The large beer garden is ideal for parties and weddings and outside bars are also catered for.

Butterly Road, Tansley, Matlock,
Derbyshire DE4 5GF
Tel: 01629 583036 (garden centre)
or 01629 582349 (restaurant)
e-mail: sales@scotlandnurseries.co.uk
website: www.scotlandnurseries.co.uk

Situated on the B6104 one mile east of its junction
with the A615 in Tansley is **Scotland Nurseries,
Garden Centre, Restaurant & Chocolate Shop**, an
oasis for any gardener. This is a large complex set high
above the village that includes a superb garden centre,
landscaping services, aquatics centre, coffee house/
restaurant and chocolate shop that offers the best in
food and drink.

The business has been family-run since 1986, and
offers everything you need for your garden - trees,
shrubs, heathers, alpines, herbaceous perennials, herbs
and soft fruit are but a few of the wonderful flora and
fauna on sale at Scotland Nurseries Garden Centre.
Set at 1,000ft above sea level, the plants are hardy.
Many of the Royal gardens including Buckingham
Palace have been supplied with plants from this
nursery.

The qualified and friendly staff are always
available to help and assist with any gardening advice.
The garden centre shop and gift shop is set within a
stone Victorian barn offering a wide array of
gardening sundries, unusual elegant gifts, soft
furnishings, books, cards and souvenirs to remind you
of your visit to Derbyshire and The Peak District.
Opening times are 9am to 5.30pm Monday to
Saturday and 10am to 4.30pm on Sundays.

The Restaurant and coffee shop offers delicious
teas, coffees, snacks, cakes and full lunches. Fruit and
cherry almond scones are made in their bakery every
morning and most of the produce used is sourced
locally. The menu specials are changed daily, Tuesday
is Senior Citizens day, special prices apply on a two
course lunch, alcoholic beverages can be served to
persons having a full meal. The Heathers Restaurant is
very popular, should you wish to have lunch booking
is advisable.

The Chocolate Shop and Café was introduced six
years ago. A chocolate emporium dedicated to all
chocoholics, it offers cakes and tea bread and of course
a wide selection of exquisite hand made chocolates.
Whilst choosing from the large range of hand made
chocolates, why not treat yourself to one of the
speciality Italian coffees on offer, cappuccino, mocha,
Americano, latte or the famous hot chocolates with
cream, chocolate shavings and marshmallows! Enjoy the chocolates with your coffee or have them
boxed as an ideal gift. Scotland Nurseries Garden Centre has full disabled and baby changing facilities.

64 THE OLD BAKERY COFFEE SHOP & RESTAURANT

11-13 The Market Place, Cromford,
Derbyshire DE4 3RE
Tel: 01629 820802

Whether you just want to call in for a quick, expertly made fresh coffee, are after a thirst quenching cold drink to accompany your lunch time snack, or evening à la carte meal, the choice at **The Old Bakery Coffee Shop & Restaurant** is sure to include something to take your fancy!

Allow Simon (owner) to indulge your sense with his delicious food prepared fresh every day with passion using local ingredients. In the evening the exceptional fine dining menu will delight, accompanied of course by your choice of wine from the extensive selection. Open 10am - 5.30pm for lunch menu, then 6pm - 8.30pm for evening menu.

66 WHITE HART HOTEL

10 Church Street, Ashbourne,
Derbyshire DE6 1AE
Tel: 01335 344711

Situated right in the heart of Ashbourne, the picturesque **White Hart Hotel** boasts four extremely comfortable en-suite guest bedrooms, available on a room only basis. Children are more than welcome here. In the bar, it has one regular real ale (Marston's Pedigree) and three guest ales, plus, of course, a wide

range of other drinks. Even if you don't stay here, it is worth having a pint here. This is an establishment that combines tradition, great service, and value for money. Open all day every day.

65 THE NATIONAL STONE CENTRE

Porter Lane, Wirksworth,
Derbyshire DE4 4LS
Tel: 01629 824833 or 01629 825403
website: www.nationalstonecentre.org.uk

Just think of STONE ... Stonehenge, gothic cathedrals, dry stone walls, precious gems, sculpture, millstones, perhaps the great debate about quarrying. But there's so much more – the sugar and steel we use, our landscapes, technology from stone axes to computer controls, the rivers, volcanoes, deserts and earth movements which created stone, even the water we drink depends on stone – we each use 5 tonnes of stone a year. Our oldest materials shaped by our oldest industry – still providing vital products, with 21st Century technology.

A dramatic site in the heart of the Derbyshire Dales on the edge of the Peak National Park and World Heritage Site is a place crammed with ancient tropical reefs, rocks and minerals, centuries of industrial history and full of wildlife treasures... a Site of Special Scientific Interest.

150 Members of the Dry Stone Walling Association from all over Britain have built 19 different sections of dry stone wall in their own local materials. Wallers and dykers from as far away as Caithness and the Cotswolds worked in their particular styles to make this wonderful outdoor museum of traditional walls. The techniques and geology of the stones are explained.

67 GALLERY CAFE

50 St. John Street, Ashbourne,
Derbyshire DE6 1GH
Tel: 01335 347425
e-mail: info@sjsg.co.uk
website: www.sjsg.co.uk

In the heart of historic Ashbourne, **The Gallery Café** is undoubtedly one of the finest cafés of its kind in Derbyshire – having won the award of Derbyshire Café of the Year 2007. It is situated in a Grade 2 listed Victorian house that was once the towns Magistrates Court, but is modern, light and airy having been fully refurbished in December 2006.

The Café uses local & Fair-trade ingredients to produce a delicious variety of home cooked food and cakes, also serving high quality coffee, teas and alcoholic drinks with meals, in a friendly environment surrounded by contemporary art. (They also have a good range of vegetarian & Gluten free food; in fact their gluten and lactose free chocolate brownies won a Bronze award in the Great Taste Awards, and their Hartington Stilton & Walnut Pâté won the Gold!

They serve delicious Spanish style Tapas on Friday evenings. Here you can enjoy a tasty little mouthful of the real Spain without having to jump on an aeroplane to enjoy it! When you begin to see the sheer range of flavours available you will, I'm sure, want to seek out the Gallery Café and take pleasure in 'the small plate with the BIG flavour'. To find out more about the Tapas evening please visit the website, and note booking is essential.

The spacious café seats 46 over two floors and is open from Tuesday to Saturday from 10am to 5pm. It sits above the St John Street Gallery, which sells contemporary paintings, sculpture and crafts from local and established artists. Living with an original work of art is a way of seeing the world differently, and stimulating your senses and mind. Buying contemporary art is not only exciting but may be less expensive than you think.

So if you're in Ashbourne, why not visit the St John Street Gallery and then head upstairs for a snack, a coffee or a meal. Children are more than welcome. All in all this would be a very 'tasteful' day out.

217

68 BOWLING GREEN INN

**2 North Avenue, Ashbourne,
Derbyshire DE6 1EZ
Tel: 01335 342511
website: www.the-bg.co.uk**

Looking for a Countryside Pub? Look no further...Graham and his team invite you to visit the **Bowling Green Inn** to sample a fine range of cask and draught ales and maybe enjoy a delicious home cooked meal in the restaurant. There is something quite special about dining in a real country pub. One that has kept its menu and décor traditional, rather than going down the gastro pub route; making everything cream and minimalist, and adding unpronounceable ingredients to their dishes. Head Chef, David Paterson concentrates on the use of the best fresh fish, meat, produce and other ingredients, all sourced locally. Food is served 12-9.30pm, seven days a week. It really is a perfectly quintessential village pub. So you are in the area - what do you do, what can you do!

Fashion outlets are around every corner in the cobbled streets of Ashbourne, from designer boutiques to high street names. So whether you are searching for trendy day wear, elegant eveningwear or beautiful lingerie you will find a shop to suit. Antique lovers will find a wealth of shops to please them here. And, specialist art galleries and shops selling pictures, crafts, sculptures and pottery make the town an ideal place to visit if you are looking for an unusual gift.

69 YE OLDE VAULTS

**21 Market Place, Ashbourne,
Derbyshire DE6 1EU
Tel: 01335 346127**

Stella Critchlow has been the hand on the pump here for almost five years and during this time she's turned **Ye Olde Vaults** into one of Ashbourne's favourite public houses. Its quite small in size within but what it lacks in size it makes up for in hospitality, tip-top condition ales, fine food and cosy B&B accommodation.

The building started out as a small timber framed structure dating to the Jacobean period circa 1620 or shortly after. It was at the end of the 18th century when the building clearly acquired its distinctive façade. Around this time the building became a public house and according to G.E Shaw's booklet *"Past and present pubs of Ashbourne"* was called the "Old Vaults". Later on to become "The Anatomised Horse" for a while, and he rightly states that this is an unusual name. One theory is that the name was inspired

by the work of a painter and horseman named George Stubbs. It was during the late 19th century that the pub was re-modernised and re-named "Ye Olde Vaults" which it is still called today.

Accommodation consists of four en-suite rooms, all with tea & coffee making facilities and colour TV, also a Full English Breakfast.

Clifton, Nr Ashbourne,
Derbyshire DE6 2GJ
Tel: 01335 342654

The scattered village of Clifton is ideally situated amidst stunning scenery, at the southern end of the Peak District National Park, 1 mile from Ashbourne. It offers excellent walking and cycling opportunities together with a local store and welcoming pub. This welcoming pub is called the **Cock Inn** and is the hub of the community. You'll love the fabulous interior, featuring low beamed ceilings, old, warm wood, a collection of cockerels on display and an open fireplace, offset by beautifully landscaped gardens with typical benches for alfresco dining. Over the summer months you can meander the day away enjoying fine food and chilled wines and beers, forgetting about the worries of work!

Husband and wife team Andrew and Lorraine Garside have been here for five years now, they keep an immaculate cellar, and were awarded the Cask Marque Beer Award. The preferred pints here are Marston's  Pedigree, Bombardier and Timothy Taylors Landlord (all real ales) plus an occasional guest ale in the winter months. Being a roadside inn, there is also a great selection of soft drinks for people who are driving. Lorraine is the cook here, producing many fine, traditional dishes that incorporate local produce wherever possible. Everything, as you would imagine, is home cooked to perfection, and the customers' favourites, with good reason, are the home-made steak pies and the roast dinners, which are served every Sunday.

VISIT THE TRAVEL PUBLISHING WEBSITE

Looking for:

- *Places to Visit?*
- *Places to Stay?*
- *Places to Eat & Drink?*
- *Places to Shop?*

Then why not visit the Travel Publishing website...

- Informative pages on places to visit, stay, eat, drink and shop throughout the British Isles.

- Detailed information on Travel Publishing's wide range of national and regional travel guides.

www.travelpublishing.co.uk

219

71 SARACEN'S HEAD

Church Lane, Shirley, nr Ashbourn,
Derbyshire DE6 3AS
Tel: 01335 360330

A Derbyshire favourite since the 19th century.

Conveniently located in a pretty little village, clustered around a fine church and a pub, the **Saracen's Head** has been welcoming visitors and locals for nearly 200 years.

Shirley is a vibrant, modern village with a fascinating history dating back over 750 years. It sits between Ashbourne and Derby, and today, Shirley manages to be both a home to many modern businesses and a picturesque reminder of bygone days. Today's residents tread the same paths as their Crusader ancestors.

Popular and imaginative food...

At the Saracen's Head, diners can expect to find modern cooking of first-rate fresh local produce offered in inventive guises. Robin Hunter, the owner, is also the head chef, he has devised an innovative menu that can't fail to please and says: *"We work really hard to put out good produce and everything is homemade, from the bread to the ice cream...We use local suppliers and all of our beef and lamb is from suppliers a maximum of three miles away".*

The menu changes regularly and offers starters, main courses, desserts and coffee and teas to suit every taste and pocket. Indeed, specials may include such varied dishes as Traditional Free Range Pork Sausages with Creamy Mash, covered in a delicious Onion Gravy to Roasted Asparagus Tart, Mustard Cream with Soft Poached Eggs & Mozzarella Trellis. In recognition of Mr Hunter's efforts, the Saracens Head was a finalist in the Derbyshire Pub of the Year Award 2008 – which is no idle boast! All food is available every lunchtime and evening, seven days a week.

Tip-top condition ales...

The Bar is truly a great place to unwind, oozing with charm now seldom found. Locals and guests mingle at ease and good conversation is king. Here you can enjoy three real ales; Abbot Ale; Old Speckled Hen and a rotating guest ale. As well as everything else you'd expect from a fully stocked bar.

The perfect place to stay...

From the end of October 2008, the Saracens Head will be offering luxury en-suite accommodation across three cottages. All have individual character befitting this charming village. Please call to make a booking.

Visit The Saracens Head and you can expect a relaxing atmosphere, the finest wines, real beers and ales together with exceptionally prepared, home-cooked food.

Osmaston, Ashbourne,
Derbyshire DE6 1LW
Tel: 01335 342371

Osmaston takes the appearance of a picturesque model village, with its brick built thatched cottages, village hall, primary school, duck-pond, church, and of course pub. The **Shoulder of Mutton** is recognised as one of the best pubs in Derbyshire. People come from far and near to sample its great food and its wonderful range of drinks. Owners Tina and Paul have chalked up 15 years here in 2008 – the building goes back centuries, though records were lost in a fire. A date stone of 1803 survives, however.

The exterior is of red brick, which gives it a charming, warm appearance. This is a friendly, welcoming establishment with plenty of authentic atmosphere and the emphasis is rightly on high standards of service and good, old-fashioned value for money. The customer is king here, and people return again and again. It is open all day in summer, with food available from midday until 2pm and from 7pm to 9pm in the evening,

Only the freshest and finest of local produce is used in the pub's kitchens, and guests can choose from a varied menu that combines the best of English cooking with influences from abroad. The Sunday roasts are particularly popular, and the place is always busy. There is a no booking policy at the Shoulder of Mutton, so you should turn up early to ensure a table. So popular is the place that the owners have recently built an extension that seats 40 people in absolute comfort. You can eat here, or in the bar, the lounge, or al-fresco in the summer months.

The bar serves a great range of drinks to suit all tastes. There is a good choice of real ales - including Bass and Marston's Pedigree - as well as keg bitters, mild, cider and lager. Plus there are whiskies, brandies, liqueurs, wines and a selection of soft drinks should you be driving. And if you are organising a party or anniversary, you could do worse than ask Tina and Paul to supply the

outside catering. They can supply food, outside bar, and all the things that make an occasion an enjoyable one. The outbuildings of the Pub house, house the local shop and post office and both are run by Tina.

Being on the edge of the Peak District there is so much to do and see in the area, from watching motor cycle racing at Darley Moor to the delights of Alton Towers. So pay the Shoulder of Mutton a visit, and sample good, old fashioned English hospitality in a friendly, welcoming pub!

221

Hulland Ward, Ashbourne,
Derbyshire DE6 3EE
Tel: 01335 370206

The Black Horse Inn dates back to the 1690's at least, and is a picturesque building that is full of 'olde worlde' charm, with colourful paintings of horses on the exterior walls, and - surprisingly - a gallows that hangs over the front door! It is on the A517, halfway between Ashbourne and Belper, close to Carsington Water, and makes the perfect base from which to explore the attractions of an area that is rich in heritage and history.

It is a free house, owned and run by Muriel and Michael Edwin for the last thirteen years, and they are proud of the reputation the inn has earned, not only among locals, but visitors as well. The interior is equally as picturesque as the outside of the building, with low beams, warm, mellow wood, open fireplaces and featured stone walls.

It has four guest rooms on offer, all en suite and all having a four-poster bed. Such is their comfort and attention to detail that they have been awarded four stars. Each has a colour TV, tea/coffee making facilities, double-glazing and central heating. The bed and breakfast tariff includes a hearty, filling full English breakfast, or something lighter if required.

Food is one of the Black Horse Inn's specialities, with Muriel presiding in the kitchen. The menu features a wide range of delicious dishes (including a wide range of vegetarian options), and in season game is very popular. Everything is sourced locally wherever possible, except for the venison, which is from Lincolnshire. On Sunday there is a carvery, which is so popular you are advised to book in advance. Food is served every lunchtime and evening.

Good drink is served every session, though there is no all day opening. Four real ales are available which change constantly, and Michael is proud of his ales, which he keeps immaculately. So much so that the inn has featured in the Good Beer Guide for many years, and is about to be featured in the CAMRA beer and bed & breakfast guide. An astonishing fact is that, since Muriel and Michael arrived at the inn, it has featured no less than 770 real ales (last count was conducted on 28/6/08). Plus, of course, there is a wide selection of beers, wines, spirits, lagers and cider, along with soft drinks if you're driving. There is plenty of off road parking, and a lovely beer garden, for when the sun shines. This is an inn that you will return to again and again!

75 MAIN SAIL RESTAURANT

Carsington Water Visitors Centre,
Ashbourne, Derbyshire DE6 1ST
Tel: 01629 540363
e-mail: enquiries@newleafcatering.co.uk
website: www.newleafcatering.co.uk

Carsington Water lies a few miles north east of Ashbourne and is one of Derbyshire's favourite recreational sites, where you can fish, sail, go walking, bird watch or just enjoy the stunning views. At the waterside you will find the Carsington Water Visitors Centre, with its **Main Sail Restaurant**. This is a light, airy place that is both stylish and modern and here you can enjoy the best of food, beautifully cooked and presented, with a backdrop of the beautiful Derbyshire countryside.

The daily specials and the menu contain many fine dishes that combine good, fresh produce with flair and imagination, and everything is freshly prepared and cooked on the premises. It is a member of Peak District Cuisine, which promotes the sourcing of locally grown food products so that diners get dishes that are fresh and flavoursome.

Why not try the New Leaf club sandwich with sliced chicken breast, garlic and spring onion mayonnaise, layered with smoked back bacon, lettuce and tomato or a Fresh seared Tuna salad served with fresh bloomer bread and butter. The trio of sausages are a must from the extensive daily specials menu, with Romany, Old English and Pork and Leek sausages, on a bed of garlic mash potato, served with a rich red wine, onion and thyme gravy and the tender lamb steaks with Rosemary and mint sauce topped with buttered leeks are wonderful with a glass of Australian Shiraz from the Arlington Estate, just one of the superb wines available from the comprehensive wine list.

You may just want to pop in for a coffee made with dark roasted Arabica beans or a cup of English Breakfast tea, but whatever you choose a warm welcome awaits at the Mainsail Restaurant.

Groups are welcome all year round and with the easy to use, pre-bookable menus, booking is simple, making the Mainsail a perfect place to bring groups of any size. Throughout December Christmas Lunches are served in the Mainsail. Each year the restaurant prepares a wonderfully evocative menu, ensuring that you enjoy a stress free time while someone else does all the hard work! Carsington Water in winter has a magic all of its own, and enjoying good food and drink while you look out over the reservoir is one of the joys of the winter months. Open every day of the year with the exception of Christmas Day, please ring for detailed opening hours.

In addition, the restaurant offers three self-catering cottages to discerning tourists, and they make the ideal base from which to explore the Peak District. Two of the cottages sleep 17, and one sleeps 9, and they represent amazing value for money. There is a minimum stay of three days, and the prices are all-inclusive.

74 THE BARLEY MOW INN

Kirk Ireton, Ashbourne,
Derbyshire DE6 3JP
Tel: 01335 370306

Standing in the quaint village of Kirk Ireton,
The Barley Mow Inn dates back to 1683,
and the rear is said to possibly be up to 100
years older. Mary Short, a friendly and
experienced
licensee, is joined by
her daughter
Jennifer, and
together they make
a wonderful family
duo. The well
stocked bar offers 5

Real Ales with Hartington IPA the regular
and 4 rotating guest ales. Snacks are available
at lunchtime for those who require something
to tide them over until tea time. Five superb
en-suite bedrooms are also provided, housed
in an old cottage and assembly room.
Available on a bed and breakfast basis, the
bedrooms offer a superb base to explore the
local village. Open 12 – 2pm daily and Mon –
Sat 7pm – 11pm, Sun 7pm – 10.30pm

HIDDEN PLACES GUIDES

Explore Britain and Ireland with
Hidden Places guides - a fascinating
series of national and local travel
guides.

Packed with easy to read information
on hundreds of places of interest as
well as places to stay, eat and drink.

Available from both high street and
internet booksellers

For more information on the full range
of *Hidden Places* guides and other
titles published by Travel Publishing
visit our website on

www.travelpublishing.co.uk
or ask for our leaflet by phoning
01752 276660 or emailing
info@travelpublishing.co.uk

77 YE OLDE GATE INN

Well Street, Brassington, Matlock,
Derbyshire DE4 4HJ
Tel: 01629 540448

Some 9 miles South East of Matlock, the
lovely village of Brassington is built on a
hillside with superb views. And at the top of
the village is **Ye Olde Gate Inn**, a gorgeous
Olde World pub that dates back to 1616. It is
supposed to be haunted!

The bar is the genuine article – low
wooden beams, roaring fires, excellent service

and a very good choice of well-kept real ales
including Marston's Pedigree, Cumberland ale and a
rotating guest ale. The menu is prepared daily by
the resident chef and pinned to the blackboard so
no two visits are the same. Food is available 12-
2pm and 6.30-8.45pm, except Mon-Tues when it is
closed at lunchtimes and though the menu is
constantly changing there is always a vast range of
tasty dishes to choose from. Well worth a visit.

Miners Hill, Brassington,
Derbyshire DE4 4HA
Tel: 01629 540222

260 Years of **The Miners Arms**...

The Miners Arms is an award winning, 260+ year old traditional country pub in the beautiful stone built village of Brassington nestling in the hills on the edge of the Derbyshire Peak District. There is a long history of lead mining and quarrying in the area, and the surrounding hillsides bear traces of the old mine workings in their grassy humps and hollows. Old mineshafts abound, and can even be found in a few gardens. The legacy of the lead mining 'glory days' is reflected in the names of some of the splendid limestone cottages which recall old mines such as 'Nickalum', 'Bees Nest' and 'Golconda'.

The Miners Arms like most of the old houses in Brassington was in its early days, part of the Manor of Brassington. Its rich history, dates back to at least 1747 when it was first mentioned in the Manor Court Roll. It was used by the Baron Court to grant licenses for miners and sort out problems.

Today, The Miners is one of only two pubs in the village and offers a warm and friendly welcome and prides itself on serving good home cooked food with vegetarian options. Lunches are served from 12.00 until 2.00 pm Tuesday-Saturday and 12.00 to 4.00 pm on Sundays. Evening meals are served from 6.00 to 9.00 pm Tuesday-Saturday. The pub is renowned for it's home made steak and stilton pies and ever popular roast dinners. Half portions are available and there is a separate children's menu. To compliment its good quality menu the Miners offers a large selection of drinks, including 3 real ales: Marston's Pedigree, Cock-a-Hoop and Ringwood Best.

During the lifetime of this edition, The Miners Arms aspires to be able to offer its customers a comfortable nights sleep, but please ring for details.

The pub is easily found just off the B5035 Matlock to Ashbourne road. The water sports centre at Carsington Water is some 3 miles to the South.

78 MIDDLEHILLS FARM

Grangemill, Matlock, Derbyshire DE4 4HY
Tel: 01629 650368 Fax: 01629 650368
e-mail: middlehillsfarm@yahoo.co.uk

Leave behind the stress and bustle of everyday life and escape to a world of beauty and tranquility with a Peak District holiday. **Middlehills Farm** is a warm welcoming family-run B&B set within the picturesque landscape of the Peak District National Park, ideally situated for visiting Bakewell and Ashbourne.

This traditional home is part of a typical farmyard setting, which also runs a seven-acre caravan & camping site. The grass site is great for families and budget conscious backpackers, combining fresh air with modern facilities and excellent meals are available locally. Or for those that appreciate solid foundations and a comfy mattress, there are two en-suite family bedrooms.

Accommodation and camping is available all year round.

79 THE HOLLYBUSH INN

Grangemill, Nr Matlock,
Derbyshrie DE4 4HU
Tel: 01629 650300
e-mail: hollybushinn@btinternet.com

Situated on the The Limestone Way, in the heart of the Derbyshire Dales and at the gateway to the Peak National Park. **The Hollybush Inn** is a 16th century erstwhile coaching inn and is Graded AA 3 Diamonds offering en-suite accommodation in tastefully decorated rooms, bar snacks and restaurant meals. Three self-catering holiday cottages are available and can accommodate up to 22 people. The Inn is completely unspoilt with the progress of time, retaining the 'oldie Worldie' character. The Hollybush is an ideal base for walkers, cyclists and tourists with good quality walks from the door and many attractions within a 12-mile radius.

Buxton Road, Tissington, Ashbourne,
Derbyshire DE6 1NH
Tel: 01335 350317
e-mail: bluebell350317@aol.com
website: www.bluebelltissington.co.uk

Discovering a delightful new pub that offers the very best in English hospitality is always special. And when it's the **Bluebell Inn and Restaurant** at Tissington, three miles north of Ashbourne, it is doubly special. This country inn, built of warm stone, has a reputation that goes far beyond its locality for great food and drink.

It consists of a bar, no smoking restaurant and function room, and has bar meals, Sunday lunches, banquets, buffets, conferences, meetings, wedding receptions and so on. The bar seats up to 52 people, and is comfortable, cosy and at the same time spacious. It offers real ales supplied by Greene King brewery, as well as a range of beers, lagers, wines, spirits and soft drinks. It is the ideal place to relax after a hard day exploring the Peak District, or planning your next trip. Hosts Ruth and Phil Sampson have a wealth of experience in the pub trade, and will make you most welcome when you visit.

With its menu containing over 40 main courses, food is important at the Bluebell, and it has achieved a fine reputation for its cuisine. The restaurant seats up to 100 people in absolute comfort, and serves home-made dishes that use only the finest and freshest of local produce wherever possible. In fact, all the meat used in the kitchens is sourced from a local farm, ensuring that you have a meal to remember. In January 2004 the inn was awarded the coveted "Peak District Cuisine" award because of the policy of using local produce,

and if you look for the "Peak District Cuisine" logo on the menu you will see which dishes this applies to. Special diets can be catered for, such as gluten-free, dairy-free, wheat-free and vegetarian.

The pub is open from 12 noon until 11pm every day from March to November, with food being served from noon until 9pm (and 8.30pm on Sundays). In November, January and February, Monday to Thursday inclusive, it closes between 3pm and 5.30pm unless booked in advance. There is a large car park that can accommodate approximately 75 cars and a large beer garden with play area.

Tissington is a historic village that continues the Derbyshire tradition of well-dressing, and there are many walks and places to visit in the area. Chatsworth House and Alton Towers are close by, as is Haddon Hall.

81 TISSINGTON HALL & GARDENS

The Estate Office, Tissington, Ashbourne,
Derbyshire DE6 1RA
Tel: 01335 352200

The Estate came into the hands of the FitzHerbert family as the result of Nicholas FitzHerbert marrying the heiress Cicely Francis in the late 15th century. The family originally came to England with William the Conqueror and settled in Derbyshire when William FitzHerbert was granted the Manor of Norbury in 1125.

The baronetcy was conferred on William FitzHerbert by George III in 1784 for acting as Minister for Woods and Rivers and for his role as a Gentleman Usher to the King. He divided his time between London and Derbyshire and was succeeded by his eldest son, Anthony, in 1791. His brother Henry inherited as a minor in 1798 and built extensively in and around the village during his 60 year tenure. Successive baronets have tended diligently to the estate and village although the total acreage has shrunk from about 4,000 acres at its peak in 1850, to 2,400 acres today. The sales were mainly enforced by twentieth century death duties and the cost of Sir Hugo's divorce in 1922.

Tissington Hall was originally built in the early 17th century, a top floor was added around 1700 and then the well-known Derby architect Joseph Pickford remodelled the west aspect around 1780 by adding a projecting central bay and open arcading on the ground floor.

The Hall and Gardens are open to the public on 28 advertised days per year. Groups, parties and societies are very welcome by arrangement throughout the year.

82 THE SOUTH PEAK ESTATE

The National Trust, South Peak Estate,
Ham Hall, Ilam, Ashbourne,
Derbyshire DE6 2AZ
Tel: 01335 350503
e-mail: john.malley@nationaltrust.org.uk
website: www.nationaltrust.org.uk

The South Peak Estate lying within what is called the White Peak area of the Peak District extends to approximately 4,000 acres. Located to the north of the market town of Ashbourne the main bulk of the estate is located within the two river valleys of the Dove and Manifold. Within the property are popular visitor attractions such as Dovedale and

Ham Park. The Estate is centred on Ham Park which contains Ham Hall (now a Youth Hostel), together with the National Trust's visitor facilities. To the north-west lies the Hamps and Manifold Valleys and to the north-east lies Dovedale stretching 7 miles to the north towards Hartington. Some of the finest Peak District limestone grasslands and dales woodland lie within

these two valleys under Trust management which are soon to be designated as Special Areas of Conservation under European leglislation. Access to the estate is available to the public all year round and visitor numbers are very high with an estimated 2 million visitors a year to Dovedale alone.

Townend Lane, Waterfall, Waterhouses,
Staffordshire ST10 3HZ
Tel: 01538 308279
e-mail: peaklion@talktalk.net
website: www.peaklion.co.uk

The Red Lion Inn enjoys a scenic location within the picturesque village of Waterfall on the edge of the Peak District National Park. Dating back to the late 1800s, it is constructed of local stone and is built into a small hill which has led to the creation of an unusual tiered beer garden. It is quite a small place but when you step inside you find a wealth of traditional character and a cosy, welcoming atmosphere.

The inn is owned and run by Sarah and Mick Lewis, an enthusiastic couple who took over here in the summer of 2008. It is their first venture into the hospitality business but they have quickly established a glowing reputation for the appetising home-made food and real ales they offer. Sarah is an accomplished cook and she tries very hard to source ingredients locally wherever possible. This means that some items are subject to seasonal availability. Sarah stresses that the Red Lion kitchen is not a *"freezer + microwave* establishment: *I cook all your meals individually and to order (have a pint while you are waiting!)"* Sample dishes include garlic and mozzarella stuffed mushrooms amongst the starters; spicy Thai chicken curry or local sirloin steak as main courses. Specialities of the house include salmon fillet with crème fraiche and lime dressing, and there are also vegetarian options. Round off your meal with one of Sarah's wonderful desserts - home-made Baileys and Malteser ice cream perhaps. Food is served from 6.30pm to 9pm, Monday to Friday; from noon until 2.30pm, and from 6.30pm to 9pm on Saturday and Sunday (until 8pm on Sunday). During the winter months, traditional roasts are served at Sunday lunchtimes.

To accompany your meal, there's a choice of 3 real ales, Bass, M&B Mild and a rotating locally brewed guest ale, as well as a full selection of other beverages.

Sarah and Mick have also introduced live entertainment on the first Saturday of every other month.

Children, pets and even horses are welcome at the Red Lion; all major credit cards are accepted; there is good disabled access throughout and plenty of off road parking.

84 BERESFORD TEA ROOMS

Market Place, Hartington, Buxton,
Derbyshire SK17 0AL
Tel: 01298 84418

Tea rooms are often countryside oasis which conjure up thoughts of home-made food and pots of tea – and this is exactly what you can expect at **Beresford Tea Rooms.** What could be better after you've completed some of the best walks in the Peak District than a refreshing cup of tea, or coffee if that is your preference, and a freshly prepared traditional sandwich.

Here you're in for a real treat, this friendly place is great for light bites and tasty snacks or a more filling meal. This bustling tearoom is also the award winning village post office –providing a focus for the community and an opportunity to meet friends. The Tea Room is open daily from March to November between 10.00am and 4.30pm and in winter from 10.30am to 3.30pm (Shut on Wednesdays during the winter months).

85 MANIFOLD INN

Hulme End, Hartington, Buxton,
Derbyshire SK17 0EX
Tel: 01298 84537
e-mail: Info@themanifoldinn.co.uk
website: www.themanifoldinn.co.uk

The superb **Manifold Inn** is a delightful 200 year old coaching inn and restaurant run by dedicated staff, under whose friendly care offers warm hospitality, excellent quality accommodation and quality fresh home cooked food. The mellow stone inn nestles on the banks of the Manifold River and is surrounded by some of England's most natural and unspoilt scenery. The welcoming bar area at The Manifold Inn provides a generous selection of real and cask ales (Timothy Taylor Landlord and Hancocks HB), lager, wine and spirits. As a free house, The Manifold Inn has embraced the ability to stock an impressive variety of beverages for the casual drinker and veteran connoisseur alike! The menu changes frequently to encompass the seasons and all meals are freshly prepared using the finest ingredients from local suppliers such as Manifold Valley Meats and Hartington Stilton.

Guest accommodation is either in the converted old blacksmith shop in the secluded rear courtyard, in the holiday cottage, or at the Inn. The beautiful holiday cottage comprises a double master bedroom with en-suite and a twin room. It has a country kitchen and a warm lounge packed full of original features and your own wood burning stove. All ten bedrooms are tastefully decorated and have en-suite shower rooms, colour TV, tea/coffee-making facilities and telephones including a junior suite with its own seating area and specially designed bed and furniture. For their less mobile guests there are two specially equipped twin bedrooms. Guests may relax in the quiet of their own lounge or join in the friendly local atmosphere of the Inn. Some disabled facilities available.

86 BIGGIN HALL COUNTRY HOUSE HOTEL

Biggin-by-Hartington, nr Buxton,
Derbyshire SK17 0DH
Tel: 01298 84451
e-mail: enquiries@bigginhall.co.uk
website: www.bigginhall.co.uk

There is no obsequious flattery at **Biggin Hall Country House Hotel**. Instead, just some fresh flowers and the owner…and that's the hallmark of this hotel; it nicely hits the spot between formality and friendliness.

Set in eight relaxing, tranquil acres of private country grounds, the hotel is a protected building of historic interest, Grade II * listed. The present owners have completely renovated it, in keeping with its original character, retaining many fine period details and marrying them with the modern attributes. Little expense has been spared, yet the overall impression is understatement. It has the warm, inviting feel of a delightful country house. The lounge has the date 1672 above the massive stone fireplace and the main entrance contains an oak panelled lobby of considerable antiquity.

Each guest bedroom is individually furnished with antiques and decorated to an exceptional standard. All have a colour TV, tea/coffee making facilities, telephone and silent fridge. As well as the "master suite" in the main house, there are six en suite double/twin rooms and a suite of two rooms sharing an adjoining bathroom. Within the recently converted 18th century courtyard there are five double/twin rooms and a two-bedroom suite, all fully en suite. The Bothy, which is attached to the main house but accessed from the courtyard, boasts two double/twin rooms, both en suite, and a two-bedroom suite with private bathroom. The Lodge, 70 yards across the lawn from the house, has one single and two double/twin en suite rooms. All guests can avail themselves of the facilities in the main house. Most people, come to Biggin Hall not 'to do' but simply 'to be'. This is life as it should be, calm and unhurried - time to talk and listen to friends and family and regain lost vitality.

Food is important in this hotel. Dinner is served at 7pm, and one of the highlights of a stay here. A classically based repertoire, though with a lighter modern focus, delivers skillfully prepared dishes using locally sourced produce, simply cooked with precision and passion. The freshness of ingredients and clear, clean flavours might be showcased in a fillet & joint of chicken wrapped in bacon with parsley butter sauce, or perhaps a starter of smoked trout & mackerel fishcakes with mild sweet chilli sauce that might almost taste of the sea. The appealing repertoire of fixed-price menus is backed up by discreet, friendly and professional service. Vegetarian options are always available, and special dietary needs can be accommodated by prior arrangement. Continental breakfasts are served between 8am and 9am, and for a modest cost you can have a full English breakfast as an alternative.

So if you're looking for somewhere really special, The Biggin Hall Country House Hotel combines luxury and informality within stunning surroundings, and affordable prices.

231

2 St Edward Street, Leek,
Staffordshire ST13 5DS
Tel: 01538 382081

Located in the heart of the historic market town of Leek, **The Swan** is the town's oldest hostelry with a history going back to the 15th century. It's an attractive half-timbered building, partly-swathed in creeper and with a coach entrance to one side reminding one of its former history as a coaching inn. Inside, the inn retains much of its ancient charm and character.

The Swan is very much a family-run pub with mine hosts, Alice and Paul, who took over here in the spring of 2008, joined by Alice's Mum and Dad in dispensing hospitality. Their hostelry is highly popular with lovers of good ales since they are recommended by CAMRA and serve excellent beers, including a wide range of guest real ales. Black Sheep, Tiger Ale and Bombardier are the regular brews, along with rotating guest ales.

The Swan offers a good choice of wholesome and appetising home-made food every lunchtime from 11am to 3pm. The menu, prepared by a skilled chef, includes a soup of the day, the Chef's own Pie of the Day, and traditional favourites such as Steak & Kidney Pudding and Gammon Steak. Vegetarian options include an Italian style vegetable lasagne served with home-made chips and Mushroom Stroganoff freshly made to order.

Hearty hot baguettes, (Steak & Fried Onion, perhaps), are available, while for lighter appetites the choice includes jacket potatoes and freshly cut sandwiches. Round off your meal with one of the delicious home-made desserts. In addition to the regular menu, daily specials are also available - Cajun Chicken, perhaps, or Oatcakes filled with vegetables and Stilton sauce. And on Sundays, traditional roasts are also available.

Booking is strongly recommended for Sunday lunch, as well as for Wednesday lunchtime since this is Market Day. In good weather, refreshments can be enjoyed in the courtyard and garden to the rear of the inn.

The Swan also caters for weddings, business conferences and private parties in its lovingly restored Georgian function room. And if you are planning to stay in this fine old town, a beautifully furnished and decorated Suite is available upstairs. Guests can stay on either a B&B or self-catering basis.

The Swan accepts all major credit cards; children are welcome and there is good disabled access to the ground floor rooms.

88 THE DYERS ARMS

3 Macclesfield Road, Leek,
Staffordshire ST13 8LD
Tel: 01538 382321
e-mail: dyersarms@btconnect.com

Leek is known as the "Queen of The Moorlands"; and its crowning glory is the **Dyers Arms**. Come in and relax in an open, friendly atmosphere where the dedicated team will create dishes to stimulate the palate and satisfy the appetite. There is an excellent printed menu offering 'Quick Snacks', 'Smart Jackets' and the 'Main Event'. Typical dishes from each section include, Hot Beef Bags with Onion Rings, Sausages and Chips and Chicken Kiev. A choice of sweets are available, please enquire at the bar. Between 12noon and 2pm every day, the 'Main Event' meals are two for just £8!

HIDDEN PLACES GUIDES

Explore Britain and Ireland with *Hidden Places* guides - a fascinating series of national and local travel guides.

Packed with easy to read information on hundreds of places of interest as well as places to stay, eat and drink.

Available from both high street and internet booksellers

For more information on the full range of *Hidden Places* guides and other titles published by Travel Publishing visit our website on

www.travelpublishing.co.uk
or ask for our leaflet by phoning
01752 276660 or emailing
info@travelpublishing.co.uk

VISIT THE TRAVEL PUBLISHING WEBSITE

Looking for:

- *Places to Visit?*
- *Places to Stay?*
- *Places to Eat & Drink?*
- *Places to Shop?*

Then why not visit the Travel Publishing website...

- Informative pages on places to visit, stay, eat, drink and shop throughout the British Isles.

- Detailed information on Travel Publishing's wide range of national and regional travel guides.

www.travelpublishing.co.uk

89 BLUEBERRYS

I Stanley Street, Leek,
Staffordshire ST13 5HG
Tel: 01538 373200
e-mail: angie.artus@unicombox.co.uk

Located in the heart of the ancient market town of Leek, **Blueberrys** has established a glowing reputation as one of the very best tea rooms in the area. When the tea room opened in November 2002, its then owners were determined that their top priority was that it should be customer-friendly. And it certainly is. The many regular customers exchange cheerful chat with the waitresses and new visitors find themselves joining in and enjoying the relaxed atmosphere. There are magazines and newspapers to browse through: paintings by local artists adorn the walls.

Angie Artus has been with Blueberrys since it opened but in early 2007 she bought the business and now personally runs it with the help of those cheerful, hard-working waitresses. And, as with the original owners, the top priority remains providing the very best customer care - as well as top quality fare.

Blueberrys menu is also customer-friendly - nothing pretentious or outrageously priced, just a good choice of wholesome and appetising food prepared with top quality ingredients from local suppliers. The day starts with a selection of breakfast dishes, ranging from a Full English to a warm croissant and preserve.

Light meals on offer include omelettes, a Mediterranean vegetable & cheese parcel, or just a straightforward sausage roll. There's also an extensive selection of sandwiches, hot or cold, baguettes, oven-baked jacket potatoes, and salads. In addition to the regular menu, daily specials are listed on the blackboard. Children have their own menu.

At tea-time, there's a traditional cream tea, or the lighter options of scones or toasted teacakes. Or you could really indulge yourself with one of Blueberry's speciality - their delicious cakes and desserts! To accompany your meal, there's an extensive choice of teas, coffees, hot chocolate, as well as a selection of milk shakes and other cold beverages.

Payment is by either cash or credit card (apart from American Express and Diners) and if you are retired, when you pay at the till your bill will be reduced by 10%. Blueberry's is open from 9am to 4pm on market days, (Wednesday and Saturday), and from 9.30am to 4pm on other weekdays. Closed on Sundays.

11-13 Stanley Street, Leek,
Staffordshire ST13 5HG
Tel: 01538 373751
e-mail: enquiries@denengel.co.uk
website: www.denengel.co.uk

The Belgians love their beer, and now it isn't always necessary to visit Belgium to taste the country's wonderful beers. You can share their enthusiasm by visiting the stylish **Den Engel Belgian Bar and Restaurant**. Opened ten years ago, and having moved to the present premises four years ago, the Belgian Bar is a popular place to sample some of the best beer and food in the Peak District and Staffordshire.

It is one of a dozen or so such bars in Britain, and has been judged as one of the best. It has certainly been voted by Tim Webb, who writes books about Belgian beer and is a noted authority, as the best he has been to outside Belgium!

It is owned by Geoffrey and Hilary Turner, and Geoff, a great Belgian beer enthusiast, makes regular trips to Belgium to keep up to date with the latest brews. This ensures that you, the customer, get to drink some fine beers at really down to earth prices! Once you've got a taste for Belgian beer,

there's no substitute for a trip over to enjoy it on its home ground.

On offer are over eleven brews, including the latest, Sparta Pils, a genuine Belgian pils lager. But you can also drink Blanche de Bruxelles, De Koninck, Gouden Carolus, Karmeliet Tripel and Liefman's Kriek. No fewer that 110 bottles line the shelves of this popular establishment, together with export Guinness, Kwak, Orval and so much more. One note of caution: Belgian beers are usually much stronger than British ones.

Opening times are Monday - Thursday open 4pm, Friday, Saturday, Sunday open 12 noon, Sunday, Monday, Tuesday close 11pm and Wednesday - Saturday close 11.30pm.

The restaurant features many beer-based dishes. It seats 30 in absolute comfort, and is open from Wednesday to Sunday from 7pm - 10pm. You can choose from a printed menu or a specials board. Menus change weekly and you are advised to book for Saturday evenings. Dishes that feature often include: Confit of Duck Leg, Pot Roasted Rabbit in Dekoninck and Traditional Flemish Stoverij with Frites (a classic Flemish variation of Beef Carbonade). A vegetarian option is always available upon request.

Geoff and Hilary endeavour to source all produce from local suppliers, the majority of their fruit and vegetables are from Gerald Harrison on Leek Market place, for meats they use both Blackhursts Butchers of Lask Edge and James of Baddeley Green.

91 | THE KNOT INN

Station Lane, Rushton Spencer, Macclesfield,
Cheshire SK11 0QU
Tel: 01260 226238
website: www.theknotinn@hotmail.co.uk

The Knot Inn is a superb hostelry in old, red brick that stands just off the A52 in the village of Rushton Spenser, between Macclesfield and Leek. It stands close to what was a disused branch railway line, and was previously called the Station Inn. It is a handsome building that dates to the 19th century, and has a well-proportioned front with fine, small paned windows and a stately entrance. Outdoor tables and wonderful floral displays enhance the whole picture during those fine summer months.

The interior is a mixture of stylish, modern furniture and fittings and old, polished wood and bare stone pillars. The dining area is especially attractive, with its comfortable seating, its carpets, the sparkling cutlery on every table and the red tablecloths.

The Inn is managed by Vin and Gina who have been hosts here since December 2006. They have created a warm, friendly place that is popular with both locals and visitors alike. Here, you feel, you can relax over a refreshing drink after a hard day exploring the Peak District and all it has to offer.

It is open every day and all day Saturday, Sunday and Bank Holiday Mondays, with the occasional Friday. At other times it is open during the usual sessions for the sale of some of the finest food and drink in the area. Four real ales are on offer. Black Sheep, Adnams and Charles Wells Bombardier are the regulars with a rotating guest ale. Plus there is the usual range of beers, wines and spirits. Each spring a beer festival is held where you can try up to 30 real ales.

Food is served daily between 12 noon and 2pm and 5.30pm and 9pm or thereabouts, while on Saturday and Sunday the times are 12 noon to 9pm. This is a popular place to eat at weekends, so you are well advised to book in advance. The food is very local, as Vin rears his own Highland cattle, and Gina's dad rears sheep and lambs. The homemade pies here, as you can imagine, are very popular. Other popular dishes are home-made steak and kidney pie, poached chicken fillet with white wine and mushroom sauce, three lamb cutlets with minted gravy and a selection of juicy steaks. You can choose off the menu or the daily specials board.

All credit cards, with the exception of American Express and Diners Club, are accepted, and children are welcome at this family-friendly inn. There is also occasional entertainment, and you should ring for details. There is a large car park, a play area, a beer garden and a patio to the side and to the rear.

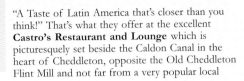

11 Cheadle Road, Cheddleton, nr Leek,
Staffordshire ST13 7HN
Tel: 01538 361500
e-mail: jamie@castros-restaurant.co.uk
website: www.castros-restaurant.co.uk

"A Taste of Latin America that's closer than you think!" That's what they offer at the excellent **Castro's Restaurant and Lounge** which is picturesquely set beside the Caldon Canal in the heart of Cheddleton, opposite the Old Cheddleton Flint Mill and not far from a very popular local attraction, The Churnet Valley Railway.

A friendly, family-run restaurant established in 2004, Castro's is the creation of Jamie, Nikki and Thom, - Thom is the chef. His menu specialises in authentic Latin American cuisine so, among the starters, along with the nachos and tapas you'll find dishes such as Gringas - strips of pork sautéed with red onion and fresh coriander, wrapped in a flour tortilla with mozzarella and cheddar cheese, and served with dressed salad leaves.

For the main course, how about Mexican-style Fajitas, Castro's Burritos or a fiery Cajun Enchilada? For vegetarians, the options include Guevara's Mushroom - fresh field mushrooms stuffed with a creamy rice, garlic and coriander filling, finished with melting blue cheese and served with freshly dressed salad. As well as these tasty Latin American dishes, the menu also offers steaks, a Surf and Turf dish, seafood alternatives and a vegetarian Bean Burger.

All the food served at Castro's is freshly prepared on the premises and the majority of the ingredients is obtained from local produce. With this in mind, there is no taste they cannot cater for, including any food intolerance or allergies. They advise contacting them directly beforehand in such cases as a precaution, to ensure that they can provide you with the most suitable meal.

To accompany your meal, a wide variety of wines, lagers, spirits and cocktails is available from the bar.

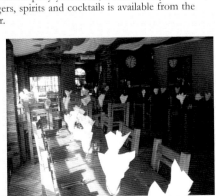

Castro's is open from 6pm, Tuesday to Saturday, and also serves lunches from noon until 3pm, Tuesday to Friday. If you're interested in sampling their Early Bird Menu, this is available Tuesdays, Thursdays and Fridays between 6pm and 7pm. Every Wednesday Castro's holds a Steak Night, with a specialist menu providing customers with a fantastic selection that includes Fillet, T-Bone, Sirloin, Rump and Chicken Steak. The restaurant can also be hired out for private parties, such as Christenings on Sundays, and can cater for up to 44 people.

Star Bank, Cotton, Oakamoor,
Staffordshire ST10 3DW
Tel: 01538 702489
e-mail: yeoldestarinn@tiscali.co.uk

Ye Olde Star Inn is a rarity nowadays - an old coaching inn that has retained its 'olde worlde' atmosphere while still offering the very modern concepts of value for money, high standards of service and a warm, friendly welcome. It dates from the 16th century, and many of the original features have been retained, such as the low, oak beams, exposed stone and dark, polished wood. Situated on the B5417 a mile of so from the centre of Oakamoor towards the A524, it is a free house owned and run by the Pickles family, who, since they came here in August 2005, have created an establishment that is popular with tourists and locals alike.

It offers three real ales - London pride and two rotating ales - as well as a fine selection of beers, wines, spirits and soft drinks for those who are driving. In addition, it serves great food, and is the ideal place for a lunch or evening meal. Food is served from Monday to Saturday between 12 noon and 2.30pm and 5pm

and 9.30pm, and on Sunday from 12 noon to 9pm. You are best to book at all times in the summer. All the family share the cooking, and there is a printed menu and a daily specials board, which takes advantage of fresh local produce in season.

Here you can enjoy homemade 'pub favourites' such as Steak and Ale Pie served with mashed potatoes and vegetables, Lamb shank and Chicken in Stilton. Treat yourself with a slice of pure indulgence; choose from the homemade Sticky Toffee Pudding, Chocolate and Brandy Pot, Homemade Sherry Trifle and many more. For those who believe you can never have too much of a good thing then there are the 'Sharing Plates', desserts so generous that two people can share, you have the choice of a Mega Chocolate Platter, Chocolate Lover's Dream or Cheeseboard. The Sunday Carvery is especially popular; there are generous slices of hot roasted meats on offer, alongside an unlimited choice of vegetables, roast and mashed potatoes, plus all the traditional trimmings.

The restaurant seats 50, and a family room is available. Children are very welcome and even have their own extraordinary 'Little Persons Menu' featuring starters, mains and treats. All credit cards with the exception of American Express and diners are accepted.

Froghall, Staffordshire ST10 2HA
Tel: 01538 754782
e-mail: info@therailwayinn.net
website: www.therailwayinn.net

The Railway Inn is a handsome, whitewashed building standing on the A52 opposite the Kingsley and Froghall Railway Station, which is on the privately run Churnet Valley Preserved Railway. It sits close to Alton towers, and is also handy for the Peak District National Park, so makes the perfect base from which to explore an area that is rich in tourist attractions and history.

Built as an inn in the late 19th century, it offers five fully en suite bedrooms, each one beautifully furnished and decorated, and two having four-poster beds. The place is ideal for those with reduced mobility, as one of the rooms, a family room sleeping up to six, is on the ground floor. The rooms are all clean, spacious and welcoming, and the tariff includes a hearty and filling full English breakfast - just right to set you up for a day exploring the area. Lighter options are also available if required.

The whole place has recently been

extensively refurbished, and has the feel and ambience of an "olde worlde" inn, with open fires in the winter months, panelled walls, exposed brickwork and carpeted floors. And being called the Railway Inn, there is some interesting old railway memorabilia for you to examine! It is very popular with locals, which is always a good sign, and you will be made more than welcome by your hosts, brother and sister team Christine and Bob, who have been here since July 2006. It is open all day, every day for the sale of a wide range of beers, lagers, cider, wines, spirits, liqueurs and soft drinks if you're driving. It also serves three to four real ales, with

Bombardier and Jennings Cumberland being the regulars and one to two rotating guest ales.

Superbly cooked food is served every day from Monday to Saturday from 12 noon to 3pm and from 6pm until 9pm. Christine and Bob employ professional chefs, and all the produce used in the kitchen is sourced locally wherever possible, ensuring freshness and great flavour. On Sunday there is a very popular carvery between 12 noon and 4pm and so good is the food that you are well advised to book on Sundays.

Children are very welcome at this family-friendly establishment, and there is ample off-road car parking space.

95 CROWTREES FARM

Eaves Lane, Oakamoor,
Staffordshire ST10 3DY
Tel: 01538 702260
e-mail: dianne@crowtreesfarm.co.uk
website: www.crowtreesfarm.co.uk

Crowtrees Farm is a delightful traditional stone building some 200 years old which

occupies a scenic location overlooking the Churnet Valley on the edge of the village of Oakamoor. It's the home of Dianne and Chris Bickle who offer quality 4-star B&B accommodation in 7 attractively furnished and decorated rooms, 6 of which are en suite; the 7th has its own bathroom. The Bickles have their own hens and you will be served fresh farm eggs for breakfast. If you are planning a visit to Alton Towers, Crowtrees Farm is ideally situated being just two and a half miles away.

97 DERBY MUSEUMS AND ART GALLERY

The Strand, Derby DE1 1BS
Tel: 01332 716659 Fax 01332 716670

Derby Museum and Art Gallery, on The Strand, in the heart of the city, houses collections covering porcelain, paintings, archaeology, geology and wildlife. Paintings by the celebrated 18th Century Derby artist Joseph Wright include portraits, landscapes, subjects from literature and scenes of industry and scientific equipment that represent this

exciting period of pioneering discovery. This is the largest collection of the artist's work in any public gallery in the world. The Museum's collection of fine Derby porcelain, produced in the city since c. 1750, is of international importance.

96 PICKFORD'S HOUSE MUSEUM

41 Friargate, Derby DE1 1DA
Tel: 01332 255363

Pickford's House Museum, in the historic Friar Gate area, is a beautifully restored Georgian house, and was the home of Derby industrialist Joseph Pickford.

The dining room, drawing room and morning room are as they might have been in Pickford's time. A Georgian bedroom and dressing room have been re-created on the first floor, while on the top floor there is a servant's bedroom. The kitchen and laundry have been reconstructed, together with

a cellar, pantry and housekeeper's cupboard, so that visitors can get an idea of what life was like for the servants working below stairs in Georgian times.

One of the cellars is equipped as an air-raid shelter of the 1940s.

98 THE HONEYCOMB ❙❙

Ladybank Road, Silverhill, Mickleover,
Derbyshire DE3 0NR
Tel: 01332 515600
e-mail: thehoneycombe@btconnect.com

The Honeycomb is a fabulous place to meet, drink and eat in Mickleover! This friendly local pub, originally opened in 1974, is perfect for a quiet drink during the week, or a lively night out on its busy  weekends! You will find 4 real ales plus a fully stocked bar and fabulous homemade pub food in the bar and restaurant. Their continued approach to providing a friendly / quality service has created the perfect atmosphere for a convivial pint and a hearty meal. Also, they are very close to the well-known Radbourne Walk.

99 THE GREAT NORTHERN ❙❙

Station Road, Mickleover,
Derbyshire DE3 9FB
Tel: 01332 514288
e-mail: thegreat-northern@hotmail.com

An historic country pub and superb dining venue, **The Great Northern** was originally built in 1890 to serve as a hotel and public house for Mickleover and Radbourne Station. Today, valued customers come from all over Derbyshire and beyond, and they still receive  the warmest of welcomes. All the staff contribute to ensuring that all customers enjoy a memorable experience at each visit. This welcoming pub is hugely popular due to its excellent seasonal menus and daily changing specials board. All the food is freshly prepared, using a wide variety of mainly locally sourced ingredients. Children welcome until 9pm.

101 THE CASTLE HOTEL ❙❙ ⊨

Station Road, Hatton,
Derbyshire DE65 5DW
Tel: 01283 813396
Fax: 01283 520649
e-mail: admin@castlehotel.org.uk
website: www.castlehotel.org.uk

Relax, unwind and enjoy the atmosphere at **The Castle Hotel,** situated in the village of Hatton, a short drive off the main A50.

Matchless service is what you should expect here, hand in hand with a fantastic menu and a wide selection of drinks. Joint owners, Mike, Sue, and Trish all pull together to make a visit here an enjoyable and unforgettable experience.

The food is a must, and the 70 seat restaurant provides a wonderful place to make the most of a meal. Dishes vary from Roast Topside of Beef & Yorkshire Pudding, Roast Leg of Pork, Supreme of Chicken Bonne Femme, Roast Rack of Lamb Rosemary and Fillet Steak Rossini to Scampi Tartare, Deep Fried Fillet of Plaice Sirlion Steak and Castle Hotel Grill and that's just for main course. The desserts on offer are equally as tempting and are a perfect way to round off a meal.

Food is served from 11.30am – 2pm and 7pm – 9.30pm every day of the week.

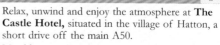

Open every session, there is always a minimum of three Real Ales with Marstons Pedigree being the regular, plus at least two ever rotating guest ales.

The quality accommodation on offer comprises of 3 guest bedrooms, each with private en-suite and much needed necessities.

Derby Road, Doveridge, Ashbourne,
Derbyshire DE6 5JR
Tel: 01889 563820

Doveridge is a peaceful, tranquil village near Uttoxeter where Robin Hood is said to have married Maid Marion, under the old yew tree in the churchyard. In this pretty village you will find the **Cavendish Arms**, housed in a substantial, well-proportioned building that has been standing for over 450 years. Whitewashed and picturesque, it was formerly two inns, the Anchor and the Cavendish, and at one time was an old coaching inn with its own stables and smithy.

Times may have changed, but the Cavendish Arms still offers superb hospitality, mouth-watering fare and unbeatable service. Friendly tenants Jackie and Dave Jones took over the charming hostelry after having successfully run a pub in nearby Tutbury for over six years. Unlike their previous pub, here they are assisted by hard working bar manageress Karen, who is always happy to help.

The interior is just as delightful as the outside, with open fires, old knick knacks and ornaments dotting the walls, plush seating and low, thick beams.

There are three real ales on offer at the bar - Marston's Pedigree, Bass and rotating guest ale. They are all beautifully kept by mine host Dave, and are very popular with both locals and visitors alike. Plus, if you prefer, there is a great range of beers, wines, spirits, lagers, cider and soft drinks on offer. Why not relax here over a welcoming drink after having explored an area that is just so rich in history and heritage?

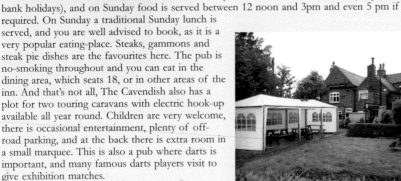

And, indeed, why not eat here as well? Jackie is a superb cook and creates some wonderful aromas that waft through the inn tempting even those who have just eaten. With dishes such as Fillet Steak, Roast Chicken, Seafood Platter, Chilli Goujons and Battered Cod and speciality dishes such as her tasty Curries and Sweet & Sour dishes you would be foolish to leave here with an empty stomach.

Food is served from 12 noon to 2pm and from 6pm until 8pm on Tuesday, Wednesday and Thursday, and in the evening from 6pm to 9pm on Friday and Saturday. There is no food on Monday (apart from bank holidays), and on Sunday food is served between 12 noon and 3pm and even 5 pm if required. On Sunday a traditional Sunday lunch is served, and you are well advised to book, as it is a very popular eating-place. Steaks, gammons and steak pie dishes are the favourites here. The pub is no-smoking throughout and you can eat in the dining area, which seats 18, or in other areas of the inn. And that's not all, The Cavendish also has a plot for two touring caravans with electric hook-up available all year round. Children are very welcome, there is occasional entertainment, plenty of off-road parking, and at the back there is extra room in a small marquee. This is also a pub where darts is important, and many famous darts players visit to give exhibition matches.

242

4 Potter Street, Melbourne,
Derbyshire DE73 8HW
Tel: 01332 863358
e-mail: enquiries@baytreerestaurant.com
website: www.baytreerestaurant.com

The **Bay Tree Restaurant** in the heart of Melbourne is one of the best known and much loved restaurants in Derbyshire. It has been in the same hands for over 19 years, and during that time its reputation has been built on good, honest cooking, fresh local ingredients and a combination of imagination and flair.

The co-owners Vicki Talbott and chef Rex Howell are determined not only to maintain the high standards they have set but improve even further on them as well. Rex admits to being somewhat severe in the kitchen if things are not 100% up to his standards but that is to his customers' advantage. The staff have almost become perfectionists and are amazingly dedicated to their work.

The restaurant is housed in a warm, old building of red brick that dates back to 1790, and which still retains many of its original features. It features in all the best food guides, and behind the 18th century brick frontage, the 70-seat restaurant has been refurbished in a cool contemporary style by designer David Wrigglesworth. You are well advised to book, as the place is as popular as ever, if not more so!

The menu changes regularly in this award-winning establishment, but always boasts the best of New World cuisine. There is always a great range of nibbles on offer, and, of course, the famous "Bay Tree Champagne Breakfasts". Favourites on their wide-ranging menus include the English breakfast grill 'for the hearty', natural smoked haddock fish cakes, and the hard-to-resist Canadian pancakes served with fresh blueberries or crispy bacon rashers.

Champagne Breakfasts are served from Tuesday to Saturday each week from 10.30am to 11.45pm. Lunches are served from 11.45am until 3pm, with dinners being from 6.30pm onwards. The Sunday hours are from 12.30pm until 4.30pm, and the restaurant is closed on Mondays.

The wine list has been carefully chosen to reflect the cooking in the Bay Tree, so there is sure to be something that will suit your dinner perfectly. And someone is always on hand to help you choose just the right wine!

There are various menus, including set price dinner menus, set-price lunch menus and à la carte menus. Children are most welcome, and all major credit cards are taken.

Celebrating your 'special day' or 'just being alive'? Here you'll get a meal that you are going to remember for all the right reasons!

103 IVY HOUSE FARM B&B AND WOODLANDS HILL COURT SELF CATERING

Stanton-by-Bridge, Derby,
Derbyshire DE73 7HT
Tel: 01332 863152
e-mail: mary@guesthouse.fsbusiness.co.uk
website: www.ivy-house-farm.com and
www.woodlandhillscourt.co.uk

Ivy House Farm B&B and Holiday Cottages
offer the very best in guest house and self-catering
accommodation to discerning holidaymakers. Set
on a working arable farm in the quiet village of
Stanton-by-Bridge, Derbyshire, Ivy House Farm
offers guests the chance to experience a traditional
farmhouse stay.

Dating back to the 17th Century and converted at the turn of the Millennium, the rooms are
aptly named after their former occupation on
the farm, including the Cow Shed, Sheep
Shed, Pig Sty and Stable. The four diamonds
rated accommodation offers excellent
amenities, with en-suite bathrooms, tea and
coffee making facilities and televisions. A
traditional décor adds to the natural charm and
character of the rooms. A hearty breakfast is
included in the tariff, and children are most
welcome.

The homely dining room lets guests enjoy
the delicious full English breakfast in comfort.
Proprietors Mary and David Kidd cater for the
preferences and tastes of all diets, with local
produce and home made bread contributing to
an excellent standard of food.

Within the adjacent courtyard is **Woodlands Hill Court**, five ground floor, self-catering
cottages, one of which is suitable for the disabled. They have been furnished, decorated and fitted
out to an exceptional standard, and sleep three to four. They come fully equipped, and the price is
all-inclusive with the exception of electricity. People should phone first for details of availability.
Local tearooms and cafés at Melbourne Hall, Calke Abbey and Staunton Harold provide quick
snacks with hearty meals found in pubs and restaurants a short drive away.

There is so much to do and see in the area around Ivy House Farm. Stanton-by-Bridge is a
sleepy, typically English village famous for its Swarkeston Bridge and Stanton Causeway. It was
here, in 1745, that Bonnie Prince Charlie abandoned his march south to take London for the
Jacobites. Derby is only a few miles away, as is East Midlands Airport and Castle Donnington Race
Track. Visitors are assured of a warm welcome on arrival and a comfortable base to enjoy this
beautiful area in the heart of England.

Whether you are visiting Ivy Farm House for an unwinding break or are travelling for a night
due to work, the idyllic scenery and laid back atmosphere ensure a relaxing time for all.

104 RISING SUN

I The Green, Willington,
Derbyshire DE65 6BP
Tel: 01283 702116

Rising Sun, is a picturesque old inn that was recently took over by Mark and Jo Shaw who have given it a new lease of life. This is a typical village 'local', full of charm and character, which acts as a focal point for the village and which always offers a warm welcome.

The spacious and comfortable bar is open all day and every day, and offers two real ales – Marston's pedigree and a rotating guest ale, which are always kept in tip-top condition. Plus there is the usual range of beers, lagers, cider, spirits, wine and soft drinks.

The food served here is delicious, and the finest and freshest of local produce is used wherever possible. The Sunday lunch is so popular; you are well advised to book.

Children are more than welcome, and dogs are allowed within the bar area. There is plenty of off-road parking, outside seating, and an upstairs function room with bar for up to 60 guests - just right for weddings, parties, anniversaries and conferences. The function room also plays host to 'The Real Music Club' on Thursdays from 8-11pm, this is a friendly and informal gathering of musicians, singers and poets, for details please log on to their website at www.real-music-club.com.

105 TRAVELLERS REST

2 New St, Church Gresley, Swadlincote,
Derbyshire DE11 9PS
Tel: 01283 216813

The **Travellers Rest** is a local community pub, situated in the village of Church Gresley, a short drive from the lovely town of Swadlincote. They serve a full selection of draught beers, wines and spirits for your enjoyment. The pub has a great atmosphere and a warm, friendly welcome making it a fantastic place for everyone to be. There is an extensive home cooked menu, so customers will never go hungry. Favourite dishes include the Steak & Ale Pie and Liver & Onions.

The Travellers Rest is a very family orientated pub, which hosts a wealth of charity and fund raising events for all the family to enjoy. There are regular themed evenings where all the staff come to work dressed up and anyone of customers who want to dress up can, its all for charity. Santa Clause also takes a visit to the pub at Christmas, there is always a brilliant party for children and the elderly while Santa brings them all presents. Christmas day lunch and Christmas parties can all be catered for.

To accommodate all customers who smoke, there is now a heated smoking shelter on the premises, along with a beer garden, which is a fabulous place to relax with a refreshing drink, while the children play happily in the children's play area. So why not get out your fancy dress costumes, get the family together and join in on the fun today.

245

106 OVERSEALE HOUSE

Acresford Road, Overseal, Swadlincote,
Derbyshire DE12 6HX
Tel: 01283 763741
e-mail: oversealehouse@hotmail.com
website: www.oversealehouse.co.uk

Whether you are en-route to a destination or wanting a long weekend...**Overseale House** is the obvious choice.

This beautiful George II country house set in 3 acres of land is the ideal place to rest, relax and visit the many attractions around the South Derbyshire area. Built in the 1770's and lovingly restored by its owners Peter and Anne Robinson. The house boasts eight bedrooms plus three bathrooms running along a central corridor, which extends the full length of the house. Each bedroom has a different style of decoration and individual fireplace.

The sitting room dates from 1760 and is the most original feature of the house. The windows are an astonishing 240 years old. The curtain valences were lost for years but were recently discovered, after a year long

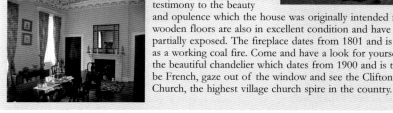

restoration, they are a testimony to the beauty and opulence which the house was originally intended for. The wooden floors are also in excellent condition and have been left partially exposed. The fireplace dates from 1801 and is still used as a working coal fire. Come and have a look for yourself and see the beautiful chandelier which dates from 1900 and is thought to be French, gaze out of the window and see the Clifton, Campville Church, the highest village church spire in the country.

108 THE BLACK HORSE

2 Top Street, Appleby Magna, Swadlincote,
Derbyshire DE12 7AH
Tel: 01530 270588
e-mail: theblackhorse@inbox.com
website: www.blackhorsevillagepub.co.uk

A far cry from the nicotine-stained boozers of old, **The Black Horse** offers fine food, sophistication and the perfect pint. In a slightly off-kilter sixteenth century grade II listed building The Black Horse is a typical village pub thanks to lovingly restored original features. Carla & Stacy, leaseholders, took over here in April 2008 and have ensured it retains a real flavour of days gone by and a relaxed and friendly atmosphere that is sure to refresh visitors however short their stay. To maintain the traditional and welcoming ambiance, they have become famous for you will not find any pool tables or jukes boxes in The Black Horse. Instead, you are free to sit undisturbed in the cosy bar area and enjoy a drink and a chat in quiet, relaxed surroundings.

Yet the emphasis here is quite simply on fantastic

real ales, which will turn even the most feminine of spritzer drinkers and food of a very high quality. Using locally sourced and organic produce the modern European dishes change with the seasons.

If you have a special occasion that requires something a little more special than your usual table for four book The Black Horse's private dining room which seats twelve. Private dining menus are available and cakes, place cards and so on can be arranged.

107 ROBIN HOOD INN

I Burton Road, Overseal, Swadlincote,
Derbyshire DE12 6LQ
Tel: 01283 760252

A short drive south east of Burton-on-Trent, adjacent to the A444, stands the village of Overseal. It is here you will find the **Robin Hood Inn**, one of the best establishments of its kind in Derbyshire. A new landlord, Allan Land took over here in June 2008 and brought with him a new buzz, more class and a warmer welcome to locals and visitors alike. The exterior is whitewashed, and has a quiet charm that is echoed in the interior. It is cosy, warm and friendly, just like a village pub should be. It is open every

day and sells two real ales – Marston's pedigree plus a rotating guest ale. There is also an excellent range of beers, wines, spirits and soft drinks should you be driving.

Bar snacks are available at all times, and great food is served in the dining area from 12 noon - 2pm Thursday to Sunday and from 6pm - 9pm Thursday to Saturday. The dining area seats 40 people in absolute comfort, and you can choose from a printed menu or a specials board. Sunday customers will see Chef's traditional lunch in full swing, with locally supplied meat and vegetables for the best value in the Derbyshire area. These come highly recommended so it is advised to book. All the produce is fresh and local, ensuring a great eating experience. All credit cards except Diners are welcome. To keep customers amused there is a pool table, Darts and Dominos, Quiz nites, Karaoke and live entertainment and that's not forgetting the large TV showing all major sporting events. There is also courtyard seating and a large off-road car park.

Don't worry if you have nowhere to stay, as there is plenty of accommodation available here all year round, if you feel you would like to stay longer to enjoy the fantastic atmosphere then please do. There are nine twin/double or family rooms. All bedrooms are en-suite, light, airy and comfortable and come well equipped with a TV, tea and coffee making facilities. The price is per room and includes Alann's hearty breakfast.

The pub has an excellent base of regular clientele as well as passing trade, why not pop in and experience the atmosphere for yourself. You may become a regular too!

109 MOIRA TEA ROOM

Moira Furnace Museum, Furnace Lane,
Moira, Swadlincote, Derbyshire DE12 6AT
Tel: 01283 226666
e-mail: moirafurnace@uk2.net
website: moirafurnace.co.uk

If you feel in need of some refreshments during your visit to the Moira Furnace Museum, you only need to head for the **Moira Tea Room**. Dine in style at Moira Tea Room, which is open all year to museum visitors and the general public. The Moira Tea Room is a great place to take a break from history and eat a modern sandwich. Enjoy a rich, hot coffee or perhaps a cold drink, together with a few items from the varied menu or one of the scrumptious homemade cakes. Open from 10am – 5pm during the summer and 10am – 4pm in the winter, the popular tea room serves a wide variety of home-cooked food, including a selection of sandwiches, delicious breakfasts, toasties, jacket potato's plus various cakes and

scones. There are also tasty daily specials and a children's menu. It is a pleasant location to meet friends or take

a break whilst visiting the museum.

The Moira Furnace was built in the early part of the 19th century, it is an iron blast furnace. The museum guided tour provides information on how the furnace worked and the lives of its inhabitants. Narrow boat trips are also available on the Ashby Canal, which runs along side the furnace.

112 CRICH TRAMWAY VILLAGE

Crich Tramway Village, nr Matlock,
Derbyshire DE4 5DP
Tel: 01773 854321
e-mail: enquiries@tramway.co.uk
website: www.tramway.co.uk

Crich Tramway Village offers a family day out in the relaxing atmosphere of a bygone era. Explore the re-created period street with its genuine buildings and features, fascinating exhibitions and most importantly, its trams.

Unlimited tram rides are free with your entry fee, giving you the opportunity to fully appreciate the Village and surrounding countryside.

Journey on one of the many beautifully restored vintage trams, as they rumble through the cobbled street past a traditional police telephone known as the 'TARDIS', the Red Lion Pub & Restaurant, exhibition hall, workshops, children's play and picnic area, before passing beneath the magnificent Bowes Lyon Bridge.

Next it's past the bandstand, through the woods, and then on to Glory Mine taking in spectacular views of the Derwent Valley.

137 Market Street, South Normanton,
Alfreton, Derbyshire DE55 2AA
Tel: 01773 810 748
e-mail: tricia333v@hotmail.co.uk
website: www.the-devonshire-arms.co.uk

Three years in, **The Devonshire Arms** in peaceful South Normanton has worn in and warmed up very nicely, and it's even more popular than ever. Tricia and Bill welcome you to The Devonshire Arms, where the prime concern is your comfort, relaxation and enjoyment. The staff are here to ensure your visit exceeds your expectations and everyone can be certain of a warm welcome. Classically old yet refreshingly new, The Devonshire Arms juxtaposes traditional décor with contemporary style, providing a venue that's hip and trendy to boot.

There's a variety of ales on tap, with local brews a speciality – such as Sarah Hughes or Dark Ruby plus three guest ales. Other beers include: John Smiths Smooth, Stones, Mansfield Original, Mansfield Dark and Manns Chestnut. For lager drinkers there's Stella, Fosters, Fosters Super Chilled and Carling. Not forgetting the cider drinkers, you can enjoy a chilled pint of, Strongbow, Woodpecker or Old Rosie.

A full food menu is available to view online at their website, but traditional favourites include: Homemade Pie, choose from Meat & Potatoes / Steak and Kidney / Steak and Ale pie topped with a rich short-crust pastry served with chips or potatoes, vegetables and gravy; Wholetail scampi in breadcrumbs, deep fried and served with tartare sauce served with chips or potatoes and garden peas; Battered or breaded Cod served with chips, tartare sauce and mushy or garden peas; Carvery with choice of meats with fresh seasonal vegetables, we carve the meat but help yourself to everything else! (Available Sunday until 3pm).

Do you have a birthday party, anniversary or engagement to celebrate? Whatever your needs The Devonshire Arms will do their best to cater for your function whether business or pleasure. Offering hot and cold buffets and refreshments together with the highest standards of service. Catering for special diets on request. Facilities include ample car parking at the rear of the pub and disabled access. Major credit and debit cards are accepted.

Located just a mile from M1 Junction 28, within easy reach from Mansfield, Derby and Chesterfield. At the gateway to the Peak District you can enjoy a refreshing drink with friends, a family meal or an organized function. Please note that children under 16 are welcome up to 9pm.

111 OLD YEW TREE INN

51 Manor Road, South Wingfield,
Derbyshire DE55 7NH
Tel: 01773 833763
e-mail: oldyewtreeinn@btconnect.com

The village of South Wingfield dates back to pre Norman times when it was known as Winefield. Nowadays, South Wingfield is better known for the hauntingly beautiful romantic ruins of it's superb fifteenth century Manor House than it is as a village, and appropriately village and manor seem almost completely detached.

This was the romantic setting for scenes from the films, 'The Virgin & the Gyps" and Zefferelli's adaptation of 'Jane Eyre', also the ruins have been featured in the TV series, 'Peak Practice' - but most famously, Mary Queen of Scots was held prisoner here on three separate occasions during the sixteenth century.

In its heyday Wingfield Manor was one of Derbyshire's, if not England's finest country houses – one of the largest and most lavish in the entire realm. It was a statement of power and wealth, designed and built to impress. The gatehouse alone was the size of a small castle - and larger than the homes of all but the richest in the land!

Set in this peaceful village, amongst all that history is the **Old Yew Tree Inn,** which is said to be one of the most haunted pubs in Derbyshire. It's a perfect destination pub in a very pleasant old style building with beams on the inside; here you're guaranteed good service with a personal touch. A range of real ales are served – usually Marston's Pedigree plus three others. The pub also does food – there are several menus providing an extensive range of dishes, choose off the printed: A La Carte menu, Table d'Hote menu, Early Doors Menu, Evening menu, Lunch menu and finally the Sunday Special. All food is locally sourced and cooked to order meaning the chefs are more than willing to cater to any special dietary requirements. A popular menu is the 'Early Doors Menu', which is served from 5pm to last orders taken at 6.30pm, favourite dishes

include: Homemade Smoked Salmon and Sweet Chilli Fishcake and Homemade Steak, Guiness & Stilton Pie. The menus are so extensive that there will be a dish to tempt any palate. Seating is limited to 36 persons inside, so it is advisable..ed to book at all times.

So whether you are looking for somewhere to hold your special event, or just want to enjoy a fantastic meal in a relaxing friendly atmosphere, The Old Yew Tree Inn, South Wingfield is the perfect choice.

Alderwasley, Belper,
Derbyshire DE56 2RD
Tel: 01629 822585
e-mail: info@bear-hotel.com
website: www.bear-hotel.com

The **Bear Inn and Hotel** is one of the oldest and most renowned Inns and restaurants in Derbyshire. Overlooking miles of countryside that spawned the Industrial revolution and the globalisation of textiles, the Derwent valley has played backdrop to many a canvas and Hollywood movie. The hotel is a well placed base camp from which to explore the delights of Chatsworth, Matlock Bath, Buxton, Derby and of course Alton Towers.

The fame of The Bear has spread in recent years, mainly as a Gastro pub of note, a hotel, carvery and real ale venue. Real Food, Real Ale, Real People, Real Derbyshire can be completed with Real History. The names and dates of all Innkeepers and owners from 1735 – 2008 are listed in the entrance hall of the Bear. Just standing beneath the beams of this beautiful English country Inn invites history to wash over you. Several fine English ales are on offer including Bass, Speckled Hen, Timothy Taylor Landlord and Hartington Ale to mention but a few.

The restaurant seats 70 with food served between 12.00-9.30pm Monday to Saturday and 12.00-9.00pm on Sunday where the carvery option comes highly recommended. Locally produced beef, lamb and pork are procured from butcher Richard Taylor (Owen Taylor) at Leesbrook just across the valley. Real Derbyshire really does mean local produce from Wirksworth vegetables to Chatsworth ice cream and Thornbridge Ales (Ashford in the Water). The Chef's specials vary from Wild Boar in apricots and red wine to various Italian and Thai specials such as lamb rump on a massala mash with Thai sauce. A good range of vegetarian dishes are also available. 2005 - 2007 saw The Bear winning the good pub food award.

The Bear has 8 rooms and 2 self-catering cottages that overlook miles of beautiful countryside. The rooms vary from premier with four-poster beds and rich fabrics, to standard rooms equally oozing character and charm. All rooms are ensuite.

The Bear is licensed for weddings and has a large function room. The Bear Hall combines venue and ambiance to make a wonderful day. The Bear has a helipad for those who choose to make a grand entrance. Alternatively, horse and carriage for the bride and groom can be arranged through Arraslea Shires.

Conferencing facilities with a range of packages for corporate clients are also available.

Alderwasley, Belper,
Derbyshire DE56 2RD
Tel: 01629 822585
e-mail: info@bear-hotel.com
website: www.bear-hotel.com

Conveniently located just yards off the A5111 Derby Ring Road, the outstanding **Greyhound Hotel** offers an excellent choice of tasty and nourishing home-made dishes. Dale and Stephen Vernon took over here in the spring of 2008. They have been together for 10 years but Stephen has been in the hospitality business for some 28 years. They have done wonders with the place - locals are flocking back and new customers are appearing all the time.

The major attraction is undoubtedly Dale's cooking. Her dishes are based on local produce wherever possible, are lovingly prepared and attractively presented. Portions are generous and the prices very reasonable. The main course menu offers a wide choice ranging from a hearty 10oz Rump Steak, through fish, chicken and pasta dishes to vegetarian options such as Mushroom Dopiaza. There's a separate choice of meals for children up to 10 years old.

Dale also offers a separate Lite Bites menu that includes hot ciabatta paninis, hot filled 10-inch Subs all topped with a generous helping of melted cheese and served with a salad garnish and dip pot. Burgers are also available as well as a variety of cold filled rolls. To accompany your meal, there's a wide choice of beverages in the well-stocked bar, including one real ale, Bass, served from the jug. Food is served from noon until 7pm, Monday to Friday; and from noon until 5pm on Saturday. On Sundays, Dale offers a Carvery with a choice of three different roasts. Such is its popularity, booking is strongly recommended. The hotel has a separate dining area seating up to 60, but if the weather is favourable there's plenty of room outside where there's also a sheltered smoking area.

This lively hostelry hosts live entertainment on Saturday evenings from 9pm, and on Sundays there's a karaoke from 7.30pm. Payment at the Greyhound is by cash only; children are welcome until 8pm; and there's good disabled access throughout.

5-7 High Street, Ripley, Derbyshire DE5 3AB
Tel: 01773 512300

The historic town of Ripley is another Derbyshire town whose past is steeped in industry. It was mentioned in the *Domesday Book* as Ripelie, and is situated about 9 miles outside the city of Derby. In the centre of town, housed above Hurst's the Chemist on the High Street you will find **Brocks Café and Bistro**, a place not to be missed for lovers of fine food. Owners Nigel and Diane invite you to sample their great menu comprised of locally sourced ingredients wherever possible.

Although a relatively young establishment, Brocks Café and Bistro has proven to be a very popular choice for locals and visitors who enjoy that 'home from home' experience. Upon entering, you are greeted with the distinctive smell of home cooking that whets appetites. Professional Chef Nigel has culinary experience spanning over 37 years, so you can be sure that the quality of the food that follows will not disappoint.

Opening hours are Monday to Saturday 9.30am – 3.00pm with closure on Sundays and at other times for private functions. Breakfast is served from 9.30am until 11.30am and lunch between 11.45am and 2.30pm. You are treated to a whole host of typical English items for breakfast, all offering good value for money, not to mention a great start to the day!

The lunch menu has a wide selection of meals with daily specials listed on the blackboard. You could enjoy the roast of the day, or perhaps some homemade fishcakes. If you are looking for a lighter bite, favourites such as wraps, omelettes, paninis and jacket potatoes are all available. For those with a sweet tooth, the dessert menu boasts much loved classics such as apple pie and custard or jam sponge. Such a great selection of sensibly priced food means that there will be something to satisfy all tastes.

A well-stocked and fully licensed bar offers a good selection of alcoholic and non-alcoholic beverages at very reasonable prices. Children are welcome.

At present there is seating for up to 50 people, but a refurbishment project is currently underway to expand the dining room area to allow for an additional 20 people. Upon completion of this project, the Brocks will be opening Friday and Saturday evenings as a bistro.

This café is definitely worthy of a visit or two!

116 BLACK BOY INN

Old Road, Heage, Belper,
Derbyshire DE56 2BN
Tel: 01773 856799

Do you remember when pubs were pubs? The **Black Boy Inn** at Heage is a gem and history leads us to believe that it has been named after King Charles II who was born with a very dark complexion and was, during the civil war, sometimes referred to as 'the black boy'. The following extract is taken from English Monarchs, The House of Stuart, "Charles' appearance was anything but English, with his sensuous curling mouth, swarthy complexion, black hair and dark eyes, he much resembled his Italian maternal grandmother, Marie de Medici's side of the family. During his escape after the Battle of Worcester, he was referred to as 'a tall, black man' in the parliamentary wanted posters. One of the nick-names he acquired was 'the black boy'."

The pub sits in a dip on the road to Belper and offers a fine selection of beers, wines & spirits and good

food. Delightful hosts, Angela and David have been here since April 2007 and are intent on ensuring that the Black Boy not only remains as an integral part of the local community, but also offers an unrivalled welcome to visitors from further afield. Food is served every lunchtime and evening, there is a choice of dishes available and are listed on the blackboards. Roast dinners are available everyday here and are extremely popular.

117 THE WHITE HART INN

2 Church Street, Heage,
Derbyshire DE56 2BG
Tel: 01773 852302
e-mail: sophieharris78@hotmail.com

The pretty village of Heage is where you will find **The White Hart Inn**, a historic 400-year-old country pub with plenty to offer. Proud owners Sophie and Luke took over the premises in July 2008 and wasted no time in undergoing a complete refurbishment. With the open log fires during winter and an ever-changing specials board of homemade food it's not surprising

that the inn is extremely popular. There are various themed evenings throughout the week from Pool Night on Tuesdays to Quiz Night on Thursdays. A large secure grassed beer garden, children's play area and an outstanding decked patio can be found to the rear.

118 EAGLE TAVERN

94 Ripley Road, Heage,
Derbyshire DE56 2HU
Tel: 01773 857235

The **Eagle Tavern** is very much a family run establishment, and this is reflected in the high standards of service and the warm welcome you get as soon as you step over the threshold! You can choose from two real ales plus a wide range of other drinks, and the food is exceptional. Choose from the menu or the specials board - you

won't be disappointed. Food times vary so please call for details. Everything is freshly cooked from local produce wherever possible. If you pay a visit, you're sure to come back!

254

119 SPANKER INN

Nether Heage, Belper,
Derbyshire DE56 2AT
Tel: 01773 853222

Situated in Nether Heage, off the A6 in the Amber Valley, the **Spanker Inn** is a real find - a traditional English pub that puts good ale, great food and a warm friendly welcome at the top of its priorities. Under the new management of delighted hosts Fiona and Andrew (who also own and run the Spotted Cow), they are determined not only to maintain the inn's fine reputation, but to build on it.

The interior is cosy and traditional, and here you can enjoy a quiet drink among the friendly regulars. It offers four real ales, the regular being Marston's Pedigree plus a vast range of rotating guest ales.

The produce used in the kitchen - meat, ham sausages etc - is all sourced from within the county, and Fish is from the Isle of Wight, ensuring freshness and flavour. Andrew is an experienced and professional chef and will oversee both kitchens, here at the Spanker Inn and the Spotted Cow so rest assured, you can expect quality cooking. People have come to enjoy his cooking so much that you are well advised to book on weekends. There is ample off-road parking, and children are very welcome.

120 DENBY VISITOR CENTRE

The Denby Pottery Company Ltd, Denby,
Derbyshire DE5 8NX
Tel: 01773 740799
website: www.denby.co.uk

The Visitor Centre is next to the Pottery in a cobbled courtyard with shops, restaurant and outdoor play area. It is open daily with activities from plate painting to cookery demonstrations.

In the museum you can see examples of pieces from Denby's rich heritage on display in the museum. A selection of Heritage Ware in the form of limited editions of Denby animals novelties, created from original moulds, are made by hand in the Craftroom and are on sale in reception.

Discover a selection of prints and original paintings by local artists in the artists gallery, and a tempting choice of gifts, jewellery, cards and home accessories are also available in the gift shop.

See hand-blown glass being created as your guide explains the processes in the glass studio. Tours are available most weekdays for a small charge and a selection of designs from The Glass Studio are on sale in reception.

Cookery demonstrations and an award winning cookware shop are among the other attractions, as well as a garden centre selling seasonal plants and gifts, a Dartington crystal factory shop and a restaurant and coffee shop.

121 THE POET AND CASTLE

2 Alfreton Road, Codnor, Ripley,
Derbyshire DE5 9QY
Tel: 01773 744150
website: www.poetandcastle.co.uk

Newly refurbished in May '08, **The Poet And Castle** boasts a very impressive range of Real Ales and ciders including local Ashover brews. Situated off the A610, it hosts a good variety of traditional, no-

nonsense pub food such as bangers & mash, meat & potato pie with real chips and mushy peas. Food is served 12.00-2.00pm every lunchtime and 6.30-9.00pm Tuesday to Saturday with a Sunday carvery 12.00pm-2.00pm (booking advisable). Bar Snacks are available all day and children are very welcome. A full roster of evening entertainment is available throughout the week including quiz nights and live music.

122 THE THORN TREE INN

21 Chesterfield Road, Belper,
Derbyshire DE56 1FF
Tel: 01773 823360

Renowned throughout Belper and beyond, **The Thorn Tree Inn** continues to entice visitors and locals alike with its fine selection of Real Ales and impeccable service. Welcoming owner and local man Mick Povey bought the premises in August 2007, and wasted no time in creating a relaxed, inviting and pleasant venue in which to enjoy a refreshing drink. There are up to 7 Real Ales to choose from, with Abbot Ale, Bass and Marstons Pedigree being the regulars but in a monthly period you can sample over 20 rotating guest ales, some from local breweries.

Very popular with lovers of sport, the inn offers Sky Sports on a large TV, Darts and a pool table, perfect if you are looking to pass the time with friends. There is also occasional live entertainment held (please ask for more details). The bar is open Mon – Thus, 4pm until close & Fri – Sun, 12 midday until close. Payment is by cash only.

120 Ashbourne Lane, Cowers Lane,
nr Belper, Derbyshire DE56 2LF
Tel: 01773 550271

The Railway is a friendly family pub located just outside the historic Derbyshire town of Belper. Belper was originally named 'Beaurepaire' (meaning beautiful retreat). If you tire of sightseeing and crave a cold pint and a homemade Steak & Ale pie, the Railway is hard to beat.

The exterior is extremely picturesque, with its whitewashed walls and hanging baskets and, with its warm wood and traditional appearance, the interior is equally as inviting. However, it is the food that draws people to The Railway. The restaurant is on a raised area, and serves some of the best home cooked pub food in the county weekdays between 12-3pm and 5pm-9pm, and all day until 9pm Friday, Saturday and Sunday. Although during the summer months food is available all day 12-9pm. You can choose from the set menu or from the specials boards, which changes regularly to include dishes that take advantage of local seasonal produce wherever possible. And as a pub food restaurant there are a fantastic variety of beers served to your liking either at the 'locals bar' or at your table. Alternatively you may prefer to select a suitable wine to suit your taste and pub meal.

Every first Wednesday of the month at The Railway is an internationally themed food night, with entertainment – you are well advised to book for these events.

Children are more than welcome at The Railway, and there is a separate children's menu and a play area outside, close to a decked seating area with heaters for those who wish to dine al fresco. Open all day, every day. Make it the next restaurant you dine at when you are having a day out in the Belper area. Belper and the district of Amber Valley offer something for everyone, glorious scenery, tranquil villages, bustling market towns and a wide range of attractions to appeal to all tastes.

You can choose from learning more about the area's vast industrial heritage, do some shopping or perhaps visit one of the many factory shops in the area. There are beautiful parks and gardens to visit; Belper River Gardens are amongst the finest in the country.

257

124 THE STRUTT ARMS HOTEL

The Bridge, Milford,
Derbyshire DE56 0QW
Tel: 01352 840 240
website: www.struttarmshotel.co.uk

The site of **The Strutt Arms Hotel** has been around for 150 years, starting life as a farm, the present building was constructed in 1901 for George Henry Strutt. An attractive building, the Strutt Arms Hotel provides comfortable, modern accommodation, quality food and a warm welcome. Ben Miller, the leaseholder since June 2008, had worked in the pub as a bar-manager for 13 years, so no lack of experience there, and he has succeeded in creating a friendly and warm pub atmosphere.

There are ten rooms available all year round, six double en-suites and four standard single, with a hearty breakfast included. There is quality, traditional pub food, made with fine local produce, available daily in the relaxing and hospitable restaurant; 12pm – 2pm & 5pm – late from Monday to Thursday and from 12pm – late on Friday, Saturday and Sunday.

The Sunday lunch is very popular and reservations are recommended to avoid disappointment. The bar has Bass, Marston's Pedigree and rotating guest ales on sale, which can be enjoyed on the comfortable leather sofa's in the lounge. There is a large off-road car-park, a riverside beer garden for the summer and full disabled facilities.

125 KING WILLIAM IV

The Bridge, Milford,
Derbyshire DE56 0RR
Tel: 01332 840842
e-mail: kingwilliam.mf@btinternet.com

Milford lies on the A6 between Derby and Belper, and it is here that you will find the **King William IV**, a pub full of olde worlde charm and character. Famed for its friendly atmosphere and service, it boasts four real ales, Timothy Taylor Landlord as the regular plus three rotating ales. There is also always available, one traditional cider, Olde Rosie. The King William IV is proud to host two beer festivals each year, one in April and one in September. During this period you can enjoy 14+ real ales, 3 ciders and live music every day!

Food available in the bar is limited to rolls and other light snacks, however there are several other establishments within walking distance offering a more extensive choice. Also on offer are three comfortable, en suite rooms (one double and two twins) that have been furnished and decorated to an extremely high standard. A traditional English Breakfast is included in the price.

There is live entertainment every Monday evening and a quiz night every Wednesday. There is pleasant walking country surrounding this location and further afield with easy access to the Peak District and Dovedale. For those interested in Industrial Archaeology, there are many relics dating from the beginnings of the industrial revolution and the use of waterpower to drive the cotton mills.

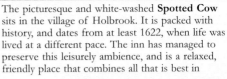

126 SPOTTED COW

12 Town Street, Holbrook,
Derbyshire DE56 0TA
Tel: 01332 881200
e-mail: info@thespottedcow.co.uk
website: www.thespottedcow.co.uk

The picturesque and white-washed **Spotted Cow** sits in the village of Holbrook. It is packed with history, and dates from at least 1622, when life was lived at a different pace. The inn has managed to preserve this leisurely ambience, and is a relaxed, friendly place that combines all that is best in English hospitality.

The customer is king at the Spotted Cow. It is owned and personally managed by Fiona and Andrew West-Hunt, who have been here since 2003, and so successful have they been that the Spotted Cow is now one of the best restaurants in the whole of Derbyshire, popular with both locals and visitors alike - which is no idle boast!

The Spotted Cow offers two luxurious bedrooms and one suite for over night accommodation. All decorated in designer style with sumptuous linens, scatter cushions and modern art. Breakfast can be bespoken at any time and all tastes from full English cooked breakfast to a lighter continental style repast can be catered for.

The Spotted Cow places great emphasis on its food. The menus are inspired both by English cuisine and foreign cuisines, with the chef, Tony, melding imagination and flair. Try the creamy garlic mushrooms, for instance, or home-made spicy salmon fish cakes for starters, or the mixed grill or medallions of fillet for lunch. And the evening menu contains such dishes as roast silverside of beef, roast breast of duck and chicken & pasta carbonara. There is also a popular Sunday carvery, though a carvery is, in fact, available every day!

127 THE PATTENMAKERS ARMS

4 Crown Street, Duffield,
Derbyshire DE56 4EY
Tel: 01332 824844
website: www.pattenmakersarms.co.uk

Dating back to the 19th Century, **The Pattenmakers Arms** is a traditional English pub where you can expect a warm welcome from friendly licensee's Claire and Scott. Choose from a wide range of drinks where regular ales on sale include Bass (by 'the jug'), Marstons Pedigree, Timothy Taylor Landlord and an ever changing selection of guest ales.

Located on Crown Street, within short walking distance from the main A6 trunk road, The Pattenmakers Arms is open every session and all day Friday, Saturday and Sunday. Good food is available over the lunch time period 12.00-2.30pm Monday to Saturday with a roast on Sundays (booking advisable). The menu comprises of no nonsense traditional 'pub grub' featuring old favourites like Ham and egg and steak and chips that are sure to satisfy.

A number of regular events are held every week, including a Friday Night Meat Raffle and Pub Quiz every Sunday Night. The Pattenmakers Arms has several teams competing in various pub sports leagues in and around the local area including Skittles, Darts, and Dominoes.

There is a function room complete with a dartboard, pool table and bar located above the main pub, which can host functions, gatherings and parties for groups of up to 30 people.

128 THE KINGS HEAD INN

I Town Street, Duffield,
Derbyshire DE56 4EH
Tel: 01332 841370
e-mail: kingsheadduffield@tiscali.co.uk
website: www.kingsheadduffield.co.uk

Formerly the chief hostelry of the village and was the billeting house for soldiers passing through the village. The last billeting there was about 1880 when a small detachment of horse soldiers spent the night there. But never has it offered hospitality quite like you can enjoy today. **The Kings Head Inn** is a traditional English pub, inside you can choose from a fine selection of beers, lagers, wines, spirits, and more, together with a warm and friendly atmosphere. Accommodation in a separate barn conversion is available at the rear of the pub. Perfect if
you are
travelling and
looking for
somewhere to
stay for the
night.

129 FINN M'COULS

35 Stanton Road, Ilkeston,
Derbyshire DE7 5FW
Tel: 01159 323139
e-mail: gaiqui@aol.com

Finn M'Couls is a good old-fashioned public house. Situated on the A6096, It offers a friendly atmosphere that is very popular with locals and
visitors alike.
Lively evening
entertainment
is provided
with karaoke
on Fridays and
live music on
Saturdays.

Sam and Marco invite you to sample a selection of Real Ales and their menu of excellent value food. Available 11.30-2.00pm and 4.30-9.00pm Monday to Friday, 11.30-7.00pm Saturday and 12.00-7.00pm on Sunday. A Monday special menu allows two people to eat for just £8 with various theme nights and specials occurring throughout the week. Children are welcome up to 7pm.

131 THREE HORSESHOES

Main Road, Morley, Derbyshire DE7 6DF
Tel: 01332 834395

This traditional, friendly inn epitomises all that is good about England's village pubs. Formerly a coaching inn, it is situated approximately 5 miles north east of Derby, in the tranquil village of Morley. The **Three Horseshoes** has been run by Laura and Richard for 6 years, and is popular with both visitors and locals alike. They have up to three real ales available, with Marstons Pedigree being the regular.

Feel free to dine in the cosy dining room, as well as the bar area or in the large beer garden. Their professional and experienced chef, Richard, has been in the business for 15 years, and he produces some truly delicious meals, using local ingredients. Choose from either the printed menu

or the specials board. The homemade Steak and Ale Pie is a favourite, as well as the ever changing dessert menu. Why not also try one of their Starters (including Chef's soup of the Day, Goats Cheese Bites, or Bacon and Black Pudding Salad), or the popular good old-fashioned pub meals (including Ham, Egg and Chips, Lasgane, Fish Medley, or a 10oz Rib-eye Steak). Food is served from Monday – Sunday (12-3pm), and Monday – Saturday (6-9pm). Need to book on Friday evenings.

Children welcome. All major credit cards taken and there is plenty of off road parking. Open all day 7 days a week.

30 Wood Lane, Horsley Woodhouse,
Derbyshire DE7 6BN
Tel: 01332 880385
e-mail: kgaskewnol@yahoo.com

Situated on the edge of the picturesque village of Horsley Woodhouse lies **The Sitwell Arms.** Dating back over a few hundred years, it was named after the Sitwell family, local landowners from Renshawe.

A picture postcard premises, where leaseholder Ken Askew took over here 12 months ago, after running a bed and breakfast business in France for 6 years. With all this customer service experience behind him you are sure to get looked after when you come to his pub. A very traditional looking place, which makes it popular with locals and visitors alike.

There are six real ales to enjoy, including Marstons Pedigree and Abbot Ale as the regulars, and the rest are rotated. Bar snacks are available at all opening times. The restaurant is open Thurs/Fri/Saturdays from 6 – 9pm and for the ever popular Sunday Lunch from 12 – 3pm. All meals are cooked freshly to order, using local produce, by the cook Ken. Booking is advisable.

Children are welcome, and can be kept occupied by the children's play area. A lovely beer garden is also available. Pay by cash and cheque only. The pub also have their own bowling green ready for customer's use. Open from 4pm – close (Mon-Fri), from 12 midday – 11pm (Sat), and from 12 midday – 10.30pm (Sundays).

132 ROYAL OAK

Green Lane, Ockbrook,
Derbyshire DE72 3SE
Tel: 01332 662378
e-mail: royaloak_ockbrook@hotmail.com

Located in the pictureque village of Ockbrook, The **Royal Oak** is a multi room traditional local which adds to the village's attractivness with its magnificent award winning floral displays during the summer. The oldest part of this welcoming hostelry dates back to 1762 when it was given the name it still bears. This is very much a family-run inn. Landlady Olive Wilson has been here 55 years and is now assisted by her daughters Sally and Jean with Husband Steve.

Jean is an accomplished chef and her appetising home-made fare provides a real magnet for lovers of good food. Her steak pie and Chilli dishes are particularly popular but whatever you choose, you won't be disappointed.

The wide choice of dishes includes steaks, fish, chicken and vegetarian options, cold platters and a selection of daily specials such as home-made beef & vegetable casserole.

The Royal Oak has been in the *Good Beer Guide* since 1976 and offers a choice of 4 well-kept real ales. The pub also hosts an annual Beer Festival in October when up to 40 real ales and ciders are available in the function room, all from a different county each year.

133 THE OLYMPIC HOTEL

Station Road, Draycott,
Derbyshire DE72 3QB
Tel: 01332 872104

Please note: there are no rooms available here. **The Olympic Hotel** is in fact a traditional country pub offering a cosy place to relax and enjoy quality freshly cooked food as well as superb ales.

Built in the mid 19th century, the Olympic at one time used by the railways with stables to the rear, Coachmen would bring and take people to and from the railway station. Today it is a popular venue for lovers of top quality home cooking.

The regular menu ranges from nibbles, snacks and salads, to mains such as Homemade Chilli Con Carne, Golden Scampi, Cheese & Potato Pie, Large Mixed Grill and scrumptious desserts. There is also an extensive specials board that is updated daily, all incorporating the best of seasonal produce. To

complement your meal there is of course a suitably outstanding wine list and choice of traditional real ales!

For a complete evening out the pub also provides a good range of entertainment on specific nights, Monday is 'Domino Night', Tuesday "Skittles", Wednesday 'Darts Night' and Thursday 'Pool Night'. There is a Skittles alley available for private functions and when the weather is right, take advantage of the spacious beer garden.

The Wharf, Shardlow,
Derbyshire DE72 2HG
Tel: 01332 793 330
e-mail: martinlynch@aol.com

The stunning canal side garden of **The New Inn** is extremely popular in the summer with locals and visitors alike, happily though this is not the only draw to this good looking pub. Also on offer is excellent food, well kept real ales and unrivalled hospitality. Shardlow, where the New Inn can be found, lies along the Trent and Mersey canal and developed quickly following the opening of the canal in 1777 and the boom of canal based trade. Full of attractive and picturesque old buildings, Shardlow has benefited from the conservation

effort during the late 1970's, which has retained several out houses built by the canal trade barons. Hidden amongst these magnificent properties is a superb setting for this great pub. Formerly cottages in the 18th century, the New Inn has now been run by Faye and Martin for 8 years and they have created a real success. The building is impressive, large and welcoming, the interior décor manages to be functional and still create a warm and cosy atmosphere for the guests and invites you to linger. Open all day everyday for business, the bar offers several rotating guest ales along with the well kept regular; Marston's Pedigree.

The menu is never anything less than tantalizing; the main courses include mouth-watering choices, such as Home-made Beef and Ale Pie, New Inn Cheese Burger, home-made Chili con Carne, Cumberland Sausage & Mash and Cajun Chicken. It is tasty traditional pub fayre from the grill, 8oz Sirloin, a monstrous 16oz Rump and 10oz Gammon steaks available. For a lighter bite, there are bar snacks on offer, Panini, baguettes, Jacket Potatoes; all with a large variety of fillings, several types of salads and an extensive children's menu. A popular day to visit is Sunday for the excellent roasts, a choice of two meats and mounds of accoutrements are supplied at a very reasonable price. The food is always made to order and produced with locally sourced ingredients where possible. Food is served between 12pm – 2.30pm & 5.30pm – 8.30 from Monday to Saturday and between 12pm – 4pm on Sunday. To avoid being turned away, a reservation is recommended during busy periods: Fri and Sat evenings. Children are very welcome until 9pm and there are full disabled facilities available.

135 THE OLD MARINA BAR AND RESTAURANT

Shardlow Marina, London Road, Shardlow,
Derbyshire DE72 2GL
Tel: 01332 799797
e-mail: m-oakey@btconnect.com
website: www.theoldmarinabar.co.uk

Mike and Carole Oakey are the proud owners of **The Old Marina Bar and Restaurant** and rightly so. The Old Marina Bar and Restaurant is about enjoying the company, the food, the surrounds and the friendly atmosphere. They cater for all needs, friends, families, young and old. It's about feeling relaxed and comfortable, whilst enjoying quality food and drink in a fantastic location. It's about local people, local produce and being part of the community. The bars fantastic family orientated atmosphere, friendly staff and gorgeous marina views makes The Old Marina a place everyone would want to spend the day.

For a leisurely lunch, an intimate dinner or a private party The Old Marina Bar and Restaurant offers mouth watering food using fresh local produce, prepared simply and served impeccably. Mick is the Head Chef! Justifiably, Mike is very proud of the food he serves and ardently protects his "fresh from market to table" reputation. He never buys pre-prepared or boil-in-the-bag and states emphatically "Our aim is to serve fresh food as fast as we can – not Fast Food!"

With over 30 years experience in the trade, Mike has prepared and cooked meals for Lords and Ladies, once being Chef for Earl Compton in Northamptonshire. He has won several awards for his cooking and offers patrons an extensive menu at reasonable prices. The mouth-watering Sunday carvery is not to be missed with heaps of fresh veg and roasted potatoes.

The Old Marina is situated in Shardlow, one of the best-preserved inland canal ports in the country, overlooking the colourful Shardlow Marina. The village is a fascinating place to explore, still busy with boats. Eat in the Dining Room or go al-fresco. The Old Marina boasts a large covered patio and an even larger full outdoor patio and eating area, where you can enjoy the gorgeous views. The Bar area serves an exceptional selection of drinks to suit all. As well as regular guest beers, The Old Marina Bar & Restaurant, has a wide range of beers and lagers including Worthington Cream Flow, Pedigree, Bass, Coors, Grolsch & Carling.

But it's not just about the selection of drinks or the fantastic food here; entertainment also plays a big part in the Old Marina and is very much appreciated by patrons new and old. Monday nights are quiz night, which kicks off at 8.30pm. Tuesday nights, swing to the sound of The Old Marina Jazz Band, plus Friday & Saturday nights host live acts.

A member of the Gourmet Society, The Old Marina Bar and Restaurant offers discounts to all society members and has a certificate award from Quality Cuisine.

117 London Road, Shardlow,
Derbyshire DE72 2GP
Tel: 01332 792728

The Shakespeare Inn & Restaurant is a Grade II-listed building standing in the village of Shardlow, just off the A50 and only three miles from J24 of the M1. Kevin and Sue Johnson and their family are delightful hosts, and their recent refurbishment programme has made the public bar, lounge and restaurant all looking very smart. Naturally, they've kept all the best bits from its original era but have combined these traditional features with a little modern flair, to create an inviting and slightly contemporary approach to dining.

Kevin's aim at the Shakespeare is to serve what they call 'Honest Food' - with substance and style - which has been sourced locally and cooked by the team in the kitchen. Essential to the operation here is a top-notch team in the kitchen overlooked by Kevin (an accomplished chef by trade), where there is an unusual attention to detail and to the quality of ingredients. They have a great, regularly changing 'Specials Menu' with exciting meat, game, poultry, and fish creations. They also have a dedicated menu containing only 'Fish Dishes' and features: Grilled Fillet of Salmon, Halibut with Lemon & Parsley and Scampi à la Crème (fresh scampi sautéed in butter with a white wine & cream sauce) to mention but a few – All dishes are accompanied by a selection of fresh seasonal vegetables and home made chips. There is an extensive choice of menus,

including those above plus 'Vegetarian & meat free options' and a comprehensive bar snack menu, which includes anything from .All Day Breakfast Brunch to Chilli Con Carne, Liver & Onions to Omelettes, or for those wanting a light bite, enjoy a simple chip butty.

Marston's Pedigree is the resident cask ale, with three regularly changing guests. Customers also benefit from free on site car parking and a well-maintained garden to sit and enjoy on those balmy summer evenings. The Shakespeare is open from 11.30am to midnight every day.

The first Friday of the month brings a popular jazz session and the pub hosts other live music evenings on a regular basis. Shardlow stands on the River Trent and the Trent & Mersey canal and was once a busy canal port. Commerce has long since been overtaken by leisure and the port is now an attractive modern marina.

So folks, come on down to The Shakespeare Inn & Restaurant - drop in for a drink, a snack or a great meal and enjoy yourselves.

90 Bondgate, Castle Donington,
Derbyshire DE74 2NR
Tel: 01332 812214
e-mail: thecrosskeys@ntlworld.com
website: www.thecrosskeyspub.com

Welcome to **The Cross Keys** and cheers! That is how to best describe The Cross Keys, "Everybody knows your name". From the moment you walk through the doors, you can feel the warmth and hospitality. The Cross Keys is a welcoming, friendly pub in the heart of Castle Donington. It is popular with locals and visitors alike, and has a sporty feel to it, as it has three teams attached to it - a rugby team, a cricket team and a football team.

Delighted hosts, Donna and Andy Moon, have been in charge for nearly 4 years, and have built on the solid reputation the pub had for its great atmosphere, its great drink and its filling snacks. You can be assured of a very warm welcome from the host and the friendly locals.

Benefiting from a recent refurbishment, the exterior is very attractive, and well-proportioned, and has colourful hanging baskets that add to its overall attractiveness.

Inside the spacious pub, evidence of the refurbishment continues with smart new toilets, newly decorated interior and a flat screen television, making it everything a good English pub should be.

Open every session from Monday to Thursday (though it is closed at Monday lunchtime except on bank holidays), and all day on Fridays, Saturdays, Sundays and bank holidays.

It serves four real ales - Deuchars IPA, Sharps Doom Bar, Marston's Pedigree and a rotating guest ale, plus a good range of beers, lagers, cider, spirits, wines and soft drinks should you be driving. Snack food is available lunchtimes and early evenings - if you're short of time why not telephone your order on 01332 812214. The local favourite is the traditional 'hand raised' Pork Pies – where you can help yourself to pickles, condiments and home made chutneys, all for a very reasonable price of £1.80. Other snacks include; Meat & Potato Pie; Peppered Steak Slice; Cornish Pasties; Small/Large portion of chips; Chip Cob with Melted Cheese to mention but a few!

In the winter months there is a quiz every other Wednesday night, and everyone is welcome (ring for details). There is plenty of outdoor seating in the courtyard, and ample parking spaces.

Donington Park racetrack is soon to be home to British F1 Grand Prix. The Park also houses the largest collection of Grand Prix cars in the world. It is only 4 miles from both the East Midlands Airport and the M1 motorway, making it an excellent location in which to stay when entering the county.

137 MALT SHOVEL INN

14 The Green, Aston-on-Trent,
Derbyshire DE72 2AA
Tel: 01332 792256
website: www.themaltshovelaston.co.uk

The Malt Shovel is an olde worlde inn found in the picturesque village of Aston-on-Trent, two miles from the well-known Swarkestone Bridge. It has a wonderfully warm and friendly atmosphere, welcoming new and old customers, making it a fantastic place for family and friends to drop in for a quiet drink. To stop all customers feeling hungry they serve a lovely traditional home cooked menu, each lunch and evening, with the produce being sourced locally where possible. The pub has recently come under new management but still, good, old-fashioned English hospitality are the watchwords here, and you'll be assured of a warm welcome if you visit!

140 THE ANCHOR INN

Station Road, Kegworth,
Derbyshire DE74 2FR
Tel: 01509 672722
e-mail: anchorpub@yahoo.co.uk

The Anchor Inn is situated in the village of Kegworth, a short drive from junction 24 of the M1. Yet, it sits peacefully in the countryside and opposite a picturesque canal. This pub is another of the four monuments in the village to the mock Tudor style of pub design, employed by Worthington and many other brewers in the 1920s. It was erected on the site of the previous Anchor that had served the trade created by the passage of commercial narrow boats through Kegworth on Soar Canal, which opened in 1778.

They have a well-stocked cellar, serving a full selection of draught beer, wine and spirits for your enjoyment along with a lovely range of soft drinks for all those non-drinkers and drivers. The pubs fantastic atmosphere and warm and friendly staff, make it a great place for everyone to be. And

not before too long, food will be available lunchtime and evenings. A printed menu will display, good traditional pub grub dishes. Please call for further information.

Ideal for walkers, cyclists or those touring the area, there are three letting rooms available, with shared bathroom. Extra facilities include a self-contained kitchen and laundry equipment. Tariff is on a room only basis.

267

139 YE OLDE FLYING HORSE

3 Churchgate, Kegworth,
Derbyshire DE74 2ED
Tel: 01509 672 253
e-mail: ivanandsarahb@btinternet.com

Kegworth is a charming old village, thought to have been founded sometime around the 8th century AD. Kegworth is located on the borders of Derbyshire, Leicestershire and Nottinghamshire, this thriving place hosts a few pubs, and standing out from the rest though is **Ye Olde Flying Horse**. Rebuilt in 1922 on the site of the former 'Flying Horse', the pub is an attractive, welcoming building and has overthrown its previously dismal reputation with the new tenancy of Ivan and Sarah. Ivan is a professional chef who has worked within the trade for 25 years, running premises in Yorkshire, Derbyshire and Leicestershire. With the help of a new menu featuring great food, well stocked bar and fun entertainment, Ye Olde Flying Horse is back on the map.

The pub is open all day every day, serving a range of real ales that you can enjoy next to one of the roaring log fires during winter. Food is served between 12pm – 3pm & 5pm – 8pm from Monday to Saturday and between 12pm – 3.30pm on Sunday. The menu offers good portions of great English pub grub at reasonable prices; Fish & Chips.; made with beer batter and served with garden peas; succulent 8oz Rump Steak served with chips, peas and onion rings; and Wild Mushroom & Asparagus Risotto: this creamy risotto is served with a jacket potato and peas, and these are merely highlights. The pudding menu beckons after the hearty main, tantalising choices include Treacle sponge with custard, deep filled apple pie with cream or the luxury chocolate sponge with a chocolate sauce. Reservations are recommended on Sunday lunchtimes, the Sunday roast is very popular amongst the locals. There are many food and drink offers available that change on a regular basis. All the food is made fresh to order and where possible includes locally sourced ingredients.

The pub is now a well known entertainment venue, everybody is welcome to the Monday night Quiz from 8pm, once a month there is live entertainment on a Saturday evening and there is a large games room with a full size pool table. The pub features a nice beer garden, a large off road car park and the village is in a prime location; close to Midlands Airport, Derby and Nottingham.

'A wonderfully friendly hostelry with top notch grub, will definitely be back!'

268

141 DONINGTON PARK FARMHOUSE

Melbourne Road, Isley Walton, Castle Donington, nr Derby DE74 2RN
Tel: 01332 862409 Fax: 01332 862364
e-mail: info@parkfarmhouse.co.uk
website: www.parkfarmhouse.co.uk

Once a fully working farm and threshing barn, **Donington Park Farmhouse** is a charming 17th century building that still retains the character of its past. The hotel and surrounding buildings are located in 20 acres of land on the beautiful Leicestershire /Derbyshire border, beside Donington Park Motor Racing Circuit. Owners John and Linda Shields, who have owned and personally run the hotel since 1983, also own the adjacent 500 acre farm and Donington Deer Park. So Venison is always featured on the menu, as well as being available for sale in frozen take-home packs (sausages, steaks, or joints).

The hotel offers a full range of dining facilities, including a Full English or Continental breakfast, tea, coffee and Bar Snacks, and the dining room is open each evening to residents and their guests for Farmhouse Suppers featuring many locally-sourced dishes including Venison from their own deer park. There's also a residential licensed bar featuring Real Ale.

The accommodation at the Farmhouse comprises 19 guest bedrooms, all are comfortably furnished with en suite facilities and fully equipped including a free-to-use broadband internet connection. Many of the bedrooms and the guests' lounge enjoy a superb view of the 12th century parish church high atop Breedon Hill.

The farmhouse has a series of original brick & timber barns which have been sympathetically restored to create a beautiful collection of rooms suitable for weddings, parties, company events and meetings.

Two of the rooms in the barn complex are licensed for civil marriages: the Hitching Room, for up to 80 guests, or The Threshing Barn, holding up to 150. Guests can enjoy the novelty of dining in style in former Pig Sties and dancing in a 17th century Threshing Barn! Finish the evening off with a Hog Roast, BBQ, disco or barn dance, great fun for all ages. The hotel can cater for parties of all sizes up to 300 guests, depending on your individual requirements. There is a large enclosed courtyard for your private use, ideal for children to play in while the adults can enjoy their party in complete seclusion.

Within the extensive grounds, the hotel owners have developed a lovely caravan site with 60 pitches, suitable for caravans, motor-homes or tents.

Lockoford Lane, Tapton, Chesterfield,
Derbyshire S41 0TQ
Tel: 01246 275 844

A short drive from the centre of Chesterfield is the small suburb of Tapton, it is here that **The Lockoford Inn** plies its trade, originally a farm and with parts dating back to the 18th century, the Lockoford Inn has recently been taken over by Vikki and Andy Greenan. Their success is virtually guaranteed with Vikki having worked on site for the past 12 years and she has become a very popular landlady indeed. Tapton is renowned for being the home of George Stephenson, whose name is synonymous with steam technology and of course constructed the world's first public railway line for steam trains to use. He was resident of Tapton House, constructed in Georgian style in the late 18th Century; it is now known as the Tapton Campus of Chesterfield College.

This popular inn is well known throughout Derbyshire, well frequented by locals and visitors, there is always something to keep guests amused, on Mondays and Thursdays the Lockoford inn hosts quiz nights, often themed; for example Body Parts or Connect 5. Every Friday night there is musical entertainment and on Saturday the live entertainment switches between

a guest singer and karaoke. Just starting up as well is the Tuesday Poker night, beginners and pros are welcome with a free buffet available.

The main draw to the pub is the food available; Vikki is a super chef and provides excellent food at very reasonable prices, offering such deals as two courses for just £3.99 for pensioners between 12pm and 2pm, Monday to Friday. Where possible, Vikki sources the food from local producers and has brought a delicious new à la carte menu in to accompany the existing choice. The specials board is updated daily with tantalising dishes, making it extremely difficult to choose! A popular choice among the locals is the Sunday Carvery, well priced and offering several types of meat with mounds of

accoutrements; the traditional Sunday lunch is served from 12pm to 5pm every Sunday. The bar is well stocked, offering local favourites Abbots real ale, John Smiths Smooth, Carling and Magner's Cider, catering for everybody's tastes.

The Lockoford Inn also has an ace up its sleeve: upstairs are three en suite, comfortably furnished rooms available all year round; with all the tourist attractions surrounding this picturesque location, the Inn is in an ideal base for visitors to the area. There is a large car park available and the Inn is open every day, all day.

143 COCK & MAGPIE

2 Church Street North, Old Whittington, Chesterfield, Derbyshire S41 9QW
Tel: 01246 454453

Old Whittington is most famous for its Revolution House, now a thatched cottage, but it once was the 'Cock & Pynot Inn' (Pynot is an old dialectic colloquialism for a 'Magpie'). Today it takes its name from the 'Glorious Revolution' that totally changed the face of English history. The national importance of the 16th century former `Cock & Pynot Inn' is signified both by its Museum status and its designation by English Heritage as a Grade 1 listed building.

Nearby and on the corner of Church Street North stands its late-Georgian successor, the **Cock & Magpie**, erected around 1790 and taking over trade from the former alehouse.

The Cock and Magpie is a warm, friendly, family-run pub. The front bar has low-beamed ceilings, cubbyholes and arches, plus paintings of animals and of the pub making it a cosy place to enjoy a convivial pint.

Choose from a full selection of draught beer, wine and spirits along with real ale and a range of soft drinks, and if you fancy a bite to eat, an excellent traditional home cooked pub menu is available, served in the lovely 80-seat

restaurant or throughout the pub. There is also a dedicated 'senior citizens lunch menu', offering a choice of soups or sweets with a main course for just £4.45 (correct May '08)!

The main menu has every base covered: there are steaks and grills, vegetarian dishes, pasta dishes, fish dishes and meat dishes, though not forgetting starters, sandwiches, 'Cock & Magpie' cobs, salads, jacket potatoes and a 'miscellaneous' section, which features cheese burgers, hot beef cob with gravy plus many more. You really are spoilt for choice! They also do a 2 for 1 Early Bird special, served from 5.30 to 7.30 Monday through Thursday and 5 till 7 Friday and Saturday. All

food is prepared to order and from local produce wherever possible.

But if that wasn't enough, and you require something in the way of amusement, then they have that too. Tuesday evening is 'general knowledge quiz night' from 9.30pm. Thursday is also a quiz night but these nights the theme is music. Then on the 3rd Sunday of each month – a well-known and much loved duet, called 'The Cadillac's' performs here.

Bolsover castle and many more attractions are situated just a short drive from this beautiful village.

Bolsover Castle, Castle Street, Bolsover,
Derbyshire S44 6PR
Tel: 01246 824 032

Originally built by the allegedly illegitimate child of William the Conqueror, William Peverel in the 12th Century, Bolsover Castle was built not for defence, but as an elegant retreat, reminiscent of an age of chivalry and romance. Ruined and restored many times throughout its history, Bolsover Castle can claim to have housed many famous historical figures including Mary Queen of Scots and Charles I. It is in this magnificent structure that **Whyld About Food** can be found, offering refreshment to the many thousands of people who visit each year.

Local couple Diane and Trevor created this superb dining establishment two years ago and it has gone from strength to strength assisted by their excellent staff. The name of the restaurant is quite apposite, as the couple's surname is Whyld. This property is ranted and raved about throughout Derbyshire and the neighboring counties and on tasting the food, it becomes quite clear why. Diane has won a number of awards at local shows for her scones and it is not just scones she is good at. The menu offers a variety of snacks and sandwiches to supplement a days sightseeing such as: homemade soup of the day, jacket potatoes with a variety of fillings, bagels, mouthwatering Panini and a selection of hot drinks. Highlights of the menu include the sandwiches, from which you can choose from Bolsover ham & Cavendish pickle, Dovedale blue cheese & real ale chutney and Chicken with onion marmalade. Similarly appealing are the Scones with jam and cream or the local Derbyshire Oatcakes. All of the produce used is purchased from local businesses and all of the meals are cooked there and then to order.

There is a small selection of wines and beers to be enjoyed with a meal or there is a choice of coffees, including espresso, latte, cappuccino and caffe macchiato, these coffees are all made with a local, unique Bolsover Roast. Alternatively there is a selection of teas and hot chocolate.

The café is open seven days a week between April 1st and November 1st, from November to March; the café is closed on Tuesdays and Wednesdays. There is seating inside or for enjoyment of the spectacular surroundings, there is seating outside. There are full disabled facilities available.

Bolsover, Derbyshire S44 6PR
Telephone: 01246 822844
website: www.english-heritage.org.uk

'By an unlikely miracle,' wrote the architectural historian Mark Girouard, 'the keep at Bolsover has survived into this century as an almost untouched expression in stone of the lost world of Elizabethan chivalry and romance.'

Dominating the countryside from its hilltop, Bolsover occupies the site of a medieval castle built by the Peverel family shortly after the Norman Conquest. Sir Charles Cavendish bought the old castle in 1612 and began work on his 'Little Castle' project. Despite its embattled appearance, his creation was not designed for defence, but for elegant living.

Sir Charles intended the house as a retreat from the world to an imaginary golden age of chivalry and pleasure. His son William, later Duke of Newcastle, inherited the Little Castle in 1616 and set about its completion, assisted by the architect John Smythson. An extraordinary survival, the exquisitely carved fireplaces and recently conserved murals and painted panelling of its interiors take the visitor on an allegorical journey from earthly concerns to heavenly (and erotic) delights.

A series of 'Caesar paintings' depicting Roman emperors and empresses has also recently returned to Bolsover. These were commissioned by William Cavendish and copied from originals by the great Venetian artist Titian - which have since been destroyed - making the Bolsover versions uniquely important.

Rotherham Road, Scarcliffe, Chesterfield,
Derbyshire S44 6ST
Tel: 01246 823 152

Situated in the picturesque village of Scarcliffe, home to the notable England cricketer Harry Elliott, the **Horse & Groom** is an imposing property offering magnificent views of the surrounding Derbyshire countryside. The owner Winston Butler has lived in the area all his life and the Horse & Groom was for many years his favourite watering hole. Winston bought the pub 13 years ago and with the help of his daughter Caroline and sons Robert and Richard, provides outstanding hospitality, ales and accommodation.

This 480 year old Inn is full of character and history, the building is imposing and the décor is fitting for such a handsome place. The Horse & Groom is open all day, every day for gossip, relaxation and well kept real ales, with 7 real ales on offer at any one time, there certainly is no shortage of choice; the 4 regulars are Black Sheep, Tetley's, Stones and Abbot, the 3 guest ales rotate and Winston reckons that the pub will go through around 200 guest ales in a year! The beers are in good

hands as well, the pub has been featured in the Good Beer Guide for the last 10 years. Occasionally there is live music of the folk variety and endowed with a superb beer garden at the rear, this place is perfect for a pint.

Scarcliffe is in a prime position, very close to a number of tourist attractions in Derbyshire, including Bolsover Castle, the Carr Vale Nature Reserve, Hardwick Hall and Poulter Country Park. If the abundance of attractions and things to see mean that you can't see them all in one day then don't worry because also on offer at the Horse & Groom is accommodation consisting of three self-catering cottages, available all year round. There are two upstairs with double beds and one ground floor which has a double bed as well as a bed settee, the cottages are spacious, comfortable and well priced. For more information about the accommodation available please contact the owners. There are full disabled facilities for guests wishing to drink, however please ring for details concerning the accommodation. Also available at The Horse and Groom are caravan and camping facilities.

Hardwick Park, Chesterfield,
Derbyshire S44 5QJ
Tel: 01246 850 245
e-mail: batty@hardwickinn.co.uk
website: www.hardwickinn.co.uk

The **Hardwick Inn** dates back to the 15th Century, beautifully built out of locally quarried sandstone; the property is situated very close to the National Trust's Hardwick Hall and the building is actually owned by the National Trust; perhaps more impressively, the Inn has been run by the Batty family since 1928; three generations later Pauline and Peter Batty run the place with the help of their daughters Sarah and Jenny and the head chef Paul Booth, who himself has worked there for 12 years. It is said that the Hardwick Inn is probably one of the best known dining and drinking establishments in Derbyshire and the long running service of the licensees and the head chef have probably been a major factor in the success of the Inn.

When entering the premises, it feels like stepping back in time, there is a traditional historic feel which is augmented by the comfortable, warm atmosphere, in the winter the roaring fires help to keep the place snug and cosy. The carvery restaurant looks glorious and offers the choice of three locally sourced meats and mounds of vegetables, Yorkshire puddings, roast potatoes and the suchlike. The menu is extensive, offering a variety of steaks, from a 10oz Rump and Sirloin to 12oz Rib-eye and 14oz T-Bone, a selection of salads, featuring seafood, poultry or just leaves and a wide assortment of starters to begin with. As well as the restaurant, a guest can opt for

some bar fayre, where guests can try some lamb from the Hardwick Estate, or the local in season game, rabbit and pheasant often feature, perhaps something from the River and Ocean dishes section or for the very hungry, the Hardwick Mixed Grill. The specials board is updated daily with sumptuous choices selected from whatever meat is in season and fresh that day. To accompany the meal, the bar is very well stocked, and features over 200 malt Whiskeys and 5 real ales: Old Speckled Hen, Theakson's Old Peculiar, Black Sheep, Bombardier and Theakson's XB.

The Bar Fayre is available between 11.30am and 9.30pm Mon – Sat and on Sunday between 12pm and 9pm. The carvery restaurant is open lunchtimes from Tuesdays to Saturdays 12pm - 2pm; and on Sundays 12pm - 1pm and 4pm - 5.30pm.

Tuesday to Saturday evenings the Restaurant is open between 7pm and 8.30pm.

Mansfield Road, Hasland, Chesterfield,
Derbyshire, S41 0JH
Tel: 01246 206 847

The **Telmere Lodge** is situated just a short drive from the centre of Chesterfield in the village of Hasland. The impressive premises had been shut for over a year before Andy, Helen and Helen's mother Mary took over as new tenants, and the Telmere Lodge has gone from strengh to strenth since. Andy, Helen and Mary are very hands on, they are always striving to make sure that each visit is one to remember by ensuring that the gardens are kept, the ales well rested and the food lovingly prepared. It is this attitude that has the locals flooding back and visitors arriving in droves.

The bar is well stocked, always present are Marston's Pedigree, Bombardier and Black Sheep, as well as one rotating guest ale, and with a very comfortable beer garden to sit in and enjoy them. The main draw of the pub though, has to be the food, Mary is

"Queen of the Kitchen" and utilises the local produce to great effect and has created a mouth- watering menu and daily specials, which depend on what meat is delivered from nearby Darley Dale. The menu includes a submenu from 'The Pie Shop' featuring; Steak & Kidney, Chicken, Ham & Mushroom, Suet Pudding and Steak & Stilton, all of which sound sumptious in their descriptions. There is such choice though; the starter menu holds tempting dishes like BBQ Spare Ribs, Smoked Salmon Wrap and the Telmere Special, which is a combination of Prawns and Crab Meat. The grill offers fresh meat daily and there are four cuts of meats from which to choose, starting at an 8oz Sirlion to a mighty 16oz T-Bone. Other dishes that stand out include a

Mushroom Tortellini Raphael, Poacher's Chicken, Portobello Steak, Poached Salmon and Smoked Haddock Florentine. And for the people lucky enough to visit on a Sunday, there are the ever popular Sunday roasts. Food is served between 12pm - 3pm & 5pm - 9pm Mon - Fri and from 12pm - 9pm on Saturday and Sunday; it is recommended that guests reserve tables for the weekend.

Thursday nights are special nights, known locally as Pie Night, the pub lays on a menu of home-cooked pies and follows it up with a quiz evening. The pub has extensive parking, a function suit available for weddings, corporate events and the suchlike and full disabled access.

Derby Road, Wingerworth,
Derbyshire, S42 6NB
Tel: 01246 232458

The Hunloke Arms is a substantial, well-proportioned inn standing just off the A61 two miles south of Chesterfield. It dates back to the 18th century and was once a well-known coaching inn, named after a lord of the manor of the day. With its fine Georgian lines and porticoed entrance, it looks every inch the grand, welcoming inn, and the mellow interior, with old wood, coloured lead glass and comfortable furnishings, fully confirms that impression. It has an excellent host in Gavin Hibbard, an experienced chef who is restoring the inn's reputation as a place to seek out for food and drink, combined with outstanding service and good value for money.

The bar is open all day every day for drinks which include 4 real ales - Deuchars, IPA, Black Sheep and a rotating guest brew - as well as a wide selection of beers, lagers, cider, wines, spirits and soft drinks.

Food is definitely the star here, served lunchtime and evening Monday to Thursday, all day Friday and Saturday and from high noon to 5pm on Sunday when a Carvery is available. The choice runs from sandwiches and light bites to burgers, grills and classic entrées like lamb's liver with onion gravy, mash & crisp pancetta, fillet of salmon with smoked salmon & chive butter sauce, and braised lamb shank with redcurrant gravy.

Everyone is welcome to join in the Tuesday and Sunday quizzes which start at 9pm, and there are occasional live entertainment evenings.

Children are made most welcome and all major credit cards are accepted.

277

150 THREE HORSESHOES

Matlock Road, Spitewinter, Nr Ashover,
Derbyshire S45 0LL
Tel: 01246 568034
e-mail: michaeljilavu@aol.com
website: www.pubonthehill.co.uk

Popular with locals and visitors alike, the **Three Horseshoes** is a well-known landmark at the 'top of the hill', four miles from Chesterfield on the Matlock Road. They serve an extensive selection of draught and bottled beers, lagers, wines and non-alcoholic beverages to accommodate everyone's needs. Also credited is its real ale list and fine selection of malt Whiskey. But the real emphasis here is on the food, *"this is not just pub food, this is Three Horseshoe's pub food"*. A long-standing feature of the menu is their proud claim to 'The Best Cod and Chips in the area'. The fish is delivered fresh from Aberdeen and beer battered. Since 2001 Michael, owner and trained chef for over 40 years, has successfully introduced an inventive Mediterranean based cuisine to complement the traditional

English flavours. So alongside sirloin steak, surf and turf, roast Gressingham duck and slow cooked shank of lamb, you might find feta cheese and Mediterranean pie, squid and prawn kebab, and specials such as paella, fried tender calamari, smoked haddock and fresh fish cakes. Together with the pubs imaginative new refurbishment and family friendly surroundings you'd be forgiven for spending the whole day there.

151 KING EDWARD VII

121 High Street, Tibshelf,
Derbyshire DE55 5PP
Tel: 01773 591019

Bless 'em all! Our various Royal families over the centuries have inspired more names and images for pub signs than any other family, quite willingly allowing themselves to adorn signs up and down the country.

So why exactly are so many pub names inspired by the monarchy? The answer is basically that their images have always been very recognisable, quite a consideration when the majority of the population could neither read nor write. A recent addition to the ranks of monarchy inspired pubs came in 2003 with the re-appearance of the **King Edward VII** at Tibshelf. For many years it was known as NUCS club but now this black and white building is an outstanding inn, where you can enjoy a cosy drink, a delicious meal, a comfortable night's sleep - or all three.

The traditional British pub hosts seven bedrooms, three of which are equipped with double beds and en-suite bathrooms. There are also four single and shared bedrooms with shared shower room and separate toilets. All of the rooms contain a range of amenities including central heating, television and tea and coffee making facilities. Prices range from £20 per person per night on a room only basis, £25 for breakfast to be included, but for £30 you enjoy bed, breakfast and a delicious home cooked meal.

Guests can relax in the evenings and enjoy a quiet drink in the bar, or join chefs Duncan and Liz with a range of traditional English dishes including large 8" Yorkshire pudding and Homemade Steak Pie on the menu. You will never be disappointed by the range of meals on offer, all homemade and produced from the finest local ingredients. There is a range of wines to choose from to complement your meal or a selection of real ales if you prefer.

For people who enjoy sport there is sport shown by Sky Sports across four big screen televisions, a pool table and darts board to have a practice in readiness for the team matches. Other entertainment includes live singers, karaoke and quiz nights.

So, if you are looking for delicious home cooked food, fine cask conditioned ales in a relaxed friendly environment then look no further.

152 BATEMAN'S MILL COUNTRY HOTEL AND RESTAURANT

Mill Lane, Old Tupton, Chesterfield,
Derbyshire S42 6AE
Tel: 01246 862296 Fax: 01246 865672
e-mail: info@batemansmill.co.uk
website: www.batemansmill.co.uk

The award winning **Bateman's Mill Country Hotel and Restaurant** is a conversion of an 18th century mill house, located in a quiet rural area on the edge of the Peak District and in easy travelling distance from many National Park attractions including Chatsworth Estate, Haddon Hall, Hardwick Hall, Bakewell and historic Chesterfield.

Owned and operated by John, Maggie and Steven Roberts since late 2004, the Hotel under their ownership has won a number of awards and accolades, including Winner Outstanding Quality Award 2005/6.

Charming classical country style bedrooms all en-suite with Sky TV, tea and coffee making facilities, trouser press, hairdryer, direct dial telephone, data access and easy accessible rooms on the ground floor. Tariffs include full breakfast with choices from a very comprehensive menu.

Chef-Proprietor John Roberts, a Member of the Master Chefs of Great Britain, produces wonderful food focusing on modern European dishes with an emphasis on local produce. The Hotel offers several dining options, from bar meals to lunches and dinners. You can eat in the ground floor bar and restaurant, first floor Millers Restaurant or for that extra special occasion in the private dining suite. John also invites you to his cookery demonstrations, held during the daytime in the hotel kitchen. A 2-course lunch and wine is included in this package – please call for details.

Menus are changed on a regular basis, with the Specials restaurant menu including dishes, such as, pan-fried scallops, with pancetta and tomato and herb oil dressing; Bresola salad, with light cured beef, fine leaves, croutons, warm poached egg and mint dressing; roast rump of local lamb, dauphinoise potatoes, red wine and thyme jus; or for dessert, warm pear and almond tart with crème anglaise; Baked fresh figs and pineapple in brandy, caramel sauce and coconut ice-cream. Lighter dishes, steaks and salads are available in the ground floor bar, which with its feature well race, open fire and exposed beams offers a comfortable setting for guests wishing to dine more informally or enjoy a drink from an extensive wine and beverage list, which includes real ales.

Families, cyclists and walkers are welcomed at the Mill, and John and Maggie provide a host of local information to assist you in visiting the area. Dogs are also welcome by prior arrangement and the owners can offer a variety of packages including discounted ticket entry to Chatsworth House (subject to availability). You are ensured a very warm welcome at this lovely hotel, which prides itself on the quality of food and service, recognised by a number of awards.

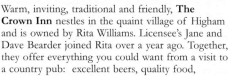

Main Road, Old Higham,
Derbyshire DE55 6EH
Tel: 01773 832310
Fax: 01773 830483

Warm, inviting, traditional and friendly, **The Crown Inn** nestles in the quaint village of Higham and is owned by Rita Williams. Licensee's Jane and Dave Bearder joined Rita over a year ago. Together, they offer everything you could want from a visit to a country pub: excellent beers, quality food, friendly, professional service, an inviting atmosphere and great company. With décor from a bygone era of charming inns, The Crown Inn has worked with the history of the building to enhance its natural beauty and create a pleasant environment that encourages patrons to linger and savour the experience.

In a previous incarnation it was the 'Black Bull Inn', for centuries the social centre of the village, and in this relatively quiet 'conservation area' of today, it is hard to believe that in the 18th century when the Derby to Sheffield coaches changed here, the Black Bull had its own ballroom - and a small theatre where touring companies regularly performed on market day!

Nowadays the pub offers quality drink, food and accommodation. The standard flagship ale is Bombardier and two other rotating guest ales accompany it. A traditional menu can be enjoyed throughout the pub for a more relaxing atmosphere. Food is served 5pm - 9pm Mon - Sat, 12 - 2pm Friday & Saturday, Carvery Sunday 12 - 3pm & Wed evening 5pm -9pm.

To keep all the customers amused, there is a Quiz night every Tuesday from 9pm, an acoustic night each Thursday as well as live entertainment on Friday's from 9pm. Karaoke nights are also held occasionally at weekends, these are always a great night for all, and everyone is welcome to have a go. For more information on up-coming events please call for details.

Also for customers who are looking to spend

the night, the Crown Inn would be more than happy to accommodate you in one of their guest rooms. There are ten rooms available in a variety of sizes, all rooms are en-suite with a TV and tea and coffee making facilities. Tariff includes breakfast. And for customers who drive, the pub has one large car park available, where you can be assured the car is left in safe hands.

This small friendly pub is much loved by locals and by anyone who has the good fortune of stumbling upon it. It is well worth going out of your way to visit.

115 Carr Lane, Dronfield Woodhouse,
Derbyshire S18 8XF
Tel: 01142 891 407
e-mail: the_miners_arms@btconnect.com

Found in the picturesque village of Dronfield Woodhouse, **The Miners Arms** has a reputation for quality cuisine and fine ales; Jenny and Mark took over two years ago and the pub's popularity has gone from strength to strength. Awarded the Cask Marque for well kept beers, the pub offers 3 real ales for the discerning customer: Black Sheep, Greene King IPA and the locally brewed Easy Rider. The menu is packed with traditional pub fayre, cooked using the best of local meat and vegetables, tempting dishes include Steak and Guinness Pie, Red Thai Chicken Curry and Sausage and Mash. The grill offers a range of steaks, from an 8oz Sirloin to a mighty 14oz T-bone cooked to the

customer's preference and served with chips, mushrooms, peas and tomato. The pub is a busy venue, providing a quiz and bingo on Tuesday and Thursday nights, and live music once a month which are very popular among the locals. The pub also lay on meal deals for pensioners during the week's lunchtimes. The pub has a large car park, a super beer garden and full disabled facilities.

HIDDEN PLACES GUIDES

Explore Britain and Ireland with *Hidden Places* guides - a fascinating series of national and local travel guides.

Packed with easy to read information on hundreds of places of interest as well as places to stay, eat and drink.

Available from both high street and internet booksellers

For more information on the full range of *Hidden Places* guides and other titles published by Travel Publishing visit our website on

www.travelpublishing.co.uk
or ask for our leaflet by phoning **01752 276660** or
emailing **info@travelpublishing.co.uk**

THE HIDDEN PLACES OF
THE LAKE DISTRICT AND CUMBRIA

THE HIDDEN PLACES OF
THE PEAK DISTRICT AND DERBYSHIRE

THE HIDDEN PLACES OF
DEVON

Tourist Information Centres

ADDERSTONE

Adderstone Services, Adderstone Garage, Belford,
Northumberland NE70 7JU
e-mail: adderstone@hotmail.com
Tel: 01668 213678

AMBLE

Queen Street Car Park, Amble,
Northumberland NE65 0DQ
e-mail: ambletic@alnwick.gov.uk
Tel:01665 712313

ASHBOURNE

13 Market Place, Ashbourne, Derbyshire DE6 1EU
e-mail: ashbourneinfo@derbyshiredales.gov.uk
Tel: 01335 343666

BAKEWELL

Old Market Hall, Bridge Street, Bakewell,
Derbyshire DE45 1DS
e-mail: bakewell@peakdistrict-npa.gov.uk
Tel: 01629 813227

BURTON UPON TRENT

Coors Visitor Centre, Horninglow Street,
Burton upon Trent, Staffordshire DE14 1NG
e-mail: tic@eaststaffsbc.gov.uk
Tel: 01283 508111

BUXTON

The Crescent, Buxton, Derbyshire SK17 6BQ
e-mail: tourism@highpeak.gov.uk
Tel: 01298 25106

CASTLETON

Buxton Road, Castleton, Hope Valley,
Derbyshire S33 8WN
e-mail: castleton@peakdistrict.gov.uk
Tel: 01629 816558

CHESTERFIELD

Rykneld Square, Chesterfield, Derbyshire S40 1SB
e-mail: tourism@chesterfield.gov.uk
Tel: 01246 345777

DERBY

Assembly Rooms, Market Place, Derby,
Derbyshire DE1 3AH
e-mail: tourism@derby.gov.uk
Tel: 01332 255802

HOLMFIRTH

49-51 Huddersfield Road, Holmfirth,
West Yorkshire HD9 3JP
e-mail: holmfirth.tic@kirklees.gov.uk
Tel: 01484 222444

LEEK

Stockwell Street, Leek, Staffordshire ST13 5HH
e-mail: tourism.services@staffsmoorlands.gov.uk
Tel: 01538 483741

MACCLESFIELD

Town Hall, Macclesfield, Cheshire SK10 1DX
e-mail: informationcentre@macclesfield.gov.uk
Tel:01625 504114

MATLOCK BATH

The Pavillion, Matlock, Derbyshire DE4 3NR
e-mail: matlockbathinfo@derbyshiredales.gov.uk
Tel: 01629 55082

MATLOCK

Crown Square, Matlock, Derbyshire DE4 3AT
e-mail: matlockinfo@derbyshiredales.gov.uk
Tel: 01629 583388

RIPLEY

Town Hall, Market Place, Ripley, Derbyshire DE5 3BT
e-mail: touristinformation@ambervalley.gov.uk
Tel: 01773 841488

SHEFFIELD

Visitor Information Point, 14 Norfolk Row,
Sheffield S1 2PA
e-mail: visitor@sheffield.gov.uk
Tel: 0114 2211900

SWADLINCOTE

Sharps Pottery Museum, West Street, Swadlincote,
Derbyshire DE11 9DG
e-mail: tic@sharpespotterymuseum.org.uk
Tel: 01283 222848

Towns, Villages and Places of Interest

A

Adlington 33
  Adlington Hall 33
Aldwark 86
  Green Low 87
Alfreton 128
  Alfreton Heritage Centre 128
  Alfreton Park 128
  Parish Church of St Martin 128
Alport 61
  Harthill Hall Farm 62
  Monk's Hall 62
  River Bradford 62
Alsop-en-le-Dale 90
  Alsop Hall 90
  Cross Low 91
  Green Low 91
  Moat Low 91
  Nat Low 91
  Parish Church of St Michael and all
    Angels 90
  Viator's Bridge 90
Alstonefield 95
  Hanson Grange 96
  Parish Church of St Peter 96
  Tithe Barn 96
Ambergate 132
Ashbourne 79
  Gingerbread Shop 80
  Grammar School 80
  Green Man and Black's Head Royal
    Hotel 80
  Market Square 79
  Owfield's Almshouses 80
  Parish Church of St Oswald 80
  Pegg's Almshouses 80
  Spalden Almshouses 81
  The Mansion 80
Ashford in the Water 45
  Ashford Hall 46
  Churchdale Hall 46
  Parish Church of the Holy Trinity 45
  Sheep Wash Bridge 45
  Thornbridge Hall 46
Ashover 169
  Cocking Tor 170
  Eastwood Hall 170
  Parish Church of All Saints 169, 170
  The Fabric 169

Aston-on-Trent 151
  Aston Hall 151
  Parish Church of All Saints 151
Ault Hucknall 164
  Hardwick Hall 164
  Parish Church of St John the Baptist
    166

B

Bakewell 38
  Agricultural Business Centre 39
  Aldern House 38
  All Saints Parish Church 38
  Alm Houses 40
  Bagshawe Hall 40
  Bakewell Information Centre 40
  Bakewell Pudding 39
  Bloomers Original Bakewell Pudding
    Shop 39
  Chatsworth 39
  Five-Arched Bridge 38
  Haddon Hall 40
  Holme Hall 40
  Lumford Mill 40
  Market Hall 40
  Old House 40
  Old House Museum 40
  Old Packhorse Bridge 38
  The Old Original Bakewell Pudding Shop
    39
  The Rutland Arms 39
Ballidon 86
Bamford 24
  Bamford Edge 24
  Bamford Mill 25
  Bamford Sheepdog Trials 25
  Cutthroat Bridge 25
  Ladybower 24
  St John the Baptist Parish Church 24
  The Derwent Dam 25
  Upper Derwent 24
  Visitor Centre at Fairholmes 25
Barlborough 160
  Barlborough Hall 160
  Barlborough Old Hall 160
  Market Cross 161
  Parish Church of St James 161
Barlow 171
Barrow-on-Trent 121
  Parish Church of St Wilfrid's 121

Baslow 28
  Devonshire Bridge 29
  Eagle Stone 29
  Old Bridge 29
  St Anne's 29
  Wellington Monument 30
Beeley 55
  Hob Hurst's House 55
  Parish Church of St Anne 55
Belper 138
  Chapel of St John the Baptist 139
  Derwent Valley Visitor Centre 139
  East Mill 139
  George Brettle's Warehouse 140
  North Midland Railway 139
  North Mill 139
  Parish Church of St Peter 140
  River Derwent 139
  The River Gardens 139
Birchover 64
  Cratcliff Tor 65
  Robin Hood's Stride 65
  Rowtor Chapel 64
  Rowtor Rocks 64
Bollington 33
  Discovery Centre 34
  Middlewood Way 34
  White Nancy 34
Bolsover 162
  Bolsover Castle 162
  Parish Church of St Mary's 163
Bonsall 72
  Bonsall Brook 72
  Parish Church of St James 72
Borrowash 147
  Parish Church of St Stephen 147
Bosley 35
  Macclesfield Canal 35
Boylestone 114
  St John the Baptist 114
Brackenfield 169
  Parish Church of the Holy Trinity 169
  Trinity Chapel 169
Bradbourne 85
  Bradbourne Hall 85
  Bradbourne Stone 85
  Parish Church of All Saints 85
  The Old Parsonage 85

Bradley 82
Bradley Hall 82
Parish Church of All Saints 82
Bradwell 23
Bagshawe Cavern 24
Grey Ditch 23
Brailsford 112
Parish Church of All Saints 113
Brassington 85
Chapel of All Saints 86
Harborough Rocks 86
Minning Low 86
Parish Church of St James 86
Rainster Rocks 86
Breadsall 110
Parish Church of All Saints 111
The Old Hall 110
Breaston 148
Millennium Sensory Garden 148
Parish Church of St Michael 148
Bretby 121
Bretby Hall 121
Brough 23
Navio 23
Buxton 5
Axe Edge 8
Buxton Museum 7
Buxton Opera House 7
Buxton Pavilion Gardens 6
Great Stables 5
Market Place Fountain 7
Opera House 7
Pym Chair 8
St Anne's Church 7
St John the Baptist Church 7
The Crescent 5
Turner's Memorial 6
Buxworth 11

C

Calke 118
Calke Abbey 118
Calver 28
Calver Bridge 28
Georgian Cotton Mill 28
On Foot Through The Peak 28
Castle Donington 151
Donington Park Museum 151
Nottingham East Midlands Airport 152
Parish Church of St Edward, King and
Martyr 151

Castle Gresley 124
Castle Knob 124
Castleton 20
Blue John Mine 21
Castleton Visitor Centre 21
Lord's Seat 20
Mam Tor 20
Oak Apple Day 21
Peak Cavern 22
Peveril Castle 20
Speedwell Cavern 21
St Edmund Parish Church 20
The Ollerenshaw Collection 20
Treak Cliff Cavern 22
Winnats Pass 20
Cauldon 103
Chapel-en-le-Frith 9
Chestnut Centre 10
Eccles Pike 10
Charlesworth 16
Melandra Castle 16
St John the Baptist Parish Church 16
Chelmorton 52
Parish Church of St John the Baptist 52
Chesterfield 156
Chesterfield Canal 157
Chesterfield Museum and Art Gallery
157
Market Hall 156
of the Parish Church of St Mary and All
Saints 156
Queen's Park 158
Shambles 156
Chinley 11
Chinley Chapel 11
Chinley Churn 11
Chinley Viaducts 11
Cracken Edge 11
Ford Hall 11
Church Broughton 115
Old Hall 115
Parish Church of St Michael 115
Church Gresley 123
Parish Church of St Mary and St George
123
Clay Cross 168
Clay Cross Countryside Centre 168
Parish Church of St Bartholomew 168
Clowne 161
Parish Church of St John the Baptist
161
Codnor 137
Codnor Castle 138, 139

Combs 9
Combs Reservoir 9
Coton-in-the-Elms 124
Parish Church of St Mary 124
Cressbrook 47
Cressbrook Mill 48
Cressbrook Dale 47
Creswell 161
Creswell Crags 162
Model Village 162
Crich 131
Crich Stand 131
Crich Tramway Village 131
Parish Church of St Mary 131
Cromford 70
Cromford Canal 71
Cromford Mill 70
Cromford Venture Centre 71
Cromford Wharf 71
High Peak Trail 71
Leawood Pumping Station 71
Wigwell Aqueduct 71
Crowdecote 54
Chrome Hill 54
Parkhouse Hill 54
Curbar 27
Cliffe College 28
Cundy Graves 27
Curbar Edge 28
Cutthorpe 171
Linacre Reservoirs 171

D

Dale Abbey 144
Dale Abbey 145
Hermit's Wood 145
Parish Church of All Saints 145
Darley Abbey 109
Abbey of St Mary 110
Parish Church of St Matthew 110
Darley Dale 59
Darley Yew 59
Mill Close Mine 60
Oker Hill 59
Parish Church of St Helen 59
Red House Carriage Museum 60
Whitworth Institute 59
Denby 136
Denby Pottery 136
Parish Church of St Mary 137
Derby 106

Allestree Park 109
Arboretum 109
Cathedral of All Saints 106
City Museum and Art Gallery 108
Derby Gaol 108
Derby Industrial Museum 107
Markeaton Park 109
Pickford's House Museum 107
Quad 109
Rolls-Royce 106
Royal Crown Derby Porcelain 106
St Mary's Chapel on the Bridge 107
Dinting 17
Dinting Arches 17
Holy Trinity 18
Donisthorpe 125
Doveridge 114
Parish Church of St Cuthbert 114
Draycott 148
Draycott House 148
Victoria Mill 148
Dronfield 172
Chiverton House 172
Cruck Barn 172
Manor House 172
Parish Church of St John the Baptist 172
Peel Monument 172
Rose Hill 172
The Cottage 172
The Hall 172
Duffield 141
Duffield Castle 141
Duffield Hall 142
Parish Church of St Alkmund 141

E

Earl Sterndale 53
Parish Church of St Michael 54
Eckington 159
Parish Church of St Peter and St Paul 159
Ecton 96
Edale 18
Edale Cross 20
Jacob's Ladder 20
Pennine Way National Trust Trail 19
The Moorland Centre 20
Edensor 40
Chatsworth House 40
St Peter's Church 41
Ednaston 113
Ednaston Manor 113

Elton 66
Grey Ladies 67
Nine Stones 67
Elvaston 148
Elvaston Castle 148
Golden Gates 149
Parish Church of St Bartholomew 149
Etwall 116
Etwall Hall 116
Parish Church of St Helen 116
Port Hospital Almshouses 116
Eyam 43
Eyam Hall 44
Eyam Moor 44
Eyam Museum 44
Parish Church of St Lawrence 44
Plague Village 43
Riley Graves 43

F

Farnah Green 140
Fenny Bentley 87
Cherry Orchard Farm 87
Parish Church of St Edmund's 87
Flagg 52
Flagg Hall 52
Flagg Races 52
Flash 102
Three Shires Head 102
Fritchley 132
Meeting House 132
Froggatt 27
Froggatt Edge 27
Stoke Hall 27

G

Glossop 16
Church of All Saints 17
Glossop Heritage Centre 17
Snake Pass 16
Grassmoor 166
Five Pits Trail 166
Great Longstone 41
Longstone Hall 41
Grindleford 44
Brunt's Barn 44
Padley Chapel 45
Grindon 94

H

Hadfield 18
Longdendale Trail 18
Woodhead Chapel 18
Hartington 97
Beresford Dale 98
Hartington Hall 98
Hartshorne 117
Parish Church of St Peter 117
Hassop 41
Church of All Saints 41
Hassop Hall 41
Hathersage 25
Atlas Works 26
Charlotte Brontë 26
Highlow Hall 26
Little John 25
Moorseats 26
North Lees 26
St Michael's Parish Church 26
Hayfield 14
Bowden Bridge Quarry 15
Church of St Matthew 15
Dungeon Brow 15
Kinder Downfall 15
Kinder Scout 14
Mermaid's Pool 16
Heage 135
Heage Windmill 136
Parish Church of St Luke 136
Heanor 138
Parish Church of St Lawrence 138
Shanakiel House 138
Shipley Country Park 138
Heath 164
Sutton Scarsdale Hall 164
Hilton 117
Wakelyn Hall 117
Hognaston 83
Parish Church of St Bartholomew 84
Holbrook 141
Parish Church of St Michael 141
Holloway 69
Lea Hurst 69
Holmesfield 172
Parish Church of St Swithin 172
Holymoorside 170
Stone Edge Cupola 171

Hope 22
  Church of St Peter 22
  Hope Agricultural Show 23
  Lose Hill 22
  Win Hill 22
Hopton 84
  High Peak Railway 84
  Hopton Incline 84
  Sir Philip Gell Almshouses 84
  Via Gellia 84
Horsley 144
  Parish Church of St Clement and St
    James 144
Hulme End 97
  Leek and Manifold Valley Light Railway
    97

I

Idridgehay 140
  Parish Church of St James 140
  South Sitch 140
Ilam 92
  Ilam Hall 93
  Ilam Park 93
  Parish Church of the Holy Cross 92
Ilkeston 142
  Charter Fair 142
  Erewash Museum 142
  Parish Church of St Mary 142

K

Kedleston 111
  All Saints Church 112
  Indian Museum 112
  Kedleston Hall 111
Kinder Scout 14
King Sterndale 52
  Christ Church 53
Kirk Ireton 83
  Carsington Reservoir 83
  Parish Church of the Holy Trinity 83
Kirk Langley 111
  Parish Church of St Michael 111
Kniveton 83
  Parish Church of St Michael 83
  Wigber Low 83

L

Lea 69
  Lea Gardens 69

Leek 99
  Blackbrook Zoological Park 101
  Brindley Water Museum 101
  Hen Cloud 101
  Kiddies Kingdom 101
  Nicholson Institute 100
  Parish Church of St Edward's and All
    Saints 100
  Ramshaw Rocks 101
  River Churnet 101
  The Roaches 101
  Tittesworth Reservoir 101
  War Memorial 100
Linton 124
Litton 47
  Litton Mill 47
  William Bagshawe 47
Long Eaton 152
  Parish Church of St Lawrence 152
Long Lane 113
  Parish Church of Christ Church 113
  The Three Horseshoes 113
Longford 113
  Longford Hall 113
  Parish Church of St Chad 113
Longnor 54
  Church of St Bartholomew 54
  Longnor Craft Centre 54
  Market Hall 54
  Market Squares 54
Lower Hartshay 135
Lyme Park 13
  Lyme Hall 13
  The Cage 13

M

Macclesfield 30
  Charles Frederick Tunnicliffe 31
  Heritage Centre 30
  Paradise Mill 30
  Parish Church of St Michael and All
    Angels 30
  Silk Museum 30
  West Park Museum 31
  William Buckley 31
Mackworth 111
  Mackworth Castle 111
  Parish Church of All Saints 111
Mapperley 143
  Nutbrook Canal 143
Mappleton 91
  Parish Church of St Mary 91

Matlock 57
  Matlock Bath 57
  Matlock Farm Park 58
  Parish Church of St Giles 57
  Peak Rail 58
  Peak Rail Society 58
  Riber Castle 58
  Snitterton Hall 58
Matlock Bath 57, 67
  Chapel of St John the Baptist 69
  Gulliver's Kingdom Theme Park 68
  Heights of Abraham 68
  High Tor 68
  Life in a Lens 68
  Parish Church of the Holy Trinity 69
  Peak District Mining Museum 68
  The Aquarium 68
Mayfield 98
  Mayfield Mill 99
  Parish Church of St Giles 99
  Parish Church of St John the Baptist 98
Melbourne 118
  Melbourne Hall 119
  Parish Church of St Michael and St
    Mary 119
Middleton by Wirksworth 72
  Good Luck Mine 72
  Middleton Top 73
  Middleton Top Winding Engine 73
Middleton by Youlgreave 63
  Lomberdale Hall 64
Milford 140
Millers Dale 50
  Litton Mill 50
  Monsal Dale Viaduct 51
  Parish Church of St Anne's 51
Milton 121
  Foremark Water 121
Moira 125
  Conkers 125
Monsal Head 46
  Monsal Dale 46
  Monsal Trail 46
Monyash 52
  Lathkill Dale 52
  Parish Church of St Leonard 53
  River Lathkill 53
Morley 144
  Almshouses 144
  Parish Church of St Matthew 144

N

Netherseal 124
  Parish Church of St Peter 125
New Mills 13
  Little Mill 14
  New Mills Heritage Centre 14
  New Mills Millennium Walkway 14
  Sett Valley Trail 14
  The Goyt Valley Way 14
  Torrs Gorge 14
  Torrs Riverside Park 14
Newhaven 91
Norbury 114
  Parish Church of St Mary and St Barlok 114

O

Oakerthorpe 129
  Oakerthorpe Nature Reserve 129
Ockbrook 147
  Moravian Chapel 147
  Ockbrook Windmill 147
Old Brampton 171
  Brampton Hall 171
  Frith Hall Farmhouse 171
  Parish Church of Saints Peter and Paul 171
Osmaston 82
  Parish Church of St Martin 82
Over Haddon 55
  Lathkill Dale Trail 55
  Mandale Mine 55

P

Parwich 89
  Parish Church of St Peter 90
  Parwich Hall 89
  Parwich Moor 90
  Roystone Grange Archaeological Trail 90
Peak Forest 49
  Eldon Hole 49
  Parish Church of King Charles the Martyr 49
Pentrich 134
  Parish Church of St Matthew 134
  Pentrich Revolution 134
Pilsley 41, 167
  The Herb Garden 167
Pomeroy 53

Prestbury 31
  Norman Chapel 32
  Parish Church of St Peter 31
  Prestbury Hall 32
  Priest's House 31
  Reading Room 32

R

Renishaw 159
  Renishaw Hall and Gardens 159
Repton 122
  Foremark Hall 123
  Parish Church of St Wystan 122
  Repton College 123
Riddings 133
Ripley 134
Risley 146
  Parish Church of All Saints 147
  Risley Hall 146
  Risley Hall Gardens 146
Roosdyche 12
  Bing Wood 12
Rosliston 124
  Parish Church of St Mary the Virgin 124
Rowsley 56
  Caudwell's Mill 56
  Parish Church of St Katherine 56
  Peacock Hotel 56
  Peak Village 56
  Toys of Yesteryear 56
Rudyard 102
  Kinver Edge 102
  Rudyard Lake 102
  Rudyard Lake Steam Railway 102
  Staffordshire Way 102
Rushton Spencer 102
  Chapel in the Wilderness 102
  The Cloud 102

S

Sandiacre 146
  Parish Church of St Giles 146
Sawley 153
  Bothe Hall 153
  Parish Church of All Saints 153
  Sawley Marina 153
Scarcliffe 163
  Parish Church of St Leonard 163
  Poulter Country Park 164

Shardlow 149
  Broughton House 150
  Parish Church of St James 150
  Shardlow Heritage Centre 150
  Shardlow Marina 150
  Trent and Mersey Canal 150
Sheepbridge 158
  Dunstan Hall 158
Sheldon 52
  Magpie Mine 53
  Parish Church of St Michael and All Angels 52
Shining Tor 8
Shottle 140
  Parish Church of St Lawrence 140
South Normanton 129
  Parish Church of St Michael 129
South Wingfield 130
  Parish Church of All Saints 131
  Wingfield Manor 130
Spondon 147
  Locko Park 147
  Parish Church of St Werburgh 147
Stanley 145
  Parish Church of St Andrew 145
Stanton by Dale 145
  Middlemore Almshouses 146
  Parish Church of St Michael and All Angels 146
Stanton in Peak 60
  Earl Grey's Tower 60
  Stanton Moor 60
Stanton Moor 61
  Nine Ladies 61
Staveley 160
  Parish Church of St John the Baptist 160
  Staveley Hall 160
  Staveley Iron Works 160
Stoney Middleton 42
  Castle Hill 42
  Middleton Dale 42
  Middleton Hall 42
  St Martin's Parish Church 42
Stretton 169
  Ogston Hall 169
  Ogston Reservoir 169
Sudbury 115
  Museum of Childhood 115
  Parish Church of All Saints 115
  Sudbury Hall 115

Sutton 34
  Raphael Holinshed 34
  Sutton Hall 34
Sutton-on-the-Hill 115
  Parish Church of St Michael 115
Swadlincote 117
  Parish Church of Emmanuelle 117
  Sharpe's Pottery Centre 117
Swanwick 133
  Parish Church of St Andrew 133
Swarkestone 120
  Parish Church of St James 120
  Swarkestone Bridge 120

T

Taddington 49
  Five Wells Chambered Cairn 49
  Parish Church of St Michael and All
    Angels 49
  Taddington Hall 50
Tansley 70
  Tansley Wood Mill 70
Taxal 9
  Shallcross Hall 9
  St James 9
  Windgather Rocks 9
Thorpe 91
  Beresford Dale 92
  Dovedale 91
  Dovedale Castle 92
  Dovedale Dash 92
  Lover's Leap 92
  Mill Dale 92
  Parish Church of St Leonard 90
  River Dove 91
  Thorpe Cloud 91
  Tissington Spires 92
  Twelve Apostles 92
  Wolfscote Dale 92
Tibshelf 167
  Five Pits Trail 167
  Parish Church of St John the Baptist
    168
  Tibshelf Ponds picnic site 168
Tideswell 48
  Eccles Hall 48
  Parish Church of St John the Baptist 48

Tissington 87
  Parish Church of St Mary 88
  Tissington Hall 88
  Tissington Trail 89
Tunstead 51
  Tunstead Quarry 51

W

Wardlow 46
  The Pingle 47
Warslow 96
  Parish Church of St Lawrence 97
Waterfall 94
  Parish Church of St James and St
    Bartholomew 94
Waterhouses 94
  Hamps-Manifold Trail 94
Wensley 64
West Hallam 143
  Parish Church of St Wilfrid 143
  The Bottle Kiln 143
  West Hallam Hall 143
Wetton 95
  Ecton Hill 95
  Manifold Valley Trail 95
  Parish Church of St Margaret 95
  Radcliffe Stables 95
  Thor's Cave 95
  Wetton Low 95
  Wetton Mill 95
Whaley 162
  Whaley Thorns Heritage Centre 162
Whaley Bridge 12
  Peak Forest Canal 12
  Roosdyche 12
  Rose Queen Carnival 12
  Toddbrook Reservoir 12
  Whaley Water Weekend 12
Whatstandwell 132
  Shining Cliff Woods 132
  Whatstandwell Walk 133
Whittington 158
  Revolution House 158
Wingerworth 167
  Parish Church of all Saints 167

Winsick 166
Winster 65
  Bank House 66
  Market House 65
  Parish Church of St John 66
  The Ore House 65
  Winster Hall 66
  Winster Millennium Tapestry 65
Wirksworth 73
  Adam Bede Cottage 74
  Babington House 73
  Carsington Water 75
  Gell's Almshouses 73
  Hopkinsons House 73
  National Stone Centre 74
  North End Mills 74
  Parish Church of St Mary's 73
  Wirksworth Heritage Centre 75
Wormhill 51
  Chee Tor 51
  Wormhill Hall 51

Y

Yeldersley 82
  Yeldersley Hall 82
Youlgreave 62
  Arbor Low 63
  Conduit Head 63
  Gib Hill 63
  Parish Church of All Saints 62
  Thimble Hall 63

TRAVEL PUBLISHING ORDER FORM

To order any of our publications just fill in the payment details below and complete the order form. For orders of less than 4 copies please add £1.00 per book for postage and packing. Orders over 4 copies are P & P free.

Name:

Address:

Tel no:

Please Complete Either:

I enclose a cheque for £ _____ made payable to Travel Publishing Ltd

Or:

Card No: Expiry Date:

Signature:

Please either send, telephone, fax or e-mail your order to:

Travel Publishing Ltd, Airport Business Centre, 10 Thornbury Road, Estover, Plymouth PL6 7PP

Tel: 01752 697280   Fax: 01752 697299   e-mail: info@travelpublishing.co.uk

	Price	Quantity		Price	Quantity
HIDDEN PLACES REGIONAL TITLES			**COUNTRY LIVING RURAL GUIDES**		
Cornwall	£8.99	....	East Anglia	£10.99	....
Devon	£8.99	....	Heart of England	£10.99	....
Dorset, Hants & Isle of Wight	£8.99	....	Ireland	£11.99	....
East Anglia	£8.99	....	North East	£10.99	....
Lake District & Cumbria	£8.99	....	North West	£10.99	....
Northumberland & Durham	£8.99	....	Scotland	£11.99	....
Peak District and Derbyshire	£8.99	....	South of England	£10.99	....
Yorkshire	£8.99	....	South East of England	£10.99	....
HIDDEN PLACES NATIONAL TITLES			Wales	£11.99	....
England	£11.99	....	West Country	£10.99	....
Ireland	£11.99	....			
Scotland	£11.99	....			
Wales	£11.99	....	**TOTAL QUANTITY:**		
OTHER TITLES					
Off the Motorway	£11.99	....	**POST & PACKING:**		
Garden Centres & Nurseries	£11.99	....	**TOTAL VALUE:**		

READER REACTION FORM

The *Travel Publishing* research team would like to receive reader's comments on any visitor attractions or places reviewed in the book and also recommendations for suitable entries to be included in the next edition. This will help ensure that the *Hidden Places series of Guides* continues to provide its readers with useful information on the more interesting, unusual or unique features of each attraction or place ensuring that their visit to the local area is an enjoyable and stimulating experience. To provide your comments or recommendations would you please complete the forms below and overleaf as indicated and send to:

**The Research Department, Travel Publishing Ltd,
Airport Business Centre, 10 Thornbury Road, Estover, Plymouth PL6 7PP**

Your Name:

Your Address:

Your Telephone Number:

Please tick as appropriate:

Comments ☐   Recommendation ☐

Name of Establishment:

Address:

Telephone Number:

Name of Contact:

READER REACTION FORM

COMMENT OR REASON FOR RECOMMENDATION:

....

....

....

....

....

....

....

....

....

....

....

....

....

....

....

....

....

....

....

READER REACTION FORM

The *Travel Publishing* research team would like to receive reader's comments on any visitor attractions or places reviewed in the book and also recommendations for suitable entries to be included in the next edition. This will help ensure that the *Hidden Places series of Guides* continues to provide its readers with useful information on the more interesting, unusual or unique features of each attraction or place ensuring that their visit to the local area is an enjoyable and stimulating experience. To provide your comments or recommendations would you please complete the forms below and overleaf as indicated and send to:

**The Research Department, Travel Publishing Ltd,
Airport Business Centre, 10 Thornbury Road, Estover, Plymouth PL6 7PP**

Your Name:

Your Address:

Your Telephone Number:

Please tick as appropriate:

Comments ☐   Recommendation ☐

Name of Establishment:

Address:

Telephone Number:

Name of Contact:

READER REACTION FORM

COMMENT OR REASON FOR RECOMMENDATION:

READER REACTION FORM

The *Travel Publishing* research team would like to receive reader's comments on any visitor attractions or places reviewed in the book and also recommendations for suitable entries to be included in the next edition. This will help ensure that the *Hidden Places series of Guides* continues to provide its readers with useful information on the more interesting, unusual or unique features of each attraction or place ensuring that their visit to the local area is an enjoyable and stimulating experience. To provide your comments or recommendations would you please complete the forms below and overleaf as indicated and send to:

**The Research Department, Travel Publishing Ltd,
Airport Business Centre, 10 Thornbury Road, Estover, Plymouth PL6 7PP**

Your Name:

Your Address:

Your Telephone Number:

Please tick as appropriate:

Comments ☐   Recommendation ☐

Name of Establishment:

Address:

Telephone Number:

Name of Contact:

READER REACTION FORM

COMMENT OR REASON FOR RECOMMENDATION:

Index of Advertisers

ACCOMMODATION

The Anchor Inn, Kegworth — p 152, 267

Ball Cross Farm Cottages, Chatsworth Estate,
nr Bakewell — p 41, 202

The Barley Mow Inn, Kirk Ireton,
nr Ashbourne — p 83, 224

Batemans Mill Country Hotel & Restaurant,
Old Tupton, nr Chesterfield — p 168, 280

The Bear Inn, Alderwasley, nr Belper — p 132, 251

Biggin Hall Country House Hotel,
Biggin-by-Hartington, nr Buxton — p 98, 231

The Black Grouse, Longnor, nr Buxton — p 54, 205

The Black Horse Inn, Hulland Ward,
nr Ashbourne — p 83, 222

Bowling Green Inn, Bradwell, Hope Valley — p 24, 188

Bull I' th' Thorn, Hurdlow, nr Buxton — p 53, 204

The Bulls Head, Youlgreave, nr Bakewell — p 62, 211

The Castle Hotel, Hatton — p 116, 241

Causeway House, Castleton, Hope Valley — p 20, 187

Cavendish Arms, Doveridge, nr Ashbourne — p 114, 242

Common Barn Farm, Rainow,
nr Macclesfield — p 34, 200

The Crown Inn, Old Higham — p 169, 281

Crowtrees Farm Bed & Breakfast,
Oakamoor — p 103, 240

Devonshire Arms Hotel, Nether End,
nr Baslow — p 29, 195

Donington Park Farmhouse, Isley Walton,
nr Castle Donington — p 152, 269

The Duke of Wellington Residential Country Inn,
Matlock — p 58, 210

Glendon Guest House, Matlock — p 57, 208

The Hollybush Inn, Grangemill, nr Matlock — p 86, 226

Horse & Groom, Scarcliffe, nr Chesterfield — p 163, 274

Ivy House Farm B&B and Woodland Hills Court
Self Catering, Stanton-by-Bridge — p 120, 244

King Edward VII, Tibshelf — p 168, 279

King William IV, Milford — p 140, 258

The Kings Head Inn, Duffield — p 141, 260

Ladybower Inn, Bamford, Hope Valley — p 24, 189

The Little John Inn, Hathersage,
Hope Valley — p 26, 190

The Lockoford Inn, Tapton,
nr Chesterfield — p 157, 270

Manifold Inn, Hartington, nr Buxton — p 97, 230

The Manners Hotel, Bakewell — p 38, 200

Middlehills Farm, Grangemill, nr Matlock — p 86, 226

The Miners Arms, Eyam, Hope Valley — p 43, 203

The Miners Arms, Brassington — p 85, 225

Overseale House, Overseal,
nr Swadlincote — p 124, 246

The Printers Arms, Thornsett, High Peak — p 15, 183

The Railway Inn, Froghall — p 103, 239

The Robin Hood, Rainow,
nr Macclesfield — p 34, 200

Robin Hood Inn, Overseal,
nr Swadlincote — p 124, 247

The Roebuck Inn, Chapel-en-le-Frith — p 10, 178

The Royal Hotel, Hayfield, High Peak — p 14, 182

Rutland Arms, Baslow — p 29, 194

Saracens Head, Shirley, nr Ashbourne — p 82, 220

Spotted Cow, Holbrook — p 141, 259

The Star Inn, Glossop — p 17, 186

The Strutt Arms Hotel, Milford — p 140, 258

The Swan, Leek — p 99, 232

Sycamore Inn, Birch Vale, High Peak — p 15, 184

The Torrs, New Mills — p 14, 181

White Hart Hotel, Ashbourne — p 79, 216

Ye Olde Cheshire Inn, Longnor,
nr Buxton — p 54, 206

Ye Olde Vaults, Ashbourne — p 81, 218

297

FOOD AND DRINK

The Anchor Inn, Kegworth   p 152, 267

The Barley Mow Inn, Kirk Ireton,
nr Ashbourne   p 83, 224

Batemans Mill Country Hotel & Restaurant,
Old Tupton, nr Chesterfield   p 168, 280

Bay Tree Restaurant, Melbourne   p 119, 243

The Bean & Bag, Bakewell   p 38, 201

The Bear Inn, Alderwasley, nr Belper   p 132, 251

The Beehive & Hague Bistro, Glossop   p 17, 186

Beresford Tea Rooms, Hartington,
nr Buxton   p 97, 230

Biggin Hall Country House Hotel,
Biggin-by-Hartington, nr Buxton   p 98, 231

Black Boy Inn, Heage   p 135, 254

The Black Grouse, Longnor, nr Buxton   p 54, 205

The Black Horse, Appleby Magna,
nr Swadlincote   p 125, 246

The Black Horse Inn, Hulland Ward,
nr Ashbourne   p 83, 222

Bluebell Inn & Restaurant, Tissington,
nr Ashbourne   p 88, 227

Blueberrys, Leek   p 100, 234

Boars Leigh Restaurant, Bosley,
nr Macclesfield   p 35, 200

Bowling Green Inn, Bradwell, Hope Valley   p 24, 188

Bowling Green Inn, Ashbourne   p 80, 218

Brocks Café & Bistro, Ripley   p 134, 253

Bull I' th' Thorn, Hurdlow, nr Buxton   p 53, 204

The Bulls Head, Youlgreave, nr Bakewell   p 62, 211

Cafe @ The Green Pavilion, Buxton   p 5, 177

The Castle Hotel, Hatton   p 116, 241

Castro's Restaurant & Lounge, Cheddleton,
nr Leek   p 102, 237

Cavendish Arms, Doveridge,
nr Ashbourne   p 114, 242

Cock & Magpie, Old Whittington,
nr Chesterfield   p 158, 271

Cock Inn, Clifton, nr Ashbourne   p 82, 219

Coffee Tavern, Pott Shrigley   p 33, 198

The Cross Keys, Castle Donnington   p 151, 266

The Crossings, Furness Vale, High Peak   p 13, 180

The Crown Inn, Old Higham   p 169, 281

Dandy Cock Inn, Disley, nr Stockport   p 13, 179

Den Engel Belgian Bar & Restaurant, Leek   p 100, 235

The Devonshire Arms, South Normanton   p 129, 249

Devonshire Arms Hotel, Nether End,
nr Baslow   p 29, 195

Dolphin Inn, Macclesfield   p 31, 197

The Duke of Wellington Residential Country Inn,
Matlock   p 58, 210

Duke of York, Romiley, nr Stockport   p 16, 185

The Dyers Arms, Leek   p 99, 233

Eagle Public House & Restaurant, Buxton   p 5, 176

Eagle Tavern, Heage   p 136, 254

The Eating House, Calver Bridge,
Hope Valley   p 28, 192

Finn M'Couls, Ilkeston   p 142, 260

Gallery Cafe, Ashbourne   p 79, 217

The Gate, Tansley, nr Matlock   p 70, 214

The Great Northern, Mickleover   p 109, 241

The Greyhound Hotel, Alderwasley,
nr Belper   p 132, 252

Hardwick Inn, Hardwick Park,
nr Chesterfield   p 165, 275

The Hare & Hounds, Simmondley Village,
nr Glossop   p 17, 185

Heights of Abraham, Matlock Bath   p 68, 212

The Holly Bush, Bollington   p 34, 198

The Hollybush Inn, Grangemill, nr Matlock   p 86, 226

The Honeycomb, Mickleover   p 109, 241

Horse & Groom, Scarcliffe,
nr Chesterfield   p 163, 274

The Horseshoe, Matlock   p 57, 208

Hunloke Arms, Wingerworth   p 167, 277

In a Pickle, Chapel-en-le-Frith   p 10, 178

The Jolly Sailor, Macclesfield   p 31, 196

King Edward VII, Tibshelf   p 168, 279

King William IV, Milford   p 140, 258

The Kings Head Inn, Duffield   p 141, 260

The Knot Inn, Rushton Spencer,
nr Macclesfield — p 102, 236

Ladybower Inn, Bamford, Hope Valley — p 24, 189

The Little John Inn, Hathersage, Hope Valley — p 26, 190

The Lockoford Inn, Tapton, nr Chesterfield — p 157, 270

Main Sail Restaurant, Carsington Water,
nr Ashbourne — p 83, 223

Malt Shovel Inn, Aston-on-Trent — p 151, 267

Manifold Inn, Hartington, nr Buxton — p 97, 230

The Manners Hotel, Bakewell — p 38, 200

The Miners Arms, Eyam, Hope Valley — p 43, 203

The Miners Arms, Brassington — p 85, 225

The Miners Arms, Dronfield Woodhouse — p 172, 282

Moira Tea Room, Moira, nr Swadlincote — p 125, 248

The New Inn, Shardlow — p 150, 263

The Old Bakery Coffee Shop and Restaurant,
Cromford — p 71, 216

The Old Marina Bar & Restaurant,
Shardlow — p 150, 264

The Old Sun Inn, Buxton — p 6, 177

Old Yew Tree Inn, South Wingfield — p 130, 250

The Olympic Hotel, Draycott — p 148, 262

The Pattenmakers Arms, Duffield — p 141, 259

The Peak District Mining Museum,
Matlock Bath — p 69, 214

The Poet & Castle, Codnor, nr Ripley — p 137, 256

Pool Cafe, Hathersage, Hope Valley — p 26, 189

The Princess Victoria, Matlock Bath — p 67, 212

The Printers Arms, Thornsett, High Peak — p 15, 183

Puss in Boots, Macclesfield — p 31, 197

The Railway, Cowers Lane, nr Belper — p 140, 257

The Railway Inn, Froghall — p 103, 239

Red Lion Inn, Waterfall, nr Waterhouses — p 94, 229

Rising Sun, Willington — p 122, 245

Rising Sun Inn, Rainow, nr Macclesfield — p 34, 199

Riverside Tea Rooms & Old Bank Cafe Bar,
Matlock Bath — p 68, 213

The Robin Hood, Rainow, nr Macclesfield — p 34, 200

Robin Hood Inn, Overseal, nr Swadlincote — p 124, 247

The Roebuck Inn, Chapel-en-le-Frith — p 10, 178

The Royal Hotel, Hayfield, High Peak — p 14, 182

Royal Oak, Ockbrook, nr Derby — p 147, 262

Rutland Arms, Baslow — p 29, 194

Saracens Head, Shirley, nr Ashbourne — p 82, 220

Scotland Nurseries Garden Centre, Restaurant &
Chocolate Shop, Tansley, nr Matlock — p 70, 215

Shakespeare Inn & Restaurant, Shardlow — p 150, 265

Shoulder of Mutton, Osmaston,
nr Ashbourne — p 82, 221

The Sitwell Arms, Horsley Woodhouse — p 144, 261

Spanker Inn, Nether Heage, nr Belper — p 136, 255

Spotted Cow, Holbrook — p 141, 259

The Star Inn, Glossop — p 17, 186

Stones Restaurant, Matlock — p 57, 207

The Strutt Arms Hotel, Milford — p 140, 258

The Swan, Leek — p 99, 232

Sycamore Inn, Birch Vale, High Peak — p 15, 184

The Sycamore Inn, Matlock — p 58, 209

Tall Trees Coffee Shop & Restaurant, Two Dales,
nr Matlock — p 59, 211

Tawney's Coffee Shop, Matlock — p 58, 209

Telmere Lodge, Hasland, nr Chesterfield — p 166, 276

The Thorn Tree Inn, Belper — p 139, 256

Three Horseshoes, Morley — p 144, 260

Three Horseshoes, Spitewinter,
nr Ashover — p 167, 278

The Three Merry Lads, Lodge Moor,
nr Sheffield — p 26, 191

The Torrs, New Mills — p 14, 181

Traveller's Rest, Church Gresley,
nr Swadlincote — p 123, 245

White Hart Hotel, Ashbourne — p 79, 216

The White Hart Inn, Heage — p 136, 254

Whyld About Food, Bolsover — p 162, 272

Ye Olde Cheshire Inn, Longnor,
nr Buxton — p 54, 206

Ye Olde Flying Horse, Kegworth — p 152, 268

Ye Olde Gate Inn, Brassington — p 85, 224

Ye Olde Star Inn, Cotton, nr Oakamoor — p 102, 238

Ye Olde Vaults, Ashbourne — p 81, 218

PLACES OF INTEREST

Avant Garde of Baslow, Baslow — p 29, 193

Bolsover Castle, Bolsover — p 163, 273

Buxton Museum and Art Gallery, Buxton — p 8, 178

Chatsworth House, Edensor — p 41, 202

The Chestnut Centre, Chapel-en-le-Frith — p 11, 179

Crich Tramway Village, Crich, nr Matlock — p 131, 248

Denby Visitor Centre, Denby — p 137, 255

Derby Museums and Art Gallery, Derby — p 108, 240

Eyam Museum, Eyam, Hope Valley — p 43, 204

Glossop Heritage Centre, Glossop — p 16, 182

Haddon Hall, Bakewell — p 40, 201

The National Stone Centre, Wirksworth — p 73, 216

Pickford's House Museum, Derby — p 107, 240

Scotland Nurseries Garden Centre, Restaurant &
Chocolate Shop, Tansley, nr Matlock — p 70, 215

The South Peak Estate, Ilam,
nr Ashbourne — p 92, 228

Tissington Hall and Gardens, Tissington,
nr Ashbourne — p 88, 228

Treak Cliff Cavern, Castleton, Hope Valley — p 22, 187

The Wind in the Willows Attraction, Rowsley p 56, 207